The Onset of Language

The Onset of Language outlines an approach to the development of expressive and communicative behavior from early infancy to the onset of single-word utterances. Nobuo Masataka's research is rooted in ethology and dynamic action theory. He argues that expressive and communicative actions are organized as a complex and cooperative system with other elements of the infant's physiology, behavior and the social environments. Overall, humans are provided with a finite set of specific behavior patterns, each of which is phylogenetically inherited as a primate species. However, the patterns are uniquely organized during ontogeny and a coordinated structure emerges which eventually leads us to acquire language. This fascinating book offers exciting new insights into the precursors of speech and will be of interest to researchers and students of psychology, linguistics and animal behavior biology.

NOBUO MASATAKA is Professor at the Primate Research Institute, Kyoto University, Japan. He has published numerous articles in journals such as *Developmental Psychology, Child Development* and *Journal of Child Language*.

T0381809

Cambridge Studies in Cognitive and Perceptual Development

Series Editors
Giyoo Hatano, University of the Air, Chiba, Japan
Kurt W. Fischer, Harvard University, USA

Advisory Board
Gavin Bremner, Lancaster University, UK
Patricia M. Greenfield, University of California, Los Angeles, USA
Paul Harris, Harvard University, USA
Daniel Stern, University of Geneva, Switzerland
Esther Thelen, Indiana University, USA

The aim of this series is to provide a scholarly forum for current theoretical and empirical issues in cognitive and perceptual development. As the twenty-first century begins, the field is no longer dominated by monolithic theories. Contemporary explanations build on the combined influences of biological, cultural, contextual and ecological factors in well-defined research domains. In the field of cognitive development, cultural and situational factors are widely recognized as influencing the emergence and forms of reasoning in children. In perceptual development, the field has moved beyond the opposition of 'innate' and 'acquired' to suggest a continuous role for perception in the acquisition of knowledge. These approaches and issues will all be reflected in the series, which will also address such important research themes as the indissociable link between perception and action in the developing motor system, the relationship between perceptual and cognitive development and modern ideas on the development of the brain, the significance of developmental processes themselves, dynamic systems theory and contemporary work in the psychodynamic tradition, especially as it relates to the foundations of self-knowledge.

Titles published in the series

1. *Imitation in infancy*
   Jacqueline Nadel and George Butterworth
2. *Learning to Read and Write: A Cross-Linguistic Perspective*
   Margaret Harris and Giyoo Hatano
3. *Children's Understanding of Biology and Health*
   Michael Siegal and Candida Peterson
4. *Social Processes in Children's Learning*
   Paul Light and Karen Littleton
5. *Half a Brain is Enough: The Story of Nico*
   Antonio M. Battro
6. *The Imitative Mind: Development, Evolution and Brain Bases*
   Andrew N. Meltzoff and Wolfgang Prinz
7. *Microdevelopment: Transition Processes in Development and Learning*
   Nira Granott and Jim Parziale
8. *Between Culture and Biology: Perspectives on Ontogenetic Development*
   Edited by Heidi Keller, Ype H. Poortinga and Axel Schölmerich

The Onset of Language

Nobuo Masataka

Primate Research Institute, Kyoto University, Japan

CAMBRIDGE UNIVERSITY PRESS
Cambridge, New York, Melbourne, Madrid, Cape Town, Singapore, São Paulo

Cambridge University Press
The Edinburgh Building, Cambridge CB2 8RU, UK

Published in the United States of America by Cambridge University Press, New York

www.cambridge.org
Information on this title: www.cambridge.org/9780521593960

© Nobuo Masataka 2003

This publication is in copyright. Subject to statutory exception
and to the provisions of relevant collective licensing agreements,
no reproduction of any part may take place without the written
permission of Cambridge University Press.

First published 2003
Reprinted 2004
This digitally printed version 2008

A catalogue record for this publication is available from the British Library

Library of Congress Cataloguing in Publication data
Masataka, Nobuo, 1954–
The Onset of Language / Nobuo Masataka.
        p.   cm. – (Cambridge studies in cognitive and perceptual development)
Includes bibliographical references and index.
ISBN 0 521 59396 4
1. Language acquisition.   I. Title.   II. Cambridge studies in cognitive perceptual
development.
P 118.M367   2003
401′.93 – dc21   2003043933

ISBN 978-0-521-59396-0 hardback
ISBN 978-0-521-04957-3 paperback

Contents

Figures

Tables

Acknowledgements

For a period of my life that lasted almost a decade, first as a graduate student and then as a post-doctoral student, I was interested in the vocal communication of nonhuman primates. Soon after entering graduate school at Osaka University I was given the opportunity by Kosei Izawa to spend ten months in the upper Amazonian basin observing free-ranging New World Primates. He suggested I make vocal recordings of the primates, an experience that was to profoundly influence my subsequent research interests. Another experience which was to affect the direction of my research in a no less profound way was the birth of my two children. I was amazed by the fact that just after birth they were already engaging in their first communications with others and that, unlike nonhuman primates, infants connect with other people by vocalization, gesture and facial expression from the very first moments of life. Even at such a very young age the ability to communicate is central to what it means to be human.

These experiences led to my fascination with questions such as why is our species the only one to have developed language? What are the species differences that make language possible? Why does language take the form it does, and not other forms? How does language emerge in infants? The outcome of my research in tackling these themes is summarized here. Several years ago the late George Butterworth became interested in my work and encouraged me to write this book. I am deeply indebted to him.

I am also very grateful for the comments and suggestions I have received while writing this book from Giyoo Hatano and Kurt Fischer. My thanks also go to the many students and colleagues who have played a crucial role in providing inspiration for my work. A short list of key collaborators who deserve recognition would include Shozo Kojima, Kosei Izawa, Hideki Sugiura, Ryo Oda, Maxeen Biben, Tomoko Nakano, Keiko Ejiri, Toshiaki Tanaka, Sachiyo Kajikawa, Sotaro Kita and Wataru Takei. There are three more names to mention, those of my wife, Motoko, and my two sons, Yuji and Morio. Without them, I might never have been inspired with the ideas presented in this book.

Finally, I acknowledge that the writing of this book was supported by the MEXT Grant-in-Aid for the 21st century COE Program (A2 to Kyoto University).

1   Introduction

This book outlines an approach to the development of expressive and communicative behavior in early infancy until the onset of a single word which is rooted in ethology and dynamic action theory. Here the process of expressive and communicative actions, organized as a complex and cooperative system with other elements of the infant's physiology, behavior and social environments, is elucidated. Overall, humans are provided with a finite set of specific behavior patterns, each of which is probably phylogenetically inherited as a primate species. However, the patterns are uniquely organized during ontogeny and a coordinated structure emerges, which eventually leads us to acquire spoken language. A dynamic model is presented where elements can be assembled for the onset of language in the infant in a more fluid, task-specific manner determined equally by the maturational status and experiences of the infant and by the current context of the action.

No doubt, communication is a social phenomenon and the most prominent feature of human speech and language. The complex organization of human societies is mediated by the ability of members to inform one another and is dependent on the exchange of information. Therefore, not surprisingly, many scientists have focused attention on how children acquire language ability.

Although children do not produce linguistically meaningful sounds or signs until they are approximately one year old, the ability to produce them begins to develop in early infancy, and important developments in the production of language occur throughout the first year of life. Unless they are hearing-impaired, infants acquire phonology during their first year. In spoken language, the acquisition of phonology consists of learning to distinguish and produce the sound patterns of the adult language. At birth, the newborn has the ability to distinguish virtually all sounds used in all languages, at least when the sounds are presented in isolation. The newborn produces no speech sounds, however. During the first year of life, speech-like sounds gradually emerge, beginning with vowel-like coos at six to eight weeks of age, followed by some consonant sounds, then followed by true babbling. By the end of the first year, children are typically babbling sequences of syllables that have the intonation contour of their target languages. Finally, meaningful words are produced; that is, the onset of speech occurs.

The factors that underlie these developments include: physical growth of the vocal apparatus, neurological development, and language experience. Language experience exerts its influence on both the perception and the production of speech sounds. Characteristics of the vocal apparatus that enable us to acquire language, features of neurological development, and features of the manner in which the experience of ambient language influences children's linguistic behavior are all uniquely human, and this uniqueness can only be adequately comprehended when we view the process of early language development from a comparative perspective. Moreover, the predisposition of humans to acquire language is not restricted to a specific modality but rather is somewhat amodal. When humans have difficulty acquiring spoken language, other possibilities can be explored – a further biological predisposition that has phylogenetically evolved exclusively in humans.

A primate behaviorist's view of language acquisition

By comparing human language with the communicative behavior of nonhuman primates, this book will take an ethological perspective in exploring the changes that occur during this earliest stage of language development. Animal societies are equally dependent on the exchange of information. Any organism that lives in complex social groupings must rely on communicating some aspects of its status to others. Such an exchange of information, the process that defines a communication system, implies the existence of a common language or a common set of rules that govern the encoding and decoding of signals in the communication system.

It is tempting to think of animal communication systems as being composed of simple invariant designators or external manifestations of some basic internal states such as hunger, pain or reproductive readiness. For nonhuman primates, however, it is known that, in addition to these states, many other individual and societal factors such as individual identities, kinship, roles, dominance relations and coalitions play an important part in social organization and social behavior. The complexity of many primate societies kindled interest in the communication systems mediating social behavior. For this reason, the objective and quantitative description of vocal communication began earlier in nonhuman primate studies than in studies of human infants.

Carpenter (1934), a pioneering researcher, introduced in his observations of howler monkeys the basic method that is still used – describing vocalizations and the situations in which they were used. Rowell and Hinde (1962) were the first to characterize the vocal repertoire of a monkey, the rhesus macaque, by publishing sound spectrograms. Winter, Ploog and Latta (1966) added a quantitative dimension to the analysis by measuring acoustic features of the sounds recorded in their colony of squirrel monkeys. Struhasaker (1967) statistically analyzed the vocalizations recorded in his field study of vervet monkeys.

As a primate behaviorist, these early pioneering works influenced my initial interest in language. Consequently, my first exposure to the study of language did not involve human infants, children or even adults. In 1979, I was living in the upper Amazonian basin in Bolivia observing groups of a free-ranging New World primate, Goeldi's monkey. While there, I recorded their vocalizations. During my observations, I found that the animals exhibited two different types of responses when group members encountered a predator and emitted an alarm call. One was to climb down to the ground and to freeze there. The other was to climb up to the highest strata in the canopy and to mob. Different types of alarm calls appeared to be associated with different types of predators and the behavioral responses were assumed to vary with call type. However, the sound spectrographic analyses that I conducted upon returning to Japan showed that the entire sample of alarm calls fell along a graded continuum. Therefore, I chose to focus my doctoral thesis on how Goeldi's monkeys perceive conspecific alarm calls. Using captive animals, I investigated their responses to experimentally produced conspecific natural calls as well as to synthesized versions of them that varied in the acoustic parameters that defined the calls under study. Although natural alarm calls showed considerable individual heterogeneity, playbacks of synthesized versions of these calls that varied in a single acoustic parameter produced gross differences in behavioral responding across a narrow acoustic boundary.

With respect to speech perception in humans, if one creates synthetic speech stimuli representing equal steps along the continuum of a single acoustic parameter (for example, voice-onset-time ranging from simultaneous voicing to increasingly delayed voicing) and plays these stimuli to subjects, subjects report the experience of hearing either of two different sounds (for example, /ba/ or /pa/) rather than a graded series of sounds. That is, they perceptually group several different stimuli as /ba/ and certain other stimuli as /pa/. There is no apparent ambiguity between /ba/ and /pa/. A given stimulus from any point on the continuum is labeled as one or the other phoneme, and the two phonemes are strictly categorized; this phenomenon is known as categorical perception. The findings I obtained on vocal perception in Goeldi's monkeys appear analogous to this categorical perception that humans demonstrate with speech sounds, though at present such a perception is thought to be restricted to speech sounds.

After earning my doctorate, I briefly conducted research in Texas, USA. There, I investigated the perception of conspecific alarm calls in a group of Japanese macaques that had been translocated from the Kyoto area of Japan ten years prior. In my work with Japanese macaques, I employed the same experimental paradigm as in my previous work with Goeldi's monkeys. I found that Japanese macaques also perceive their conspecific alarm calls categorically, as demonstrated in human speech perception. From my studies, I learned that what is perceived as a single unit of behavior by human observers (i.e., what is heard as a single class of vocalization, in this case) may not actually be perceived as such by members of other species. These findings, together with similar results with other nonhuman primate species (see Snowdon 1982, for review), were rather astonishing because previous researchers attempting to construct vocal repertoires for nonhuman primate species (e.g. Rowell and Hinde, 1962) have noted the complex call structure of animals that was highly variable both between individuals and within the repertoire of a single individual. That is, many calls could not be easily categorized into discrete classes but rather call structures seemed to intergrade with one another. Researchers have assumed that in many cases these intergradations corresponded to hypothetical underlying motivational continua, thus the intergrading call structure was said to map a continuous motivational system. Despite this sort of variability and complexity, findings like my own suggest that we must be very cautious about how we define units of behavior in nonhuman primates. Based on such reflection, thereafter, primatologists working with vocal communication started to seek new methodologies that could reconcile the continuous variability in calls with the discrete messages they appear to carry. In addition, they successfully expanded the notion of vocal communication in traditional ethology. In so doing, they sought to elucidate the evolutionary continuity between nonhuman primate vocalization and human language.

Implications and limits of the traditional ethological approach to communication

The term "ethology" refers to the biological study of behavior (Tinbergen, 1951). It has been claimed that the discipline of ethology offers a unique integration of a unifying theory, evolutionary biology, with a methodological heritage, naturalistic observation (Blurton-Jones, 1972; Charlesworth, 1980). The operational translation of the evolutionary perspective on to behavior was provided by an early pioneer of ethology, Nicholas Tinbergen. Tinbergen (1951) defined ethology as follows:

the science [of ethology] is characterized by an observable phenomenon (behavior, or movement), and by a type of approach, a method of study (the biological method). The first means that the starting point of our work has been and remains inductive, for which description of observable phenomena is required. The biological method is characterized by the general scientific method, and in addition by the kind of questions we ask, which are the same throughout Biology and some of which are peculiar to it. (1951: 411)

The modern synthetic theory of evolution provides an integrative framework for many disciplines and content areas. Naturalistic observation provides not only essential descriptive data but it also serves as an invaluable source of ecologically valid hypotheses. Current ethology does not stress biological determinism but rather a multilevel perspective that can expand and enrich our understanding of development. Tinbergen argued that the question, "Why does this animal behave in this way?" included four different questions in the "why." The first question asks why the animal performed a particular behavior now, the question of immediate causal control of the behavior. The second question asks how the animal grew to respond in that particular way, the question of individual development. The third question asks why this kind of animal does this particular behavior, the question of survival value or function of the behavior. Finally, there is the question of why this group of animals came to solve this problem of survival in this way, the question of evolutionary origins of the behavior.

Until the mid-1980s, virtually all investigators interested in the vocal communication systems of nonhuman primates were concerned with the problem of human language in terms of these four questions. Those engaging in research with nonhuman primates looked for clues to illuminate the evolutionary background and biological heritage of human language. These kinds of clues, hints of the rules by which socially important information is encoded into and decoded from speech sounds, are especially relevant to hypotheses on the origins of human language since there are no fossil records available and one has to rely on comparative studies alone. The uses of vocalizations and their relationship to social behavior may be investigated when both the auditory and social parameters of behavior are available. In fact, in many nonhuman primates, certain features of the social situations in which the sounds are emitted are accessible to the investigator.

The approach to language that I adopt in this book might surprise those who have little knowledge about recent advances in primatology with respect to vocal communication. For example, linguists and developmental psychologists who regard language as a capability beyond the reach of animal research subjects might conclude that primate vocal communication falls outside their own purview as investigators and scholars. Such reactions would not be unexpected given that mainstream modern linguistics has been more concerned with theories of grammar than social communication and ecologically valid models of language use. Further, language has also been defined in very abstract terms and treated by many linguists as though it were synonymous with generative morphology and syntax.

By considering the general characteristics of vocal systems and how they are used, a number of primatologists interested in communicative behavior have recently revived the traditional ethological paradigm in order to place the interspecies comparison of vocal sounds in perspective for nonhuman primates. The conceptual framework for this book is inspired by the theories and methods of this recently expanded ethology as well as by current knowledge about vocal communication in nonhuman primates. The arguments raised and the paradigms developed in recent research also contribute to our understanding of the nature of linguistic capacity and are particularly indispensable to understanding how preverbal human infants acquire language. However, before I explore arguments surrounding language development in human infants, I will outline recent advancements in research on nonhuman primate vocal communication. A focus on such research will help show why evolutionary and comparative perspectives as formulated in the discipline of ethology are crucial to guide a program of developmental research on humans in general. Indeed, this is particularly important in that recent trends in developmental psycholinguistics research cast nonhuman primates in a more interesting light than ever before.

It is now recognized that language, whether spoken or signed, rests on several different types of motor and phonetic learning systems and a range of potentially contributory precursive behaviors (Bullowa, 1979; Papoušek, Jürgens and Papoušek, 1992; Oller, 2000; Speidel and Nelson, 1989). Hence, it is now deemed legitimate to investigate infants' cognitive and neural development as well as their social perceptual experiences in the quest for understanding how and why they begin to speak. Such an approach is also a theoretical necessity. That is, if infants engage in behaviors that facilitate language before they possess the cognitive capability to fully appreciate its existence, then their behaviors must be motivated by one or more non-linguistic factors (Locke and Snow, 1997). Merely owning the genes of a species known to possess the capacity for language would be insufficient. Linguists have argued that language requires specialized mental mechanisms that are encapsulated or dissociated from other, more generalized processing systems. However, linguists have not yet presented actual evidence for this. I propose that an ethological approach to language development provides one possibility for a breakthrough on this issue.

Discrepancy between ethologists' traditional view and linguists' view of human speech

In his formulation, Tinbergen aptly recognized that a full understanding of behavior includes both proximate and distal "causes" and that one must always view individual animals within the ecological context of the species. In sharing this view, my purpose in this book is in part to illustrate how Tinbergen's formulation can be used to direct research on a class of common, but puzzling infant behavior: language acquisition. That a combination of evolutionary biology and naturalistic observation potentially has much to offer our understanding of human behavior has been pointed out a number of times over the past few decades. However, Tinbergen's formulation has only been successfully extended to human behavior, more specifically, human language, in just a few investigations. As partial explanation for this, Tinbergen also cautioned that one should not confuse questions asked at one level with those asked at another. For example, Blurton-Jones (1972) argued that the persistence of unproductive nature–nurture arguments in behavioral research is a consequence of the confusion between issues of development and those of adaptation and evolution. More importantly with respect to communicative behavior, it must be acknowledged that ethologists have not understood how linguists distinguish human language from nonhuman communicative behavior on the one hand, and that linguists have not understood the significance of the ethologists' view of language on the other.

Traditional ethology conceived of animal communication as genetically fixed, developmentally immutable, stereotyped activity. Within the communicative repertoire of a species there were thought to be only a relatively small number of invariant signals (Moynihan, 1970) that were used in an equally small number of motivational or contextual situations (Smith, 1977). Although the critical importance of context in the interpretation of signals has been recognized for many years, the prevailing view that has been provided of communication in nonhuman animals has been of a restricted signal repertoire and a restricted set of communicative referents.

According to the traditional ethological view, which assumes discontinuity between human and animal communication, human communication is not stereotyped and is considerably modifiable during development. Human communication employs a signal repertoire of enormous size compared with the repertoires of nonhuman species. Human communication has signal invariants that are easily perceived by human recipients even though it is often difficult for humans to discern the physical structure of signals. If one ascribes to this view, one cannot analyze human communication from an ethological perspective. Earlier studies of sounds produced by nonhuman animals (other than primates) also confirmed that these sounds could be regarded as a sort of fixed action pattern. Before sound spectrum analysis became possible in the 1950s, all sounds were identified by labels that were often idiosyncratic to the person who used them. With the new method, different individuals were now able to agree on the pattern of a signal based on its objective and permanent representation. Pioneering sound spectrographic analyses revealed that many of the vocalizations recorded from a number of bird species could be easily discriminated from one another. However, as noted by Rowell and Hinde (1962), nonhuman primate vocalizations frequently appeared to intergrade with one another and hence were not clearly classifiable into discrete categories.

Therefore, in the ethological view, nonhuman primate vocalizations should be classified into the category of human communication because of their signal feature of forming a graded continuum. However, the ethologists were so naive regarding linguistics in general that they failed to appreciate that the human system does not necessarily use continuous units exclusively. On the contrary, although language employs continuous parameters whereby small changes in acoustic value result in corresponding changes in transmission value (e.g., as one raises one's voice gradually, one may sound increasingly angry or upset), such continuous variations merely correspond to "paralinguistic" signaling. They are not regarded by linguists as playing a role in differentiating lexical items. Linguists concluded that while nonhuman primate vocal communication systems appear in some cases to rely heavily on signal dimensions that vary continuously for communicative value, human vocal communication systems maintain a fundamental distinction between dimensions that are manipulated continuously for paralinguistic effect and segmental features. Moreover, in linguistics, the latter are treated as phonetic units and are interpreted categorically in terms of their lexical effect.

A typical expression of this sort of linguistic view of nonhuman primate vocalizations and human language is Hockett's (1960) characterization of human language, as a communication system, in terms of "design features" (e.g., "discreteness" and "duality of patterning"). According to Hockett, the human system possesses discreteness in that the alphabet-level (segmental phonetic) units have categorical values. That is, a change in the acoustic characteristics of one sound segment (say the b in "bay") is regarded as irrelevant from the standpoint of transmission value (meaning) unless it precedes a shift to a new meaning category (say "pay"). Human language usually includes lexicons of thousands of words constructed from such discrete alphabetic/phonetic units. Nonhuman vocal communication systems often include an inventory of discrete calls or call types (e.g., one for threat, one for affinity, one for alarm). However, their categorical lexicon is usually small in number of meaningful units by comparison with human languages, and importantly, as already noted, it is usually characterized by stereotypy.

The power of the human system to create an extensive lexicon lies in its dependency on the duality of patterning referred to by Hockett. According to Hockett, duality of patterning concerns individual alphabetic units of the human phonetic/phonemic system that are independent of meaning; duality of patterning refers to the fact that these units can be recombined and reordered to construct different units of meaning. Thus the words act, cat and tac(k) all share the same phonemic units while lexically they are entirely distinct.

It is important to emphasize the "recombinability/reorderbility" characteristic implied by this duality because recombinability enables a small number of phonemic units to be utilized to create an enormous lexicon, by merely stringing the phonemic units in unique patterns. With respect to potential recombinability, studies of nonhuman primate vocal systems appear to show either that no restructuring is possible or that changes are far more limited than those that can occur in human speech. A system that has no recombinability is restricted to a lexical inventory size, which can be no greater than the number of discrete units in the system.

Thus, the use of continuous variations of sounds for communicative purposes that has been recognized in nonhuman species is indeed shared by humans, but in humans continuous variation is only used as a paralinguistic component of vocal communication and not as a component of language itself. Humans also apparently differ from nonhuman primates in making greater use of the categorical features of sound in their vocal communication. Linguists have assumed that through the acquisition of such distinct means, humans exclusively are equipped to produce and use language. The evolution of language is thought to have occurred some time after the emergence of vocal communication like that found in living nonhuman primates, for instance after the acquisition of a unique vocal apparatus as bipedal walkers. In order to produce sounds with the features needed for language, sounds generated by the air stream must be morphologically chopped by vibrating vocal folds.

Methodological characteristics of ethology in investigating nonhuman primate vocalizations

Hockett initially proposed his model in order to criticize naive comparisons between nonhuman sounds and human language. However, having rejected the position of traditional ethologists, one might revisit the original question: how are nonhuman sounds similar to or different from the sounds of human language? Hockett's model provides a framework for discussing only how the sounds "function" (similarly or differently in humans and nonhuman species) but it does not really address the issue of the relationship between human and nonhuman sounds per se. In order to investigate how preverbal infants come to produce sounds that characterize human language, a purely acoustic description of preverbal infant vocalizations could still be meaningful. In this regard, findings obtained from comparisons between the vocal sounds of humans and nonhuman primates could offer an important perspective.

Further, mostly owing to our ever-developing knowledge of human speech perception, the distinction between discrete and continuous vocalizations has blurred recently. Knowledge concerning human speech perception came first from findings on categorical perception, a topic in which I was interested in my doctoral work. Namely, several of our speech sounds appear to form a continuous distribution when examined spectrographically and yet we rarely have difficulty distinguishing the category into which a particular sound falls. Findings such as these make it difficult to apply the graded-discrete distinction between the signals of primates (humans included) versus the signals of other animals as was done in the earliest nonhuman primate vocalization studies. Whether a repertoire appears large or small depends on how one characterizes signals and how one deals with graded signals. Along with improvements in the detection of signals, early estimates of repertoire size have been altered; while obviously valuable in itself, this has made it even more difficult to draw any conclusions about repertoire size.

In response to the oversimplified dichotomy between animal and human communication, primate behaviorists have sought methods to identify more precisely each call type within a vocal repertoire. As a result, advancements have been made in the techniques used to analyze vocalizations. These advancements fall primarily into three domains that I will discuss presently: (1) contextual analysis, (2) sorting techniques, and (3) playback techniques.

Contextual analysis

First, there came to be much more detailed analysis of the contexts in which calls occurred than in previous investigations. For example, in his study of Japanese macaques, Green (1975) found that one call type, the coo call, actually consisted of several variants, each of which was associated with a different behavioral situation. In classical studies of primate vocalizations (e.g., Rowell and Hinde, 1962) data comprised a few representative sound spectrograms on the graded nature of calls. Actual isolation of discrete vocalizations based on physical characteristics was difficult because of this variability and because this variability was interpreted as representative of a behavioral continuum of arousal or motivation. In his study, Green therefore isolated additional sources of variability in the vocalizations of Japanese macaques. He sorted spectrograms into categories of similar appearing acoustic patterns and found that these categories represented vocalizations uttered in similar social contexts. Social contexts were differentiated by various factors such as age, biological state (e.g., "estrous female") and dominance relationships. His success in grouping calls according to their acoustic characteristics, which could then be correlated with social context, provided further support for the argument that vocalization variability is a function of behavioral categories.

Subsequently, for a number of vocalizations in other primate species that had been classified as single types, other researchers have found that an apparently unitary call type can further be divided into several variants (e.g., pygmy marmoset trills, Snowdon and Pola, 1978; cotton-top tamarin chirps and long calls, Cleveland and Snowdon, 1982). My own findings with Goeldi's monkey alarm calls provide another example. Examining the correlation between different structural variants and different behaviors is one way of discriminating call types.

Sorting techniques

The second important area of methodological advancement concerns the development of sorting techniques. Indeed, in order to find variant and functionally meaningful forms within a category formerly classified as unitary, it is necessary to establish reliable sorting techniques for the sounds.

In general, analyses of animal vocalizations have largely been dependent upon sound spectrographs that provide a visual analog of vocalizations. At the onset of the analysis, an investigator would typically attend to the set of characteristics that appear most salient, at least to him or to her. Then, the investigator would proceed to sort the spectrograms into categories based on those particular structural differences. Thus, by using different criteria for sorting, different investigators could conceivably generate different numbers of vocal signals. For example, it is possible that one investigator might sort only according to obvious differences in call type whereas another may sort according to minor or subtle differences in call structure. The repercussions of this difference between investigators can be quite striking.

As such, I will discuss two important points concerning sorting techniques. First, while most of the early studies of primate vocalizations employed only quantitative sorting techniques, qualitative techniques (e.g., visually inspecting sound spectrographs and anecdotally classifying them into several types) have been used to supplement the quantitative techniques (Smith, Newman and Symmes, 1982). When examining subcategories or variants within a larger category, quantitative statistical techniques can be useful. Quantitative techniques can help identify the acoustic parameters that differentiate call variants and address questions concerning whether or not the differences the investigator has perceived in sorting are indeed valid. If no quantitative basis is available to support a finer division of call types, then over-classification is likely to occur. Overlooking true call variants that distinguish different populations is also likely to occur. Second, the use of quantitative techniques enables one to distinguish the parameters that determine differences in the content of the call from the parameters that identify the individuals or population making the call.

Early research pioneers used a calibrated graticule to obtain measures of the temporal and frequency parameters for each spectrogram (Snowdon, 1982). Later, owing to technological advances, it became possible to enter natural vocalizations directly through its analogue-to-digital converter and sample them. The sequentially digitized samples are stored in sequential order there. Discrete Fourier Transforms are obtained by applying a Fast Fourier Transform to the digitized representations of vocalizations. Then, using call context as one variable and individual animals or other factors as other variables, resulting digitized values can be subjected to univariate or multivariate analysis of variance or discriminant analysis. Through this method it is possible to determine which parameters, if any, vary depending on the behavioral situation and which, if any, vary between individual animals. However, the fact that statistical techniques may occasionally reveal a degree of complexity in vocal structure which qualitative sorting ignored does not automatically mean that this greater acoustic complexity is functionally significant in the communication system of the animals – that must be determined empirically.

The determination requires three steps. First, one must determine that the vocal structure shows a significant association with the behavioral and social context in which a call is produced (the process described above as "contextual analysis"). Second, one must form hypotheses about call function. Finally, most importantly, one must test whether or not the statistically significant associations between variants of calls that are classified into a single category and the contexts in which they are recorded really imply that the associations are biologically significant. In order to verify the associations, it must be demonstrated that conspecific animals really perceive the variants differently. That said, I have now touched on an important issue that research primatologists have fervently sought to address and I will elaborate on it further in the section to follow.

Playback technique

Primatologists have attempted to use playbacks of calls in appropriate and inappropriate contexts to solve the problem of contextual relevance. Ideally, the identification of a certain number (e.g., five) of vocal structure categories or subcategories will be accompanied by the identification of the same number (e.g., five) of types of social-behavioral situations in which calls are uttered, with a perfect association of one given call structure with one social-behavioral situation. But the normal state of affairs is far from ideal; one call type may appear in more than one situation and one situation may be associated with more than one call type (Gouzoules, Gouzoules and Marler, 1984). In order to verify that conspecifics really perceive the variants differently, it is crucial to demonstrate empirically that they respond differently to the variants. For this purpose, auditory playback experiments have been developed. Snowdon (1982) summarizes the theoretical implications of this experimental paradigm as follows:

One hypothesizes which behavior should occur following a call in situation A and which behavior should occur following a call in situation B. One can establish that call X is given functionally in situation A by playing back call X in situations A and B. Animals should give their normal responses to call X only in situation A and not in situation B if call X is most closely associated with situation A. Playback of call X in situation A should also be more effective at eliciting appropriate behavior than playback of call Y. (p. 215)

Snowdon further pointed out several advantages of the playback technique. The playback technique offers experimental data to resolve questions that could be answered at best roughly by the use of correlational techniques. One can conduct experiments both in captivity (i.e., in a closed captive population that preserves the normal social structure found in nature) and in free-ranging situations (i.e., in a population of animals in their natural habitats). In captivity, behavioral responses occurring with regularity to natural emissions of the stimulus are defined as criterion responses to the experimental playback of the signals. The advantages of this sort of experiment stem from the fact that natural social groups are investigated, thus typical responses to signals are likely to occur within normal social contexts. Moreover, one can identify individual animals and record their individual responses with high precision.

However, the playback technique does have some limitations. First, it is often difficult to get animals to respond repeatedly to a playback stimulus. For example, for effective simulation, the speakers must be well concealed in parts of the environment where other members of the social group are likely to be. Further, stimulus presentation must be kept within relatively low frequencies to avoid habituation to the stimuli. Second, it is possible that the behavioral response one observes might not be an accurate reflection of what the animals can discriminate. There might be signals that the animal can differentiate but which do not always lead to differential spontaneous overt behavioral responses. Therefore, the method might produce a bias toward finding categorization of stimuli rather than differentiation of stimuli. One might discover that sounds, which are easily discriminated in an operant conditioning situation, may not normally lead to different "natural" behavioral responses by the animals and so would not appear to be discriminable using the playback technique.

Nonetheless, for determining how animals naturally respond to signals in their normal environments, it is an extremely powerful method. Indeed, the best evidence for discrimination provided by the methods of studying animal perception that were traditionally used in experimental psychology (i.e., discriminative conditioning and the habituation-dishabituation paradigm), may not be the most appropriate data for understanding natural processes in animals because the traditional methods present the sounds to animals outside of the normal context in which these sounds would normally be produced. Therefore, researchers have employed playbacks in free-ranging situations in order to compensate for the disadvantages of the playback experiment in captivity. Obviously, when executed, this paradigm is more difficult than other methods employed in perception studies. Experimenters must make certain that all animals are within audible range of the playback stimulus. As with playbacks used with captive populations, it is necessary to camouflage playback equipment so that animals will respond to playbacks normally. Despite the technical difficulties, this paradigm has the greatest ecological validity in that everything is natural except for the stimuli being played back. For this reason, several primate investigators have made tremendous efforts to conduct field playback experiments and with a great deal of success.

Methodological advantages of ethology in investigating human language development

Only by use of the playback method is it possible to determine the biologically relevant acoustical components comprising a vocalization in nonhuman animals. As argued by Snowdon (1982), in other paradigms adopted in traditional experimental psychology, nonhuman animals are more likely to base discrimination simply on "acoustic" features which are ecologically irrelevant for themselves rather than on so-called "phonetic-like" features of the stimuli (described in detail below), because of the lack of a normal context and because of the parameters typically used for stimulus presentation. He proposed that "most operant studies with animals will produce evidence for a failure to categorize stimuli. That is, most stimuli will be more or less equally discriminable as the discrimination is likely to have been based on 'acoustic' features" (p. 412).

Just as Snowdon referred to biologically relevant features of nonhuman vocalizations as phonetic-like, an analogous phenomenon has been reported in the speech perception of humans. For example, researchers have reported several experiments that challenge the notion that categorical perception is something special and speech-specific. Pisoni (1977) has shown that categorization by voice-onset-time occurs with pure tones; thus phonemes of speech are not necessary for categorical perception. It has also been shown that categorical discrimination can be made continuous if subjects are given the appropriate set (e.g., by sequencing the presentation order of stimuli as they would occur on the relevant acoustic continuum). Moreover, continuous perception appears by minimizing the memory load during the discrimination task; that is, when subjects are simply asked to detect a change in stimuli rather than whether the last sound heard is more similar to a first or a second comparison sound (Pisoni and Lazarus, 1974). These findings imply that speech perception is similar to perceptual categorization in other modalities. Namely, there is a labeling function that is categorical and a discrimination function that may be categorical or continuous depending on the method of stimulus presentation and the demands of the experimentation task.

In contrast to other areas of developmental psychology, the human language research literature pays little attention to the preverbal period. This is partly because conventional units of linguistic analysis are not useful for such study. Indeed, the conventional units may not always be defensible or optimal, even though much of the current understanding of speech and language development is based on conventional linguistic units such as words, syllables, phonemes and phonetic features. Consequently, the terminology used to describe preverbal vocalizations has varied between researchers. Van der Stelt and Koopmans-van Beinum (1986) called it the "descriptive chaos in studies on infant sound production" (p. 140). Although various problems have created this confusion, it must be true that linguists confronting the subject of infant vocalizations are daunted by its inherently chaotic characteristics: babies produce many different sounds. As long as they depend upon the conventional units of behavioral analysis, scientists may resist examining these chaotic sounds. Such resistance may have contributed to the long-held but false view that babbling is a phenomenon entirely unrelated to speech, the latter being dominated by an innate linguistic capacity that only comes into play at the point when real words are acquired (Jakobson, 1941).

However, the descriptive chaos in studies on infant sound production cannot be overcome by simply adopting systematic linguistic or prelinguistic categories. For instance, as pointed out by Delack (1976), a universally accepted definition of babbling was obvious but descriptions changed with the discipline of the researcher because the processes underlying the development of sound production are not simple. Nevertheless, the adult listener is able to recognize haphazard linguistic categories. Delack (1976) suggests "an early link between perception and sound production which implies a continuity of sound-meaning correlation has been overlooked by many investigators" (p. 494). This is precisely the view adopted by primatologists struggling with the problem of distinguishing "phonetic-like" features from "acoustic" features of vocalizations.

A primary advantage of the primatological approach to early language development is that it can help clarify the appropriate units of behavioral analysis. At least, it makes us keenly attentive to the assumptions that underlie the choice of such units. This is not surprising, not only for primate behaviorists but also for ethologists as a whole. The perspectives presented by primate behaviorists are shared with ethologists in general because both usually undertake their investigations of behaviors in nonhuman species by conducting longitudinal observations of the target behaviors under naturalistic circumstances. It is a commitment to natural history as a starting point for behavioral studies that is a hallmark of the ethological approach. The assembly of the "ethogram" (or catalogue of behavior in its natural context) is essential for any comparative study and also provides the basis for further ecological or causal analyses (Eibl-Eibesfeldt, 1970).

Advantages of an evolutionary view on language

Another advantage of the ethological approach is that it offers a useful evolutionary perspective on emerging behavior. As will be argued later in more detail, with respect to the vocal tract, it is inappropriate to think of the infant mechanism as being simply a scaled-down version of the adult structure. Although data on vocal tract development remain sparse, existing data suggest that the infant's vocal tract differs substantially from that of the adult. The infant's vocal tract is not only shorter (thereby accounting for absolute differences in dimensions and configurations) but it also differs in the relative or proportionate size of its subdivisions. These anatomical differences may impose restrictions on the degree to which the units and dimensions of adult language can be used to characterize infant vocalizations.

As the universalist theories of Jakobson (1941), Smith (1977) and Stampe (1973) fall under criticism, the redefinition of data, concepts and issues in infant language acquisition is well underway. The major criticisms of these theories (Locke, 1993; Oller, 2000) are as follows: empirical evidence violates the predicted orders of acquisition; language acquisition is not adequately explained by a process of successive acquisition of phonetic oppositions; and cognitive development is ignored. Further, these theories generally predict a gradual convergence on, or progression toward, an adult system, when in fact phonology acquisition is characterized both by regression and by overgeneralization. These theorists apparently view the development of an organism as a continuous process of adaptation to the environment in which it lives.

Charles Darwin was perhaps the first and most noteworthy scientist to adopt this adaptation-to-the-environment view of the processes underlying language acquisition in human infants. Of course, Darwin is often credited with establishing the scientific approach not only to language acquisition but also to the entire discipline of developmental psychology. Although his major interests were in the theory of evolution, he could also be considered the first developmental psychologist. Indeed, in 1877 he published a short paper, "A Biographical Sketch of an Infant", describing the development of his infant son, Doddy. In the paper, he reported that his son "understood intonation and gestures" before he was a year old, whereas his linguistic competence was still very limited. In addition, he was impressed by the playfulness of his son and by his capacity for emotional expression.

In his studies of his own infant son, Darwin particularly sought to understand the evolution of innate forms of human communication. Underlying his studies is the notion that one can best understand development as the progressive adaptation of the child to the environment. Thus, this very commonly held notion could now be traced directly to Darwin and the influence of evolutionary theory. The introduction of systematic and objective methods to the study of development, another of Darwin's contributions, also must not be overlooked. His studies of development were always undertaken on the basis of actual observation of developing children, and the major biological foundations of behavioral development were virtually laid after the publication of Darwin's study. Nevertheless, many studies conducted in the field of psychology after Darwin have remained philosophical or anecdotal despite his work. Objective and quantitative investigations are crucial to understanding behavioral development in nonhuman animals because they never talk. This perspective has spawned the development of a scientifically driven discipline to study the vocalizations of nonhuman animals on a "purely" acoustical level. Some scientists working in the field of nonhuman animal vocalizations, myself included, have therefore come to develop interests in the vocalizations of preverbal infants.

In a larger sense, pragmatic and interactive data combined with a comparative, evolutionary perspective on language in relation to human biological adaptation complete an ethological paradigm that emphasizes natural selection. The evolutionist paradigm, such as the one initiated by Darwin, regards infant language acquisition as a particularly human progressive adaptation of brain and behavior to varied and distinct environments. An infant is thought to develop from exhibiting a particular range of expressive resources in spontaneous exploratory productions to exploiting those expressive resources on the basis of experience in gaining control over expressive skills in language. Such a view is also in harmony with the paradigmatic notion that human language evolved as a tool that helped generalist hominids to survive and exploit diversity in the physical and social environment. Diversity is potentially life threatening to species that are too behaviorally and ecologically specialized to learn and to adapt to new environmental habits and niches. Developmentally, the cognitively based theory of language acquisition characterizes the infant as an active seeker and user of information. The infant actively solicits linguistic information and tests and revises hunches.

Interestingly, recent comparative studies (e.g., Hauser, 1996) suggest the existence of cognitive parallels in the development of human and nonhuman primates. The capabilities we share with nonhuman primates are the first capabilities to develop in human infants. Here the significance of ethological approaches to human language acquisition becomes clear. For example, much of nonhuman primate socialization revolves around affective signaling by voice and by face and this also applies to the interactions of human infants. Both groups of primates (i.e., human and nonhuman) retain their capacity to communicate on that level. Humans additionally take on more arbitrary and codified means for communicating. Therefore, investigations of interactions between infants and people who are talking should be important for understanding language development because language develops in a social context. Physical cues, particularly the vocal variations of caregivers, help define infant social development. As infants orient to the cues, these cues may start them down a developmental growth path that leads to language acquisition. If this scenario is true, the question of how infants acquire language becomes a relevant ethological issue and this book presents evidence for this very proposal.

Structure and function of nonhuman primate vocalizations

As previously argued, findings emanating from new analytic techniques for nonhuman primate research have led us to re-evaluate the traditional view of human/nonhuman differences in vocal ability. Snowdon (1982) summarizes four major functional levels of variability in vocalizations throughout the primate order: (1) individual variability, (2) population variability, (3) localization variability, and (3) "phonetic-like" variability.

Individual variability

It has been known for some time that substantial individual variability exists in the form of nonhuman primate calls in several species (Rowell and Hinde, 1962; Marler and Hobbette, 1975). However, until recently it has not been clear that conspecifics really perceive and make use of the variation. Playback studies reveal this to be the case. Japanese macaque mothers show selective responses to playbacks of recorded vocalizations of their offspring and differences in the calls of mothers are responded to selectively by their infants, even those younger than one month old (Perreira, 1986; Masataka, 1985). The same phenomena were confirmed in rhesus macaques (Hansen, 1976) and in squirrel monkeys (Kaplan, Winship-Ball and Sim, 1978). In a field experiment, Cheney and Seyfarth (1980) played "lost" calls of infants to groups of mothers, all of whose infants were out of sight, and found that mothers responded selectively to calls of their own infants. Interestingly, other mothers appeared quite aware to whom the infants were related, as evidenced by the observation that recorded calls of other infants caused them to look at the infant's mother. A playback experiment using chimpanzee pant-hoot calls and control sounds showed that chimpanzees discriminate between calls of familiar and strange animals as well as between male and female pant-hoots (Bauer and Philip, 1983). Finally, in their study of pygmy marmoset contact calls, Snowdon and Cleveland (1980) found individually distinctive acoustic features in the calls that elicited differential individual responses upon playback.

Population variability

It is common to find dialects or geographical variations in acoustic patterns of vocalizations between different populations, in birds and humans. Also, for nonhuman primates there is a growing literature documentating population differences in vocal structure. Maeda and Masataka (1987) undertook a quantitative acoustic analysis of long calls of red-chested moustached tamarins from the primary forest of northwestern Bolivia and found that their acoustic structure varied between populations. Because there was no evidence to suggest underlying genetic differences between the populations, the authors concluded that vocal variability was comparable to dialects. Subsequently, a playback experiment revealed that animals really perceive the difference between the acoustic quality of long calls recorded from their natal populations and those recorded from alien populations (Masataka, 1988). In terms of long calls, researchers have confirmed similar findings in chimpanzees and Japanese macaques (Masataka and Fujita, 1989; Kajikawa and Hasegawa, 2000).

Essentially, animals perform these vocalizations most frequently when they are separated during travel from conspecifics living in the same groups. Antiphonal calling takes place mostly among affiliative individuals. The vocalizations of individuals living in alien groups, in general, provoke vigorous avoidance responses in hearing animals. Such behavior would serve functionally to encourage intragroup cohesion and intergroup spacing.

Localization variability

This form of variability concerns changes in call structure that occur in association with the distance of callers from other animals in their groups. Several studies have examined the design features of vocalizations, namely, those acoustic features of sounds that maximize or minimize detectability in a given environment (Waser and Waser, 1977; Wiley and Richards, 1978). Frequency modulation is a very important acoustic cue for sound localization (Brown, Beecher, Moody and Stebbins, 1979). For instance, Pola and Snowdon (1975) found that pygmy marmosets used three trill variants that were physically different from one another and yet appeared to convey identical behavioral messages. These trill variants could be ordered according to their cues for sound localization. In a subsequent field study in Peru, Snowdon and Hodun (1981) reported that the most localizable trill variant was heard most frequently when calling and responding animals were far apart, whereas the least localizable variant was used by animals in close proximity. A similar variation in call structure depending on distance between animals has been observed in the calls of captive cotton-top tamarins (Cleveland and Snowdon, 1982).

Masataka and Symmes (1986) recorded isolation calls of captive squirrel monkeys by separating infants from their natal group members and then permitting vocal contact between the "lost" baby and the group at systematically varied distances. Separated infants gave longer calls at greater separation distances from their natal group members and responding adults and juveniles similarly extended the length of their vocalizations. In the longer variants, a high-frequency element was prolonged. At first this appears rather disadvantageous for long-distance sound transmission. However, in the habitat occupied by squirrel monkeys, insect noise in the range 5–8 kHz operates to mask some portions of vocalizations and to produce the unlikely result that higher frequencies are better distance signals. The longer variants enjoy the advantage of relatively clear acoustic channels in noisy environments – an example of the net advantage of a "frequency window" in ambient environmental noise.

"Phonetic-like" variability

With respect to the three types of variability described thus far, the results described are arguably not very surprising. Intelligent, long-lived primates, who spend most of their lives in close proximity to relatives and fellow group members, would readily learn to associate individual vocal characteristics with other attributes of social and environmental relevance. This is similar to our attention to the paralinguistic elements of human speech. More interesting, then, would be the discovery of "phonetic-like" elements in nonhuman primate vocalizations. A series of playback experiments seriously challenged the long-held view that nonhuman primates communicate primarily about internal states and that they communicate relatively little, if anything, about external objects or events.

Since Struhsaker's (1967) early fieldwork in the mid-1960s, primatologists concerned with the origin of language have had an interest in the calls of vervet monkeys. This is because vervet monkeys give acoustically different alarm calls to at least three types of predators (to large mammalian carnivores like leopards; to eagles; and to snakes such as pythons). Further, each call type is associated with an adaptively appropriate escape response; for example, when on the ground, leopard calls lead the monkeys to seek refuge in the trees whereas snake calls lead them to search the ground. In their playback experiment with free-ranging animals, Seyfarth, Cheney and Marler (1980) played recorded alarm calls (in the absence of actual predators) and filmed the monkeys' responses to the calls. They found that subjects looked in the direction of the concealed loudspeaker and responded to each type of call with an appropriate escape response. Analysis of the filmed material also revealed that individuals responded largely independently of one another. Moreover, alarm call specific responses were elicited regardless of the sender's or responder's age or sex and response type was not affected by manipulation of the length or the amplitude of the playback calls. Thus, the conclusion that some vervet monkey calls have semantic qualities concerning external objects or events seems difficult to escape.

This sort of "representational"-like behavior has been reported in other non-human primate species including gibbons (Tenaza and Tilson, 1977), ringtail and ruffed lemurs (Macedonia, 1990), and Goeldi's monkeys (Masataka, 1983a). As already noted, in free-ranging Goeldi's monkeys, freezing and emission of warning calls are recognized as the two most consistent types of responses to two different, naturally occurring types of alarm calls. Playback of synthesized versions of these calls varying in frequency range actually produced differential behavioral responding with a slight change of the acoustic parameter, suggesting an underlying perceptual boundary. Similar findings have also been reported for macaque vocalizations and for pygmy marmoset calls that are thought to represent external objects as well. The phenomena appear closely analogous to the manner in which humans perceive speech. Taken together with findings on the semantic quality of calls that are perceived categorically, these findings reinforce the emerging view that at least some monkey vocalizations possess "phonetic-like" features.

Admittedly, the four sources of variability discussed here do not represent all possible sources of variability within monkey calls. However, the findings obtained so far suggest that all or some of the sources of variability between calls can usually be identified in any call type and that when identified, the calls are separated from one another acoustically. For example, if cues (phonetic-like, individual, populational and localization) are perceived in a call by humans, they are also perceived by monkeys based on independent acoustical features that correspond to each cue. This is analogous to the acoustic relations between phonetic features and paralinguistic properties of speech sounds.

The ethological perspective on the evolution of vocal communication in primates

Scientists working with sounds or vocalizations of nonhuman species point out that the phonatory apparatus, as it evolved toward its human form, is paralleled not only by an increase in the vocal repertoire but also by an overall increase in voluntary control over vocal or sound production. At the simplest level of vocal communication a subject reacts innately to a specific stimulus with a specific call. In classical ethological terms, this could be called a vocal "fixed action pattern," evoked by an innate releasing mechanism. Under such circumstances, neither the vocalization, which represents a genetically preprogrammed motor pattern, nor the eliciting stimulus, which elicits vocalization without any prior experience, has to be learned. At this level of vocal communication, voluntary control is hardly recognized. In cases where voluntary control is completely wanting, vocalizations from the vocal repertoire correspond to elicited reactions, comparable to isolation calls in response to separation from conspecifics. Nonetheless, individual variability in vocalizations is apparent even in the absence of voluntary control, due to individuality in the morphological characteristics of the vocal apparatus.

In cases where responses are elicited involuntarily, animals would exhibit antiphonal calling immediately on hearing a particular call. However, in cases where responsive vocal production is somehow under voluntary control, as described next, perception of individuality in the hearing call, if it could develop, would allow the call receiver to take action on a more socially relevant basis. Moreover, if vocalizations uttered by animals, as a consequence of heightened arousal caused by being separated from other group members by great distances, are modified involuntarily so that acoustic properties that could serve to localize the sound are exaggerated, the evolution of the voluntary modification could be facilitated also.

The next more complex level of communication involves the situation where a subject reacts with a genetically preprogrammed vocal motor pattern but the eliciting stimulus is learned. In other words, the subject has to learn the appropriate context in which to perform a particular vocal utterance that, until then, had been used more or less indiscriminately. Most of the monkey calls and a number of the nonverbal emotional vocal utterances of humans seem to belong to this category. The alarm calls of vervet monkeys and squirrel monkeys are among the most intensively investigated examples of this sort. With respect to the alarm calls of vervet monkeys, their acoustic quality has been found to be genetically preprogrammed. However, Seyfarth and Cheney (1986) have shown evidence of observational learning and social reinforcement in the comprehension and usage of the three types of calls. Juvenile animals give the calls in response to a variety of objects. For example, they might emit eagle alarm calls to starlings, to hawks, to falling leaves, etc. On the other hand, adults make alarm calls only to martial eagles, their only aerial predator, and infants often wait to call until after an adult has given an alarm.

Ring-tailed lemurs can learn to respond to the alarm calls of other species. Oda and Masataka (1996) have shown a gradual development of infant lemur responsiveness to alarm calls of sympatrically living sifakas, another species of prosimian. Infants living in groups with considerable exposure to sifaka alarm calls respond to the sifaka calls whereas infants living in groups with no exposure to the sifaka do not. The study demonstrated that animals living in groups with considerable exposure to these alarm calls actually comprehend the meaning of the calls. The development of the categorical perception of calls also requires experience with hearing the sounds. Japanese macaques with no exposure to alarm calls only perceive their variations continuously while those with abundant exposure to alarms perceive the same variations in a categorical manner (Masataka, 1983b).

For some mammalian species, such as the cat, the dog, the sea lion, the dolphin and several species of primates, it has been experimentally demonstrated in captivity that they can be trained to master vocal conditioning tasks. That is, they can learn to emit a species-specific vocalization for a food reward when a conditioned stimulus is presented (and to refrain from vocalizing during presentation of a different stimulus). Such species clearly have some voluntary control over vocalization. This control, however, is limited to the initiation and suppression of vocalization; it does not extend to the acoustic structure, which is still genetically determined.

The third and most complex level of vocal communication involves learned vocal motor patterns uttered in response to learned stimuli. In this case, there is not only voluntary control over the initiation and suppression of an utterance, but there is also voluntary control over the acoustic structure of the utterance. The possibility of population variability emerging in vocalizations arises. This level of communication is the common communicatory mode of humans. Among nonhuman primates, Japanese and rhesus macaque coo calls are typical examples of this level; Masataka and Fujita (1989) found learning of allospecific vocalizations in cross-fostered monkeys. In the study, one Japanese macaque was cross-fostered by rhesus parents and two rhesus macaques were cross-fostered by Japanese monkey parents. The cross-fostered monkeys imitated food calls of their foster parents. Other monkeys tested in a playback paradigm responded to the calls of their cross-fostered conspecifics as they would to the calls of the foster species. Moreover, the brain structures involved were found to differ depending on the levels at which vocal communication took place. Producing learned vocal motor patterns requires a number of brain structures that are not necessary to produce innate vocal utterances. The capacity to voluntarily initiate or suppress vocalization depends upon brain structures that are not required for the production of unconditioned vocal reactions. In parallel with the hierarchy of levels of complexity in vocal communication, there is a hierarchy of brain structures underlying the different levels of vocal communication.

However, species' brain volumes have been shown to positively correlate with the size of the group in which the species lives, at least among nonhuman primates (Dunbar and Bever, 1998). Based upon this finding, a hypothetical scenario has been presented concerning the evolution of human language. According to Dunbar's argument, language has become progressively more complex in tandem with the increasingly pressing demands of larger group sizes. In Old World monkeys and apes, particularly, contact calling functions as a kind of grooming-at-a-distance. As time-budgets became increasingly squeezed, the animals might have kept up a steady flow of vocal chatter. Eventually, the content in these communications would have been irrelevant: rather along the lines of those formulaic greetings so common in our own conversations.

As group sizes began to drift upward, beyond the sizes to which living species of monkeys and apes are currently limited, vocal grooming began increasingly to supplement physical grooming. Dunbar and Bever (1998) hypothesized that this process would have begun around two million years ago with the appearance of *Homo erectus*. Increasing emphasis was being placed on vocal as opposed to physical grooming for group cohesion. Eventually, even this form of communication would have exhausted its capacity to maintain group cohesion. A more efficient mechanism for bonding might be required to allow group size

Table 1.1 *Comparison of three-stage-evolution of vocal communication in animals and three-stage-development of language in human children*

Stage	Key characteristics	Example	
		Animal	Human child
1st	Genetically preprogrammed pattern of vocalizations are elicited as a response to a specific stimulus	Isolation calls are uttered when separated from conspecifics. When lost from other group members, free-ranging lemurs are predisposed to utter this type of vocalization, whose acoustic pattern is invariate and species-specific.	Due to the increase of "arousal" or "level of excitement", species-specific pattern of vocal expression is evoked. Young infants start crying whenever it is functionally required to bring the infants to closer proximity with their caregivers.
2nd	While produced vocalizations are preprogrammed, contexts in which they are produced or responses to them are learned	While some prosimians' alarm calls are predispositionally different according to the differences of types of predators, the difference is learned by sympatric related species. Sympatrically living lemurs can perceive two types of sifaka's alarm calls differently, which are produced according to aerial and terrestrial predators, respectively, but lemurs with no contact with sifakas cannot.	Although the acoustic pattern of speech-like vocalizations by three-month-olds is invariate, they are capable of volitionally controlling its production. After vocalizing spontaneously, the infants, waiting for the mothers' responses, vocalize again in bursts if the mothers are unresponsive.
3rd	Learned vocal motor patterns are produced in response to learned stimuli	In free-ranging groups, affiliated macaques exchange coo calls with one another, volitionally modifying the acoustic feature of the calls. Japanese macaques match pattern of frequency modulation of coos to that of the preceding calls of others if they attempt to respond to the calls.	Nine-month-olds learn the pattern of the use of different pitch contours as a means of signaling different communicative functions. Rising terminal contours are used by them with utterances that demand a response such as request and protests, whereas nonrise is used with functions that label external objects.

to continue its upward drift. At this point, communicative systems resembling human language are assumed to appear. Such a view of the evolution of language is partially in line with the view of language development adopted in this book where I emphasize social communication and ethologically valid models of language usage.

Combining ethological data and dynamic system approaches to the development of action

This scenario of a three-stage evolution of vocal communication appears to share common features with the ethological scenario for the development of language. Three stages are also recognized in the developmental process through which infants' prespeech sounds are transformed into intelligible speech. First, there are natural categories of sounds that emerge when the oral, facial, respiratory and ingestive apparatuses combine and activate at specific stages of anatomical and functional maturation. Second, genetically preprogrammed perceptual mechanisms, together with the input of caregivers, allow infants to respond selectively to the sounds. Through experience with the responses, infants learn to give their vocalizations voluntarily under specific circumstances. Finally, infants select from the universe of possible natural categories of sound patterns by matching their own motor output to the sounds of the ambient linguistic environments.

In this book, in order to elucidate the details of the transitional process through the first to the third stages that are depicted in the ethological scenario, the conceptual framework of a dynamic systems approach to the development of action (Fogel and Thelen, 1987; Thelen and Smith, 1994) will be combined with ethological data. This conceptual framework addresses how complex systems like the human vocal system change over time. In the dynamic systems approach, actions are regarded as a set of relationships between properties defined across child and environment. For example, actions such as walking arise in response to forces from the environment and from muscles as well as according to how skillfully the child functions in performing a specific task. In this view, actions are softly assembled, online, by marshaling the dynamic properties of the body relative to how a particular task is perceived.

The principles of dynamic systems are very general and can be applied both to the assembly of behavior in real time and to the emergence of behavior in ontogenetic time. That is, in real time, these principles speak to how articulators cooperate to produce consonant–vowel syllables as well as to how infants progress, in ontogenetic time, from vegetative to speech-like vocalizations. The dynamic systems approach is especially powerful because it focuses not only on the products or end states, but also on the processes that give rise to new forms of behavior and development. In contrast, perhaps as an historical consequence of long-lasting debates with behaviorism, ethologists are often overly preoccupied with a genetically deterministic view of behavior and discussions of how the behavior develops ontogenetically. Therefore in the book, I combine ethological data on early language development with the dynamic systems interpretation of behavioral development.

In the next chapter, I will look at one of the first steps in the process of language acquisition, the onset of vocal turn-taking. If caregiver–infant interaction is critical to infants' language acquisition, and if caregiver–infant alternations of behavior form an important component of interaction, then we must attend to the phenomenon of vocal turn-taking. A rudimentary form of vocal turn-taking behavior has been observed among nonhuman primates (Masataka and Biben, 1987; Sugiura and Masataka, 1995), and it is thought to have been phylogenetically inherited by humans. Further, I argue that in humans the practice of vocal turn-taking facilitates the acquisition of a native language even during early infancy because in order to perceive and reproduce sound patterns, infants must have good perceptual access to the material to be reproduced. Also, to respond contingently, caregivers must hear the infant's reproductions of their speech with some clarity. In fact, several investigators have found a marked increase in vocal turn-taking between twelve and eighteen weeks of age (Ginsburg and Kilbourne, 1988). Studies suggest that at this age, infants begin to inhibit their own vocalizations if their mother is speaking and to fall silent if their mother starts to speak.

2 The development of the ability to take turns

In looking at the linguistic behavior of preverbal infants, I will describe their conversational abilities during the first four months of life. Obviously, the ability to participate cooperatively in shared discourse is fundamental to social development in general, and particularly to the development of communicative behavior. In a conversation, one person talks, the other listens and then responds, and the cycle is repeated in a "give-and-take" exchange. One can observe verbal conversational behavior in young children, and if one expands one's category of "conversational behavior" to include nonverbal behavior, then one can also observe such conversations in very young preverbal infants. Indeed, adults often appear to engage in conversation with infants. The adult talks, the infant smiles or vocalizes, the adult responds, and the sequence continues. Structurally these conversations closely resemble the response–reinforcer relationship. Rather than functioning to reward or strengthen infant behavior, social reinforcement may function to create a "give-and-take" conversational environment for the adult and infant.

To what degree are infants able to perceive responses from caregivers as contingent stimulation? Does social reinforcement really serve to establish a conversational environment? How can we demonstrate this experimentally? When do infants come to acquire such conversational abilities? The present chapter will be devoted to answering these questions. However, before I discuss conversational interaction between human infants and their caregivers, I will first provide a review of vocal turn-taking behavior in nonhuman primates since there appears to be phylogenetic continuity between the two phenomena. Over the past few years, my colleagues and I have found evidence of vocal turn-taking in two species of nonhuman primate. One is a New World primate, the squirrel monkey, and the other is an Old World primate, the Japanese macaque. While a variety of vocal repertoires has been known in the roughly 4,000 species of mammals as well as numerous species of passerine birds, at present this faculty has been observed only in the two species mentioned.

Turn-taking abilities of squirrel monkeys living in a captive group

In nonhuman primates, bonds among group members are achieved and maintained primarily through social grooming. Although the origins of this phenomenon are not fully understood, grooming is thought to bond social groups because it allows animals to establish a rapport with one another and hence to develop trust. Grooming is regarded as crucial to the stability of primate groups over time. Indeed, evidence exists that groups that do not groom as frequently as they should are more likely to fragment during foraging or even to undergo rapid fission. However, this creates a problem for animals living in large groups because time spent grooming turns out to be more or less linearly related to group size. Based on this relationship, Kudo and Dunbar (2001) estimated that a group of 150 animals would have to spend approximately 40 percent of the day grooming. This amount of grooming time is not really feasible. Indeed, in primates, there is some suggestion that grooming time reaches an asymptotic value at around 20 percent of total time because they need to spend a great deal of their time foraging for food and traveling between one feeding site and another. Consequently, there appears to be a serious time allocation problem that is likely to limit group sizes to around 80–100 individuals.

However, exceptions exist. Some primates live in larger groups of as many as 200 individuals: for example, squirrel monkeys and Japanese macaques. They must have encountered that grooming constraint, and they must have coped with it, when the need to evolve larger groups arose. Grooming as a strictly dyadic activity was limited in that they could not groom several individuals at once. A more efficient mechanism for social bonding was required, and hence a turn-taking pattern of contact call exchange evolved in these species.

In 1987, we first reported on our series of investigations on turn-taking behavior in nonhuman primates, specifically a captive group of squirrel monkeys (Masataka and Biben, 1987). However, long before our report was published, temporal alternation of calling had been known to occur in a number of bird species. This is usually referred to as antiphonal calling. In most species, a fairly strict alternation of calling takes place within mated pairs. That is, the male and female bird alternate their singing with such antiphonal perfection that no one would guess that two birds were involved unless one saw them or unless one happened to come between them and heard the sound coming from two different directions.

The squirrel monkey is classified as a small-sized New World primate; the body weight of the adult male rarely exceeds 400g. As previously mentioned, squirrel monkeys forage in large groups of up to 200 individuals which include multiple adult males and adult females. In contrast to monogamous bird species where antiphonal calling occurs only within mated pairs, in squirrel monkeys a single type of contact call is uttered abundantly within the larger group. This is known as a "chuck" call.

Chuck calls may function to keep animals within a group in close vocal contact. Studies conducted prior to our own noted that the calls are often heard in rapid sequences involving two or occasionally more animals and therefore it was concluded that their calling might not be distributed randomly among group members (Smith et al., 1982a; Smith et al., 1982b). However, the possibility that the timing of call exchanges between individuals other than mated pairs might be as exact as the temporal "rules" governing antiphonal calling between mates had not been considered.

Following Armstrong (1963), many authors have proposed one particular function for antiphonal calling within a mated pair – to strengthen the pair bond. With regard to squirrel monkeys, Smith, Newman and Symmes (1982) conducted vocal recordings of chucks in six captive groups, simultaneously observing all of the social interactions that occurred in the group, and found that affiliated individuals were more likely than nonaffiliated individuals to emit chucks consecutively. This supports the bonding hypothesis but it means that the action of "exchanging" chucks has to be perceived by the calling individuals themselves. However, squirrel monkeys live in large groups. The likelihood that chuck calls will take place at any given moment increases as the number of callers increases. Even if a caller perceives a vocal response immediately after his/her own vocal utterance, how does the caller perceive the specific group member with whom he/she has exchanged calls? This was the first question we attempted to answer.

We conducted a total of 200 minutes of vocal recordings on a group of ten squirrel monkeys, simultaneously observing all the agonistic and affiliative interactions that occurred in the group during the recording. The complete data set contained 2,998 chucks. All the vocalizations were sound-spectrographically analyzed and the intervals separating two consecutive chucks were also measured. The caller was identified at the time the call was recorded in 1,758 calls (59 percent). In order to attribute the remaining 1,240 vocalizations to individual callers retrospectively, statistical evaluation of the parameters of the vocalization's acoustic structure was used. Previous studies have shown that a unique combination of such parameters characterizes each individual (Smith, Newman and Symmes, 1982; Biben, Symmes and Masataka, 1986), permitting reliable attribution of the source of any vocalization. In this study, too, chuck call structures showed distinct individual differences so we were able to classify unidentified sonagrams by matching them with identified sonagrams. Intervals separating two consecutive chucks were defined as the time from the end of one chuck to the beginning of the next. If a chuck-chuck interval was separated by non-chuck vocalizations, the data were not included in further analysis; in all, there were thirty-two instances of this.

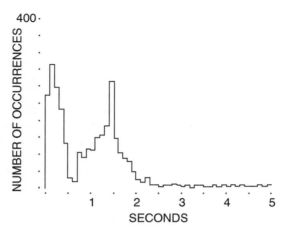

Figure 2.1   Distribution of intervals between sequential chucks by different callers (cited from Masataka and Biben, 1987).

Logically, chuck-chuck sequences were categorized into two different types: sequences involving two different individuals and sequences involving the same individual. In the latter case, the same individual would utter two consecutive chucks. When chuck-chuck sequences were plotted against inter-chuck intervals, their distributions were found to differ considerably according to the category into which each sequence had been classified. The distribution of inter-chuck intervals from two different individuals showed a bimodal pattern (fig. 2.1), with one peak at short intervals (0.1–0.2 sec) and another peak at relatively longer intervals (1.4–1.5 sec). Chucks seldom occurred at intervals of 0.6–0.8 sec. Only 3 percent of intervals were longer than 5 sec, confirming the high level of rapid vocal exchange that occurs in this species when living in relatively large groups. With respect to the distribution of inter-chuck intervals from single callers, we found one peak at relatively longer intervals (1.4–1.5 sec) (fig. 2.2) but the second peak was totally absent. We reasoned that when one caller emits two consecutive chucks in sequence, the second chuck is not likely to be produced by the caller in response to its own preceding chuck. This patterning led us to predict that chuck-chuck sequences involving two different animals might contain two different types of sequences. If two chucks were separated by relatively short intervals, the second chuck in the sequence might be produced as a response to the first one, and if two chucks were separated by relatively long intervals, they were probably uttered independently of one another.

To test this notion, we conducted analyses to examine how well the identity of the second caller could be predicted from the identity of the first caller in

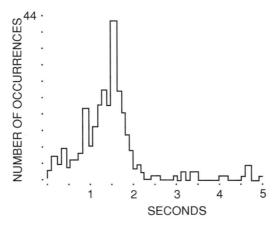

Figure 2.2   Distribution of intervals between sequential chucks by same callers (cited from Masataka and Biben, 1987).

two chuck sequences. Based on the patterns described above, we undertook this analysis on two different datasets classified according to criteria defined as follows: (1) two consecutive chucks where a second chuck followed a first chuck by intervals longer than 0.5 sec (N = 2033) and (2) two consecutive chucks where a second caller followed a first caller by intervals of 0.5 sec or less (N = 964). Table 2.1 shows the distribution, by caller, of chuck sequences characterized by inter-chuck intervals longer than 0.5 sec. This distribution did not deviate significantly from that predicted by chance alone. Table 2.2 shows the distribution of chuck sequences characterized by inter-chuck intervals of 0.5 sec or less. This distribution did show highly significant deviations from what would be predicted by chance alone. In part, deviations owed to the fact that short-interval repeated calls by the same caller were very rare in all instances; however, deviations from expected values in table 2.2 would have shown significance even if these single-caller data were excluded. Concerning this single-caller finding, it is possible that squirrel monkeys are physically unable to utter two or more chucks within 0.5 sec. To test this possibility, we looked for cases where the same individual uttered two chucks within a given 0.5 sec period, with the two chucks separated by one or more calls of other animals. If squirrel monkeys were incapable of rapid repetition, such sequences should have occurred very rarely or not at all. However, overall sixty-eight such cases were found in the datasets.

Since previous studies had reported that chuck calls were more likely to be exchanged between group members that were affiliated with one another, we decided to examine correlations between the distributions of chucks occurring between two different individuals and the distributions of affiliative and agonistic

Table 2.1 *Distribution of two consecutive chucks separated by intervals longer than 0.5 sec by caller*

Preceding caller	Following caller									
	M	Y	O	P	G	V	E	W	B	Z
M	30 (30.3)	28 (33.6)	37 (26.4)	36 (34.2)	35 (33.5)	15 (14.8)	25 (25.3)	14 (17.0)	32 (29.2)	12 (19.7)
Y	20 (20.1)	22 (22.3)	18 (17.5)	22 (22.6)	22 (22.2)	7 (9.8)	17 (16.8)	17 (11.3)	16 (19.4)	14 (13.1)
O	36 (33.2)	32 (36.9)	28 (29.0)	37 (37.5)	41 (36.8)	18 (16.3)	24 (27.8)	19 (18.7)	39 (32.1)	16 (21.7)
P	26 (31.3)	36 (34.8)	37 (27.3)	36 (35.3)	36 (34.6)	10 (15.3)	26 (26.2)	14 (17.6)	32 (30.2)	20 (19.7)
G	37 (27.3)	29 (30.3)	23 (23.8)	26 (30.6)	29 (30.2)	12 (13.3)	21 (22.8)	16 (15.3)	28 (26.3)	17 (17.8)
V	5 (11.3)	22 (12.6)	7 (9.9)	14 (12.8)	10 (12.6)	11 (5.6)	5 (9.5)	6 (6.4)	6 (11.0)	13 (7.5)
E	17 (19.6)	17 (21.8)	14 (17.1)	23 (22.1)	24 (21.7)	9 (9.6)	22 (16.4)	12 (11.0)	16 (18.9)	17 (12.8)
W	23 (17.6)	21 (19.6)	15 (15.4)	16 (19.9)	19 (19.5)	9 (8.6)	14 (14.8)	10 (9.9)	14 (17.0)	13 (11.5)
B	24 (24.9)	27 (27.6)	12 (21.7)	34 (28.1)	26 (27.5)	9 (12.2)	25 (20.8)	14 (14.0)	32 (24.0)	14 (16.2)
Z	15 (17.4)	25 (19.3)	12 (15.2)	19 (19.7)	16 (19.3)	14 (8.5)	16 (14.6)	9 (9.8)	10 (16.8)	16 (11.4)
Total	233	259	203	263	258	114	195	131	225	152

$G = 87.48$, $df = 81$, $0.10 < P < 0.50$; expected values (in parentheses) calculated from marginal totals.

Table 2.2 *Distribution of two consecutive chucks separated by intervals of 0.5 sec or less by caller*

Preceding caller	Following caller									
	M	Y	O	P	G	V	E	W	B	Z
M	1 (4.0)	11 (5.1)	3 (10.1)	5 (7.2)	15 (7.5)	10 (6.2)	1 (3.4)	0 (3.0)	1 (2.0)	4 (2.4)
Y	16 (14.7)	3 (18.6)	84 (37.2)	29 (26.6)	16 (27.4)	13 (22.9)	10 (12.6)	3 (10.9)	9 (7.4)	4 (8.7)
O	6 (10.2)	25 (12.9)	4 (25.9)	30 (18.5)	21 (19.0)	12 (15.9)	11 (8.8)	8 (7.6)	12 (5.1)	1 (6.1)
P	8 (8.8)	8 (11.2)	24 (2.3)	3 (15.9)	23 (16.4)	18 (13.7)	14 (7.6)	1 (6.5)	7 (4.4)	6 (5.2)
G	20 (12.6)	19 (15.9)	27 (31.9)	25 (22.7)	1 (23.4)	37 (19.6)	2 (10.8)	16 (9.3)	6 (6.3)	7 (7.5)
V	12 (8.8)	15 (11.1)	9 (22.1)	20 (15.8)	25 (16.2)	3 (13.6)	5 (7.5)	12 (6.4)	0 (4.4)	10 (5.2)
E	4 (5.4)	4 (6.8)	28 (13.5)	5 (9.7)	3 (9.9)	5 (8.3)	3 (4.6)	15 (4.0)	3 (2.7)	8 (3.2)
W	3 (4.3)	8 (5.4)	5 (10.8)	2 (7.7)	16 (7.9)	8 (6.6)	8 (3.6)	0 (3.1)	0 (2.1)	4 (2.5)
B	3 (3.7)	2 (4.7)	16 (9.4)	10 (6.7)	5 (6.9)	7 (5.8)	3 (3.2)	0 (2.7)	0 (1.9)	1 (2.2)
Z	3 (3.5)	1 (4.4)	2 (8.8)	8 (6.3)	6 (6.4)	9 (5.4)	14 (3.0)	1 (2.6)	0 (1.7)	0 (2.1)
Total	76	96	192	137	141	118	65	56	38	45

$G = 388.80$, $df = 81$, $P < 0.001$; expected values (in parentheses) calculated from marginal totals.

interactions within the study group. We compared the distribution of two consecutive chucks with the distribution of affiliative interactions among group members and the distribution of frequencies of agonistic interactions among group members, respectively. We made independent comparisons on each of the two datasets we created. The dataset composed of two consecutive chucks with inter-chuck intervals of 0.5 sec or less showed a highly significant positive correlation with affiliative interactions, confirming our previous prediction. On the other hand, the dataset composed of two consecutive chucks with inter-chuck intervals longer than 0.5 sec did not exhibit any such correlation. Neither of the two datasets revealed significant correlations with agonistic interactions.

These results strongly indicated that the second chucks in two-chuck sequences that involve two different callers are of two different types: second chucks of short-interval two-chuck sequences occur in response to the first chuck, whereas second chucks of longer-interval two-chuck sequences occur independently of the first chuck. When squirrel monkeys respond to chucks emitted by members of their own group, they appear to do so within a certain length of time, approximately 0.5.sec in the present group. Moreover, when two consecutive chucks were produced by the same caller, the second chucks rarely occurred within 0.5 sec, but rather tended to occur after longer intervals. This suggests that when a squirrel monkey utters a chuck spontaneously, it remains silent for a short interval; only after no response has occurred within a certain period of time will the caller utter a second chuck. Thus, vocal production by squirrel monkeys is at least to some extent under voluntary control. Further, squirrel monkeys appear to have some sort of "rules" governing their vocal exchanges.

The rules seem to be, if squirrel monkeys try to respond to chucks given by group members, they should do so within 0.5 sec; otherwise, they should not vocalize at all during that 0.5 sec period. This rule, especially keeping silent after hearing a first chuck, could allow squirrel monkeys themselves to determine, when they hear two chucks consecutively, whether the caller of a second chuck is responding to the first chuck or not, even in large groups. This rule allows for the efficient transfer of information among members in large groups and so functions to strengthen the psychological bonds among them. Arguably, this is analogous to rudimentary forms of human conversational exchange.

Flexibility of turn-taking in free-ranging Japanese macaques

Our findings that we have discussed thus far on squirrel monkey chuck exchanges were the first to report on the temporal flexibility of vocal behavior in nonhuman animals. Extending on this previous work, we sought to examine similar types of calls in other nonhuman primate species. Therefore, in a follow-up study we chose to focus on the coo calls of Japanese macaques. Acoustically, the coo call has a basically tonal structure with a high degree of variability. In terms of coo calls by Japanese macaques, as with chuck calls by squirrel monkeys, most members of a group utter these calls in calm and relaxed situations.

Because Japanese macaques have been investigated intensively in free-ranging situations since the late 1950s, researchers have accumulated knowledge about various aspects of their behavior. In free-ranging situations, these animals appear to maintain within-group contact vocally when visual contact is difficult to achieve. They are also able to recognize the individuality in vocalizations (Masataka, 1985). Mitani (1986) studied the patterning of vocalization exchange in a free-ranging group of Japanese macaques and described a "network" of vocal exchanges. The most frequent exchanges were found among females of the same kinship. In his study, Mitani defined "a vocal exchange" in terms of the rather subjective determination by an observer that two vocalizations, each vocalized by a different animal, occurred consecutively. Thus, the evidence he presented remains suggestive. However, based on Mitani's findings, it seemed likely to us that Japanese macaques, like squirrel monkeys, respond vocally to a group member if two coos from different individuals follow each other within a short interval. Hence, we began to investigate temporal patterns in the occurrence of consecutive coo calls for Japanese macaques as we had previously done with squirrel monkeys. In so doing, we took precise measurements of every interval separating two consecutive coo vocalizations.

Since 1990, in a continuing research project, we have accumulated extensive vocal recordings and observations of social behavior in two groups of free-ranging Japanese macaques. The groups are the Yakushima-P group and the Ohirayama group. For about the past forty years, the two groups have been geographically separated by more than 700km and have been without any contact.

Animals in the Yakushima-P group range over approximately 40ha of mountain forest on Yakushima Island, south of Kyushu. Maruhashi (1980) has studied the group without provisioning them since 1973. All of the individuals are recognized and the kinship relationships among them are known. During our study, the group consisted of five adult females (six years and older), two juvenile females (three to five years), one immature female (zero to two years), six adult males, three juvenile males, and one immature male.

The Ohirayama group was originally a translocated group. The original members of the group were captured together in 1957 on Yakushima Island and then immediately flown to Mt. Ohirayama, Aichi Prefecture, on the Japanese mainland. During our observations, the group was made up of fifteen adult females, five juvenile females, nine immature females, eleven adult males, nine juvenile males, and fifteen immature males.

We collected data by the focal animal sampling method, with a given observation session lasting for sixty minutes. In an observation session, the observer stood near the focal animal and aimed a hand-held microphone at the animal to record all vocalizations (vocalizations of the focal animal as well as those of other group members), the identities of callers, and behavioral correlates. Observations were made when most group members were located within visible or audible range (one to approximately twenty-five metres). If an animal that uttered a vocalization could not be identified, the caller was treated as "unidentified" for subsequent data analysis. A total of twenty-three and eighty-four observation sessions were conducted with the Yakushima-P and Ohirayama groups, respectively. Generally, the frequency of vocal emission varied considerably among individuals. Thus, the data collection method was designed to provide a similar number of vocalizations for each individual in a group. From this corpus of recordings, we extracted five-minute continuous segments during which vocal exchanges were successfully recorded. Then we randomly chose forty-three and forty-two segments for spectrographic analysis for the Yakushima-P group and the Ohirayama group, respectively. All of the vocalizations included in these segments were subjected to spectrographic analysis according to the same procedure that we previously employed in our study on squirrel monkeys.

Sequences of two consecutive coos were classified into two categories: (1) sequences of two consecutive coos where the second coo was uttered by a different caller than the first, and (2) sequences of two consecutive coos uttered by the same caller. In each sequence, the inter-coo interval was defined as the time from the end of a coo to the beginning of the next coo. Fig. 2.3 presents overall distributions of intervals with respect to the two types of sequences in both the Yakushima-P and the Ohirayama groups. As in the squirrel monkeys, for both populations of Japanese macaques the distributions of intervals between two different animals were bimodal, with one peak at short intervals and another peak at relatively longer intervals. Coo calls occurred rarely at intervals of one to four seconds. We took these distribution patterns as evidence that coos occurring with short intervals are responsive to preceding vocalizations and that coos occurring with longer intervals are uttered independently of preceding calls.

This interpretation was supported by the distributions of intervals within the same caller. These distributions were also basically bimodal, with one peak at short intervals and another peak at relatively longer intervals. However, the short interval peaks in the distributions of one-caller intervals did not overlap with the short interval peaks in the distributions of two-caller intervals in each population. In the Yakushima-P group, 70 percent of second coos in two consecutive coo sequences involving two different animals were distributed between 0–0.7 sec; the same proportion were distributed between 0–0.6 sec in the Ohirayama group, 0.1 sec earlier than in the Yakushima-P group. With regard to two consecutive coo sequences uttered by the same animal, 89 percent of those occurred at intervals of more than 0.8 sec in the Yakushima-P group whereas

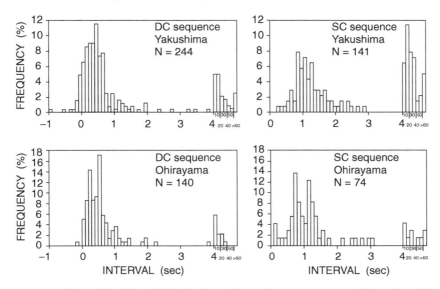

Figure 2.3   Overall distributions of intervals between sequential coos by different callers (DC sequences) and of intervals between sequential coos by same callers (SC sequences) in the two Japanese macaque populations (cited from Sugiura and Masataka, 1995).

in the Ohirayama group 81 percent occurred at intervals of more than 0.7 sec, again 0.1 sec earlier than in the Yakushima-P group.

These results strongly indicated that the second coos in two consecutive coo sequences involving two different animals are of two different types. It also suggested the second coo that is separated by shorter intervals from the preceding call occurs in response to the first coo, whereas the second call that is separated by longer intervals occurs independently of the first coo. In the latter case, the second coo can be regarded as having occurred "spontaneously." In these two groups, the second coos in two consecutive coo sequences emitted by one animal rarely occurred during the periods in which most second coos occurred in two consecutive coo sequences emitted by two different animals. The results indicated that when an animal spontaneously emitted a coo, she remained silent during the period when group members were likely to respond. When no animals gave a vocal response, she emitted yet another coo to address the other animals. Obviously she had the ability to perceive the length of the interval between her spontaneous coo and a responsive coo of a group member, if one occurred. Moreover, when no responsive coo came after her spontaneous utterance of a coo, she was able to produce another coo as if to "request" possible vocal responses from others – a behavior that we did not observe in our squirrel monkeys.

The intervals in two consecutive coo sequences emitted by two different animals were significantly longer for the Yakushima-P group than for the Ohirayama group. Genetic differences between the two groups might be used to explain this observation. However, the original members of the Ohirayama group were translocated from Yakushima Island and only a few generations had passed since the separation. Furthermore, a recent study on the genetic variation in local Japanese macaque populations revealed that genetic variability in the monkeys on Yakushima Island is extremely small (Nozawa et al., 1991). Thus, it would be difficult to assume great genetic differentiation between these two populations.

Another factor that might account for the group differences is the duration of the calls in the two consecutive coo sequences. The differences in the distributions of absolute inter-call intervals between the two consecutive coos, where the interval is defined as the time from the end of the first coo to the beginning of the second one, might not be meaningful. If the distributions of coo durations did differ between the two populations, the difference of the distributions of inter-call intervals (as we defined them here) might have been an artifact of the difference in the distributions of the coo durations themselves. However, the durations of first or second coos in two consecutive coo sequences emitted by two different animals were not statistically different between the two populations, so this explanation can be rejected.

Rather, the result may reflect differences in the number of potential respondents. The number of individuals in the Yakushima-P group was smaller than in the Ohirayama group. Animals in non-provisioned groups, such as those in the Yakushima-P group, were more likely to be dispersed during feeding or group progression than animals in provisioned groups. The fact that animals are more likely to be spaced out over great distances in non-provisioned groups than in provisioned groups might account for the interval differences. Okayasu (1987) reported that coo call exchanges occurred most often over distances of 5–30m in the Yakushima-M group, a group that inhabits an area geographically adjacent to the Yakushima-P group. In the Ohirayama group, fifty-six out of seventy-four (76 percent) coo call exchanges occurred at distances from 0–5m (Sugiura, 1993). In parallel with an average increase in inter-individual distances, a greater time lapse between the two coos in an exchange would be required in order to maintain within-group contact. Therefore, it seems that Japanese macaques are able flexibly to alter their "temporal rules" for regulating coo exchanges.

Flexibility in the acoustical features of coos and their usage

Flexibility in Japanese macaques' coo calling behavior does not merely relate to temporal features but also to acoustic quality and to social usage. Since the distributions of intervals between two consecutive coos emitted by two different animals are bimodal, one could ask whether the acoustic properties of the coos in short- versus long-interval sequences also differ. That is, because one can regard coos following short intervals as responsive to their preceding coos, one might hypothesize considerable similarity between responsive and preceding coos. On the other hand, because coos following longer intervals can be regarded as spontaneous vocalizations, acoustic similarity between these coos and those preceding them would likely be smaller. Therefore, we conducted correlation analyses comparing the acoustic features of two consecutive coos that followed each other, for both short and long intervals. The median interval between two consecutive coos uttered by the same caller was 1.1 sec, when the data of the Yakushima-P group and those of the Ohirayama group were pooled, so the entire dataset for each population was divided into two subsets according to the following criteria:

(1) two consecutive coos that occurred at intervals shorter than 1.1 sec and
(2) two consecutive coos that occurred at intervals longer than 1.1 sec.

Since Japanese monkey coo calls are extremely tonal and their fundamental-frequency elements are spectrographically distinct and are usually the most dominant frequency component, we established nine parameters with respect to the fundamental frequency elements of each vocalization for acoustic measurement: duration, maximum frequency location, minimum frequency, start frequency, maximum frequency, end frequency, maximum minus minimum frequency, maximum minus start frequency, and maximum minus end frequency (see fig. 2.4).

When correlation analyses were performed using these parameters, only one parameter showed a significant positive correlation between the acoustic features of first and second coos, in one of the two data subsets. The maximum minus minimum frequencies of the two coos were positively correlated with one another, when the two coos were given by two different callers within a 1.1 sec interval. When we examined whether inter-individual differences were present in the parameters, all of the parameters except maximum minus minimum frequency were found to be individually heterogeneous.

Individual voice recognition is a well-known phenomenon in social species, particularly in birds and nonhuman primates, as a means of maintaining within-group contact. For example, Japanese macaques have the ability to use individual differences in vocalizations to distinguish the identities of group members (Masataka, 1985). Thus, the fact that most of the acoustic parameters we examined were individually different should not be surprising.

In addition, apart from the parameters we already examined, there is at least one parameter encoded in coo calls that Japanese macaques are able to modify flexibly in line with the context. This additional parameter concerns modulating the frequencies of continuous tonal elements that comprise coo calls. When an

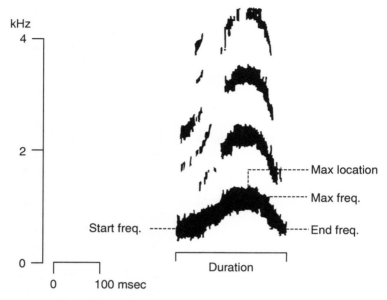

Figure 2.4   A representative sonagram of a Japanese macaque coo call, in which the acoustic parameters measured for acoustic analyses are indicated (cited from Sugiura and Masataka, 1995).

animal attempts vocally to respond to a preceding coo it has heard, it adjusts the range of frequency modulation in its own responding coo to resemble that of the preceding call. This phenomenon could be regarded as a rudimentary form of vocal matching, which is known to be an important ability for human preverbal infants in acquiring spoken language.

One might ask whether or not such vocal flexibility develops during ontogeny. To test the possibility that it does, we examined whether or not the similarity of frequency modulation between the first and the second calls in two consecutive coo sequences emitted by two different callers within 1.1 sec of one another was influenced by the caller's age. We examined the relationship between age and similarity in the following two data subsets:
(1) two consecutive coos where the individualities of both callers were identi-
    fied, and both callers were adults, and
(2) two consecutive coos where the individualities of both callers were identi-
    fied, and one caller was an adult but the other was immature.
When the results of the correlation analyses were compared for the two subsets, a strong positive correlation was found between first and second callers in their frequency modulation in the adult–adult subset, but not in the adult–immature subset. Young animals, unlike adult animals, did not alter this acoustic quality

of their coos. Hence, it appears that long-term experience is necessary for the development of such an ability.

Flexibility in coo vocal behavior is also seen in the use of vocalizations. Mitani (1986) investigated the effects of behavioral context and proximity on call production in a free-ranging group of Japanese macaques inhabiting Yakushima Island. He collected his data during periods when monkeys were most active; that is, between 0600 and 1100 and between 1400 and 1800. Sampling was designed in order to provide equal observation times for each animal in the study group. For each focal animal, he recorded all vocalization occurrences. Additionally, he noted the focal animal's activity when calling as well as its proximity to other group members within a 3m radius. Focal animal activities were organized into three categories: resting, moving and foraging. When Mitani compared calling frequency across these three contexts, he found that the animals more frequently uttered coos while resting and moving than while foraging. No significant differences in call frequencies were found between resting and moving. With respect to the effects of proximity, more calls occurred when other animals were absent than when they were present. Finally, Mitani compared the number of exchanges of coo calls with the number of occurrences of grooming bouts in all possible dyads within the group. He found that the more often a dyad exchanged vocalizations, the less often they tended to groom one another.

Although squirrel monkeys and Japanese macaques share similar temporal rules regulating within-group vocal exchange, it is interesting to note that the findings on coo usage in Japanese macaques discussed thus far contrast greatly with the findings on chuck usage in squirrel monkeys. First, observations of captive (Smith, Newman and Symmes, 1982) and free-ranging (Boinski and Mitchell, 1995) groups of squirrel monkeys show that chucks are emitted in abundance regardless of the types of activities in which callers are engaged. Second, squirrel monkey dyads exchange calls irrespective of the distance between the two animals. Third, and perhaps most importantly, the greater the affiliation between two squirrel monkeys, the more often they tend to exchange chucks.

Such species differences might to some extent be attributable to differences in the characteristics of the groups in which each species lives. For instance, in Japanese macaques there is very high intra-group feeding competition whereas such competition is low in squirrel monkeys. Indeed, in free-ranging Japanese macaque groups more than 80 percent of agonistic interactions occur over access to food resources (Furuichi, 1983) whereas such interactions are rarely observed in squirrel monkeys (Boinski and Mitchell, 1995). In a foraging situation, it appears to be disadvantageous for a Japanese macaque to vocalize and draw the attention of other group members. Moreover, macaques inevitably become more cohesive when foraging than when resting and moving because their food resources are distributed in several spatially restricted "patches." This situation is also likely to influence their vocal production.

Basically, Japanese macaques are more likely to exchange coos when they are physically unable to maintain contact with one another. This pattern is most apparent in the negative correlation Mitani (1986) found between the frequencies of grooming and coo exchanges among group members in Japanese macaques. Without doubt, social communication among group-living nonhuman primates involves nonphysical contact as well as physical contact. While in squirrel monkeys, chuck production is a mode of expressing affiliative motivation towards conspecifics in addition to physical contact, i.e., acoustic contact and physical contact complement each other; in Japanese macaques coos are produced to maintain group cohesion instead of physical contact, i.e., the one replaces the other. In Japanese macaques, vocal production is not bound by the emotional state of the caller. A plausible functional explanation for flexible vocal usage in Japanese macaques is that group members share a spatial map of group dispersion which fuels a sense of whether they are more separated or more densely spaced in relation to one another. The map generated by each individual Japanese macaque provides an assessment of its gross distance from all others. On the basis of this map, if an individual perceives itself to be separated from others, it becomes more vocally active. Similarly, Japanese macaque group members share a map of the network of physical affiliative interactions and, based on this map, they attempt to exchange coo calls with individuals with whom they share less physical contact. Thus, unlike chuck production in squirrel monkeys, coo production in Japanese macaques is not bound by the presence or absence of conspecifics in the physical world. Japanese macaques are able to "address" conspecifics that are present in the mental images each macaque individually generates.

The coevolution of neocortex size, group size and rudimentary forms of language in primates

The above findings are consistent with arguments surrounding the coevolution of neocortical size, group size and language in humans (Dunbar, 1993). Primate brains are larger relative to their bodies than the brains of any other animal species (Jerison, 1973). One might expect animals with large bodies to have larger brains simply because they have more muscle mass to coordinate and manage. However, primates have much larger brains than other mammals of the same body size; for instance, chimpanzee brains are about five times larger than expected for mammals of similar body weight (Kudo and Dunbar, 2001). As humans, we have brains that are approximately eleven times larger than our body size would predict. Much of the increase in human brain size is taken up with the neocortex, the thin layer, barely seven cells deep, that wraps around the outside of our old mammalian brain.

Two independent papers have addressed the question of why primates have large brains (Sawaguchi and Kudo, 1990). They showed that among primates neocortex size is related to social group size and not to ecological variables such as diet or ranging pattern. These results have since been confirmed by others (Barton, 1996) and have also been demonstrated to apply to bats and carnivores (Barton and Dunbar, 1997). The hypothesis that the selective pressure for the evolution of large brains among primates lies in the complexity of their social behavior is now well established and is becoming increasingly accepted. The hypothesis is now usually referred to as "the social brain hypothesis" (Byrne, 1995; Vauclair, 1997).

Byrne (1995) argued that primate societies differ from those of all other animal species in the extent to which they use complex political ploys such as deliberate deception and manipulation of others. In their own field studies of baboons, for instance, Byrne and his colleagues observed a young juvenile watching an adult female digging for roots. Roots are difficult for young animals to obtain because great strength is required to pull them from the ground. The juvenile waited until the female had just managed to free the root from the soil and then gave a loud scream. The scream was the kind usually emitted by juveniles when older animals are attacking them. On hearing the scream, the juvenile's mother immediately rushed over and attacked the female who then ran away, leaving her root for the juvenile. It seems as though the mother had misinterpreted the situation. She heard her juvenile scream as though being attacked and, because the other female was the only other animal near her offspring, she appeared to identify this female as the culprit. Without stopping to find out what had happened, she immediately attacked the poor innocent female.

This sort of behavior is known as tactical deception. In tactical deception, an actor (in this case, the juvenile) tries to manipulate the behavior of another animal (its mother) to achieve some desirable goal (inducing the other female to give up her root). Interestingly, such behavior turns out to be surprisingly common among monkeys and apes while it is rare or even absent among prosimians and other mammals; both of the latter two species groups are characterized by relatively small brains. Accordingly, it is argued that the enormous computing demands involved in knowing about a multitude of other individuals and their interactions with one another and then manipulating that complex knowledge are what have led to the evolution of large brains in the primate lineage. In this context, social grooming is not efficient because of its dyadic nature as an activity. If grooming serves as the means of acquiring social knowledge because it allows individuals to know one another, and if the time available for social grooming is limited, then there are only two ways of increasing the efficient use of this time. Either individuals must become able to groom more social partners in the same amount of time, perhaps by grooming each one more briefly, one after another, or individuals must become able to transfer more information during their periods of interaction.

Vocal contact calls have some design features that are especially useful in this context. First, they allow one to interact with several individuals almost simultaneously. In addition, establishing temporal rules regulating vocal exchanges enables individuals to keep contact with one another in large social groups. The number of possible dyads exceeds 10,000, if 150 individuals live in one single group. Attempting to keep track of so many social relationships would be virtually impossible if it were done merely by direct physical affiliative interaction, such as through grooming. However, with vocal exchanges, because the time invested in each individual is very brief, temporal rules offer the possibility of dramatically increasing the number of relationships that group members can manage. Moreover, the rules allow them to acquire social information not only through episodes of direct interaction in which they themselves are involved but also through interactions in which they are not involved, because an individual can hear vocal exchanges between others (including both allies and nonallies). In other words, different primates may use the same amount of time for social interaction but some species may use it more efficiently than others by developing temporal rules for affiliative vocal exchanges. This is in line with the argument that human language evolved to facilitate bonding within large social groups, by enabling individuals to exchange information of relevance to the social environment (Dunbar, 1996). As discussed below, this has been phylogenetically inherited by humans and has provided them with the basis to evolve language.

Contingency awareness in infants

In human infants, temporal rules for affiliative exchanges play an important role in maintaining their interactions with caregivers from a very early age. In the field of infant studies, this issue has long been investigated as a question of contingency awareness. In contemporary literature on infant social development, it is widely assumed that certain optimal infant–caregiver social structures are required to facilitate the child's social, emotional and cognitive development. Further, most attempts to operationalize the concept of optimal social structure emphasize the importance of sequentially dependent responding between infant and caregiver during their social interactions. A typical example of this emphasis has been called social contingency (Watson, 1985). The skill of conversational turn-taking in particular has been regarded as one of the major milestones in early interactional development before the onset of true language.

The ability to participate cooperatively in shared discourse is fundamental to social development in general. Thus, in the 1970s and the 1980s numerous casual observational studies were conducted which revealed that by the time infants are eight or nine months of age, they and their parents have achieved remarkably smoothly coordinated interactive sequences in terms of their use of vocalizations and gaze. Turn-taking is consistently described as an essential characteristic of these social structures. In these studies, the function of turn-taking has been examined from the vantage point of its benefits to infant development. Stern et al. (1982) proposed that the primary function of turn-taking is to provide infants with the opportunity to learn the structure of conversations, the 'dialogic mode'. Watson (1972) conceptualized turn-taking as a game that provides an opportunity for the infant to gain a sense of control with positive affective responses such as smiling. Kaye (1982) similarly suggested that turn-taking allows the infant to gain finer control over the adult's behavior.

As research proceeded, vocal interactions involving younger infants were occasionally found to be as smoothly coordinated as those involving eight- to nine-month-old infants. Ginsburg and Kilbourne (1988), on the basis of their longitudinal observations of several infants from one to forty-two weeks and from thirteen to forty-four weeks of age, reported that turn-taking began between twelve and eighteen weeks of age. Simultaneous vocal production by caregivers and infants took place frequently between seven and thirteen weeks; however, its frequency declined dramatically thereafter. Papoušek and Papoušek (1989) further confirmed this finding. Apparently the tendency to take turns continues to increase steadily as infants grow and the earlier turn-taking is assumed to be maintained mostly by the efforts of caregivers. Adults were largely responsible for the early development of coordinated structures in interactions with their infants. They played the more active role or took the initiative in providing the temporal structure for taking turns, by providing social stimulation contingent upon the infants' responses.

There are several reasons for this. Anecdotal evidence has emerged that mothers pay close attention to the voices of their infants from the very first postnatal moments. Mothers appear to depend upon vocal information to identify their infants and to gain information about their health and emotional states. They themselves report that they use their infants' vocalizations as social signals and that they adjust their own utterances to conform to those of their infants. Adults are said to use cues such as exaggerated pauses to help infants learn to take turns. Initially, infants lack the central capability to make the rapid adjustments required for voluntary turn-taking (Elias and Broerse, 1989). During the very early period, infants' vocal production occurs in the form of periodically occurring bursts (Schaffer, 1977). Between these bursts the mother skillfully inserts her own actions and by doing so, she is attempting to provide some temporal organization for her interaction with the infant. This is in line with the theory of social learning that presupposes that infant vocalizations are reinforced by contingent social stimulation.

Several contemporary theories of infant development suggest that exposure to response contingent and non-contingent stimulation during infancy can have important implications for a child's cognitive, emotional, and social development (e.g., Locke, 1993; Bates et al., 1996). Exposure to response contingent stimulation has consistently been found to have positive affective properties, to increase the infant's motivation to participate in contingency relationships, and to produce a generalized ability to detect the presence of contingent relationships. In contrast, exposure to non-contingent stimulation is argued to reduce the infant's motivation to participate in contingency relationships and to impair the infant's ability to detect contingent relationships. The impact of response contingent stimulation has been examined conventionally in the context of operant conditioning research with infants; for example, via a transfer paradigm whereby infants participate in either a response contingent or a non-contingent operant learning procedure. Their performances are then compared on a subsequent (usually similar) operant contingency task. Prior experience with response contingent stimulation is predicted to facilitate performance on the subsequent task, whereas prior exposure to the non-contingent stimulation is predicted to impair performance. Positive facilitation is generally interpreted as evidence for a learned generalized sense of control; and negative effects are interpreted as evidence for a lack of control.

When the early vocal turn-taking of infants was examined on the basis of this experimental paradigm, the plausibility of social learning explanations for turn-taking was found to be questionable. Bloom and Esposito (1975) reported that social stimuli, which have traditionally been used as reinforcers of vocal responses, were equally effective as elicitors of vocal responses. In their study, three-month-old infants received two consecutive five-minute periods of adult stimulation. In both periods, the adults talked, smiled and touched the infants and in a natural manner tried to elicit vocalizations from them. In the first period, the infants received the adult stimulation immediately after producing the vocalization. In the second period, infants experienced the same amount of stimulation from the adults, but independent of the vocal productions of the infants themselves. When the researchers compared the two experimental conditions in terms of the number of vocalizations produced by the infants, no significant differences were found. In a subsequent experiment on three-month-olds by Bloom (1977), in the first period, the adult became unresponsive for five seconds contingent upon each vocalization by the infant (time-out, negative reinforcement). In the second period, the infant experienced the same number of time-out periods at the same intervals but independent of vocal responding. When the number of vocalizations produced by the infant was compared across the two experimental conditions, again no significant differences were found, indicating that negative reinforcement did not suppress infant vocal rate either.

However, these results do not necessarily negate the possibility that infants perceive differences between caregiver contingent stimulation and non-contingent stimulation. Both Bloom and Esposito (1975) and Bloom (1977), reported that the temporal distribution of the infants' vocal behavior was differentially affected by reinforcement contingencies, not the rate of vocal responding. In these experiments, infants produced more bursts of vocal responses during non-contingent stimulation periods and more pauses between vocal responses during contingent stimulation periods. These results indicated that the infants were already aware of the quality of the contingent stimulation. In spite of the contingency awareness, the rate of vocal production was not differentially affected by adult stimulation whether it was provided contingently or not. A possible explanation accounting for these seemingly conflicting results might be that infants become more vocally active simply because they are in the presence of socially active partners, though this argument would simultaneously negate any effect of conversational turn-taking on the later social development of infants.

The functional significance of vocal response bursts in non-contingent circumstances

Subsequently, I tested a total of forty-eight three- and four-month old infants by providing contingent or non-contingent stimulation (Masataka, 1993a). The aim of this study was twofold. The first purpose was to attempt to replicate Bloom's previous study. However, in my experiment infants were tested at home whereas Bloom conducted her investigation in the laboratory. Further, in my study, contingent and non-contingent responses were administered by the infants' own mothers, while in Bloom's study the experimenter administered them. Second, since Bloom conducted her research exclusively on three-month-old infants I sought to extend my work into the fourth month and to add a longitudinal dimension to this study.

Therefore, each participant was tested twice: first, when aged three months (range two months and twenty-six days to three months and ten days) and then again thirty days later. Each infant was studied in a room at his or her own home. Video tape recorder (VTR) cameras simultaneously recorded the infant's behavior as well as the behavior of his or her mother. Throughout the sessions, mothers adopted a face-to-face position and maintained eye contact with their infants, who lay in a supine position in a crib.

In the first test, undertaken when the infants were three months old, equal numbers of mother–infant dyads were randomly assigned to the two groups, the contingent group and the random (non-contingent) group. Mothers of infants in the contingent group responded to their infants only after a vocalization, thereby engaging in conversational turn-taking with their infants. However, mothers of infants in the random group responded to their infants on a prearranged schedule and independently of the timing of their infants' vocalizations. These mothers responded to their infants in the same manner and at the same intervals as their counterparts in the contingent group, cued by audio-taped signals delivered

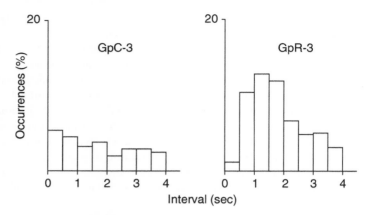

Figure 2.5   Distributions of intervals between two consecutive 3-month-old infant vocalizations in the contingent group (GpC-3) and the random group (GpR-3) (cited from Masataka 1993a).

through an earphone. This timing produced a violation of conversational turn-taking for infants in the non-contingent group.

When I compared the vocalization rate per minute for infants who experienced turn-taking with those who experienced random responses, I found a statistically significant increase in the score from baseline to interaction across experimental conditions. The difference was significant irrespective of the group (i.e., contingent or random) to which the infant was assigned. Hence, the results confirmed previous findings that positive reinforcement does not specifically enhance vocal production by infants. The group x treatment interaction was not significant. However, the temporal organization of vocal production was patterned differently across the experimental conditions. When a burst was defined as two consecutive infant vocalizations within an interval shorter than two seconds, the percentage of vocalizations qualifying as bursts was 21.5 percent for infants in the contingent group and 37.2 percent for infants in the random group. There was a significant difference between the two groups in their percentage of bursts. Fig. 2.5 shows the distributions of intervals shorter than four seconds between consecutive infant vocalizations, for both groups. Note that in the random group, bursts often occurred with intervals between 0.5 and 2.0 sec. Intervals were seldom shorter than 0.5 sec.

The second test was conducted when the same infants were four months old. All twenty-four infants of the contingent group in the first test and eight infants of the random group, a total of thirty-two participants, were newly assigned to a contingent or a random group, at random, in matched pairs. Mothers interacted with their four-month-old infants in the contingent and random groups in the same manner as they had when the infants were three-month-olds. The remaining sixteen infants from the first test formed a third group, another

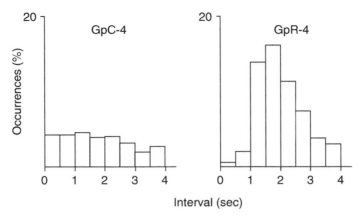

Figure 2.6   Distributions of intervals between two consecutive 4-month-old infant vocalizations in the contingent group (GpC-4) and the random group (GpR-4) (cited from Masataka 1993a).

non-contingent control. For each of these sixteen infants, the mother responded in the same manner and at the same time interval as for the random group in the first test. The infants were assigned to this group in order to examine whether the random responsiveness of exactly the same temporal pattern would produce differences in their vocal behavior when they were four months versus when they were three months of age. This third group is called "the second random group" below for convenience and to distinguish it from the other random group ("the first random group").

When I compared the vocalization rate per minute of infants who received contingent stimulation with that of those who received one or the other of the two different patterns of random stimulation, I again found only an overall statistically significant increase in the score from baseline to interaction. The difference was independent of whether the infant was assigned to the contingent group or to either type of random group. The treatment effect was not signifi-cant. With respect to the temporal distribution of the infants' vocal production, the percentage of consecutive vocalizations uttered by infants with intervals shorter than 2 sec (i.e., bursts) was 20.7 percent for infants in the contingent group and 37.5 percent for infants in the first random group. This difference was statistically significant. These findings appeared roughly consistent with the re-sults of the experiments conducted with three-month-old participants. However, detailed examination revealed differences in vocal production between the ages of three and four months.

Fig. 2.6 presents the distributions of intervals between two consecutive infant vocalizations when the infant was tested at four months of age. Note that for the infants in the first random group, bursts occurred most often with intervals of

1.5 and 2.0 sec and that the very short bursts (with intervals of 0.5 and 1.0 sec) that had occurred at three months were now rare. The percentage of consecutive vocalizations produced by the infants with intervals shorter than 1.0 sec was 12.2 percent in the random group when tested at the age of three months compared with 2.9 percent in the first random group when tested thirty days later. This difference was statistically significant. This age-related difference in infant responses becomes more robust when one compares the vocal production of infants in the random group at three months of age with infants in the second random group at four months of age. In these two random treatment conditions, infants received non-contingent stimulation of exactly the same temporal organization throughout the six-minute testing period. But, at four months of age, the resulting bursts often occurred with intervals longer than 1.0 sec, rather than at intervals between 0.5 and 1.0 sec as they did at three months of age. The percentage of consecutive vocalizations produced by the four-month-old infants with intervals shorter than 1.0 sec was 2.2 percent, whereas the percentage was 11.0 percent when the same infants were in the random group at the age of three months. The difference was statistically significant. When comparing mean length of vocalizations uttered by infants at the age of three versus four months, no significant differences were found. Thus, the age-related difference in burst intervals was not due to the possible change that could have occurred in the vocal behavior of the infant between the first and the second testing. Rather, when stimulated non-contingently, these results suggested that infants tended to utter packets or bursts of vocalizations. Moreover, the intervals within such vocalization bursts also varied according to the infants' age. What is the significance of these findings? The clue to answering this question relates to the manner in which mothers responded to infant vocalizations when instructed to stimulate the infants contingently. Regardless of whether the infant was tested at the age of three months or at the age of four months, the instructions that mothers were given in the contingent stimulation setting did not differ. The mothers were required to interact with their infants with a smile, a light touch on the abdomen, and the phrase, "Hi (baby's name)" simultaneously whenever a vocalization was uttered by the infant. Nevertheless, when I compared the distributions of intervals between the end of infant vocalizations and the beginning of the mothers' contingent responses for infants at three versus four months of age, I found a significant change in the mothers' behaviour. As presented in fig. 2.7, the mean duration of this interval was 380 msec (maximum: 724 msec) when infants were three months old, and 73 percent of the intervals were distributed between 0 and 500 msec. However, at four months of age, the mean duration of this interval was 609 msec (maximum: 788 msec), which is statistically greater than the value for three months of age, and 52 percent of the intervals were distributed between 500 msec and 800 msec. Thus, the average duration of the interval after which mothers provided contingent responses

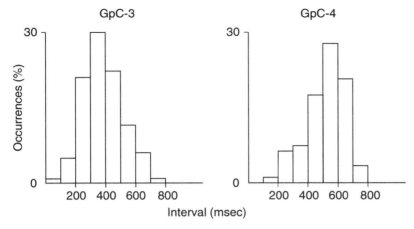

Figure 2.7   Distributions of intervals between the beginning of infant vocalization and the beginning of the mother's contingent response in the contingent
group of 3-month-olds (GpC-3) and in the contingent group of 4-month-olds
(GpC-4) (cited from Masataka 1993a).

tended to increase and this tendency paralleled infants' tendency to lengthen
the intervals separating their own consecutive vocalizations.

That the interval after which mothers responded contingently to their infants
became longer as the infant grew older is not all that astonishing in itself. It has
been suggested that memory span is positively related to age in infancy (Hirsh
and Watson, 1966). At the age of three months, contingency is probably only
effective when it is provided quickly, and mothers are attentive to the maximum intervals over which infants actually perceive their mothers' actions as
contingent upon their own vocalizations. These results highlight the sensitivity
of the caregiver, in developing the caregiver–infant communication system, to
the infants' maturing capabilities. Furthermore, the degree to which intervals
between infants' consecutive vocalizations varied with age, in the contingent
condition, corresponds exactly to the degree to which intervals separating each
infant vocal production and the maternal response varied with age, in the non-
contingent condition. These findings suggest that after vocalizing spontaneously
the infant waits for the mother's response. The length of time that the infant
waits is determined by the infant's recent experience with the mother. In other
words, at each age stage, the infant possesses knowledge about how long he or
she should wait for the mother's response. If the mother is noncontingently responsive, the infant does not wait for the mother but vocalizes in short intervals
or in bursts. Thus, infants are able to adjust their pattern of vocal production
flexibly, according to their mothers' pattern of responses.

The results support the anecdotal evidence mentioned earlier, that infants between the ages of twelve and eighteen weeks are less likely to begin vocalizing while their mothers are speaking than when they are silent (Ginsburg and Kilbourne, 1988). Three- to four-month-old infants are more capable of voluntarily controlling their vocal production than has been commonly assumed. Even when mothers gave random stimulation to their infants, they maintained their infants' attention and infants focused their attention on their mother's activity. Under such random circumstances, infants can take the communicative initiative by producing rapid bursts of responses, requesting their mothers to respond contingently. By engaging in such activity, the infants' vocalization rates in the random condition were equivalent to those recorded in the contingent condition. Consequently, it was difficult to determine quantitative differences in the effects of adult contingent social stimulation independent of infant vocal activity.

Developmental precursors of vocal turn-taking

Even in the absence of contingency, attention-getting acts by caregivers facilitate the vocal behavior of infants; however, in a different manner than contingency does. In the absence of contingency, infant vocal behavior is quite similar to the coo call behavior of Japanese macaques. What differentiates the behavior of human infants from that of macaques may merely lie in the length of time required to develop this ability for turn-taking: the ability is evident in three-month-old infants in humans while in macaques it takes five years to develop, namely until sexual maturation. Turn-taking with contact calls has never been observed among infants or juveniles in Japanese macaques or in squirrel monkeys. How then do humans become so skillful at turn-taking so early in infancy?

Infants younger than three months of age seldom utter non-cry vocalizations. They appear to first learn turn-taking through a mode other than the vocal. Locke (1993) proposed the possibility that turn-taking has its origins in the characteristic pattern of sucking behavior that is biologically predisposed in human infants. Although the number of living mammal species currently exceeds 4,700, Wolff (1968) pointed out that the pattern of sucking in human infants is unique.

Wolff classified human sucking behavior into two distinct categories according to its temporal organization: "nutritive mode" and "nonnutritive mode." He defined sucking in the nutritive mode as sucking that occurs as long as the infant receives liquid milk intake from a nipple or bottle. Sucking behavior performed by all mammal species other than humans falls into this category. He defined sucking in the nonnutritive mode as sucking that occurs when milk intake is blocked or when the infant sucks a blind nipple. While the nutritive mode is characterized by a continuous stream of sucking with equal peak intervals between successive sucks, the nonnutritive mode is characterized by a regular alternation between periods of sucking in bursts and pausing. The manner in which bursts and pauses alternate varies primarily according to the infant's age. In their subsequent comprehensive study, Johnson and Salisbury (1975) found sucking in the burst-and-pause pattern of the so-called "nonnutritive mode" to be a much more prevalent form of sucking for human infants than sucking in the continuous pattern of the so-called "nutritive mode," even when receiving liquid milk intake. Bowen-Jones et al. (1982) and Lucas et al. (1979) provided further support for this finding. They found that the mode of sucking changed from the nutritive mode to the nonnutritive mode as feeding continued, commonly relatively soon after the onset of the feeding. Therefore, the pattern of repeated burst–pause repetition is supposedly more common for humans as a species-specific milk-intake behavior.

Determining the functional significance of the pauses that separate bursts in the uniquely human pattern of sucking behavior has been puzzling because feeding in such an intermittent mode appears less efficient for milk intake. For newborn infants, time spent awake is limited to just 25–30 percent of the day and in the case of breast feeding the amount of milk they can take in is extremely restricted. Nevertheless, pauses are interspersed with bursts even in the sucking of newborn infants. Pausing should not be necessary because in newborns, swallowing and breathing can occur concurrently with sucking. Fatigue appears to be ruled out as an explanation for pausing, because infants pause no longer on the second breast than on the first; nor is there any increase in the pause durations over the time course over which each feeding session takes place.

Kaye (1977) found one consistent effect of pauses in sucking. When a pause occurs, the mother discovers it immediately. She forms the impression that sucking by the infant needs to be restarted. She attempts to accomplish this by jiggling the infant (if breast feeding) or by jiggling the bottle (in case of bottle feeding). Thus, jiggling by the mother is performed exclusively during intervals that separate bursts of sucking by the infant. The precise effect of this jiggling on infants' resumption of sucking and how the resumption in turn affects subsequent jiggling by the mothers were also examined (Kaye and Wells, 1980). Kaye and Wells (1980) observed fifty-two mother–infant dyads in naturalistic bottle-feeding situations when the infants were two days and then two weeks old. They calculated the conditional probability of a burst of sucks as a function of time – either after a pause, after the onset of jiggling, or after the offset of jiggling. Results of the study revealed that the cessation of jiggling was a more reliable predictor of the resumption of sucking than jiggling itself. Contrary to the mothers' expectations, jiggling was actually found to forestall sucking. An experiment in which bottles were jiggled according to a predetermined controlled schedule demonstrated that jiggling ceased because of a contingent response by the infant, rather than to the mother's anticipation of the sucking.

In the earliest period of life, there appears to be an exchange of turns between caregivers and infants in the context of feeding. Namely, the caregiver responds to the infant's pause by jiggling and the infant responds to the end of the caregiver's jiggling with bursts of sucking. Further, following the birth of their infants, mothers were found to shorten each bout of jiggling as the first two weeks progressed. Turns with shorter duration probably come to be exchanged more often between the caregiver and the infant. It is then possible that vocal turn-taking ability emerges at the end of this steadily increasing developmental tendency for caregiver and infant to alternate their jiggling and sucking contingently.

Masataka (1993c) conducted a study in order to update Kaye and Wells' findings and also to examine the effects of jiggling–sucking exchanges on later caregiver–infant interactions. In the experiment, Masataka (1993c) exposed forty-five infants either to contingent stimulation, random stimulation, or no responsiveness using jiggling by their mothers. The infants were tested twice, once at two weeks of age and again at eight weeks of age. In each experimental session, the participant infant was bottle-fed by its mother. The feeding nipple was attached to a pressure transducer that in turn was connected to an integrator located in a chamber adjacent to the experimental room. The integrator recorded the pressure of each suck. A session consisted of a five-minute nourishing period followed by a six-minute test period. The forty-five infants were randomly assigned to one of the three groups: contingent, non-contingent and unresponsive. The mother wore headphones through which she heard the experimenter's instructions. Once the session started, the mother and the infant were left in the experimental room and the experimenter entered the chamber where the integrator was located. During the first five-minute nourishing period, the mother was told to feed her infant as she normally would when they were alone together. Once the test period began, she was asked to follow the instructions that she heard through the headphones. When an infant in the contingent group was being tested, the experimenter watched the integrator carefully and instructed the mother to jiggle the nipple whenever a burst of sucking ceased. She was required to jiggle it for a three-second period. When an infant in the noncontingent group was being tested, the experimenter instructed the mother to jiggle the nipple independently of the timing of the infant's sucking burst or pause and rather according to a predetermined schedule. Again, each jiggling bout lasted three seconds. Mothers of infants in the unresponsive group were instructed to remain unresponsive throughout the session.

Each mother–infant dyad was tested again exactly forty-two days after their first testing session. All of the forty-five dyads were randomly reassigned to the contingent, non-contingent or unresponsive group. Mothers assigned to each of the three groups were instructed to interact with their infants in the same manner as the previous participants in that group had been instructed. Using recordings from the integrator, in a given experimental session a computer calculated the total duration of infant sucking, the total number of bursts, and the length of the pause separating two consecutive bursts.

When results of the first testing were compared for the three groups, the total duration of sucking throughout the testing period did not differ between the groups. The total number of bursts also did not differ between groups. However, the temporal pattern of the bursts was significantly different. Fig. 2.8 presents distributions of intervals separating two consecutive bursts (between the beginning of one burst and the beginning of the next) for the three groups. For the contingent group, the peak of the distribution was located between 0.8 and 0.9 sec and the score tended to decline equally whether the score increased over 0.9 or decreased from 0.8. The mean interval was 0.86 sec. For the non-contingent and unresponsive groups, the peak was located between 0.4 and 0.5 sec and the distributions were skewed towards the range of 0.2 to 0.5 sec. The mean intervals were 0.47 sec and 0.48 sec for the non-contingent and unresponsive groups, respectively. The distribution of the contingent group was found to be significantly different from that of the non-contingent and that of the unresponsive group. The distributions of the latter two groups did not differ significantly from one another. We calculated a distribution of intervals that might be expected if bursts occurred randomly throughout the testing period. When each of the three group distributions was compared with this distribution, the results for the contingent group were found to be significantly different from the expected distribution. There were more long intervals than would be expected by the random model. However, the distributions of the non-contingent group and the unresponsive group did not show a significant deviation from the expected distribution. In both latter groups, bursts occurred at random. When stimulated contingently, then, series of bursts do not occur independently of one another: but two-week-old infants are able to repeat bursts and pauses in regular cycles. However, in the absence of contingent stimulation, this regularity was not sustained.

In the second testing session, six weeks after the first testing, the total duration of sucking and the number of bouts throughout the testing period again did not differ across the three experimental groups. When the total durations of sucking by each infant between the first and second testing sessions were compared, again no significant differences were found. When we compared the number of bouts for each infant between the two sessions, the number of bouts in the second testing was found to be significantly higher than the number of bouts in the first testing. Infants therefore tended to repeat bursts of shorter duration with greater frequency at the age of eight weeks than at the age of two weeks. For the contingent group, the peak of the distribution of inter-burst intervals was between 0.5 and 0.6 sec and the mean interval was 0.57 sec, much shorter

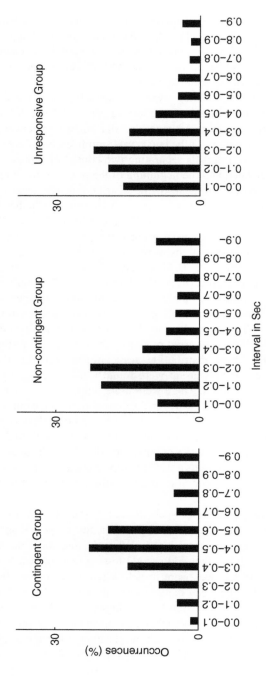

Figure 2.8 Comparison of distributions of intervals between two consecutive bursts in sucking by 2-week-old infants among three experimental groups.

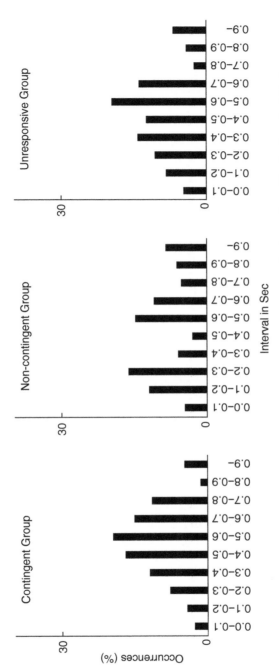

Figure 2.9 Comparison of distributions of intervals between two consecutive bursts in sucking by 8-week-old infants among three experimental groups.

than the values obtained at the first testing. The difference clearly corresponded to shortening the duration of individual sucking bursts. Otherwise, the pattern of the distribution for the contingent group at the age of eight weeks was very similar to that for the contingent group the age of two weeks. For the non-contingent group, however, the second distribution pattern was quite different from the distribution pattern at the first testing. It was basically bimodal, with one peak with at a relatively short interval (0.25–0.3 sec) and another at a longer interval (0.55–0.6 sec). The second distribution for the noncontingent group was significantly different from that for the contingent group. Its mean interval was 0.46 sec. Although this average is not significantly different from that of the non-contingent group in the first testing, other features of the two non-contingent distributions differed significantly from one another. For the second non-contingent group in the second testing, twenty-eight of the intervals were shorter than 0.3 sec and 34 percent were longer than 0.55 sec. When this distribution was compared with the random distribution of intervals, the two were found to be significantly different. However, the peak of the distribution for the non-contingent group at shorter intervals coincided with the peak of the expected (random) distribution. The peak at relatively longer intervals coincided with the peak of the distribution of intervals in the contingent group.

In the second testing session, when the mother remained unresponsive the distribution of intervals between bursts showed a very different pattern from that of the unresponsive group in the first testing session. Further, its pattern was very similar to that for the contingent group in the second testing. The peak was located between 0.5 and 0.6 sec and the mean interval was 0.53 sec. Both the distribution and the mean score did not differ between these two groups. This time, the pattern of intervals for the unresponsive group was significantly different from that of the non-contingent group.

The communicative function of "first cooing"

The results of the above experiment suggest that at two weeks old, the infant's resumption of a burst in a burst–pause sequence is entirely dependent upon the contingency delivered by the caregiver, in the form of jiggling. Consequently, when infants were stimulated at random according to a predetermined schedule of jiggling, the pattern of temporal distributions of bursts simply followed the pattern generated by the random stimulation. The random pattern was also evident when the mother remained unresponsive. On the other hand, when the infant was stimulated non-contingently at the age of eight weeks, its response was to some extent dependent upon normally established contingencies, but partly determined by some form of spontaneous temporal regularity. At the age of eight weeks, similar patterns were even more robust in the distribution of intervals for the random group. The pattern was no longer random but rather essentially the same as that observed when infants were contingently stimulated. Even when caregivers were unresponsive, the infants maintained a regular repetition of burst and pause like that exhibited in the presence of contingent jiggling from caregivers.

Then, first noncry vocalizations appear around the age of eight weeks. In the jiggling experiment, the participating infants occasionally refused to keep sucking the nipple during testing. The number of occurrences of such activity was as follows for the three groups: three occurrences in the contingent group, five occurrences in the noncontingent group and sixteen occurrences in the random group. Refusals were observed significantly more often when the caregiver was unresponsive to the infant than when the caregiver responded to the infant. Whenever the infant ceased sucking, the mother was instructed to induce sucking again as soon as possible. In all instances, this was achieved within five seconds. During the intervening period, however, the infant often uttered noncry vocalizations. In twenty-one of a total of twenty-four such instances, they cooed. Crying was not heard at all. In an interview conducted after the completion of the testing session, mothers often reported that when their infants vocalized they got the impression that "the infant was somehow attempting to communicate." During interaction with the caregiver after birth, perceptual abilities develop in the infant that enable precise estimation of the length of time after ceasing a burst of sucking until the probable occurrence of jiggling. The length of time is determined by the infant's recent experiences with the caregiver. After stopping their bursts, infants learn to wait for the jiggling. If caregivers remain unresponsive, infants then coo. The vocal production serves to solicit a pause response from the caregiver (i.e., the infant is requesting a response).

The traditional literature has assumed that the intonational envelope is the earliest and most basic unit of interpersonal signaling in the vocal mode. The use of intonation contour as a means of signaling different communicative functions was first reported in the infant in the single-word stage (Dore, 1974; Halliday, 1975). Subsequently, the finding was extended to the vocal behavior of preverbal infants.

Flax et al. (1991), having longitudinally observed three infants, found that at the age of ten months, vocalizations with rising pitch contours were more likely to be associated with requests than vocalizations with non-rising pitch contours. We will explore this issue in greater detail in chapter 4. In brief, differentiated, and probably purposeful production of vocal variants in terms of pitch contours has been presumed to be a first step in signaling different communicative functions for preverbal infants. Contrary to this assumption, however, my experimental findings suggest the possibility that at a much earlier period (i.e., at the onset of cooing), purposeful vocal communication is likely to occur in a specific context (i.e., requesting responses from others).

This phenomenon may be explained in terms of "arousal" or "level of excitement" in the infant because in the absence of the expected responses from caregivers, the infant's level of excitement or arousal presumably increases, which in turn autonomically induces vocal production. The precise contribution of arousal level to these findings is difficult to assess. In infants just beginning to coo, sucking rate tends to increase in parallel with increases in arousal level (Vihman and Boysson-Bardies, 1994). We did not find this result in the present random experiment. If the infants had become very highly aroused, the type of vocalization they uttered should have been cry rather than noncry vocalizations. Functionally speaking, crying should be heard as often as noncry vocalizations, because crying is supposed to elicit parenting behavior most effectively. Simultaneously, the vocalizations should have been accompanied by a variety of motor actions including movements of the arms and legs, increased rigidity of the torso, or characteristic facial movements such as lowering and drawing of the brow. Nevertheless, cooing was uttered alone without such nonvocal behavioral correlates.

Other possible explanations for the finding of early coo requests should be considered. In seeking to account for the finding, one might consider two relevant models: the semanticity model and the level-of-arousal model. The semanticity model asserts that even very young infants occasionally utter vocalizations containing sufficient information to elicit distinct and apparently adaptive responses from recipients, who behave as if the vocalization designated specific objects or events in the external world. The level-of-arousal model asserts that internal levels of arousal produced by the environmental context determine the production of vocalizations. Distinguishing between semanticity and level of arousal might be a difficult task for scientists engaged in naturalistic observations of animal communicative behavior in that the semantic-affective (arousal) dimension represents a continuum along which vocalizations can vary. That is, no vocalization is either totally semantic or totally affective but rather consists of both a semantic component and an affective component.

In the language of psychological learning, this semantic-affective debate in terms of the production of vocalizations has been classified as distinguishing between operant versus respondent behavior. However, this classification does not imply equivalency. It is not the case that semantic equals operant and affective equals respondent. Rather it is implied that the production of a semantic signal must be an operant response whereas the production of an affective signal must be a respondent. In Skinnerian terms, a respondent is a response innately connected to a clearly specifiable stimulus. It entails an extremely high correlation between presentation of the stimulus and the occurrence of the response. In addition, respondents occur independently of their consequences. In contrast, an operant is "an identifiable part of behavior of which it may be said, not that no stimulus can be found that will elicit it . . . but that no correlated stimulus can be detected upon occasions when it is observed to occur" (Skinner, 1957, p. 21). An environmental stimulus may "set the occasion upon which a response may occur . . . but it does not elicit the response" (Skinner, 1957, p. 22).

On the basis of these assumptions, operant control or the semanticity of vocal production could be demonstrated typically if organisms must learn to emit a specific call in response to an arbitrary stimulus, and to withhold vocalizing in response to a second arbitrary stimulus in order to get reward and in some instances to avoid punishment. Indeed, this is what happened for mother–infant interactions in the above experiment, because when the infant vocalizations were heard, the mothers often responded immediately by jiggling. No doubt, the jiggling acted as a contingent response to the preceding vocal behavior. The cooing operant was enabled when a possibly incidental utterance of cooing by the infant following unresponsiveness to an inter-burst pause in the infant's sucking was interpreted as having a communicative function by the mother. The mother's interpretation may be totally incorrect. However, precisely because mothers interpret their infants' vocal productions in this manner, the vocalizations come to be modulated and volitional control over them starts to develop in infants.

A dynamic view of the development of turn-taking

Concerning the development of motor actions in animals and humans, several nonlinear dynamical models of the neuro-musculo-skeletal system have been presented. In dynamic terminology, when systems self-organize under the influence of an order parameter, they settle into one or a few modes of behavior that the system prefers over all other possible modes. This preferred behavioral mode is called an attractor state. The state space of a dynamic state can be expressed as an abstract construct of a space whose coordinates define the component of the system. They define the degrees of freedom in the behavior of the system. In these nonlinear dynamical views of motor activities, the development of behavior is generally regarded as the process of increasing the complexity of movement by increasing the number of independent degrees of freedom (Thelen and Smith, 1994). However, as demonstrated by developmental changes in the sucking patterns of infants during the first eight weeks, a process of reducing degrees of freedom could occasionally precede their subsequent increase, at the initial onset of the behavior. Such movements are usually known as general movements in neonates (Prechtl, 1990). In addition to a number of reflex-like movements, immediately after birth infants are reported to exhibit a variety of specific motor actions without obvious external stimuli. These motor actions are thought to occur "spontaneously." General movements are defined as gross movements involving the whole body, lasting from a few seconds to a minute, a variable sequence of arm, leg, neck and trunk movements, and also oral movements such as sucking. Their temporal pattern of occurrence appears basically random. They also vary in intensity, force and speed and their onset and end are gradual. In their development, as infants come to acquire voluntary control of movement, such activities disappear.

At the initial stage, the components of the system that execute motor activities in infants are extremely poorly organized such that each of the components is activated independently from the others. The relationship between the components can best be described as "chaotic." Thereafter, the movements change into a stable pattern of activity in which their function is specifically recognizable. The process is one of decreasing of degrees of freedom.

Concerning the sucking behavior of newborns, too, the alternation of burst and pause is an intrinsic property of their system (Finan, 1999; Hayashi, Hoashi and Nara, 1997; Pouthas, Provasi and Droit, 1996). We may be allowed to assume the presence of a rhythm generator that executes the behavior, but it is inherently unstable and it does not attain dynamic stability without interacting with the environment. In this instance, responses to sucking behavior by caregivers are what is meant by the "environment." When a pause separates bursts, caregivers are likely to perform jiggling. Jiggling is perceived contingently by the infant and it serves as a marker that regularly "punctuates" burst–pause sequences. The temporal property of cyclicity within the generator that controls sucking behavior develops with the aid of appropriate caregiver responses to the initially random pattern of burst–pause repetitions; and through a reduction in degrees of freedom, the generator appears to acquire characteristics as a "limit cycle attractor." The process then proceeds to the next stage, in which infants develop the ability to maintain regular sequences of bursts and pauses without any external stimulation; hence, a spontaneous feature emerges (Paul, Dittrichová and Papoušek, 1996).

Jiggling by caregivers acts as the initial trigger for the rhythm oscillation of the sucking controller. In this vein, Rovee-Collier and associates (Rovee-Collier and Gekoski, 1979; Rovee-Collier and Hayne, 1987; Rovee-Collier, 1990) conducted a long and systematic series of experiments. In their experiments, three-month-old infants were placed on their backs and their ankles were attached to a mobile suspended overhead by a ribbon. If the infants kicked their feet spontaneously, the mobile would move. The researchers reported that within minutes after the experiment began, the infants learned the contingent relationship between the kicking of their feet and the jiggling of the mobile. Jiggling of the mobile appears to be very attractive to the infants because they experience moving contingently with the mobile. The faster and harder the infant kicks, the more vigorously the mobile jiggles. Thus, not only the visual and auditory nature of jiggling but also its tactile and proprioceptive nature appear to make this movement highly reinforcing for young infants.

Next, a failure of the caregiver to jiggle evokes a new behavior in the infant; it shakes up the stable system and necessitates reorganizing the components that comprised the stable system. In response to the absence of the jiggling, namely the caregiver's violation of an "interactional rule" with the infant, the infant learns to utter noncry vocalizations. Once the infant learns to vocalize under such circumstances, he or she experiences vocal responding from the caregiver. New mappings are established through different takes on the caregiver–infant interaction. Achieving this freedom from context-boundedness, means that the formation of a proto-conversational framework is achieved between infant and caregiver. With this achievement, the infant begins developing the ability to produce truly speech-like vocalizations; this will be discussed in the following chapter.

3   Cooing in three-month-old infants

A three-month-old infant is lying in a crib. Slowly, the infant turns its head and eyes to each side as its gaze moves around the laboratory walls. The caregiver approaches the infant and leans over the crib in a face-to-face posture. The infant's gaze shifts across the caretaker's face and then settles on the caregiver's eyes. As the infant stares, its gross body movements cease. The infant's eyes brighten. The arms, legs and trunk produce a slight twitch and without even moving its mouth, the infant utters a short and soft vocalization. Hearing the infant's vocalization, the caregiver immediately raises her eyebrows, opens her mouth widely, and with one full nod of her head, inspires audibly. Then, the caregiver says the name of the infant. In response, the infant, still staring intently at the eyes of its caregiver and without moving its body, utters another sound. This time however, the infant's mouth is open and moving, the duration of the vocalization is considerably longer, and in sounds from the infant's mouth. In response, the caregiver asks, "Are you talking to me?"

In chapter 2, we presented evidence that infants develop the ability to participate in vocal interaction with adults before they are three months of age. Vocal communication between infants and adults is a synergistic social system. Therefore, my purpose in chapter 3 is to explore the effects of this system on the early development of vocal production in infants.

Developmental change in the vocal apparatus

In chapter 2, I described experiments designed to investigate the components comprising the communication system of three-month-old infants and their caregivers. In these experiments, the temporal structure of infants' vocalizations was examined under contingent and random vocal play conditions. Two distinct patterns were discovered. In these studies, adults talked to pairs of infants using identical frequency and expression and at the same moment in the session. The adults' vocal responses were contingent upon the vocalizations of the infant in one condition and random with respect to the vocalizations of the infant in the other condition. Differences in terms of the presence or absence of turn-taking (i.e., contingency) had no effect on how often the infants vocalized. The adult's turn-taking or random vocalization did, however, affect the temporal pattern of the infant's vocal production. The infants produced intermittent bursts of sound when adult vocalizations were random and separated their vocalizations with distinct pauses when adults adopted a turn-taking pattern. Since infants' speak–listen patterns appear to reflect those of adults, it has been argued that infants possess the ability to maintain conversational turn-taking. What has not yet been addressed is the effect of this ability on the infant's subsequent vocal development. Indeed, what does the infant learn from the adult through such conversational vocal play?

Actually, seeking to answer this question has served as the predominant motive for experimental studies on turn-taking ability in three-month-old infants. However, before we address that issue, we must consider the degree to which infants can vary their voice quality. While the ability to vary one's voice quality is virtually limitless in adults, this ability is highly limited by biological immaturity and the lability of vocal sound production in three-month-old infants. Over the past two decades, researchers (e.g., Jusczyk, 1997; Kent, 1992; Lieberman, 1984; MacWhinney, 1999; and Oller, 2000) have provided a careful and close look at the anatomical, neuro-motor and respiratory factors that determine the quality of vocalization in early infancy. In this literature it has been commonly noted that the newborn has a short vocal tract and a flat oral cavity that is filled to capacity by a large tongue, which can only move forward and backward in concert with the jaw. The epiglottis is in contact with the palate and, although this barrier prevents the aspiration of food, it also renders the infant an obligate nose-breather and a producer of highly nasal sounds. The movement of the vocal apparatus (tongue, lips, jaw, velopharynx) that is so important for variety in sound production is highly restricted in the infant. The duration of a vocalization (a function of respiratory control) is restricted by the position of the chest cavity relative to the spine, limited rib cage and abdominal movement, and limited lung capacity.

However, the aforementioned features of the newborn's vocal system change rapidly and dramatically at a specific stage; the threshold is known to be at three months of age. Oller (2000) described this threshold as the transition from quasi to fully resonated nuclei. Nwokah et al. (1994) viewed the threshold as arising partially from the development of laughter and referred to it as the transition from comfort sounds to vocal play (this issue will be discussed in further detail in chapter 6). Netsell (1981) described the threshold as the transition from neonate to "yabbler." Netsell suggested that the development of speech-motor control, associated with the tongue, mouth, jaw and respiratory patterns, produced speech-like sounds at three months that were initially the result of the infant's accidental opening and closing of the mouth while phonating. One of the sounds that infants produce in this manner could be described as "yeah." Using spectrographic analyses, Tankova-Yampol'skaya (1973) described the transition as the onset of intonation and suggested that adults perceive early intonation as a sign of infant communicative intent. Researchers tend to vary in terms of the manner in which they describe the changes that occur. However, the general consensus among researchers is that the larynx begins to drop, resulting in the extension of the pharyngeal length of the vocal tract; the epiglottis then becomes disengaged from the palate, thus permitting oral resonance. Respiratory control begins to develop with the aid of neuro-motor control and the skeletal repositioning of the rib cage. The tongue, jaw and lips begin to have increased movement and independence. These changes occur almost simultaneously in infants around the age of three months. After these changes occur, infants are able to utter new types of speech-like vocalizations, not heard prior to the changes.

Bloom and colleagues referred to these speech-like vocalizations as "syllabic sounds" (Bloom, Russell and Wassenberg, 1987, p. 215). These sounds have greater oral resonance and pitch variation. They are often produced towards the front of the mouth with the mouth open and moving. To adults, these vocalizations sound relaxed and controlled. Bloom et al. referred to the vocalizations produced before the onset of syllabic sounds as "vocalic sounds." In contrast to syllabic sounds, vocalic sounds have greater nasal resonance and are produced towards the back of the mouth. Vocalic sounds are perceived as more uniform in pitch and more effortful than syllabic sounds.

The effects of contingent stimulation on the quality of infant vocalizations

Having established these two vocalization categories, Bloom et al. classified the vocalizations produced by infants in an experiment on the effects of contingent and non-contingent stimulation. Infants were assigned to one of two groups wherein they received either contingent or random vocal stimulation during a six-minute period. The researchers hypothesized that young infants would utter a greater proportion of syllabic speech-like sounds during social interaction which maintained the rules of turn-taking (contingent) as compared with episodes in which the rules of turn-taking were violated (non-contingent).

Before stimulation began, the vocal activity level of each infant was measured for a two-minute period. The data showed that vocal activity levels did not differ quantitatively or qualitatively between infants before stimulation. As a proportion of all recorded vocalizations, syllabic sounds comprised between 35 percent and 40 percent. However, once stimulation began, a striking group difference appeared for the two experimental conditions. When adults maintained a turn-taking pattern of vocal interaction, the rate of vocalic sounds decreased dramatically and, thereby, infants produced a greater proportion of syllabic sounds. Infants that experienced random stimulation did not exhibit this pattern.

To investigate more fully the effects of turn-taking on the quality of vocalizations, the researchers examined changes in the mean number of syllabic and vocalic sounds over the time course of the experimental session. When the mean numbers of syllabic and vocalic sounds were compared for each minute of the session, infants receiving contingent stimulation were found to increase their number of syllabic sounds and to decrease their number of vocalic sounds as the session progressed. The rate of syllabic sounds exceeded 50 percent and during the final two-minute period. Bloom (1988) subsequently duplicated her own findings, as did Masataka (1993a) and Masataka (1995), thus this is a well-demonstrated phenomenon.

However, when stimulating the infant vocally, adults verbalize. The sounds that caregivers uttered should thus be classified as syllabic sounds. Therefore, a plausible explanation for the above findings is that the quality of caregiver vocalizations influences the quality of infant vocalizations, and that the influence is effective only when the caregiver's vocalizations are delivered contingent upon the vocal production of the infant. Clearly, the results of this series of experiments provide partial support for this argument. It remains possible, however, that contingent stimulation alone is effective in increasing the infant's proportion of syllabic sounds regardless of the actual quality of the vocalizations delivered as contingent stimulation.

Bloom (1988) tested this possibility. In her study, infants once again experienced either vocal turn-taking or random stimulation. This time, however, instead of a syllabic sound, adult responsiveness consisted of a smile, a light touch to the abdomen and a vocalic sound. When all infant vocalizations were counted and then coded as syllabic or vocalic sounds under these conditions, turn-taking was indeed found to facilitate a speak–listen pattern of infant vocalization. Nonetheless, in the absence of the verbal component of the adult's response, turn-taking had no special facilitative effect on syllabic sounds. During both turn-taking and random nonverbal interaction, the infants increased their total rate of vocalizing but they continued to produce fewer syllabic as compared with vocalic sounds. Although the quality of adult vocalizations does influence the quality of infant vocalizations, the influence must be unidirectional, not bidirectional. The adult's behavior works only in the direction of facilitating the production of speech-like vocalizations in infants.

No doubt, each infant becomes able to utter speech-like sounds only after the requisite anatomical, neurophysiological, respiratory and motor development has occurred. Therefore, turn-taking interaction with the caregiver only provides an opportunity for adult speech to influence acoustic features of sounds that the infant itself can already produce. But why would verbal stimulation play a special role in increasing syllabic sounds while vocalic stimulation play no special role in increasing vocalic sounds?

The question seems to relate to the nature of a phenomenon that has been treated to date as an "early form of imitation." Piaget (1951) classified vocal imitation into several types. As its earliest form Valentine (1930) lists reflexive imitation (e.g., the tendency to cough when someone else coughs), the "innate" tendency in early infancy to imitate not specific sounds but sound making, and the tendency for certain activities to "monopolize" the infant's attention. Similarly, Tomkins (1962) suggested that the earliest vocal imitation might develop through the process of contagion, which has an emotional basis, and concluded that the infant's earliest vocal productions could well be classified as a form of vocal contagion. Assuming that the increase in syllabic sounds resulting from contingent verbal stimulation is a product of vocal contagion rather than "imitation" (in the cognitive-representational sense), one might find an answer to the question of why vocal contagion occurred only when verbal stimulation was offered by caregivers in a turn-taking fashion. The verbal stimulation no doubt consisted of speech sounds that had been quite familiar to the infants since birth. Actually, the infants would have been exposed to the sounds even before birth (i.e., during the prenatal period) (DeCasper et al., 1994). Three-month-old infants are also able to discriminate contingent from noncontingent adult stimulation. However, contingent stimulation is not enough to facilitate vocal contagion in infants at this age; in addition, the stimulus provided must itself be familiar to them. Finally, the stimulus has an emotional basis because of the relationship between caregiver and infant. These are the conditions for contagion noted by Piaget and Tomkins. The question remains, however, of why syllabic stimulation plays a special role in infant vocal behavior only when it is provided contingently.

In this regard, Locke (1993) suggested that subcortical mechanisms under-lie this and other early forms of imitation, which are responsive to kinesthetic stimulation. For instance, movement might be an important contributor to the "imitation" of visual displays. Similar subcortical processes might also play a role in early vocal contagion; these processes might shed light on why vocal contagion occurs only when the verbal stimulus includes turn-taking. Verbal stimulation causes the infant to pause longer between vocalizations. Perhaps it is only through the provision of these intervals that infants might receive the subcortical response needed for them to mimic features of adult verbal behavior. This subcortical activity is thought to generate a state of arousal that Valentine (1930) described as "monopolizing" the infant's attention. In other words, it is suggested that just as vestibular stimulation (rocking) low-ers the newborn's state of arousal and increases visual orientation, turn-taking similarly affects three-month-old infants' arousal and attention. This could explain why adult vocal stimulation enhances syllabic sound production in three-month-old infants only when it provides turn-taking in combination with speech sounds.

Why the human vocal system changes around three months of age

To appreciate the significance of the vocal contagion occurring around three months of age, we must consider the cost-benefit tradeoffs of this vocal apparatus, which allows human adults to produce speech sounds, compared with the vocal systems generally found in nonhuman animals. Several investigators (e.g., Lieberman, 1984) have examined the similarities and differences in the upper respiratory tracts of humans and other mammals. These researchers found that the position of the larynx, or voice box, in the neck is paramount in determining the way an animal breathes, swallows and vocalizes. Two general anatomical patterns have been recognized, each with its own functional consequences. The first is known as the basic mammalian pattern. In virtually all mammals, except humans, the larynx is high in the neck throughout their entire lives, lying roughly opposite the first to third cervical vertebrae. In this position, the larynx is able to lock into the nasopharynx, which is the air space towards the back of the nasal cavity. This position allows the larynx to provide a direct passageway for air between the nose and the lungs. If an animal with this basic mammalian vocal anatomy swallows any liquid, the liquid flows around either side of the interlocked larynx and nasopharynx, through channels known as the piriform sinuses, before finally reaching the esophagus and stomach. Because they possess separate pathways for food and air, animals with this basic mammalian vocal anatomy, without exception, are able to swallow and breathe simultaneously. However, this pattern severely restricts the array of sounds an animal can produce. The pharynx, an air cavity surrounded by membranes and musculature, is located above the larynx. The pharynx is part of the food pathway and is also able to modify the sound. As long as the pharynx is positioned high in the neck, there is little space for the pharyngeal cavity. Consequently, there is little room for modifying the initial or fundamental sounds generated at the vocal fold.

The second anatomical pattern, the unique vocal system of human adults, provides a marked contrast with the basic mammalian pattern. In adult humans, the position of the larynx corresponds to the fourth to almost the seventh cervical vertebrae, a position considerably lower than that found in other mammals. In this position, it is impossible for the larynx to lock into the back of the nasal cavity and hence to separate the breathing and swallowing pathways. Consequently, the respiratory and digestive tracts cross above the larynx, which has unfortunate drawbacks. For example, food can easily become lodged in the entrance of the larynx, block the airway, and cause suffocation. In addition, it is absolutely impossible for adult humans to drink and breathe simultaneously without choking. As compensation, however, the descent of the larynx into the neck has produced a greatly expanded pharyngeal chamber above the vocal folds. This difference can be regarded as an anatomical feature of enormous value because sounds emitted from the larynx can be modified to a greater degree than is possible for other nonhuman mammals.

Anatomically, the difference in the position of the larynx for the basic mammalian pattern versus the human pattern relates to the shape of the bottom of the skull, i.e., the basicranium. Given that the basicranium serves as the roof of the upper respiratory tract, this should not be surprising. Across the mammalian orders, two basic skull/larynx configurations have been found to exist. In one the basicranium is fairly flat while in the other it is markedly arched or flexed. In the first configuration, which is characteristic of all mammals except human adults, the larynx is positioned high in the neck, while in the second configuration, which is found only in human adults, the corresponding larynx is positioned low in the neck. However, the vocal systems of human infants under three months of age, are classified not into the second configuration but rather into the first. Indeed, their larynxes are positioned relatively high in the neck, much like those of other mammals. Actually, with respect to the upper respiratory tract, young human infants possess the functional anatomy of nonhuman primates. Around three months of age, the larynx of the human begins to descend lower into the neck, as previously described.

It should be obvious why the vocal system that is unique to human adults is not also possessed by newborns. The production of speech sounds is always accompanied by the risks associated with not being able to simultaneously breathe, swallow and vocalize. If newborns were morphologically designed to produce speech sounds, they would face tremendous difficulty in consuming milk or they could die by choking. The change at three months of age can be seen as a product of compromising between the benefits and costs of having a uniquely human vocal system. Thereafter, infants are able to utter truly speech-like vocalizations. However, this does not necessarily mean that infants come to produce such vocalizations exclusively. They still produce nasal (vocalic) sounds as abundantly as speech-like (syllabic) sounds. Contingent verbal stimulation by adults serves to facilitate infants' production of speech-like sounds.

Another reason to assume some role for vocal contagion for infants' earliest acquisition of speech-like vocalizations comes from evidence that such imitation is not unique to humans, but rather can also be extended to nonhuman primates. Hauser (1992) recorded vocalizations of rhesus monkeys (*Macaca mulatta*) under free-ranging circumstances and examined the idiosyncratic acoustic qualities of each animal's vocalizations relative to the animal's genetic relationship to other animals. The type of vocalizations Hauser chose for study was very similar to the call we have been studying in Japanese macaques, the coo call. Further, the rhesus monkey is a species that is phylogenetically closely related to the Japanese macaque. The coo call is heard abundantly in calm and relaxed situations, and is assumed to function to keep a group of animals within the audible range of vocalizations. Hauser conducted his research on rhesus monkeys living on the island of Cayo Santiago, Puerto Rico, where studies of the animals have been conducted for over half a century and information about the matrilineal kin relationship of each animal is available for the whole period; i.e., the animal can be classified into one of 405 matrilines.

Vocal recordings of eight to nineteen coos from randomly chosen animals in the Cayo Santiago group revealed that the acoustic quality of coos from the members of one matriline differed systematically from the quality of coos of other matrilines. The acoustic basis for distinguishing one matriline from another seemed, at least to human ears, to be the degree of nasality in the vocalizations. That is, one matriline sounded very "nasal" while others did not sound so "nasal." Thus, although rhesus macaques are basically nasal breathers, the proportion of nasal airflow used in producing vocalizations is to some extent flexible; adult usage is probably a product of the environment in which immatures develop. Like Japanese macaques, rhesus macaques are also inclined to exchange coos within groups. This sort of vocal exchange could then serve as contingent stimulation for young infants, so vocal contagion could be the basis of developing matriline-specific qualities in their vocalizations.

Interestingly, in three- to four-month-old human infants, the acoustic basis that is crucial for distinguishing syllabic sounds from vocalic sounds is also the degree of nasality. This distinction was first developed by subjective ratings. During the process of establishing definitions of infant vocalizations as syllabic and vocalic, certain sounds were found to be more appealing to adult listeners than others. Naive observers made comments such as "this baby sounds as though he is really talking" in reaction to some of the sounds, but not to others.

To determine the acoustic variables that contributed to such an impression, Masataka and Bloom (1994) conducted a quantitative acoustical (spectrographic) analysis of those vocalizations that had been classified as either syllabic or vocalic in subjective ratings. In the analysis, two videotapes of three-month-old infants were examined, one of twenty-four Canadian infants (twelve males and twelve females) and one of twelve Japanese infants (six males and six females). Each of the infants was involved in interaction with its mother under naturalistic conditions. First, two trained raters categorized each vocalization as either syllabic or vocalic. Thereafter, each vocalization was submitted for acoustical analysis. Using the sonagraph, twelve acoustic parameters were obtained with respect to the fundamental frequency element of the vocalization. However, except for duration, none of them was significantly different between the two categories.

Finally, the researchers measured the degree of nasality in the infants' vocalizations. Using Fast Fourier Transformation, a power spectrum was generated at fifty-ms intervals throughout the vocalization and for each power spectrum, the frequency and amplitude of all harmonics were recorded. When the power spectra for syllabic versus vocalic sounds were compared, the presence of interharmonic energy was obvious in vocalic sounds but not in syllabic sounds. It is known that this energy is a pure reflection of nasal air flow (Huffman, 1990). Moreover, when the frequency-amplitude slope is computed, the slope generally decreases (becomes flatter) as nasal coupling increases; the presence of coupling is buttressed by the simultaneous recording of nasal airflow. Thus, when a regression line was computed for all peaks of the harmonics of these infants' vocalizations, it was found that the slope of the regression line was significantly different depending on whether the vocalization was classified as a syllabic sound or as a vocalic sound. Essentially, the same acoustic parameter – degree of nasality – determines both the acoustic features distinguishing syllabic from vocalic sounds in human infants and the kin-specific vocal quality of coo calls of rhesus monkeys.

The possibility that this "denasalization" was a crucial point for the emergence of the uniqueness of human speech as an acoustic signal is in line with Lieberman's theory (Lieberman, 1984). Lieberman proposed that the structure of the human vocal tract provides a selective advantage over other configurations because it can produce sounds that are not nasalized and that nasalization causes utterances to be less readily identified by listeners. Because the human vocal tract is denasalized, it comes to produce quantal sounds (e.g., /a/, /u/, /i/) defined by distinct spectral peaks, resulting in fewer perceptual errors. Thus, speech sounds are better suited for communication than other sounds are and they provide a significantly greater rate of data transmission than other communicative sounds.

Evolution of the uniqueness of speech in humans

The vocal system that is characteristic of modern humans is thought to have appeared only with the arrival of *Homo sapiens* some 300,000 to 400,000 years ago. This view is based on measurements of ancestral hominid fossils and subsequent reconstructions of the approximate level of the larynx and associated structures in ancestral hominids. Examination of the basicrania of original fossil australopithecine remains that were housed in collection reveals that these earliest hominids had vocal tracts much like those of living monkeys or apes. Consequently, the earliest hominids would also have had the ability to swallow liquids and to breathe simultaneously and, more importantly, they likely possessed a very restricted vocal repertoire compared with that of modern humans. Their larynges were positioned relatively high in the neck, which would have made it impossible for them to produce the sounds that modern human adults produce. Although these early hominids might have developed some sort of vocalization-dependent communication system, the repertoire of sounds that they would have been able to produce would have been extremely restricted compared with modern human adults, and would have been rather similar to that of living rhesus macaques. In this sense, rhesus macaques, with their acoustically variable coo calls, can be regarded as living models for reconstructing the processes underlying the emergence of uniquely human speech from its ancestral forms.

Formant frequency patterns play a primary role in human speech and the vocal tract shapes that correspond to most of the different sounds of human speech are well documented (Lieberman, 1984). For production, many speech sounds require a vocal tract configuration that is unique to humans and a nearly ninety-degree connection between the pharyngeal and oral cavities. At this angle, the tract is partitioned into two independent sections, which allows the body of the tongue two degrees of freedom. The human tongue can move up or down (modifying the size of the oral cavity) and forward or backward (modifying the pharyngeal cavity). For instance, when the vowel [a] in the word "father" is pronounced, a set of muscles encircling the pharynx, the pharyngeal constrictors, shrinks and pulls the tongue back. The tongue can be pulled forward by the genioglossus muscle to produce vowel sounds like [i] and can be pulled backward and up in the vocal cavity to produce vowel sounds like [u]. However, because nonhuman primates' pharyngeal cavities are short and positioned high in the neck, the range of vowels they can produce is quite limited when compared to adult humans. The range is just as restricted in three-month-old human infants as it is in nonhuman primates. The ability to perform more adult-like vocal tract movements is acquired by human infants as they develop. Such development is achieved through the process termed "true vocal imitation" – a process that should be distinguished from "early vocal imitation" or "vocal contagion," which will be discussed in the next chapter.

It is a little known fact that the nasal cavities and sinuses can also play an important role in the acoustics of the vocal tract (Frant, 1960; Dang and Honda, 1997; Dang et al., 1998). Because these cavities are mostly encased in bone, their acoustic properties are relatively static during a given vocalization. The nasal passage, much like the oral cavity described previously, is basically a tube of varying cross-sectional diameter. The nasal tract stretches from the nostrils back to the oropharyngeal port, which is where the pharynx branches into the nasal and oral cavities. A movable flap of tissue called the velum controls the coupling between these two cavities. If human adults are to produce a purely oral sound, the velum must close off the nasal tract. Human adults are able to perform this movement under voluntary control; even rhesus macaques and three-month-old human infants can perform this movement, albeit with a much lower degree of voluntary control. The ability voluntarily to control this velum movement is acquired developmentally in infants exposed to speech; it is the earliest form of learning in sound production. The vocal contagion described above appears to play an important role in this acquisition.

This contagion is possible only if the infant receives verbal stimulation in a contingent manner, i.e., verbal responses, and only if there is an emotional connection between the infant and the person(s) with whom it is interacting. "Intuitive parenting" is a term that has been often applied to caregivers' behavior in providing preverbal infants with linguistic input (e.g., Papoušek and Papoušek, 1989). Briefly, it is thought that without knowing it, adult caregivers behave in ways that provide infants with a modeling framework, by performing models that can be imitated and giving extensive corrective feedback to infants' vocal practice. The timing of the presentation of the models corresponds to the order in which the elementary prerequisites for speech develop. The caregiver is a natural, nonconscious, yet excellent teacher, who establishes optimal conditions for teaching interventions. Among other things, caregivers devote their main efforts to the most important means of adaptation, gradually ordering and adjusting their teaching tasks to infant constraints, and effectively motivating their infants. For this intuitive teaching, preverbal vocal signals, facial expressions and other bodily gestures are used. Typically, empathetic matching in the vocal and facial expression of emotional feelings is thought to provide infants with feedback that may function as a "biological echo" or a "biological mirror" and may influence the development of the self-concept. However, before the quality of the caregiver's response exerts any effect on the preverbal infant, the infant first "picks up" a modeling/imitative frame from the action of responding itself, and consequently, the readiness to produce speech-like sounds is to some extent accomplished.

The role of selective reinforcement

While verbal responding by caregivers is necessary for increased production of syllabic sounds in infants, the infants' syllabic sounds themselves represent only one feature of the vocal communication system because infants also utter vocalizations spontaneously and their vocalizations have been found to have causal effects on adults' speech. In a series of experiments (e.g., Bloom's and my own) it was found that infants uttered syllabic and vocalic sounds with almost equal frequency during baseline periods, i.e., in periods without any caregiver stimulation. Infants entered these studies with the ability to produce cooing sounds that could be labeled as either syllabic or vocalic. Since the infants had a preexisting vocal repertoire, their vocalizations could be altered even without having to rely on the introduction of novel material via contagion. In the contingent stimulation condition, participating caregivers were required to respond to their infants' vocalizations whenever they were heard, regardless of the type of the vocalization.

The question arises as to why adults in naturalistic contexts maintain conversational turn-taking with nonverbal infant partners apart from contributing to the infants' development. It is useful to look at infant–adult vocal communication not only from the perspective of child development but also from the perspective of adult social psychology. For example, adults are often found to experience difficulty and fatigue in trying to maintain a conversation with an individual who cannot speak their own language. Adults face a similar problem when they try to communicate with young infants; parents cope by searching for infant behaviors that can be construed as active social participation (Fraiberg, 1977; Robson, 1967). Authors such as Fraiberg (1977) and Robson (1967) have examined infant gaze (eye contact) and have found that it provided assurance to the parent that the infant is a "person" with mutually positive feelings. Ferguson (1964), who was concerned more directly with the quality of infant vocalizations, suggested that when infants participate in turn-taking, they produce vocalizations of a quality that helps adults to continue the conversation. Indeed, adults often say to infants, "You sound as though you are trying to tell me something. What are you saying?" This question reflects the adult's attribution of a speech-like quality to the sounds. Even turn-taking in infant–adult vocal communication may encourage maintenance of the adult's role in preverbal interactions, beyond its direct effects on the pattern and quality of infant vocalizations. This notion is consistent with Berger and Cunningham (1983) who, while studying vocal interactions between parents and their developmentally delayed infants, found that parents have more difficulty in maintaining turn-taking with Down syndrome infants than with normally developing infants; Down syndrome infants are delayed in the onset of speech-like vocalizations.

Influenced by these studies, Bloom and Lo (1990) examined the possibility that the quality of infant vocalizations might differentially facilitate adults' conversations with them. They hypothesized that an adult would be more likely to create a favorable impression of an infant when the infant utters syllabic sounds than when the infant utters vocalic sounds. If so, by maintaining the rules of turn-taking, adults affect the quality of infant sounds in a way that facilitates the continuation of the conversation. In order to determine empirically whether syllabic and vocalic sounds differentially elicit communicative responses from adults, it would be ideal to enlist infants as "confederates" in an experimental study and ask them to emit syllabic sounds to one group of adults and vocalic or other types of sounds to another group. In lieu of such cooperation by young infants as experimenters and as a first step in determining how prelinguistic sounds affect adults' impressions of their infants, Bloom and Lo sought to assess whether adults favor particular infant vocalizations. They reasoned that if adults have a preference for syllabic sounds over vocalic sounds, they would react differentially to the quality of an infant's vocal contributions to a conversation. This notion posits a link between behavioral preference and selective reinforcement. Through selective reinforcement, certain types of sounds or syllables produced by preverbal infants may encourage parental participation, which in turn leads to the increased frequency in syllabic sounds.

The sixty Canadian adult participants in their study were presented with videotapes of twenty-four three-month-old infants engaging in social communication. All participants were randomly divided into two groups. The stimulus tape was made up of segments from twenty-four different infants, each of whom vocally interacted with a female adult. Each segment was thirty seconds long and was separated by an interval of twenty seconds. Each infant, clothed in the same white cloth, was filmed lying in a supine position while the adult smiled and vocalized with the infant. Of the twenty-four infants, three represented each of the eight possible combinations of three dichotomous characteristics: vocal quality (syllabic/vocalic), facial attractiveness (high/low), and gender (male/female). During the thirty-second segment, the infants produced an average of 6.7 vocalizations. However, twelve of the twenty-four infants produced syllabic sounds exclusively while the other twelve produced vocalic sounds exclusively. The average number of vocalizations did not differ between syllabic sound-producing infants and vocalic sound-producing infants.

The stimulus tape was constructed from videotapes of past studies (Bloom, 1988; Bloom et al., 1987). Four research assistants independently rated forty-six infants, who appeared in six-minute videotaped sessions, as either high, medium or low on facial attractiveness. Attractiveness was indicative only of an infant's photogenic appearance on the videotape segment; the segment was judged without audio feedback so that the raters would not be influenced by the infant's facial attractiveness as a function of facial configurations that represent syllabic and vocalic sounds. Infants were selected who had been rated by at least three observers as high in attractiveness or as low in attractiveness.

The thirty adult participants in each of the two groups viewed the stimulus tape together in a room equipped with a video monitor and individual desks. Both groups were told that they would see short video segments of twenty-four infants and that after watching each segment they were to quickly complete a set of scales for each infant. They were not to compare infants but rather were asked to indicate their immediate reaction to each infant. Two different sets of scales were prepared for the two groups. For one of the two groups, a questionnaire assessed the adult's reaction to the infant on the basis of five characteristics: pleasant, friendly, fun, likeable and cuddly. The questionnaire listed each characteristic followed by a five-point rating scale. It contained a set of characteristics and scales for each infant and the following instructions: "after viewing each infant, please circle the number that corresponds to your feeling about that infant. Do not compare among the infants. Just indicate how you felt about the infant whom you just saw on the monitor." For the second group, a questionnaire assessed the adult's desire to interact with the infant as well as ratings of nonsocial attributions of the infant. A set of seven-point scales was provided for rating each infant on the following six items:

I would like to hug this baby (strongly disagree – strongly agree)
I would like to vocalize with this baby (strongly disagree – strongly agree)
This infant is: (not likely to be successful in the future – likely to be successful in the future)
This infant is: (not intelligent – very intelligent)
This infant is: (not sociable – very sociable)
This infant is: (not cute – very cute)

When the adult's total score was calculated across items for each infant, the range of possible scores that adults could assign was 5–25 and 6–42 for the two questionnaires, respectively. In each of the questionnaires, inter-item reliabilities were very high, which allowed the researchers to calculate a mean score (across items and across the three infants who represented one of the eight combinations of vocalization, attractiveness and gender) as the dependent variable for each participant. Results revealed that regardless of the type of questionnaire used, adults preferred infants who produced syllabic sounds (fig. 3.1). The preference was independent of differences in infant facial attractiveness and gender. No doubt, adult preference for attractive infants mirrors earlier demonstrations of preference for certain infantile facial configurations as well as more positive facial expressions such as smiling (Power, Hildebrandt and Fitzgerald, 1982; Stephan and Langlois, 1984). The experiment showed that beyond visual cues, certain acoustic cues embedded in infant vocalizations can also influence adults' impressions. Further, the type of infant vocalization that is favored by adults is exactly the type that, when it occurs, is positively reinforced through contingent verbal stimulation in a turn-taking pattern by caregivers.

Cross-cultural universality of adults' preferences for infant vocalizations

Subsequently, Bloom, her colleagues and I examined whether or not the above findings on adult preferences could be generalized across differences in parental parity and in language. Guided by studies on infant crying, we first examined whether or not individual factors associated with the listener interact with the quality of noncry vocalizations in influencing adult perceptions. Research on infant crying provides comparable evidence that the quality of pre-linguistic vocalizations can affect adults' perceptions and attributions about an infant

(Lester and Boukydism, 1985). For example, variation in the pitch of their cries has been shown to influence the degree to which adults perceive particular infants as "difficult" (Zeskind, Klein and Marshall, 1992) or "sick" (Zeskind and Barr, 1997). These studies have also identified listener factors that may interact with cry quality in influencing adult perceptions. Further, the experience of parenting (i.e., parity) is said to engender unique sensitivity and responsivity in parents to acoustic features of infant cries. Basically, mothers are more keenly attuned to the interpersonal features of parent–infant interaction than nonmothers (Locke and Snow, 1997). Thus, on the hypothesis that qualitative differences in infant noncry vocalizations would have a greater effect on the social perceptions of parents versus nonparents, we repeated the Bloom and Lo study and controlled for the amount of parental experience by selecting parents and nonparents who all had extensive experience in caring for infants. However, parents and nonparents did not differ in their preference for infants who produced syllabic sounds.

Next, we tested the possibility that cultural factors might influence our perceptions and attributions of infants as communicative partners. For example, the Kaluli of Papua, New Guinea, consider it unacceptable to impute the motives or feelings of another (Schieffelin and Ochs, 1983). They respond only to the literal content of speech and since infants cannot verbally express themselves, adults see no reason to speak to infants or to regard infants as social and communicative partners. Therefore, it would seem that due to cultural dissimilarities, the quality of infant vocalizations would not affect the perceptions of the Kaluli as they would the perceptions of the Canadian adults we tested. How do other cultures that are relatively similar to Canadian but different in the vocal components of early interaction react to differences in prelinguistic vocalizations? We sought to determine how universal were the perceptions of Canadian participants in the Bloom and Lo study.

Our first step in answering this question was to compare the perceptions of our English-speaking Canadian subjects with the perceptions of Italian-speaking subjects. We made this comparison for two reasons. First, in a practical sense, it was possible to evaluate a similar sample of Italian participants. Second, the manner in which Italians perceive a series of words in a sentence is thought to be different from the manner in which English speakers do. Generally, in Italian, emphasis is expressed through the position of the word in a sentence rather than through prosodic stress. Consequently, Italians pay less attention to prosody in speech than English-speaking Canadians do. We reasoned that such a perceptual difference would be reflected in differences in the perception of syllabic and vocalic sounds. All study participants were university undergraduate psychology students. There were two groups of thirty adults; each group included an equal number of males and females. We presented the same videotape that was used in the previous experiment to these two groups. The Canadians in this study also completed the same two questionnaires used in the previous experiment. The questionnaires were translated into Italian for the Italian participants. Results of the experiment revealed that Canadians and Italians do not differ in their preference for syllabic over vocalic vocalizations.

Nonetheless, a preference for syllabic sounds over vocalic sounds might not necessarily lead adults to provide infants who are vocalizing syllabic sounds with selective positive reinforcement. Thus, to connect the "missing link" between adults' impressions of infants and their performance of contingent stimulation, we conducted acoustical analyses on the vocalizations of twelve three-month-old infants who were interacting with their mothers under natural circumstances. All noncry, nonvegetative infant vocalizations that we recorded were dichotomously categorized as "responded-to" or "not-responded-to": if the mother's utterance occurred within three seconds after the infant's vocalization, the infant's vocalization was categorized as a responded-to vocalization; otherwise, the vocalization was considered not-responded-to. With respect to these vocalizations, we did not classify in terms of syllabic versus vocalic sounds. For each infant, we obtained an average of 10.4 responded-to vocalizations and an average of 8.8 not-responded-to vocalizations.

We analyzed these responded-to and not-responded-to vocalizations acoustically according to exactly the same procedure used to analyze syllabic and vocalic sounds in the vocal preference experiment (Masataka and Bloom, 1994). The results were found to be remarkably parallel to those of the previous study. As compared with responded-to sounds, the slope of the regression line was significantly flatter for not-responded-to sounds, suggesting that not-responded-to sounds were more nasal. The mean score of the parameter for the not-responded-to sounds was extremely similar to that of the vocalic sounds in the previous analysis whereas that of the responded-to vocalizations was similar to that of the syllabic sounds. Mothers did respond differentially to sounds depending on their degree of nasality; perceptions of this acoustic property may then enhance the adult's tendency to conceptualize, and to react to, the infant as a communicative partner.

Finally, coming full circle, we presented adults with both responded-to and not-responded-to vocalizations and sought to determine whether these sounds actually evoked different social attributions. Because we wanted to know whether the adults' social attributions were based on nasality of the vocalizations, we selected twenty-four vocalizations from the sample we collected of naturalistic vocal recordings. Twelve of the twenty-four were responded-to and the remaining twelve were not-responded-to vocalizations. They differed from one another in terms of the degree of nasality but were similar in other acoustic parameters. When the stimulus tape was presented to 100 adults, social favorability ratings for responded-to vocalizations were higher than ratings for not-responded-to vocalizations. Adult listeners also preferred infant vocalizations that were responded to by mothers under naturalistic circumstances, based on their acoustic properties alone.

Cultural-specificity of preference of infant behavior

Taken together, the above findings suggest that adults attribute greater intentionality to syllabic infants and that this phenomenon is somewhat generalizable irrespective of differences in parity and culture. Of course, we do not presume that this is the only possible means of selectively reinforcing infant vocal production. The Kaluli do not vocalize with their young infants but they talk on behalf of their infants in vocal exchanges with older siblings. They hold the infant facing towards the sibling and use a special register to speak for the infant. Although no information is currently available for the Kaluli concerning the quality of infant vocalizations, there is one point that is particularly important for our discussion of adults' preferences for infant vocalizations. When the Kaluli mother spoke to the infant, she used a nasalized voice rather than one having greater oral resonance. Given the young obligate nose-breather's own nasality and the lack of contingent verbal response, the mother's impersonation of vocalic sounds was well selected. Certainly, biological factors in early vocal communication (e.g., the quality and development of infant vocalization) have some influence on all early social systems. However, the Kaluli's cultural taboos against the attribution of feelings and intentions to others precluded verbal responses to prelinguistic vocalizations. It would not be very astonishing if the Kaluli mother showed a preference for vocalic sounds over syllabic sounds. Such parental attitudes would affect the behavior of their infants, eventually resulting in the transmission of the attitudes from parents to their offspring. Therefore, the example of the Kaluli reminds us of the possibility that cultural factors, which in part reflect a society's psychological predispositions, might also determine many of the selective features of early communication.

Indeed, when we compared the vocal preferences of Japanese and Canadian adults, we found an instance of the application of cultural rules when responding to preverbal infants. Clues to the finding emerged when we examined how nonvocal characteristics of infants who were vocalizing affected adults' impressions of the infants. As in our previous study, we presented Canadian adults with a videotape of twenty-four thirty-second segments of three-month-old vocalizing infants. The participants were divided into three groups. Although twelve infants produced syllabic sounds and twelve infants produced nasalized vocalic sounds in the stimulus tape, this time we varied the conditions of tape presentation across the groups as follows: A/V (audiovisual), Audio-only, Video-only. All groups gave higher ratings to syllabic infants independent of the modality of presentation. Thus, visual as well as auditory cues to syllabic vocalizations affected adult reactions.

Subsequently, based on the hypothesis that mouth movement was the visual cue influencing adults' more favorable impressions of syllabic infants, a video-tape of sixteen thirty-sec segments was presented to the three groups of adults (A/V, Audio, Video). The tape was constructed with dubbing so that all com-binations of acoustic (syllabic/vocalic) and visual (mouth moving/not moving) conditions were presented. The condition of tape presentation differed for the three groups: Audio/Video, Audio-only, Video-only. In the absence of audio cues (Video-only group), infant mouth movements influenced the adult ratings, indicating adults' use of this nonvocal behavioral feature in forming impres-sions of an infant as a social and communicative partner. This phenomenon is reminiscent of the "McGurk Effect," that the visual input of mouth movement during the production of a phoneme influences the auditory perception of the sound (McGurk and MacDonald, 1976).

This perceptual effect is known to be robustly demonstrable in Western cul-tures but in Japanese cultures, unless the speech sound is severely degraded, visual cues are less important for deciphering speech (Sekiyama and Tohkura, 1991). Thus, we conducted a study to determine if the findings we obtained with our Canadian sample could also be replicated with a Japanese sample. We prepared three groups of participants made up of Japanese adults; to each of the groups we presented one of the stimulus tapes: A/V, Audio-only, or Visual-only. Results revealed that although Japanese participants gave higher ratings of favorable impressions and communicative intent to infants whose mouths moved as well as vocalized, the preference for mouth movement was significantly weaker for Japanese than for Canadians.

The Japanese pay less attention to features of the infant's mouth than Canadians do. This observation appears consistent with the speculations of cultural anthropologists (e.g., Lebra, 1976; White, 1993) who propose that the Japanese may reduce arousal by avoiding face-to-face visual inspection during verbal exchanges. Compared with Americans, Japanese mothers have been reported to spend less time looking at their infants' faces during caregiving (Caudill and Weinstein, 1969; Zahn-Waxler et al., 1996). Unlike American Sign Language, in Japanese Sign Language facial cues play a minor role in transmit-ting the linguistic meaning of signs (Masataka, 1992b). These data underline the notion that the impressions adults form of preverbal infants are constructed on the basis of adult cues to speech: sound quality and facial gestures. Further, the relevance of these speech cues is modulated by adults' cultural patterns of communication. Adults credit infants with socially favorable qualities and communicative intent based on features of speech that will not be functionally part of the child's language for many months to come. However, by means of the sort of reinforcement that adults provide, in the future the child will eventually come to acquire language that is functionally equipped with these very features.

Selective reinforcement of manual action

Adults' preferences with respect to vocalizing infants concern not only the quality of the vocalizations and the accompanying facial movements, but also manual actions. The types of manual activities performed by three-month-old infants are classified into the following four categories (Fogel and Hannan, 1985): (1) spread where all fingers are extended and held, (2) index-finger extension where only index finger is extended and held, (3) grasp where the hand is holding an object, clothes, self, or mother, and (4) curl where any other movement or positions including fist, partial spreads, and rhythmically moving fingers are included. Among the four, only index-finger extension is known to co-occur temporally with the production of cooing. Moreover, manual activity varies according to the quality of co-occurring vocalizations. Masataka (1995), having observed fourteen infants during a total of fifteen-minute spontaneous face-to-face interactions with their mothers, found that index-finger extension occurred frequently in sequence with syllabic sounds, but rarely in sequence with vocalic sounds. In a subsequent experiment, the infants experienced either conversational turn-taking or random responsiveness from their mothers. As already described, in the turn-taking condition, the infants produced a higher ratio of syllabic versus vocalic sounds. As a consequence of this effect, the occurrence of index-finger extension, which originally showed a strong tendency to co-occur with syllabic sounds, increased as well. The manual action was inadvertently conditioned as infant vocal activity was contingently stimulated.

Until recently, the pointing gesture had been thought to emerge near the end of the first year of life. The general consensus had been that pointing differentiates from the movements of reaching or grasping, partly in order to economize the movement as a gesture needed for signaling and partly as a conventionalization of the adult expression learned through imitation and shaping (Bates, Camaioni and Voltera, 1975; Murphy, 1978; Leung and Rheinghold, 1981; Bruner, 1983; Masur, 1982). This assumed that cognitive developments at this age – the ability to carry out, plan and signal intentions – induce the child to learn the new behavior of pointing. However, I scored the average number of occurrences of indicative gestures, reaching attempts, index-finger extensions and pointing in ten infants while interacting with their mothers and being presented with a standard set of toys, every month until the age of fourteen months (Masataka, 2003). The rate of occurrence of indicative gestures and reaching attempts was stable over the age range of this study. If pointing developed from either of these two behaviors, we would expect to find pointing superseding both over the course of development. In contrast, the frequency of index-finger extension tended to increase until the emergence of pointing and, after the onset of pointing, it sharply declined. This strongly suggests that index-finger extension might be a developmental precursor of pointing. The underlying reason as to why this possibility has been ignored relates to the fact that learning the pointing-like motor action is an inadvertent process.

Furthermore, the action of index-finger extension and the production of syllabic vocalizations are selectively reinforced by contingent verbal stimulation by caregivers. On the stimulus tapes in our previous experiments on adults' preferences for infant vocal behavior, we controlled only for one facet of infant behavior: the quality of their vocalizations. This time, I controlled for the infants' types of manual action: six of the twelve infants producing syllabic sounds performed index-finger extension but the remaining six did not, and six of the twelve infants producing vocalic sounds performed index-finger extension but the remaining six did not. There was no significant difference in the total number of manual actions performed by the twelve infants irrespective of whether they were uttering syllabic or vocalic sounds. Other than index-finger extension, the total number of occurrences of other motor actions (spread, curl, grasp, mouthing, smiling, and gazing at) did not significantly differ across four cohorts of infants, i.e., according to the quality of vocalizations (syllabic/vocalic) and the presence/absence of index-finger extension.

When we measured preference in 100 adults using the same procedure as before, we found a significant main effect for the quality of vocalizations. As shown in fig. 3.1, infants producing syllabic sounds were preferred over infants producing vocalic sounds. There was also a significant main effect of index-finger extension, but an interaction between the two factors was also significant. As long as infants on the stimulus tape were those who produced vocalic sounds, preference scores did not differ regardless of whether or not they were demonstrating index-finger extension. However, among infants uttering syllabic sounds, preference scores for infants who were demonstrating index-finger extension were significantly higher than for infants who did not demonstrate this manual activity.

Perception of affordance in infant behavior

Various aspects of behavior in three-month-old infants could be selectively reinforced by caregivers, and mechanisms for this reinforcement are embedded in adults in the form of a sense of preference. This is not a totally new notion. In the 1940s, Konrad Lorenz, the founder of classical ethology, argued that caregiving behavior should be elicited in adults by the physical design and typical behavior patterns of human infants (Lorenz, 1943). He stated that when confronted with these patterns, adults experience a positive affective feeling, which in turn

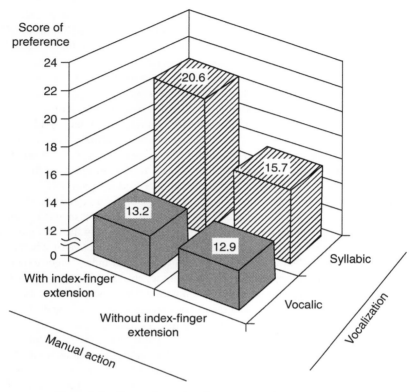

Figure 3.1   Comparison of preference scores in terms of the quality of vocalization and of manual action.

results in caregiving behavior by adults. The physical characteristics Lorenz listed are: a large head in proportion to the body; a protruding forehead that is proportionately large relative to the size of the rest of the face; large eyes below the midline of the total head; short and thick extremities; a rounded body shape; soft elastic body surfaces; and round and protruding cheeks. Additionally, he argued that these physical attributes are further enhanced by such behavioral characteristics as clumsiness. With respect to the physical design of the infant, subsequent experimental studies have confirmed adult preference for these features (e.g., Sternglanz, Gray and Murakami, 1977); this preference is consistent across a wide variety of environmental conditions such as adults' social class and their experience with children.

Importantly, the physical characteristics Lorenz mentioned have not evolved under selective pressure to elicit parenting behaviors from adults, but rather partly as a consequence of differences in the tempos of growth among various body organs. For instance, the head and eyes grow earlier than the nose and mouth in infants so that the proportions of head and eyes relative to nose and mouth are largest when infants are born and are likely to decrease with development. Nevertheless, adults show a strong preference for infants with such features. This suggests the presence of a perceptual mechanism in adults that has evolved to stimulate caring for infants, by promoting emotional preferences for infantile traits. The softness and roundness of infants' skin is simply attributable to the fact that their skin has suffered very little fatigue. Clumsiness is a symptom of immaturity with respect to motor actions. Overall, there are no known signal functions associated with the evolution of such infantile characteristics, but perceiving them serves an adaptive function for adults, who are thereby provided with information that guides biologically and socially functional behavior.

The effects of infantile traits on adults are not necessarily restricted to preverbal infants. Overall, children with the facial structures that Lorenz (1943) identified as infantile are perceived to have more childlike traits than more mature-faced peers. In particular, more baby-faced children, ranging in age from six months up to early adolescence, are perceived as more socially dependent, intellectually naive, physically weak, honest and warm than more mature-faced peers. They are also judged as less likely "to be able to follow complicated instructions" and "to know right from wrong the way an adult does" (Zebrowitz and Montepare, 1992, p. 1151). All of these effects held when the child's age was controlled and made known to perceivers. Indeed, the impressions created by these infantile traits are characterized by a baby-face overgeneralization across the entire lifespan. When portraits of baby-faced aged persons were presented to study participants, they were perceived as having more childlike traits than their mature-faced peers (Zebrowitz, 1990).

Apparently, caregiving behaviors are not mechanically elicited by infantile traits through something akin to an "innate releasing mechanism" as depicted by classical ethology. The perception of infantile traits is social, where social perception is focused on detecting structural invariants and dispositional properties such as abilities. Alley (1981) found that perceivers report a greater desire to protect from attack and to cuddle stimulus persons whose head shape or bodily proportions are infantile than those who have a more mature appearance. Alley also found a greater desire to protect, but not to cuddle, persons with an elderly craniofacial appearance than young adults. McArthur and Baron (1983) reported that persons with more babyish faces were perceived as less likely to turn a cold shoulder to attempts by university students as participants at friendly conversation. They were also perceived as less able to move several boxes of the participants' heaviest books and more likely to be the kind of roommates who comply with all the participants' wishes about furniture arrangement, quiet hours and so forth.

Beyond creating impressions, the variation in children's and adults' appearance of facial maturity can have social consequences. For example, the perception of mature-faced versus baby-faced children as being more able to follow complicated instructions, more likely to know right from wrong, more shrewd, and as having greater physical strength often leads parents to assign more demanding tasks to these children and to judge their misbehavior more harshly. Baby-faced and mature-faced adults are often given jobs requiring traits that are stereotypically associated with their appearance (Zebrowitz, Tenenbaum and Goldstein, 1991). Further, mature-faced defendants are more likely than baby-faced defendants to be perceived as having committed an intentional offence (Berry and Zebrowitz-McArthur, 1988; Zebrowitz and McDonald, 1991). When baby-faced defendants admit to an offense, they are punished less severely for negligent acts than those whose faces appear more mature, presumably because they look like they "could not help it"; however, they are punished more severely for premeditated acts, perhaps because judges are particularly disturbed by behaviors that violate their appearance of benignity (Berry and Zebrowitz-McArthur, 1988).

The assumption of attunement in the perception of infant affordances

Overall, these findings suggest that infantile properties can be viewed as properties that modulate sensory input in a manner that reveals the individual's affordances. Within the ecological approach to perception (Gibson, 1979), the units of information in structures are basically events. Events provide perceivers with structured information that supplements the information that is available in static stimuli. Certain properties of an entity change during an event while others remain the same. Those elements of an entry that remain the same are referred to as structural invariants. For instance, the shape and color of an object remain the same as it rotates. Similarly, the physical design of babies (e.g., size of the head, size of the eyes, protrusion of the cheeks, etc.) remains the same when they smile or cry. On the other hand, the types of change to entities that occur during events are referred to as transformational invariants. The behavior of organisms is obviously included in this category. For example, a particular type of biomechanical movement is recognized as walking. Similarly, the quality of cooing, the particular style of mouth movement, and the particular style of manual action are all dynamic, changing forms of stimulus information. Transformational invariants can be treated as parameters, just as structural invariants have been, that affect adults' overall preference for an infant with whom they are interacting.

If the argument about preference for infantile traits proposed by Konrad Lorenz is directly applied to the adults' preference for infants in relation to transformational invariants, the logical consequence might be that since more immature features elicit caregiving in adults, more immature qualities of infant vocalizations should provoke stronger preference in adults. The facts are quite contrary to this prediction as the more mature type of cooing is preferred. Similarly, index-finger extension is not regarded as an infantile manual action but rather could be considered more adult-like when compared with other manual activities. This seeming contradiction can be resolved if we interpret the phenomenon of preference for infant behaviors from the ecological position. The perception of affordances depends upon the perceiver's attunement, that is, the particular stimulus invariants to which the perceiver attends.

Affordances are referenced on perceivers. This highlights a basic tenet of the ecological approach, that perception requires certain compatibilities between the perceiver and the perceived. At the most fundamental level, there must be a match between the receptor ability of organisms and the stimulus information to which they are perceptually sensitive. Indeed, perceptual systems are thought to have evolved specific sensitivities to the types of structured information available in a given ecological niche. However, the concept of perceptual attunement is not restricted to biologically preprogrammed sensitivities shaped under evolutionary pressure. The stimulus information to which perceivers are attuned may vary according to their perceptual learning, goals or expectations (Gibson, 1966). The influence of perceptual learning on attunement may be easily understood if we imagine the example where the forest is perceived quite differently through the eyes of a naturalist than through the eyes of a city dweller. Cross-cultural differences in susceptibility to perceptual illusions also provide evidence for the role of perceptual learning. This includes the McGurk effect and the adult preference for infant mouth movement when vocalizing is somewhat analogous to this effect.

Even the physical design of the typical infant, when it is shown to an adult, is perceived as affording compliance in accordance with the adult perceiver's own wishes. Perceptions vary depending upon the perceiver's own social power, and the person who has no desire to elicit compliance does not perceive that particular affordance (McArthur and Baron, 1983). A perceiver's own action potential can exert a strong influence on the detection of affordances. Most notably, perceivers may be blind to those structural or transformational invariants that have no behavioral utility to them (i.e., that do not have any relevant affordance). We are all familiar with the example of the Inuit who differentiate several varieties of snow perceptually. In traditional Inuit life, each snow structure undoubtedly affords different activities. Such phenomena can occur in the social realm as well as the nonsocial; for example, adults' preferences for three-month-old infants who perform particular styles of movements may derive from their own communicative activities with the infants.

Adult perceptions of the three-month-old infant as a social, communicative partner have adaptive significance for both the adult and the infant. These perceptions are engendered by the stimulus properties of the infant's voice and motor actions: "dynamic, changing, multimodal stimulus information" (McArthur and Baron, 1983, p. 215). The degree to which the infant's behavior affects the adult's perception is modulated by the adult's characteristics and the adult's cultural perspective. When something similar to the adult's characteristics occurs in the infant, adults show a strong tendency to overassimilate them to their own characteristics. The infant also learns to perceive affordances in the adult's responses through such interactions and to match the quality of its own action with the quality of the social situation – as the adult assesses it. Consequently, the infant develops the use of behaviors with the characteristics that underlie intentional communication in the true sense, and uses them with adults who then interpret those behaviors as intentional. This could be a first step for the infant in developing intentional communication and in developing cultural variation in their communicative behaviors.

Adults' cultural perspective is based on cultural aspects of the behavior that they themselves perform. When interacting with an infant, adults continually monitor the properties displayed by the infant. Whenever adults detect properties that match the quality of their own behavior, they positively reinforce those properties. The style of movement is what underlies the adult's perception of the infant as a communicator. The ultimate source of information for this perception is not something triggered or guided by objects and events external to the perceiver, not even the infant's movement; rather, the perceiver's own performance of movement is an important contributor. This view of movement as perception is very different from the traditional view of afference and efference, but from a Gibsonian perspective, movement is what allows discrimination and discovery of the invariants in the environment that are necessary for adaptive actions. It is movement that provides dynamic sampling of stimulus attributes (Bushnell and Boudreau, 1993). In terms of the properties of invariants, we have thus far mentioned conventional attributes of nonsocial objects such as flow, edges, textures, surface and weight. However, there is no reason to restrict invariants to the nonsocial domain; indeed, they can also be extended to the social domain.

The phylogenetic origin of adult preferences

The process of "phenotype matching," which nonhuman animals use in kin recognition, can be discussed as a rudimentary basis for forming adult human preferences. This is a process by which an individual animal learns its own cues (such as "recognition pheromones"), then matches its own cues with those provided by other individuals in order to classify them as kin or nonkin. A preference is then shown for kin over nonkin. The question of how kin recognition is achieved in the absence of obvious opportunities to learn the phenotypic characteristics of kin has long been the subject of debate and, at present, the process of phenotype matching is taken as the most plausible explanation.

Studies of cascade frog (*Rana cascadae*) tadpoles may be particularly relevant to this discussion because of the various rearing regimes employed (Blaustein and O'Hara, 1981, 1982, 1983). In the first series of experiments, frogs reared with siblings as well as those reared in a mixed group of siblings and nonsiblings equally preferred to associate with siblings rather than nonsiblings. In later experiments, frogs reared in total isolation from an early embryonic stage and those reared only with nonkin preferred to associate with unfamiliar siblings rather than unfamiliar nonsiblings. Additionally, tadpoles reared with siblings or in isolation preferred to associate with full-siblings over half-siblings (either maternal half-siblings or paternal half-siblings) and with half-siblings over nonsiblings (either maternal or paternal). These experiments reveal that tadpoles can discriminate between individuals of varying degrees of relatedness regardless of whether they are reared in a mixture of siblings and nonsiblings, in isolation, with full-siblings, or with nonkin only. Blaustein and O'Hara interpreted the results as a possible example of phenotype matching. According to proponents of phenotype matching, tadpoles reared in isolation could learn their own cues and later match their own phenotypes with those of other individuals, even totally unfamiliar ones, and then choose their associates on the basis of the degree of match. With respect to tadpoles, the features that actually serve as cues for matching have not yet been determined.

Phenotypic matching is known to occur extensively in nonhuman primates. Nonhuman primates are thought to achieve matching through various communicative behaviors. For example, the long calls of a New World primate, the red-chested mustached tamarin (*Saguinus labiatus*) show acoustical variations between populations. The variations occur independent of underlying genetic differences and are regarded as dialects. Animals learn dialects postnatally. Generally, in small New World primates, long calls are frequently emitted by animals separated from other conspecifics during travel and antiphonal calling occurs, mostly among affiliated individuals (Masataka and Biben, 1987). Long calls inform resident male–female pairs of the presence of intruders (possible immigrants). Among groups of tamarins living in monogamous groups, the bond between the reproductively active male and female is partly maintained by the exclusion of other males and females. Playbacks of unfamiliar male calls provoke eviction responses (i.e., aggressive behavior towards the sound source) in males but not in females, and vice versa. The female of the resident pair is likely to vocalize antiphonally in response to the long calls of male intruders unless her partner evicts them successfully.

Masataka (1988) conducted an experiment with adult male and female tamarins from three different populations in Bolivia that were spatially separated from one another by distances of less than 26 km. Masataka played unfamiliar long calls for the tamarins from natal and alien populations. The study was conducted in order to determine whether or not the tamarins responded differentially to them. The results revealed that female tamarins respond selectively to male long calls from their natal populations. Among nonhuman animals, current evidence suggests that geographical variation in communicative behaviors occurs most prevalently in the primate order. Young individuals that learn communicative variants distinctive to their local population use them to recognize their "home deme." This form of selectivity encourages individuals to remain with their natal populations and probably to adapt to their natal environments more successfully. It serves as one psychological mechanism that could serve as a basis for maintaining cultural transmission of behavior patterns. Human adults' tendency to recognize their own behavioral qualities in infants, and to prefer infants on that basis, is perhaps derived from this mechanism.

Perception of infant behavior without awareness

Adults' preferences for certain infant behaviors, which serve as selective reinforcement, essentially comprise some sort of perception-without-awareness phenomenon. For instance, when adults are asked why they prefer infants that utter syllabic sounds over those that utter vocalic sounds, they are unable to articulate a plausible reason. This phenomenon is relatively well known as latent perception among cognitive psychologists, particularly those who are interested in visual information processing. Gibson (1966) has pointed out that an enormous amount of visual processing is necessarily carried out automatically and without awareness. The best known evidence favoring the perception-without-awareness hypothesis might be that involving a priming procedure whereby reaction time to a target stimulus is facilitated by the presentation of a preceding, semantically related stimulus (Meyer, Schvaneveldt and Ruddy, 1975; Marcel, 1983). In these studies, the priming effect was compared across two conditions. In the threshold condition, a backward pattern masking procedure was used to degrade the visibility of the priming stimuli to the point that participants were unable either to identify the primes or to make presence-absence judgements significantly above chance. This condition served to evaluate perceptual processing in the absence of awareness where awareness was defined as the ability to make a discriminated verbal report. In the second condition, the same primes were presented without the mask; this condition served to measure perceptual processing when participants were aware of the primes. Two critical findings were observed in these masked-prime studies. First, significant priming occurred even when the primes were masked. Secondly, the magnitude of the priming effect was independent of the presence or absence of the mask. In other words, even though the mask reduced verbal report accuracy to a chance level, it had little or no effect on the size of the semantic-priming effect. The results indicate that complete lexical perception can occur independently of awareness.

Prior to these findings, the course of perceptual processing had been assumed to be linear, sequential and hierarchical (Posner, 1969). Linear and sequential aspects had construed different kinds of representations as being derived one from another in a particular structural and temporal order. The hierarchical aspect had conceived of this order as either synthetic, "higher level" information being derived from "lower level" information, or analytic, where perception proceeds from the general to the specific. Interpretations of Reicher's (1969) and Wheeler's (1970) results on the superiority of letter identification in the context of a word provide good examples that are consistent with this theory. These researchers proposed the analytic hierarchical notion that somehow the "wordness" of a word is processed before its component letters. Similar inferences are drawn from studies of visual search (Merikle and Reingold, 1988; Neely, 1977), for instance, that the category of a character can be analyzed before its identity. One assumption associated with the synthetic hierarchic notion is that if "higher level" information is reportable or voluntarily usable, then all "lower level" information must also be. The converse of this is that a higher level of representation may be interfered with or prevented while lower levels or earlier stages of representation are left intact.

It was on this latter assumption that backward masking had often been used and interpreted, i.e., that if processing of a visual stimulus was sufficiently interfered with at a stage of precategorical representation, descriptions derived from that representation could not be achieved. Another example involving the synthetic assumption was the interpretation of reaction time data from same-different judgements in terms of a linear hierarchy of stages (e.g., physical, name, category); this relied on the assumption that a participant's response could be based on a specific stage of processing which was uncontaminated by any higher stage of processing. However, Meyer et al. (1975) and Marcel (1983) argued that backward masking is no longer regarded as the one technique whereby one can halt stimulus processing at a certain stage and eliminate contamination by any further automatic processing. Backward masking does not appear to impede such processing because participants' verbal reports reveal some aspects of conscious experience and its limits but hardly anything about perceptual processes themselves.

There are several reasons why, in some ways, it can be extremely misleading to rely on conscious percepts in seeking to understand perceptual processing. First, the language of representation generated at nonconscious and conscious levels might be quite different. Second, as Nisbett and Wilson (1977) suggest, even tachistoscopic stimuli or one's own sensations probably tell us more about people's beliefs about sensation and cognition than about those processes themselves. Third, paying attention to stimuli, which is required by most psychological self-report studies, may well induce a psychological/attentional state quite inimical to revealing automatic nonconscious processes. People attempt to base their behavior on notions of rationality. If the task is one of reading or reporting, one normally does not report a word that comes to mind unless one is conscious of having seen one. Further, paying attention to the outer world and being prepared to act are likely to narrow one's attention and preclude awareness of what has only an inner source.

Another well-known example of latent perception is the subliminal mere exposure effect. The subliminal mere exposure paradigm has afforded a ready means of examining the extent to which subliminal and marginal phenomena influence cognitions and attitudes towards unfamiliar stimuli. In this experimental paradigm, participants are typically exposed to slides of abstract geometric figures at both subliminal (usually 4 ms) and supraliminal exposure durations in the laboratory. The participants' attitudes toward the subliminally presented stimuli become significantly more positive with repeated exposure, even when participants are unaware that exposure has occurred. Subsequently, this effect was extended to more naturalistic situations and to the social domain. For example, Bornstein, Leone and Galley (1987) demonstrated that similar attitude changes are produced by subliminal and supraliminal exposure to photographs of actual persons. They also found that attitudes towards a person encountered in the natural environment of the psychology experiment are enhanced by subliminal exposure to a photograph of that person. This suggests that decisions made in interpersonal and social situations can be based in part on subliminally or marginally perceived stimulus qualities. To some extent, social cognitions, interpersonal judgements, and object choices can be influenced by properties of stimulus objects of which we are unaware. Bargh and Pietromonaco (1982) also found that subliminal verbal stimuli significantly influence impressions of those about whom one has little or no previous information.

This sort of latent perception is apparently involved in the adult's process of impression formation about infants and in the adult's selective reinforcement of specific infant behaviors. Occasionally, the adult is unaware of the presence of a stimulus configuration in an infant that greatly influences his or her response to the infant. Further, the adult is often unaware of his or her response and unaware that the stimulus has affected the response. When asked to report on their cognitive processes, that is, on the processes mediating the effects of a stimulus on a response, adults do not seem to do so on the basis of any true introspection. Rather, their reports are based on a priori implicit causal theories, or rational judgements, about the extent to which a particular stimulus is a plausible cause of a given response. Accurate reports are found only when influential stimuli are salient and when the stimuli are regarded as plausible causes of the responses they produce.

Overall, adults' responses to very young infants are automatically triggered by stimuli provided by the infant in somewhat of a "bottom-up" manner. Adults' perceptual mechanisms for responding do not work in a hierarchical manner. Indeed, the latest literature (e.g., Tanaka and Shimojo, 1996) suggests inter-independence of two information decoding processes in our visual and audi-tory perception: the spatial orientation or localizing process, which requires information about the presence and global location of the target stimulus, and the feature analysis process, which requires information about fine features of the stimulus. In dealing with infant behavior, the latter process is involved in adult perception but the former one is not. Adults are unaware of which features of the infant they respond to or how they respond. When interacting with an infant, logically, the number of infant features that can be detected is large. Tremendous effort would be required if adults were consciously to deal with all these features and to respond to some of them selectively. Adults would also have to acquire formidable amounts of knowledge and practical learning about caregiving before having infants. In order to economize this process, our perception of infant behavior is mediated by a specific filtering mechanism that is apparently a product of natural selection.

A dynamic account of early learning in cooing

Immediately after birth, human infants are mainly tactile beings. They spend most of their time in close contact with their caregivers. Through such contact, a sufficient body temperature is provided to the infants. At this point, infants still lack the motor ability needed to establish and maintain close contact by themselves. Consequently, they have evolved expressive actions that signal caregivers about their physiological discomfort (i.e., crying), just as caregivers have evolved sensitivity to those signals. In such situations, adults manipulate extrinsic control parameters for inducing a state of calm, through holding and the provision of nipples on which to suck. Obviously, the primary function of these actions is the infant's survival. Nonetheless, even under these well-defined circumstances, newborn infants create a semblance of dialogue by inserting pauses with their bursts of sucking, as previously described in chapter 1. Adults respond to the behavior by inserting jiggling into the pauses. By the age of eight weeks, the mechanical exchange of jiggling and bursts of sucking has changed the infant's behavior, leading the infant to take more initiative in dialogues. In response to the absence of the jiggling expected during pauses, infants come to produce spontaneous cooing. It appears that the infant's cyclic alternation of action and pauses in sucking follows a somewhat endogenous activation level.

Once the infant begins to utter speech-like vocalizations, dialogue begins to be created by exchanges of facial expressions and vocalizations; all this has taken place within approximately three months of the infant's birth.

Over this period, the infant also becomes free of the phylogenetic constraints imposed by the morphology of the vocal apparatus, which had constrained the production of true speech-like vocalizations. Concurrently, infants' visual perceptual ability develops dramatically during the three-month period, from the neonatal state in which their eyes have a fixed focal length so that only objects that are 21 cm away are perceived in sharp focus. Studying this development depends in part on the stimulus characteristics that catch the infants' attention. At first, infants' attention is directed particularly at stimuli that move, that have contrasting contours, and that contain a number of discrete elements. However, during the first month, increasing familiarity with frequently encountered stimulus configurations paves the way for a new phase. This is typically experimentally demonstrated with three-month-old infants using cards painted to resemble a human face (Fantz, 1963). Although newborns do not attend particularly to the stimulus, they come to strongly prefer it after a few months. As a consequence of this change, the infant becomes able to initiate and maintain bouts of mutual gazing, which would give adults the impression that the infant has become a more active social partner. Infant social smiling, distinguished from physiological smiling, tends to occur when looking at adults. Adults enjoy sharing a steady gaze with the infant as well as responding vocally to infant cooing whenever it occurs. This responding serves as contingent stimulation to the vocal production of the infant and the stimulation affects not only the quantity of vocal production but also its quality.

The amount of time that an infant spends out of close contact with caregivers shows a dramatic increase as the infant develops. Neonates can only survive within a limited range of body temperature because their physiological capability to thermoregulate functions poorly, so the deposition of subcutaneous body fat takes dramatic precedence over the increase in muscle tissue in the first few months of life. This morphological change underpins our impression that babies become more rounded in shape, soft-elastic in body surface, and clumsy in motion. Adults prefer babies with these features to those of younger infants (Sternglanz et al., 1977). This observation again provides evidence contrary to the classical ethology interpretation of "babyishness," that caregiving behavior for infants is triggered by the stimulus configuration via an innate releasing mechanism embedded in adults. Indeed, if adults' impression of babyishness were truly mechanically triggered for the purpose of infant protection, that impression should be stronger in interactions with newborns than in interactions with older infants. Actually, however, the occurrence of this preference and its accompanying preference is time-locked, yoked to adults' interactions with three- to four-month-old infants.

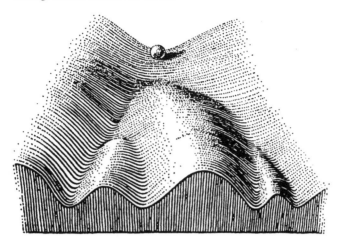

Figure 3.2   Waddington's (1957) epigenetic landscape. The ball represents some tissue at an early stage in ontogeny; its development is represented by the ball descending through the landscape.

The fat/muscle ratio should be regarded as a control parameter that allows the infant's existing abilities to become dynamically reorganized in order to permit the emergence of a skill that the infant did not manifest previously. During this period, due to a lack of postural control, infants interact with adults exclusively in a supine position. The baby with the fat/muscle ratio characteristic of this period and positioned in this manner looks extremely cute and very effectively draws the adult's attention. This impression induces the adult to sensitively frame the infant's behavior. This is a process of behavioral differentiation, usually known as "canalization." The process can be understood most appropriately on the basis of a diagram of the epigenetic landscape (fig. 3.2) originally depicted by C. H. Waddington (1957). In the diagram, a ball represents the developing organism. The layout of the hills and valleys along which the ball may roll represents possible pathways for development. Constraints on the movements of the ball are imposed by the landscape, as the ball progresses downhill. As the ball progresses, it encounters some steep valleys, and between each of them, high hills. The hills represent environmental perturbations that could knock the ball off course. Conversely, if the ball drops into a deep valley, it would be very difficult to leave the valley.

Cultural diversity of behavioral development can be represented by the diversity of this epigenetic landscape. The ontogenetic landscape for the emergence of behavioral diversity across cultures may begin with the prenatal period, which is depicted at the top of the landscape. During this period, the landscape is mainly a relatively flat terrain. There are few behavioral attractors during the prenatal period. Infants might simply show some of stereotyped and stable motor actions, which are depicted by narrow wells. However, the ball soon comes upon junctions between the valleys in the epigenetic landscape. These junctions represent critical points in development because further development can take one of several forms depending on the environmental factors that exist at a given time. The transition points between adjoining valleys can also represent movement between stages and the slope of the valleys can represent the rate of the developmental process with shallow valleys representing rapid change and transition from one mode of organization to another.

The infant encounters the first major transition point in the epigenetic landscape of behavioral development at the age of three to four months. Then, perceptual preferences by adults for specific types of infant behavior serve as attractor valleys wherein those specific behavioral configurations are selected. Moreover, the quality of adult reactions to infant behavior triggered by the adult preferences can enhance the amount of push the infant receives to go down that specific valley. This process will be described in the next chapter.

4   The development of vocal imitation

In chapter 3, we saw that the first step in vocal learning for preverbal infants is to acquire the ability to produce those qualities of cooing that are truly speech-like. This is accomplished through a give-and-take vocal exchange between the infant and the caregiver. Infant vocal production receives contingent stimulation from caregivers and is selectively reinforced. In terms of reinforcement, caregivers possess specific preferences for infant behaviour. Once infants come to utter truly speech-like cooing, this, in turn, affects the vocal behaviour of caregivers. Given caregiver preferences, in what ways do they tend to speak to infants? Then how do these specific utterances affect infants' vocal production?

Considerable scientific attention has been focused on the vocal quality of adults' early communication with their infants, for example, Ferguson's (1964) classic descriptions of the register of baby-talk. However, the functional significance of adult communication qualities for vocal development in very young infants is not yet fully understood. In this chapter, evidence will be presented suggesting the importance of one specific feature of the adult's response to early infant cooing – echoic responding – for the development of vocal imitation in the infant. Previously, the term echoic responding had been used to refer to a primitive form of infant imitation. However, when caregivers respond to infants in an echoic manner, infants listen to the ambient language and attempt to produce sound patterns that match what they hear. In other words, infants acquire the specific inventory of phonetic units and prosodic features employed by a particular language in part through the process of "true vocal imitation," which is distinguished from "vocal contagion," described previously in chapter 3. The notion was inspired in part by my previous research on vocal learning in nonhuman primates, which will be the first topic discussed below. *Homo sapiens* is not the only mammal to display such flexible vocal behavior; the ability to acquire a species-specific vocal repertoire by hearing the vocalizations of adults and mimicking them is shared with a few nonhuman primates species. Therefore, the preadaptation in our species for the flexible development of speech production is also present to some degree in other primates.

Evidence for vocal imitation in nonhuman primates

Studies on the development of vocal production in nonhuman primates can be divided into two interrelated areas: how species-specific calls develop and how nonhuman primates come to temporally modify acoustic features of a specific type of vocalization in particular circumstances. In terms of how species-specific calls develop, Masataka and Fujita (1989) showed, through cross-fostering experiments on Japanese and rhesus macaques, that infants of each species learn the production of one species-specific call (i.e., the coo). In this study, cross-fostering was initiated within twenty-four hours after the subjects' birth. When the monkeys were tested at one year of age, the coo calls of Japanese and rhesus macaque infants reared by their biological mothers differed from each other in terms of a single acoustic parameter. However, at one year of age, the calls of the Japanese macaque infants fostered by rhesus females differed from those of Japanese macaques reared by Japanese macaque mothers, but resembled those of rhesus macaques reared by their rhesus mothers. Similarly, the vocalizations uttered by the two rhesus macaques fostered by Japanese macaque females differed from those of rhesus macaques reared by their rhesus mothers, but were similar to those of Japanese macaques reared by their Japanese macaque mothers. Elowson and Snowdon (1994) reported a similar phenomenon in pygmy marmosets, a small-sized New World species (*Cebuella pygmaea*). They experimentally placed two unfamiliar populations of this species together in a common acoustic environment. After the acoustic contact, two parameters of the frequency of contact calls changed, in parallel, in both populations.

On the issue of changes in acoustic properties over a brief period, the issue relevant to this chapter, no studies other than ours have been reported. Again, our study examined the coo call vocal behavior of Japanese macaques. As described in chapter 2, monkeys utter coo calls somewhat voluntarily in response to preceding coos within a certain time interval. Some acoustic features of responding coo calls appeared to change to match those of the preceding coo calls, over the course of successive call exchanges among group members. However, in our correlation analysis comparing acoustic features of two consecutive coos, we did not evaluate the acoustic similarity of the calls at the individual level. Two possible explanations remain for their similarity: (1) individuals whose coo calls already have acoustic features similar to those of preceding calls might respond more often than individuals whose calls are less similar; or (2) individuals might modify the acoustic features of their coo replies, matching them to those of preceding calls that they have just heard. Therefore, we conducted a playback experiment at the individual level, designed to examine whether Japanese macaques match the acoustic features of their replies to those of prior auditory stimuli.

In the experiment, each female subject was presented with a set of stimuli consisting of six or eight calls that had been recorded from one of the adult females in the same group. For each experimental trial, a speaker was hidden approximately 15–20m away from the subject. At a distance of 15m from the speaker, the mean sound pressure level of the stimuli was controlled (43.4 dB). An experimenter stood about 10m from the speaker and waited until all the monkeys were silent for at least five seconds before presenting the stimuli, in order to prevent any other vocalizations from having an effect on the subsequent calls of the female subjects. To control effects of the stimulus animal's presence, the experimenter also made certain that the female whose calls were being used as playback stimuli stayed at least 15m away from the subject. If the female subject uttered coo calls during the ten seconds that followed the playback, the trial was regarded as successful. When the subject uttered two or more coos in a trial, the first coo was used exclusively for the analysis. In the analysis, the time interval was measured from the end of the stimulus to the onset of the subject's coo call in each successful trial. For each coo call, the same set of parameters employed in our previous acoustic analysis was determined spectrographically.

As a first step, in order to examine whether individual subjects responded to stimulus calls, the interval between the end of a stimulus and the beginning of the subject's subsequent coo calls was plotted, using the log frequency method (Sibly, Nott and Fletcher, 1990). If the occurrence of calls depended only on the occurrence of a stimulus, the distribution of time intervals between the stimulus and the subsequent calls would have been represented by an exponential distribution and the graph would have formed a straight line with a negative slope. However, this pattern of results was not obtained (fig. 4.1). For each subject, the majority of calls were uttered within a brief interval of approximately 0.3–1.5 sec. Few calls were uttered within intervals of less than approximately 0.3 sec or more than approximately 1.5 sec. This distribution of intervals indicated that two types of coo calls were involved in the successful trials: the "response call," which was elicited by the stimulus, and the "random call," which occurred independently of presentation of the stimulus. The results are quite consistent with those of our previous observations and since a certain length of time is necessary for a response, "response calls" should occur within a relatively brief delay after presentation of the stimulus. Within a certain time interval after the brief delay, "response calls" should occur frequently. Calls uttered a very short time after the end of stimulus presentation and those uttered after a long interval would be uttered independently of the stimulus and would thus be called "random calls."

Vocal matching by Japanese macaques

Two types of coo calls were classified according to the interval between the stimulus and the call. First, the shortest interval before a response call was determined, taking account of the minimum reaction time and the delay in sound

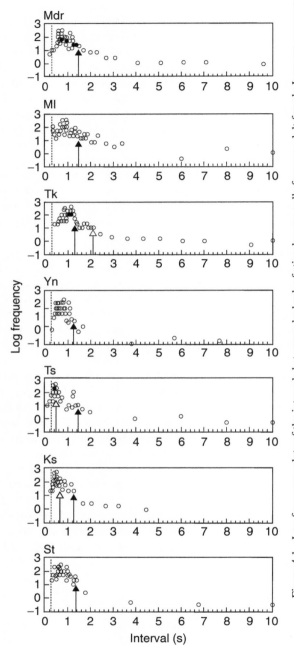

Figure 4.1 Log frequency plots of the intervals between playback of stimulus coo calls from an adult female Japanese macaque and the response coos of seven females. Each dotted vertical line indicates 0.3 sec, the minimum start of response calls. Closed and/or open arrows indicate "abrupt change points," and closed arrows indicate the end of response calls (cited from Sugiura, 1998, with the author's permission).

transmission. In an experiment on rhesus macaques, the minimum time from a stimulus presentation to a motor reaction was estimated to be approximately 0.2 sec (Saslow, 1972). In the present study, the distance between the playback speaker and the subject plus the distance between the experimenter and the subject was approximately 30m longer than that between the experimenter and the speaker. Therefore, a subject's call was recorded with a delay of approximately 0.1 sec after it was emitted. Adding the two intervals, the shortest possible response interval was defined as 0.3 sec. Consequently, calls that occurred within 0.3 sec of the end of the stimulus were classified as "random calls" and those that occurred 0.3 sec or later were classified as "response calls."

The longest interval before response calls was determined from the distribution of intervals. To determine the appropriate criterion for this interval, the "abrupt change point test for exponentially distributed bout length" was used (Haccou and Meelis, 1992). Since the distribution of intervals differed significantly between subject females, these criteria were determined for each subject. One or two significant "abrupt change points" were found for all subjects between 0.3 and 10 sec (see fig. 4.1). For four subjects for whom only one "change point" each was found, the point marking the longest interval before the subject's coo calls was chosen (mean = 1.43 sec). For the other three subjects for whom two "change points" each were found, the "change point" closer to the mean "change point" for the other four subjects was chosen as the longest interval delimiting a response call. Thus, in sum, calls that occurred at or after 0.3 sec but before the longest interval were classified as response calls and calls that occurred within 0.3 sec or after the longest interval were classified as random calls.

Data were subjected to linear regression analysis to determine the effects of the acoustic properties of the stimuli on the acoustic properties of the response calls. A regression analysis was conducted for each of the seven subjects individually so that these effects could be examined at an individual level. As shown in fig. 4.2, results of the analysis revealed that for response calls, five subjects' response calls had significant positive regression with the stimulus calls for a single acoustic parameter – maximum minus start frequency. One of the remaining two subjects' response calls had a significant regression for duration and a nearly significant regression for maximum minus start frequency. Only one animal had no significant positive regression. For random calls, only maximum minus start frequency showed a significant regression and only in two subjects, one of them negative. Therefore, only one subject's random calls showed a positive regression for any parameter, which could have occurred by chance. In contrast to response calls, the acoustic features of stimulus coo calls thus had no significant positive effect on the acoustic features of random calls in the majority of subjects.

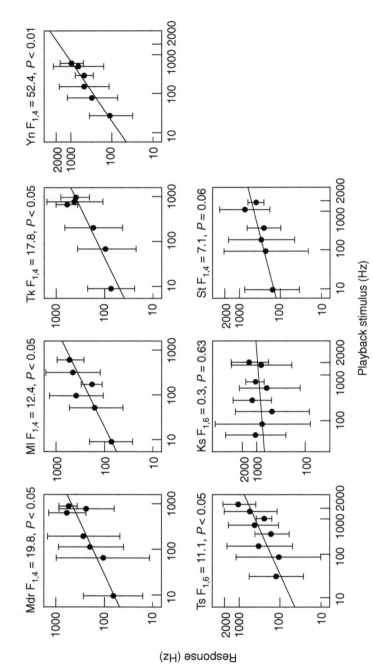

Figure 4.2 Regression of the maximum minus start frequency of the response coos of seven Japanese macaques on that of the playback stimuli (coo calls from an adult female). Mean and standard deviations for coos in response to each stimulus and regression lines are indicated (cited from Sugiura, 1998, with the author's permission).

Overall, for most subjects, the frequency range of response calls from the start to the maximum frequency was significantly influenced by the frequency range of the playback stimuli. These results strongly demonstrated that these female Japanese macaques matched the acoustic features of their coo calls with those of the stimulus calls to which they responded. Further, these Japanese macaques modified the acoustic features of their calls, particularly the range of frequency modulation in the fundamental frequency component, under natural conditions. Assuming that the basic function of the vocal exchange of coo calls is to locate group members and maintain contact with them, individual identification in the calls would be important but flexibility in the calls would be problematic. However, it should be noted that in terms of contributing to individual identification, some parameters, such as start frequency, are relatively stable within individuals and quite different between individuals (Mitani, 1986) while other parameters, such as maximum frequency, are highly variable even within individuals. In fact, Japanese macaque mothers are able to recognize the coos of their own infants on the basis of this stable parameter (Masataka, 1985). Thus, a stable acoustic component at the beginning of the call codes individuality while other components, such as the maximum frequency, code additional information.

A possible functional reason for macaques' matching the acoustic features of their coo calls with those of the preceding call to which they are responding is to indicate that the call is given as a response to the preceding caller. Occasionally, two or more callers utter responding coo calls successively or simultaneously during a vocal exchange. In such situations, acoustic cues in the responses might help the initiating caller to discriminate between a true response and an independent call. Another possible function for matching relates to locating coo calls, which depends on frequency modulation. In exchanging coo calls, Japanese macaques might use the same frequency range because that range is most suitable for the ambient noise level and the distance between callers in a given situation.

The extent to which subjects matched acoustic properties varied in the present study. One of our macaque subjects showed only weak regression in maximum minus start frequency and another showed no evidence of matching at all. A possible factor that influenced the degree of matching was the age of the subject. These two non-matching macaques were either subadult or juvenile while the two who showed strongly significant regressions were full adults. This strongly suggests that macaques come to acquire vocal matching abilities as they develop.

As already described in chapter 2, in some nonhuman primate species, including Japanese macaques, vocal exchanges are more likely to occur between affiliated individuals. In previous investigations, social grooming has been considered the most convincing indicator of affinity between individuals. However, in Japanese macaques, social grooming is not sufficient to evaluate affiliations because it is virtually restricted to within kin groups whereas vocal exchange often occurs between kin groups. In particular, the older females of different kin groups frequently exchange coo calls (Mitani, 1986). Thus, vocal matching in such exchanges might be a rudimentary form of communication that fulfills a phatic function, which is presumably an underlying function of human conversation.

Analyzing imitation in human infants

The results of our comparative study of Japanese macaque and human mother–infant pairs (see chapter 2) revealed remarkable parallels between the early stages of turn-taking ability in human infants and affiliative vocal exchanges in Japanese macaques. I therefore decided to investigate human infants' abilities for vocal matching for those acoustic parameters on which macaques showed vocal matching. Discriminant function analysis was employed to analyze statistically the acoustical relationship between infant vocal productions and caregiver utterances in mutual vocal exchanges (Masataka, 1992a). I have discussed several aspects of prelinguistic infant–caregiver interaction that emphasize the importance of parental responsiveness to infant vocalizations as a crucial prerequisite for successful reciprocal communication. Particularly in spontaneous interactions with their preverbal infants, caregivers treat infant sounds as a means of communication and they both match and model their infants' speech-like vocal sounds. Thus this imitative form of caregiver responsiveness seems to serve as a contingency for infant vocal production. In order to understand how vocal imitation develops in preverbal infants, this possibility should definitely be examined. However, the modal range of vocalizations that young infants produce in short-range face-to-face interactions with their caregivers has not received adequate attention, partly owing to difficulty in evaluating equally the reciprocal effects of caregivers' and infants' utterances to one another. For instance, infant vocalizations have been regarded as inconspicuous random sounds rather than meaningful vocal signals, but parental utterances have been treated as meaningful although they too are frequently void of lexical items. In this regard, discriminant function analysis was expected to be a powerful method for the equal treatment of parental utterances and infant sounds, regardless of the presence or absence of lexical content.

Discriminant function analysis is a multivariate statistical procedure that has proven very useful in classification problems. For problems of sorting individual observations into two or more groups (if equality of within-groups covariance matrices can be assumed), linear functions can be derived using variables that have been measured and cases with known group membership. Measurable acoustic characteristics of infant vocalizations or parental utterances could serve as criterion variables for deriving linear discriminating functions. If a set of predictor variables were successfully established for this group of sounds, then discriminant function analysis might help discern which, if any, variables discriminate between preestablished criterion groups. Thus, if an infant employed relatively discrete classes of vocalizations according to different types of maternal utterances, or if a mother produced different utterances according to relatively discrete classes of infant vocalizations, robust multivariate acoustic differences should be found in the infant vocalizations (or maternal utterances) used according to the acoustic features of maternal utterances (or infant vocalizations).

Moreover, discriminant function analysis can be used to investigate qualitative changes in the pattern of vocal exchanges as a function of the infant's age. If the quality of both infant vocalizations and maternal utterances were stable over a study period, discriminant function analysis could reveal how "incorrect" exchanges occur between infant and mother by measuring the probability with which the infants' vocalizations were classified in the wrong context. This could reveal changes in the pattern of maternal responses to infants' vocal production as a function of infant development, as well as ontogenetic changes in infants' own vocal behaviour in response to maternal utterances.

Participants were ten first-born infants (six males, four females) and their mothers who had uncomplicated prenatal and perinatal histories. The mothers were all monolingual and spoke Japanese exclusively. All of the mothers were full-time housewives between twenty-two and twenty-eight years of age. Each of the mother–infant dyads was observed at home on three consecutive days when the infants were eight weeks old. Thereafter, three-day recordings were continued weekly until the infants were twenty-seven weeks old. Each of the mother–infant dyads was recorded while interacting together freely. Recordings were made with the mother seated in a chair next to a studio-quality portable tape recorder. Each mother held her infant in her lap. The mother and the infant each wore a high-quality lapel microphone. Input from the two microphones was mixed and recorded on one channel of the tape recorder. The observer instructed the mother to talk to her infant as she normally might when they were in private. The mother and infant were left alone in the room for the duration of the recording and were recorded for fifteen minutes in a given recording session. Each mother–infant dyad underwent a total of three sessions in a given recording day. In each session, vocal interactions were defined as being composed of episodes, each of which was composed of a series of rounds of utterances that was set off by periods of silence longer than five minutes. As a unit of acoustic measurement, an utterance was operationalized as a continuous mother or infant vocalization bounded by pauses longer than 0.3 sec.

Each episode could be classified into two categories according to which member of the dyad initiated the episode, the mother or the infant. If the mother initiated the episode, it was defined as "mother-initiated interaction"; if the infant initiated the episode, it was defined as "infant-initiated interaction." Subsequent separate analyses were performed on each category of interaction. For each, an analysis was exclusively conducted on the initial move by the mother (in mother-initiated interactions) or by the infant (in infant-initiated interactions) and the corresponding immediate response (i.e., by the infant or by the mother). The acoustical relationship between the initial move and its corresponding response was investigated.

For maternal utterances, acoustical measurements were made with regard to both their suprasegmental (prosodic) and their segmental (phonetic) features. Pitch contour and vowels were classified to represent suprasegmental and segmental features respectively. For pitch contour, a sonagram was produced for each maternal utterance and pitch contour was classified into five types: rising, falling, flat, bell-shaped (falling in the beginning and rising thereafter) and complex. To classify pitch contour types, we inspected the visual displays of the fundamental frequency over time, as represented by the sonagrams. Two raters classified all of the utterances; inter-rater reliability was greater than 90 percent. For vowel classification, two raters heard each utterance through a headphone. Raters were asked to specify the vowel pronounced in each of the utterances using five vowel categories in the Japanese language: /a/, /i/, /u/, /e/, and /o/. When an utterance consisted of more than one syllable, raters were asked to classify the vowel located in the first syllable for mother-initiated interactions and the vowel located in the final syllable for infant-initiated interactions. This was done based on the assumption that the acoustical relationship between the maternal utterance and the infant vocalization, if any, would be most evident in the acoustical element of the maternal utterance that was closest, temporally, to the infant's vocalization.

In terms of infant vocalizations, a total of sixteen acoustic parameters were measured. They included twelve parameters relative to fundamental frequency (F0) elements of the vocalizations, as follows:

1. DUR: Duration
2. PF: Peak frequency attained in the vocalization
3. PFL: Peak frequency location (as percentage of duration)
4. AVF: Arithmetic mean of frequencies in the midsection of the vocalization
5. FSL: Average slope existing over the first 50ms
6. TSL: Average slope existing over the final 50ms
7. SF: Start frequency in the vocalization
8. EF: End frequency in the vocalization
9. ES: End minus start frequency
10. MF: Minimum frequency in the vocalization
11. PM: Peak minus minimum frequency
12. MFL: Minimum frequency location (as percent of duration)

In addition to these twelve parameters, the following two parameters were measured:

13. Overall arithmetic mean of frequencies in the first formant of the vocalization (F1)
14. Overall arithmetic mean of frequencies in the second formant of the vocalization (F2)

Formants are frequency regions in which the amplitude of acoustic energy is high, reflecting natural resonances created in the vocal tract. Formants are numbered, i.e., F1, F2, and so forth, from the lowest frequency upward. F1 and F2 were included in the present analysis because they are known to be the most important formants for vowel identification. Unlike F0, F1 and F2 are known to be stable with respect to frequency modulation. As described below, the vowels contained in the maternal utterances recorded in the present observation were mostly divided into /a/, /i/, and /u/. The vowels produced by adults are distinguished by the relationship between these two parameters. Concerning each of the infant-initiated and mother-initiated interactions, discriminant analyses were independently performed on suprasegmental and segmental features of the utterances.

Acoustic relationships for prosodic features in infant-initiated interactions

For analysis of prosodic features, discriminant analysis using the Statistical Package for the Social Sciences (SPSS) was performed (Nie et al., 1975). For infant-initiated interactions, we first sought to determine whether or not any acoustical variants of the infant vocalizations consistently preceded specific pitch contours of subsequent maternal utterances. In other words, we examined whether or not any prosodic feature of infant vocalizations could be predicted retrospectively from maternal vocalizations.

Three criteria were used in determining how variables were entered into the discriminant analysis. First, in order to assess the contribution of the acoustic variables over and above infant's age, age (AGE) was entered as the first variable in this analysis, followed by the sixteen acoustic variables outlined above. Second, F ratios were computed for each of the acoustic variables before the first step, and then before and after each subsequent step. An F value of 4.0 or greater was required for a variable either to be entered into the analysis (F to enter) or to be retained in the analysis once entered (F to remove). This requirement screened out variables that were less efficient discriminators than others. Variables with an F value of 4.0 or higher were entered into the analysis on the basis of Rao's generalized distance measure (Rao, 1948), which is the maximal average D2 (Mahalanobis' distance) for all group pairs. The variable that contributed the largest increase in this distance measure (in combination with the other variables already entered in the analysis), i.e., that maximally separated infant vocalizations following or preceding different types of maternal speech, was the next variable entered into the discriminant analysis.

Discriminant analysis creates a number of functions (one fewer than the number of groups or, in this case, pitch contour types for maternal utterances) based on Fisher's original solution to the discriminant problem. These functions can be used to classify individual cases into groups. However, these functions can be rather difficult to interpret (particularly in the present case, where several linear functions were expected). Therefore, standardized canonical discriminant function coefficients were employed as a means of identifying variables important in distinguishing among the groups. Four discriminant functions were used to classify the cases into one of the five groups according to Fisher's classification procedure. Canonical correlations may be used to transform variables used for discrimination into classification functions and it was these functions that were used to classify individual vocalizations by source. This procedure guarantees that the first classification function (most heavily weighted) always contained the best single combination of discriminant variables, whereas the last function (least heavily weighted) contained the poorest combination of discriminant variables. A total of 1,854 episodes that were submitted to the discriminant function analysis were split randomly into two equal independent samples. The results obtained from the first half of the total sample were cross-validated against the other half of the sample.

Data from the discriminant analysis performed on the first half of the random sample of infant vocalizations showed that the percentage of variance attributable to each of the four discriminant functions was: function 1, 74.5 percent; function 2, 20.2 percent; function 3, 3.8 percent; and function 4, 1.5 percent. The canonical correlation measures were: function 1, 0.96; function 2, 0.84; function 3, 0.54; and function 4, 0.42. Canonical correlation measures the association between each of the discriminant functions and a dummy function indicating group membership. The square of this correlation is the proportion of variance attributed to group membership. These results show that both of the first two functions are highly associated with the group membership variable. With respect to the contribution of each variable to the four discriminant functions used to reclassify the vocalizations in the first sample, function 1 was found to consist almost entirely of information from PFL and 69 percent of the variance was accounted for by this function. Function 2 accounted for 25 percent of the total discriminant variance. The two variables, FSL and TSL, were its most significant contributors. The values for FSL and TSL were quite similar in absolute value, indicating their equal efficiency as discriminators. Functions 3 and 4 were less important overall discriminators and approximately 3 percent of all cases were correctly classified as a result of

Table 4.1 *Mean values of the three key acoustic variables of infant vocalizations across five pitch contours of following maternal utterance*

Variable	Following maternal utterance				
	Rising	Falling	Flat	Bell-shaped	Complex
PFL(%)	89.6	14.2	53.3	28.7	66.2
FSL(Hz/50ms)	2.4	−7.5	0.3	−18.5	14.9
TSL (Hz/50ms)	16.0	−8.8	−1.6	14.3	−7.3

The variable abbreviations mean peak frequency location by PFL, average slope existing for the first 50ms by FSL, and average slope existing for the final 50ms by TSL.

the inclusion of these functions. AGE was not an important contributor. Overall reclassification accuracy was 72.6 percent.

Table 4.1 presents mean values for the three acoustic variables in those infant vocalizations that this discriminant analysis accurately predicted to have been uttered prior to each maternal utterance contour type. In particular, infant vocalizations preceding maternal utterances with rising contours were characterized by having their peak frequency located at the end of the vocalization, whereas the opposite was true for infant vocalizations that preceded maternal speech with falling contours. When mothers responded to infant vocalizations using utterances with flat contours, the infants' peak frequency occurred near the middle of their vocalizations. When maternal responses showed bell-shaped contours, their infants' peak frequency was likely to occur in the first third of the vocalization. When maternal utterances showed complex contours, mean PFL value was approximately 66, which means that their infants' peak frequency was likely to occur in the final third of the vocalization. Furthermore, infant vocalizations preceding bell-shaped maternal speech were characterized by a sharp downward frequency shift at their onset (FSL) and an upward shift at their end (TSL), while infant vocalizations preceding complex maternal speech were characterized by a sharp upward frequency shift at their onset and downward shift at their end. When preceding speech with a flat contour, no such distinctive frequency change occurs in either the onset or the end of the vocalizations.

The cross-validation analysis, in which the discriminant profiles derived from one random subsample of vocalizations were used to classify the second subsample, revealed that the contribution of variables to the four discriminant functions was virtually identical to that described earlier. Function 1 consisted almost entirely of the information from PFL. With respect to function 2, FSL and TSL were the most significant contributors. Function 3 and function 4 were made up of mostly of DUR and PF, and PF, respectively. The overall classification accuracy was 69.3 percent. This cross-validation produced strikingly similar results to the discriminant analysis on the first random sample. Moreover, when the proportion of cross-validated vocalizations that were misclassified was plotted as a function of infant age, the age effect was significant. Proportions of misclassifications were likely to increase with age.

The above results indicated that in infant vocalizations to which mothers responded with different prosodical variants, structural variability could be characterized by a set of quantitative physical parameters. When the classification functions are used to reclassify original data, the accuracy with which group membership can be predicted and the degree of overlap among groups can be demonstrated. An unreliable estimate of the accuracy of predicted group membership may result, however, if the number of variables approaches the number of cases in each group. In this situation, spurious correlations between measurement variables and group membership may occur. This can result in a "shrinkage" of classification accuracy when the classifying equations are applied to independent samples. The success of my cross-validation indicates that the results were not an artifact of using the same dataset to derive the profiles as to test reclassification accuracy, a commonly cited misuse of discriminant analysis (Fletcher, Rice and Ray, 1978). The best way to differentiate infant vocalizations preceding maternal speech characterized by each of the five pitch contours was PFL, a measure of peak frequency location. The combination of the variables FSL and TSL (measures of average slopes existing during the first and final 50ms) also displayed pronounced discriminatory power. Overall, infant vocalizations appeared to resemble subsequent maternal speech in terms of pitch contour (i.e., when an infant uttered a vocalization of rising contour, the mother's subsequent utterance was also likely to be of rising contour). The most likely explanation for these results is that when responding to spontaneous vocalizations uttered by their infants, mothers are likely to match or model their infants' pitch contours. Mothers' responses can be described as "echoic."

The discriminant analysis classification procedure offers a potentially powerful tool for studying chronologically related changes in vocal usage. The present results indicated that the percentage of cross-validated vocalizations that were misclassified increased with age. Ostensibly, this means that the statistically significant relationship between acoustic features of infant vocalizations and immediately following maternal utterances becomes weaker as the infant develops. However, infant age itself was not the important contributor. Rather, infants' vocalizations remained acoustically very similar across age levels, at least with regard to prosodic features. Thus, the "echoic" characteristics of

Table 4.2 *Mean values of the two key acoustic*
variables of infant vocalizations across three
vowels in preceding maternal utterance

Variable	Following maternal utterance		
	/a/	/i/	/u/
F1(Hz)	1085	804	653
F2(Hz)	2548	3059	2456

The variable abbreviations mean overall arithmetic mean of
frequencies in the formant by F1, and overall arithmetic mean
of frequencies of the second formant by F2.

maternal responses to infant vocalizations appear most robust when infants
are young and the echoic tendency becomes less robust as the infants grow
older.

Acoustic relationships for segmental features
in infant-initiated interactions

Subsequently, I conducted a similar discriminant analysis on the same sample
of infant-initiated interactions, but this time to determine whether or not any
acoustical variants of infant vocalizations consistently preceded specific segmental features of maternal utterances. In the analysis, AGE was again entered
as the first variable but it was not found to be an important contributor. When
each of the maternal utterances was classified according to the five types of
vowels, /a/, /i/, and /u/ each accounted for more than 30 percent of the total
sample whereas /e/ and /o/ each accounted for less than 3 percent. Therefore,
the following analysis was performed only on those mother–infant vocal interactions in which the maternal utterances involved either /a/, /i/, or /u/. The
analysis examined whether any acoustic variants in infant vocalizations could
be predicted retrospectively from maternal speech characterized by segmental
elements involving a vowel /a/, /i/, or /u/.

Using data from the discriminant analysis performed on the same first random
subsample of infant vocalizations used in the previous analysis, only function 1
was found to be highly associated with the group membership variable. Function 1 consisted of information from both parameters of F1 and F2; 94 percent
of the variance was accounted for by this function. The values of F1 and F2
were quite similar in absolute value, indicating their equal efficiency as discriminators. Function 2 was a less important overall discriminator. Table 4.2
presents mean values for the two key acoustic variables in those infant

vocalizations that were accurately predicted by this discriminant analysis to have been uttered prior to maternal speech with each of the three key segmental features. Infant vocalizations preceding maternal speech with the vowel /a/ were characterized by a relatively greater F1 score and a relatively smaller F2 score. Infant vocalizations preceding maternal speech with the vowel /u/ were characterized by relatively smaller F1 and F2 scores. Infant vocalizations preceding maternal speech with the vowel /i/ were characterized by the highest F2 scores. The F1 scores in these infant vocalizations were intermediate between those vocalizations preceding maternal speech with the vowel /a/ and those preceding maternal speech with the vowel /u/. The corresponding cross-validation analysis revealed that the contribution of variables to the two discriminant functions was virtually identical. Overall classification accuracy was 58.6 percent. When the proportion of cross-validated vocalizations that were misclassified was plotted as a function of infant age, again, the age effect was found to be significant. Again, proportions of misclassifications were likely to increase with age.

Acoustically, the space encompassing vowels forms a "vowel triangle" whose points are determined by the vowels /i/, /a/, and /u/. These three vowels, termed "point" vowels, occur in all the world's languages. The classic study by Peterson and Barney (1952) on seventy-six English-speaking adults showed that when the vowel /a/ was pronounced, its F1 frequency ranged between 600 and 1200 Hz and its F2 frequency ranged between 1000 and 2500 Hz. When the vowel /i/ was pronounced, its F1 frequency was much lower than when the vowel /a/ was pronounced, i.e., it ranged between 200 and 600 Hz, but its F2 frequency was higher, ranging between 2000 and 3500 Hz. When the vowel /u/ was pronounced its F1 frequency was similar to that of the vowel /i/, between 200 and 600 Hz, but its F2 frequency was lower than either /a/ or /i/, between 500 and 1500 Hz.

I measured F1 and F2 for those vowels in maternal speech, within infant-initiated interactions, that I classified into /a/, /i/, or /u/. For maternal speech classified as /a/, the average F1 and F2 were 1063 Hz and 1549 Hz, respectively. For maternal speech classified as /i/, the average F1 and F2 were 442 Hz and 2861 Hz, respectively. For maternal speech classified as /u/, the average F1 and F2 were 482 Hz and 899 Hz, respectively. Statistically, the F1 value associated with /a/ was significantly higher than that associated with /i/ or with /u/ and the F2 value associated with /i/ was higher than that associated with /a/ or with /u/. The results clearly confirmed previous findings. Moreover, vowel triangle comparisons between infant vocalizations and maternal speech were also consistent with these findings. Those infant vocalizations that preceded maternal speech with the vowel /a/ were distinguished from others by higher F1 values. Infant vocalizations that preceded maternal speech with the vowel /i/ were distinguished from others by higher F2 values. Mothers appeared to respond to infant vocalizations by uttering vocalizations that were similar in their F1/F2 frequency relationship to the F1/F2 frequency relationship exhibited by infants in their vocalizations. For example, when infants uttered vocalizations that sounded /a/-like, mothers responded to them with speech containing the vowel /a/. When infants uttered vocalizations spontaneously, mothers performed echoic responding not only with respect to the prosodic dimension but also with respect to the phonetic dimension. The tendency was most robust when infants were young and was likely to decline as they developed.

Acoustic relationships for prosodic features in mother-initiated interactions

Subsequently, I performed similar analyses on the interactions that were initiated spontaneously by mothers. I explored the possibility that the acoustic features of infants' vocalizations that followed maternal utterances with different prosodic or phonetic variations would be distinguishable. Overall, a total of 1,644 episodes of mother-initiated interaction were analyzed. This sample was then split into two equal subsamples.

The first analysis examined prosodic features. Maternal speech was classified into five categories according to its intonational shape, or pitch contours: rising, falling, flat, bell-shaped or complex. If an infant employs relatively discrete classes of vocalizations according to these types of maternal speech, robust acoustic differences should occur between infant vocalizations associated with the different maternal pitch contours. Indeed, the analysis revealed structural variability in infant vocalizations characterized by a set of quantifiable physical parameters. With regard to the first subsample of the entire dataset, function 1 was made up almost entirely of PFL and 82 percent of the variance was accounted for by this function. Function 2 accounted for 21 percent of the total variance. The two variables FSL and TSL were the most significant contributors. The values of both parameters were similar to one another. The third and fourth functions were less important overall discriminators; approximately 6 percent of all cases were correctly classified as a result of the inclusion of these functions. AGE was not an important contributor. Overall, reclassification accuracy was 74 percent. These results were strikingly similar to the results obtained from the analysis on the infant-initiated interaction described earlier.

Table 4.3 presents mean values of the three key acoustic variables in those infant vocalizations that were accurately predicted by this discriminant analysis to have been uttered following each of the five different contour types of maternal speech. Obviously, the results were amazingly similar to those obtained from the analysis on the infant-initiated interaction (see table 4.1). The cross-validation analysis revealed that the pattern of contribution of variables for the

Table 4.3 *Mean values of the three key acoustic variables of infant vocalizations across five pitch contours of following maternal utterance*

Variable	Preceding maternal utterance				
	Rising	Falling	Flat	Bell-shaped	Complex
PFL(%)	92.7	11.1	49.4	25.7	70.0
FSL(Hz/50 ms)	1.8	−5.8	0.4	−13.3	15.2
TSL(Hz/50 ms)	19.2	−10.5	−0.8	16.9	−9.4

See table 4.1 for the variable abbreviations.

four discriminant functions was virtually identical to that described above and that the rates of misclassification significantly decreased with age. Two possible explanations might account for the present results. First, mothers may have become adept at predicting what type of vocalization their infants were about to utter, prosodically (probably from what was uttered in the last interaction), and matched their initial vocalization to the infant response they expected. Alternatively, infants may have come to utter specific vocalizations in response to different pitch contours in preceding maternal speech. Since the present study was correlational rather than experimental in design, it is not possible to determine which explanation, if either, is correct. However, each sample of maternal speech that was analyzed was always temporally separated from any preceding vocal behavior by more than five minutes. Because of the relatively long pause, it seems unlikely that previous experience with infant vocalization affects the pitch contour of maternal speech at the onset of subsequent interaction. More importantly, these findings parallel the results we obtained from our analysis of vocal exchange in Japanese macaques; it is difficult to view this similarity as merely incidental.

Moreover, in infant-initiated interactions, prosodic matching also occurred between infant vocalizations and maternal speech. Age had a significant effect but this tendency was likely to be less robust as the infants developed. The results might lead us to conclude that the effect of previous experience with infant vocalizations on the prosodic features of subsequent maternal speech, if any, becomes less distinctive as infants grow older. With respect to the present sample, cross-validation produced similar results to our discriminant analysis on the first subsample. This age effect was also significant. However, this time, misclassification rates were likely to increase with age. In mother-initiated interactions, matching tended to occur more frequently as infants developed. It would be difficult to explain the results in terms of the mothers' expectations of infants' responses.

Table 4.4 *Mean values of the two key acoustic variables of infant vocalizations across three vowels in preceding maternal utterance*

Variable	Following maternal utterance		
	/a/	/i/	/u/
F1(Hz)	1065	873	718
F2(Hz)	2460	2897	2333

See table 4.2 for the variable abbreviations.

Acoustic relationships for phonetic features with mother-initiated interactions

A final discriminant analysis was conducted on infant-initiated interactions to determine whether the acoustic features of infants' vocalizations that followed maternal utterances with varied phonetic characteristics would be distinguishable. Maternal speech was classified into five categories according to its phonetic features, i.e., /a/, /i/, /u/, /e/, and /o/. If an infant employed discrete classes of vocalizations according to these types of maternal speech, this would be revealed by the analysis.

As in infant-initiated interactions, classifying all maternal utterances according to the five vowel types produced rates for /a/, /i/, and /u/ that were each greater than 30 percent, while rates for /e/ and /o/ were each smaller than 3 percent. Therefore, analysis was performed exclusively on maternal utterances characterized by the vowels /a/, /i/, or /u/. In the analysis, function 1 was comprised of information from the F1 and F2 parameters; 90 percent of the variance was accounted for by this function. The second function was not an important contributor. Although AGE was entered first in the analysis, it was found to be a relatively unimportant contributor. Table 4.4 presents mean values of the two key acoustic variables in infant vocalizations that were accurately predicted to have followed the three vowel variants of maternal speech. The results are quite similar to those shown in table 4.2. For infant vocalizations following maternal speech with the vowel /a/, the F1 value was relatively higher and the F2 value was relatively lower. In response to maternal speech with the vowel /i/, infant vocalizations were characterized by the highest F2 value. When infant vocalizations responded to maternal speech with the vowel /u/, both the F1 and F2 values were relatively low.

When measuring F1 and F2 scores associated with maternal speech, average F1 and F2 values were 1115 Hz and 1622 Hz, respectively, when maternal speech vowels were classified as /a/. When maternal speech vowels were classified as /i/, the average F1 was 460 Hz and the average F2 was 2703 Hz. When maternal speech vowels were classified as /u/, the average F1 and F2 were 471 Hz and 904 Hz, respectively. The F1 of /a/ was significantly higher than that of /i/ or that of /u/. The F2 value of /i/ was higher than that of /a/ or that of /u/. The vowel triangles formed by the maternal speech and by the following infant vocalizations were found to be extremely similar. This suggests that when responding to maternal speech, the F1/F2 relationships in infant vocalizations tend to match those in preceding maternal utterances.

Results of the cross-validation analysis were virtually identical to those described above. Overall classification accuracy was 61.5 percent. When the proportions of cross-validated vocalizations that were misclassified were plotted as a function of infant age, the effect of age found to be significant, and the rates were likely to increase with age. The results were quite similar to those obtained from the analysis of mother-initiated interactions with respect to prosodic features.

With regard to vowel-like phonetic features, the ability for vocal imitation during early infancy has been reported on the basis of an experimental study (Kuhl and Meltzoff, 1996). In this study, seventy-two infants (twenty-four in each of three age groups: twelve-, sixteen- and twenty-week-olds) were tested for vocal imitation. They were seated in an infant seat facing a three-sided cloth-covered theater, the front panel of which displayed a video screen. Once the infant was secured by a seat belt, a stimulus tape was presented and any vocalizations the infant produced were recorded for a five-minute period. The stimulus was video footage of a female speaker pronouncing /a/ as in "hop," /i/ as in "heap" and /u/ as in "hoop." Thus, Kuhn and Meltzoff presented auditory-visual face-voice stimuli to infants because they considered both the face and the voice necessary to establish a "sufficiently natural situation to induce the infant to produce speech" (1996, p. 2436).

Using this procedure, a total of 224 vocalizations, including vowel-like utterances, were recorded. When these vocalizations were analyzed spectrographically, developmental changes were found in vowel production. The acoustic characteristics of infant vocalizations became more separated in vowel space relative to acoustic differences in the stimulus, from twelve to twenty weeks of age. At twelve weeks of age, F1 and F2 distributions for infant vocalizations mostly overlapped whether or not they were produced in response to a stimulus with an /a/, /i/, or /u/. However, at sixteen weeks of age, overlapping decreased significantly, and at twenty weeks of age, it reached its lowest. The infants' vowel triangles developed to become virtually identical to the model female's vowel triangle. This suggests that infants, when listening to a particular vowel, come to produce vocalizations resembling that vowel as they develop. The results of our discriminant analysis are consistent with those of Kuhl and Melzoff (1996). The decrease in the rate of misclassification in the cross-validation analysis must have been induced by development of the ability for vocal imitation for phonetic features. In turn, this suggests that the same tendency seen in our analysis with respect to prosody could be due to the development of the ability for vocal imitation of suprasegmental features.

Relationship between rates of misclassification for infant- versus mother-initiated interactions

The results of discriminant analyses on infant-initiated and mother-initiated interactions have been presented separately thus far. However, at the level of each individual infant, the rate of increase in misclassification rates for infant-initiated interaction actually changed significantly as a function of the rate of decrease in misclassification rates for mother-initiated interaction. In the above analyses, developmental changes in misclassification rates were statistically examined using pooled data from all participants. However, as shown in figs. 4.3 and 4.4, there is individual variation in this pattern.

With regard to prosodic features, misclassification rates for infant-initiated interaction changed significantly as a function of age in six mother–infant dyads (NM, FA, SP, DK, LT and OY) whereas no such change occurred in the other four dyads (RE, WD, FE and UT). In the first six dyads, rates showed a sudden increase between infant ages of thirteen and twenty weeks. Exactly when the change took place varied from dyad to dyad, but in each of the dyads, it occurred rather abruptly so that a distinct change point could be determined. Concerning the phonetic feature in infant-initiated interaction, in contrast, developmental change was characterized by a sudden increase in misclassification rates, but only in the latter four dyads, between infant ages of sixteen and twenty-one weeks. This suggests that the degree to which mothers made echoic responses to spontaneous infant vocalizations is likely to be biased to only one or the other of the phonetic or the prosodic feature of the infant's vocalizations. That is, maternal responsiveness takes on one of two distinctive patterns defined by these two different acoustic qualities. If maternal responsiveness was distinctive, the degree to which it was echoic was relatively greater during early periods: echoic maternal responding was less likely to occur as the infant developed. Further, this change occurred abruptly.

In mother-initiated interaction, on the other hand, misclassification rates changed significantly in every participant dyad, in terms of both prosodic and phonetic features. Without exception, the rates showed a sudden drop between the ages of twelve and twenty-one weeks. Again, exactly when the change took place varied from dyad to dyad; but in each of the dyads, the change happened rather abruptly so that an abrupt change point could be determined in terms of either of the two acoustic qualities. This suggests that the degree to which infants matched the qualities of their vocalizations to those of immediately

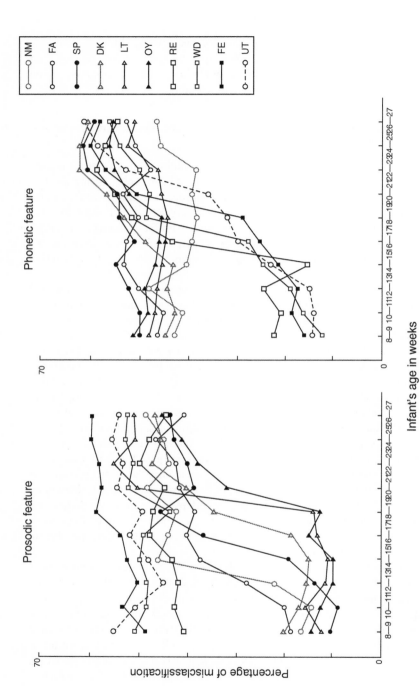

Figure 4.3 Percentage of cross-validated vocalizations that were misclassified in each dyad in the discriminant analysis on the infant-initiated interaction as a function of the age of the infant in the dyad.

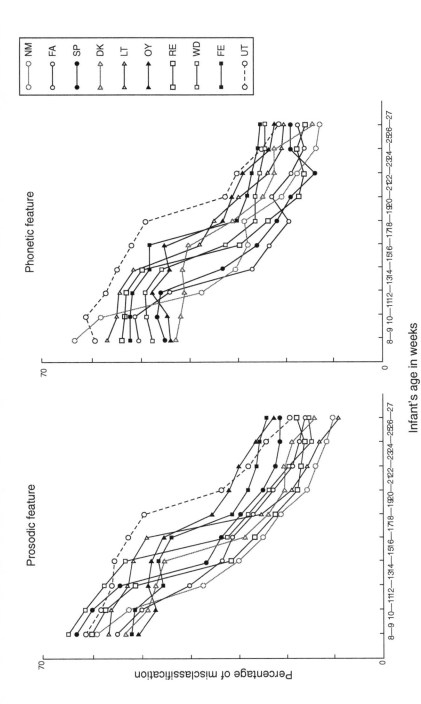

Figure 4.4 Percentage of cross-validated vocalizations that were misclassified in each dyad in the discriminant analysis on the mother-initiated interaction as a function of the age of the infant in the dyad.

Table 4.5 *Abrupt change points (infant's age in weeks) determined in the discriminant analyses*

Dyad	Infant-initiating interaction		Mother-initiating interaction	
	Prosodic feature	Phonetic feature	Prosodic feature	Phonetic feature
NM	13.9	–	12.6	13.3
FA	14.5	–	13.4	13.6
SP	16.2	–	15.0	17.3
DK	18.0	–	17.2	17.7
LT	19.3	–	17.8	16.6
OY	20.7	–	18.1	18.3
RE	–	16.5	13.6	15.0
WD	–	17.8	16.4	15.8
FE	–	20.2	19.3	18.1
UT	–	21.1	20.6	19.7

preceding maternal utterances did not vary in terms of the prosodic and phonetic features, i.e., vocal imitation occurred equally with respect to these two
properties. The tendency was for vocal imitation to become robust as the infant
developed, indeed suddenly so. Table 4.5 shows the abrupt change points with
regard to the infants' age in weeks that could be determined in the discriminant
analyses.

When comparing the score for prosodic features of mother-initiated interaction with that for phonetic features, for the same interaction for each dyad, a
highly significant positive relationship was found, i.e., the earlier the change
point occurred for one of these two features, the earlier it occurred for the other.
Concerning the six dyads for which change points could be determined via the
prosodic features of infant-initiated interactions, the change point score for each
dyad showed significant positive correlations both with the change point score
determined via the prosodic feature in the mother-initiated interaction and with
the change point score determined via the phonetic feature of mother-initiated
interaction. For each of the remaining four dyads for which change points could
be determined via the phonetic features of infant-initiated interaction, a positive linear relationship was also found between that change point score and
the change point score determined via the prosodic or the phonetic features of
mother-initiated interaction. Moreover, considering the change points identified via infant-initiated interactions for all ten dyads, whether determined via
prosodic or phonetic features, the score for each dyad was again found again
to correlate positively with the change point score determined via prosodic
and phonetic features in mother-initiated interaction. That is, within individual mother–infant dyads, the earlier the infant's vocal imitation developed in
terms of both prosodic and phonetic features, the earlier the mother's echoic

responding to her infant's vocalization decreased, in terms of either of these two acoustic features.

Effects of maternal echoic responding on the development of infant imitation

These results have several implications for our understanding of the development of infant vocal imitation. First, echoic responding by mothers plays an important role in facilitating infant imitation. Imitation had been regarded as an activity requiring cognitive abilities that take most of the first year to develop (Piaget, 1951). However, more recently, newborn infants have demonstrated the ability to match the behaviors of others (Meltzoff and Moore, 1983). For example, with regard to one adult behavior, newborns have been reported capable of matching its pattern closely. Infant matching of adult tongue movements has been demonstrated repeatedly in several different laboratories for infants a few hours old to six weeks of age (see Anisfeld, 1984; Butterworth and Harris, 1994, for review). It has consistently been reported that infants match two specific oral gestures modeled by adults: tongue protrusions and mouth openings. Controversy remains as to the mechanisms underlying the matching, but that the behavior occurs in a social context is undisputed. For instance, Legerstee (1991) examined the role of person and object in eliciting such behavior. Twenty-seven infants, five to eight weeks of age were randomly assigned to two conditions: person condition and object condition. In the person condition, infants were presented with tongue protrusions and mouth openings modeled by an adult; in the object condition, infants were presented with these gestures simulated by two objects. Infants in the person condition selectively reproduced the mouth opening and tongue protrusion gestures, whereas infants in the object condition did not; this suggests the important role of the person in eliciting early infant matching.

Evidence for cross-modal matching very early in infancy is also accumulating. By one month of age, infants already match the oral feel and the sight of textured pacifiers (Meltzoff and Borton, 1979) and they show oral-visual transfer with rigid and elastic cylinders (Gibson and Walker, 1984). Infants are able to match temporal with spatiotemporal qualities of stimuli heard and seen, e.g., puppets with sounds (Spelke, 1979), sponges and blocks with their sounds (Bahrick, 1983), etc. The development of this perceptual competence is significant for vocal imitation because auditory-visual perception is particularly useful for perceiving the communicative actions of other persons. Spelke (1990) suggested some aspects of auditory-visual coordination that might allow very young infants to learn to use speech to communicate. Immediately after birth, when hearing a voice, infants are already able to locate the person who is vocalizing. This basic coordination between vision and hearing enables the infants to seek out a visual object to help locate the sound source. They soon learn to associate faces with voices. They develop the ability to determine whether or not a person they can see speaking is the source of the voice, by perceiving the synchrony between the face and the voice. Subsequently, infants begin to have specific expectations about which face goes with which voice, at least with respect to highly familiar caregivers, and to exhibit particular preferences for specific combinations of voice quality and facial configuration. Simultaneously, when watching the facial movements that accompany the act of speaking, infants often attempt to match those motor patterns. In addition, as demonstrated by Eimas et al. (1971), they are already well equipped linguistically to recognize speech and to distinguish phonemes.

What motivates infants to attempt vocal imitation appears to be their awareness of auditory equivalences between their own vocalizations and those of their mothers, especially their mothers' echoic responses. In other words, to facilitate their infants' perceptual development, mothers respond to infant vocalizations in an echoic manner. This does not imply that maternal responding exerts effects on infant behavior exclusively by means of the acoustic features that make their response "echoic." Although the actual acoustic feature used to create an echoic response can vary from individual to individual, it is the infant's perception of the equivalence between a given acoustic feature of its mother's response and its own vocalization that is important, regardless of what particular acoustical property the two physically share. The infant's perception of equivalence would be sufficient for the infant to begin imitating.

When vocalizing, a hearing infant inevitably receives auditory feedback from its vocalization. At the same time, the infant must perceive the proprioceptive sensation derived from vocal production. Immediately after vocalizing, the infant hears its mother producing an utterance and it sees her facial movement accompanying the utterance. If the infant perceives an equivalence between its own vocalization and the maternal response, the infant might spontaneously attempt to produce a vocalization that is acoustically similar to the maternal utterance, possibly on the basis of knowledge about sensation from its own vocal apparatus that was generated when it created a particular type of sound.

This idea is supported by the finding that some of the ten mothers I tested responded echoically to their infant's infant vocalizations prosodically, while others did so phonetically. Why choose one acoustic feature to create an echoic response but not the other? Table 4.6 presents data that serve as a clue to answering this question. One possibility might be that each mother attended to that acoustic feature of her infant's vocalizations that initially her infant was already more likely to use to imitate maternal utterances. When misclassification rates for mother-initiated interaction (see fig. 4.4) were considered for each dyad when the infant was eight weeks old, and compared between prosodic and phonetic features, no significant difference was found. Initially, the infants' overall

Table 4.6 *Likelihood (%) with which each infant of the dyad, at 8 weeks of age, vocalized further in response to the maternal response to spontaneously given infant vocalization when the maternal responsiveness was classified as being echoic by the discriminant analysis and when it was not echoic*

Dyad	Maternal response		
	Echoic, reflecting the infant's prosodic feature	Echoic, reflecting the infant's phonetic feature	Non-echoic
NM	36.2	14.5	12.1
FA	26.9	14.3	11.0
SP	48.7	27.5	19.9
DK	35.0	14.9	10.9
LT	27.8	15.6	12.1
OY	20.4	9.3	7.1
RE	23.6	41.8	17.0
WD	25.2	43.3	24.7
FE	16.4	33.2	17.4
UT	27.3	39.1	21.3

tendency to imitate maternal utterances appeared to be indifferent to differences between these acoustic features. However, for infant-initiated interaction, when comparing the likelihood with which each infant spontaneously vocalized further in response to the maternal response between the two acoustic properties, a robust difference was found. In the six dyads in which the maternal echoic response reflected the prosodic features of infant vocalizations, the likelihood of the infant's vocalizing further at eight weeks of age was significantly higher only when maternal echoic responses reflected the infant's prosodic features. In the other four dyads, this likelihood was significantly higher only when maternal echoic responses reflected the infant's phonetic feature. At this early stage of mother–infant preverbal vocal interaction, the infant's tendency to remain responsive after the onset of mother–infant vocal interaction varied individually according to how well the acoustic quality of the maternal utterance reflected the quality of the infant's own vocal activity. Each mother was also sensitive to the idiosyncrasy and adjusted her response so that she could effectively maintain the interaction with her infant.

A dynamic view of the development of vocal imitation

Taken together, when responding to spontaneous infant vocalizations, maternal responses are likely to be echoic, either prosodically or phonetically. The type of echoic response performed is determined by the mother on the basis of her evaluation of her infant's readiness to remain vocal in terms of each acoustic feature. If vocal production is viewed as a special case of skilled motor behavior, some useful notions about speech control might be gained from recent work on motor behavior in general. In this context, a skill can be defined as an organization of movement that is purposeful. Bruner (1990) viewed the development of a motor skill as the construction of serially ordered acts, the performance of which is modified to achieve diminishing variability, increased anticipation and improved economy. In order to acquire the motor control necessary for voluntary vocal production, infants must solve what is known in studies of motor behavior as the degree of freedom problem. Infants must assemble a heterogeneous array of individual movements into a unitary coordinated action that produces sounds perceived as contextually relevant by adults. Certainly, a number of motor actions take part in vocal production. Kent and Murray (1982) explained the bioacoustic bases of prosodic features. A falling pitch contour, for instance, is the result of decreased subglottal air pressure towards the end of an infant's vocalization, with a concomitant reduction in vocal fold length and tension. A rising pitch contour is the result of increased subglottal air pressure towards the end of an infant's vocalization, with a concomitant increase in vocal fold tension. The acquisition of the skill to effect such varied and purposeful laryngeal articulation is crucial.

Creating vocalizations that vary in their phonetic properties requires different forms of motor coordination than creating vocalizations that vary in their prosodic properties. The articulation model introduced above comprises combinations of two formant frequency values, with movement of the jaw having a primary effect on the first formant frequency (F1) and movements of the tongue having a primary effect on the second formant frequency (F2). Acoustic variability /a/, /i/, and /u/ has been determined using these dimensions, as previously described. Producing the acoustic properties corresponding to the vowel /i/, for instance, requires only a small jaw opening, spread lips and high-front tongue position. The extreme vowels on the triangular acoustic surface appear to mark the boundaries of the infant's articulatory acoustic potential. Radiographic analysis has revealed that unlike front vowels, the production of back vowels (/a/, /u/) is more difficult for infants because it requires them to learn a different tongue–jaw relationship from that employed for the front vowels (Kent, 1981).

Before beginning to acquire any motor skill, the degrees of freedom are usually already constrained by the infant's existing morphological and dynamic properties at a number of levels. For instance, muscles, including the vocal fold and the tongue, are intrinsically elastic and neural mechanisms to detect and respond to muscle stretch appear to be functional early in life. Infants have anatomical and physiological limits on the cyclic repetition of inhalation and exhalation that determines subglottal air pressure. These characteristics are more or less individually variable, designated as the infant's intrinsic dynamics, which would reflect individuality of vocal behavior at the very initial phase of mother–infant interaction shown in table 4.6. They act both as constraints on vocal imitation and as informational raw material from which each infant must assemble an action to achieve voluntary production of purposeful variable vocalizations. Moreover, once infants transduce their intention into imitative action, they must correctly scale their action to match the model presented. To solve both the degree of freedom problem and the scaling problem would not be easy for them. Under such circumstances, maternal echoic responding acts as an attractor to provoke imitation by infants. It occurs at a specific level, which varies from individual to individual. Different styles of maternal responsiveness converge on the same selected solutions by enabling the infants to perceive the action of vocal imitation itself.

In dynamic systems terms, perception is defined as the "discrimination of an object or an event through one or more sensory modalities, separating them [sic] from the background or from other objects or events" and perceptual characterization as "a process by which an individual may treat non-identical objects or events as equivalent" (Edelman, 1987, p. 26). An infant is born with a large, but not infinite, potential state space for any set of attributes. As the infant develops, the attractor basin shifts to more specific sites within the space with respect to its function; the attractor basin emerges by selection, via the infant's perception of the world and actions it produces. The basins can be more or less stable depending on the particular collection of behaviors. Thus, the dynamic view of development postulates individual differences as

the range of possible state spaces the state can occupy and the range of possible trajectories between stable attractor states. Individual similarities, in turn, tell us about the constraints and limitations of that space and how different individuals may have converged on the same selected solutions. Individual pathways toward similar performances describe the ways the components can be assembled and the dynamics of how the space can be explored. (Thelen and Smith, 1994, p. 145)

Self-produced movement plays a very important role in this theory owing to its time-locked association with external stimuli. Due to this time-locked property, it is reliably linked with those stimuli, which in turn provide stable and persistent basins of attraction. In Edelman's terms, equivalence emerges in the mapping between two disjunctive processes, "the category is the mapping, and it need not be between an object and a response nor lead to positive or negative consequences . . . the mapping – the categories – self-organize through their reciprocal interaction with one another" (Thelen and Smith, 1994, p. 143). Thus the above findings indicate that through interaction with caregivers, having been exposed to others' real correlated actions, some global mapping was selectively strengthened. We see this process as the development of imitation in infants.

5 How infant-directed speech influences infant vocal development

As previously discussed, from early infancy, vocal communication most often takes the form of a give-and-take exchange. Turn-taking of this nature is very important for infants in developing the ability to imitate. Moreover, temporal patterning is neither the only nor the most salient characteristic of these interactions; in addition, caregivers prefer specific characteristics of infant vocalizations, especially those that occur in cooing vocalizations. However, what receives selective preference is not simply the infant vocalization, but actually the vocal characteristics of both partners' vocalizations. Indeed, with respect to early communication, scientists have devoted considerably more attention to adult than infant vocal quality. When an adult says "hi" and then addresses an infant by name, the "hi" is typically uttered at the highest pitch and in two syllables, with a falling intonation. Adults typically utter the infant's name with an exaggerated and rising melody. Conventionally, we know that most adults and children use this speech style when speaking to infants and, almost intuitively, we know that, given a choice, infants prefer to hear speech of this sort. In this chapter, we will address an important issue relating to this vocal interaction system. We will address the functional significance of speech style as a selective response in adults and as selectively attended to by infants.

Antecedents of motherese in nonhuman primates

Although it has been commonly observed that adults tend to speak to infants in an odd and characteristic fashion, it was Ferguson (1964) who first offered a coherent description of the linguistic and the paralinguistic features of adults' child-directed speech. Ferguson found that across the languages he investigated, which included English, Spanish, Arabic, Comanche, Giyak and Marathi, elevated pitch and exaggerated pitch excursions were the most prominent characteristics used. Since Ferguson's work, this speech style, commonly referred to as "motherese," has been the focus of considerable research. Most studies included the claim that adults speak to children in a high-pitched, even "squeaky" voice. Interestingly, this phenomenon is not only observed in human caregiver–infant communication, but also in nonhuman primate adult–infant communication, particularly between mothers and infants.

The bond between mother and infant is as strong in most nonhuman primate species as it is in humans. With the exception of callitrichid species, only one infant is born at a time and it is carried full-time, for at least the first few months of life, on the mother's ventrum (or back); the infant ventures off its mother's body for brief periods over the months that follow. Even after the baby begins to explore independently, it returns for extended periods to the mother's ventrum (or back) for rest, nursing and protection. In some species, the mother may not be the only caregiver; other adult or subadult females may act as "aunts," for instance, providing all functions of the mother and perhaps even adopting the infant if its mother dies. Indeed, from its first day of life, a newborn infant is frequently an attractive stimulus drawing the attention of females other than its mother. Females typically inspect infants by sniffing, nuzzling and looking at them while the infants nurse or sit on their mother's back or under her ventrum.

Apparently, vocalizations are an important means through which the bond between infant and caregiver is maintained. The infant directs some calls at its caregiver in order to solicit care. For example, infants who become separated from their mothers emit loud, easily localized and individually recognizable peeps, which are commonly referred to as "isolation calls." Uttering such vocalizations usually elicits prompt retrieval by caregivers. However, that caregivers use particular calls abundantly in the presence of infants is less well known. Such "caregiver calls" were first reported in squirrel monkeys by Dumond (1968) who attributed the calls to mothers and aunts in several contexts of infant care during the birth season. Subsequently, Biben, Symmes and Bernhards (1989) conducted a detailed acoustic analysis of these vocalizations. They found that caregiver calls were highly variable acoustically. They also found that calls made during retrieval were particularly complex and that the only features which distinguished these calls from other vocalizations were duration, elevation of pitch and exaggeration of pitch excursion. Therefore, the authors speculated that when retrieving infants, squirrel monkey caregivers modify vocalizations that, without these acoustic exaggerations, would be uttered in other contexts.

The coo calls of the Tonkean macaque (*Macaca tonkeana*), one of the seven species of the genus Macaca inhabiting Sulawesi, Indonesia, offer a further example. As is the case of Japanese macaques, the term "coo" is frequently used to describe some vocal patterns of various macaque species. Coo commonly refers to a group of basic vocalization patterns that serve a within-group vocal monitoring function. Tonkean macaques are no exception in this; for this species, three basic "coo" patterns are recognized according to the structural features of the vocalizations (Masataka & Thierry, 1993). All of them comprise harmonics.

The first variant, termed a "low coo," is characterized by a low basic frequency (the fundamental-frequency element is a low 200 Hz), little frequency modulation, and comparatively short duration. The call sounds rather nasal. The second variant, termed a "clear coo," is quite tonal; the fundamental-frequency element starts at approximately 500 Hz and shows a prominent peak around 1 kHz point and the duration is longer than 0.2 sec. The final variant, termed "harsh coo," demonstrates frequency modulation as wide as the clear coo but the overall frequency is much higher and the highest frequency point is well beyond 1500 Hz.

All three variants can be heard from every group member, mainly in the following five behavioral contexts: (1) calm situations, including antiphonal and non-directed calls; (2) interactions with group mates that were not otherwise associated with affiliative, agonistic or play behavior; (3) attending to the adult male in the absence of other overt interactions; (4) prior to food provisioning or during the actual consumption of food; and (5) interacting with a mother or with her infant. When group members are spaced at very short inter-individual distances, low coos are uttered. As the distance increases, calls grade into clear coos and then into harsh coos. In addition to the five aforementioned contexts, coos are also uttered when caregivers attempt to retrieve infants; however, harsh coos are emitted exclusively under these circumstances. In harsh coos recorded in attempts to retrieve infants, frequency modulation was the greatest, particularly in the latter half of the call, and the peak frequency occasionally reached 3 kHz. Harmonic structure was prominent, with at least the third or fourth harmonic evident. These retrieval harsh coos were recorded when an infant was not in physical contact with a caregiver; after hearing one of two such calls, the infant was observed immediately to move closer to and to cling to the caregiver.

In most macaque species in which vocal communication has been studied, what is perceived by humans as a single class of coos has often been reported to be perceived by conspecifics as more than one category. For instance, in pigtailed macaques (*Macaca nemestrina*), a species known to be phylogenetically close to Tonkean macaques (Fooden, 1975), twelve classes of coos have been described. Each class of coos occurs in association with different contexts, thus possibly conveying different messages to listening conspecifics. On the other hand, the coo variants identified in Tonkean macaques could be regarded as sorts of "localization variants" of the vocalizations. All of the variants are thought to serve essentially as short-distance location calls. Individuals modify acoustic features of the vocalizations according to the distance between themselves and group mates. Obviously, audibility must be increased as distance increases. Additionally, localizability must be increased as distance increases because at short distances, cues for locating other animals are perhaps available through other modalities such as vision or olfaction and localization errors are not greatly magnified.

The three variants of coos that we have specified in Tonkean macaques could provide differing cues for sound localization while providing similar behavioral information. According to standard views on sound localization (Thurlow, 1971), there are two major cues used for sound localization: differences in sound amplitude between the two ears and differences in temporal cues between the two ears. With respect to temporal cues in particular, frequency modulation has been shown to aid in auditory localization. Therefore, Tonkean macaques use coo calls that are fairly difficult to localize when they are located at short distances from one another and they use coos with more cues for sound localization when they are located farther from one another. A similar pattern of coo vocal production has been reported in lion-tailed macaques (*Macaca silenus*) (Hohmann and Herzog, 1985) and long-tailed macaques (*Macaca fascicularis*) (van Schaik & van Noordwijk, 1985).

A possible explanation for the differential vocal production of variable coo variants may be attributed to differences in "arousal level" for calling individuals: i.e., the acoustical difference found in coos over different spatial distributions might be owing to the fact that individuals located at great distances from group mates tend to be more aroused or frustrated than those located nearby. If this explanation is plausible, arousal differences could manifest in other aspects of the calling individual's behavior. For instance, one might predict that the rate of calling would increase or that the frequency of other nonvocal behavior would change as an individual becomes more excited. However, no such findings have ever been reported. On the contrary, as already described, Japanese macaque adults somewhat voluntarily control frequency modulation of the tonal elements in the coo calls that they vocalize. As the inter-individual distance with group mates increases, they may voluntarily modify acoustic features of their calls to enhance localizability. That the most localizable coo variant is uttered exclusively for infant retrieval supports this possibility. When caregivers appeared to be trying to attract the attention of their infants, they uttered most localizable coo variants regardless of the actual distance separating them from their infants. This no doubt parallels the prosodic modification in motherese in humans.

The importance of prosodic modification
in infant-directed speech

In humans, the expressive power of prosodic features in speech directed at preverbal infants is now considered to be more important for language acquisition than was earlier assumed. It was Lewis (1936) who attributed an important role to prosody in the development of both comprehension and production in the first two years of life. Lewis argued that young infants are selectively responsive to the "strong affective character" of intonation in adult speech and that prosodic information is initially more salient than phonetic information in the development of language comprehension. However, the view that intonation can be "understood" has characterized ethologists studying animal communication, particularly those studying vocal communication in nonhuman primates, more than researchers interested in human communication. In research on human linguistic communication, language has been regarded as the medium of meaning, with prosody relegated to peripheral status. Primatologists argued that some nonhuman primate species use pitch and pitch modulation in order to convey meaningful information about intentions and emotional states. Certainly, the evolutionary advances achieved by macaques in their use of prosody-like components to reveal intentions and motivations is majestically upstaged by the evolutionary advances achieved by human language; however, one should not underestimate the enormous extent to which human prelinguistic infants still rely on prosodic information to become able to use the semantic power of language.

Meanwhile, there is a growing literature on the paralinguistic or prosodic features of parental speech directed at infants. These features represent modifications to normal speech that include the use of higher pitch (Fernald and Simon, 1984; Garnica, 1977), simple but broad pitch contours (Fernald, 1984; Locke, 1994), longer pauses between utterances, and a slower tempo (Fernald, 1984). Of course, what is modified is not restricted to the prosodic properties of speech. Linguistic modifications to parental speech include fewer words per utterance, more repetition and expansion, better articulation, and decreased structural complexity (Ferguson, 1964; Fox and Calkins, 1993). Nonvocal characteristics are modified as well, including exaggerations to facial expressions, postural adjustments and rhythmic body movements (Kaplan et al., 1995; Stern et al., 1983). Investigators have attempted to disentangle this complex set of features to determine which are crucial to language acquisition in preverbal infants. They have concluded that vocal modifications to prosody are the most prevalent features of parental style, as compared with nonvocal modifications. Such vocal modifications occur in the infant-directed speech of parents and nonparents (Locke, 1994), familiar adults and strangers (Hirshberg and Svejda, 1990), and even preschool children (H. Papoušek and M. Papoušek, 1991). Although the precise characteristics of the vocal and nonvocal modifications vary with the age of the infant being addressed (Stern et al., 1983) and the communicative context (Papoušek, Papoušek and Bornstein, 1985; Stern, Spieker and MacKain, 1982; Stern et al., 1983), the use of a special style has been well documented in the speech directed toward infants from birth to twenty-four months of age (Moon, Cooper and Fifer, 1991). Moreover, convincing evidence for the importance of the prosodic features of infant-directed speech in determining infants' preference derives from a series of experimental studies undertaken by Fernald and her colleagues.

Fernald (1984) argued that the most highly salient feature of motherese for infants is its exaggerated pitch contour. This claim is consistent with three independent lines of evidence. First, psychoacoustic research with adults suggests that relatively simple pitch contours may be processed and remembered more effectively than the more complex and variable pitch contours of normal adult speech (Hirsh and Watson, 1996). Second, research on the vocal expression of emotion strongly indicates that the exaggeration of pitch range enhances the communication of positive affect in speech to infants (Banse and Sherer, 1996; Patterson, Muir and Hains, 1997). Finally, normal prenatal exposure to maternal speech profoundly influences the early development of speech perception (DeCasper et al., 1994). While the intensity of maternal speech *in utero* nears its intensity *ex utero*, the acoustical component of speech that is most efficiently preserved and readily perceived in utero is pitch contour.

Fernald (1985) investigated the hypothesis that pitch contour is the most prominent feature of motherese with respect to infants' perception. An operant head-turn procedure was used to condition four-month-old infants to turn in one of two directions in order to receive either infant-directed speech or adult-directed speech by their mothers. Infants showed clear preferences for infant-directed speech on the basis of voice quality alone. Subsequently, Fernald and Kuhl (1987) measured infant listening preferences to experimentally manipulated components of speech. In these stimuli, the lexical content of the speech was totally eliminated and each of the three major acoustic correlates of intonation was isolated: (1) fundamental frequency, which correlates with pitch; (2) amplitude, which correlates with loudness; and (3) duration, which is related to speech rhythm. These three variants were extracted from natural infant-directed speech and from natural adult-directed speech, both of which had been recorded from the same group of English-speaking women. Four-month-old infants were tested in an operant auditory preference procedure. In the procedure, a conditional head-turn (>30 degrees) to one side was rewarded by one of the three stimuli extracted from infant-directed speech, while a head-turn to the other side produced the same variant of the stimuli but one that was extracted from adult-directed speech. Confronted with stimuli totally devoid of linguistic content, the infants showed a strong listening preference for the fundamental frequency patterns but not for the amplitude or duration patterns of motherese. It was suggested that the fundamental frequency characteristics of infant-directed speech are highly salient to infants and that based on those features infants exhibit an auditory preference for motherese over nonmotherese speech.

Affective role of infant-directed speech

The exaggerated pitch excursion of motherese certainly provides young infants with a dynamic form of auditory stimulation that is high in both perceptual contrast and perceptual coherence. This is called the "attention-getting property" of infant-directed speech. However, another functional category for this register was subsequently proposed – affective salience – which was experimentally demonstrated by Werker and McLeod (1989). In their study, they initially compared infants' degree of preference for infant-directed speech between two conditions, when the speech sounds alone were played or when video recordings of a mother actually addressing an infant were presented. Under both experimental conditions, infants exhibited strong attentional responsiveness to infant-directed speech; hence the results were in line with Fernald's findings. However, when the video stimuli were presented, the infants responded to them positively from an affective as well as an attentive standpoint. Consequently, the possibility arose that infants' preference for infant-directed speech cannot be fully explained in terms of its attentional property alone.

In order to examine this new possibility, four five-month-old and seven nine-month-old infant participants were videotaped while they watched videotapes of a woman either talking to an infant or talking to an adult. The infant participants' videotapes were coded for their affective responsiveness as well as their attentional responsiveness. Attentional responsiveness was measured by calculating the percentage of the total time the stimulus was displayed on video that the infant participant spent looking at the video screen and affective responsiveness by asking two raters how attractive infant participants were while they were watching the video. Each of the two raters was independently told to attend to infants' facial features as well as their vocalizations and to rate each infant with a set of nine-point scales on the following three dimensions: Communicative Intent ("How much do you think the infant was trying to communicate?"); Social Favorability ("How interested do you feel the infant was?"); and Emotionality ("What is your feeling about the infant's emotional state?"). The higher the scores the infants received on each dimension, the more positive the emotions they were judged to be experiencing. Response scores representing the video in which a woman was talking to an infant significantly exceeded those representing the video in which she was talking to another adult. When addressing infants, adults frequently use nonvocal behaviors, such as smiling, in order to express positive affect. These nonvocal behaviors are expected to influence infants' responses to the acts addressed to them – in particular, to elicit positive responses. Therefore, to examine such possible confounding effects on their findings, Werker and McLeod next presented video stimuli to infants in which the woman's infant-directed speech or her adult-directed speech was paired with a neutral still face (the same face was used in both conditions). Even though affective information stemming from nonvocal behavior was eliminated, the results revealed that infants still showed strong affective responsiveness to the video of the woman addressing an infant. This suggests that the acoustic features embedded in motherese per se evoke positive affective responses in infants.

During infants' first six months of life, caregiver–infant communication primarily serves an affective function; it changes to serve a referential function in the second half of the first year (Malatesta and Haviland, 1985; Malatesta-Magai, 1991). Pronounced pitch modulation in infant-directed speech would mainly cue infants to prepare for social engagement when listening to the speech. The salience of the speech facilitates the establishment of an emotional relationship between the caregiver and the infant.

Even though preverbal infants do not glean meaning from individual words, they are nonetheless very responsive to speech because they attend to the musical components of the caretaker's utterances and these have affective meaning for them. In this sense, infant-directed speech can be referred to as musical speech. Such a view has recently spawned new interest in musical activity; a number of investigations have attempted to relate characteristics in the perception and production of motherese to the perception and production of singing. Trehub, Trainor and Unyk (1993) first demonstrated that infant-directed singing differs from singing performed in the absence of an infant. In their study, English-speaking and Hindi-speaking mothers were recorded singing a song in the presence of their own infants and singing the same song in the absence of their infants. Although some differences were noted across the two languages (e.g., Hindi mothers were likely to sing soothing songs while English mothers often sang rousing play-songs), adult raters from both language-cultures distinguished the infant-directed song from the non-infant-directed song. Trainor (1996) replicated these findings.

In a subsequent study, the singing that mothers performed when their infants were present was compared with their attempts at singing as if their infants were present when they actually were not (Trehub et al., 1997). A variety of adult raters (e.g., university students, mothers, professional childhood educators) were able to distinguish infant-directed singing from the simulated sample. It appears that infants need to be present to elicit the full range of infant-directed features; further, these modifications to normal singing appear to be "intuitive," without an accompanying awareness of performing them.

Several forms of experimental evidence that may account for the salience of infant-directed singing have also been presented. First, infant-directed singing may serve to attract the infant's attention to the singing person. In Trainor's (1996) study, fifteen mothers were recorded singing a song to their own infants and singing the same song in the absence of the infants. Subsequently, Trainor had six mothers present songs to their infants in a looking-time preference procedure. For five of the six mother–infant pairs, infants looked significantly longer at their mothers in order to elicit the infant-directed version of the song than they did to elicit the infant-absent version, suggesting that infant-directed versions of the song attracted the infants' attention more than the infant-absent versions did.

Trainor et al. (1997) sought to discern the acoustic features characterizing infant-directed singing. Acoustic differences between infant-directed and non-infant-directed singing were examined in six play-song and four lullaby pairs of recordings from Trainor (1996). The analysis was based on measures related to two acoustic dimensions: voice quality and clarity of musical structure. Measures of voice quality included: (1) mean pitch; (2) jitter or frequency perturbation; (3) shimmer or amplitude perturbation; (4) pitch variability; and (5) relative intensity of low, mid and high frequencies. Measures of clarity of musical structure included: (1) timing deviation at the ends of phrases; (2) accent structure represented as relative intensity of stressed and unstressed syllables; (3) accent structure represented as relative duration of stressed and unstressed syllables; (4) accent structure represented as stressed syllable duration relative to phrase length; (5) relative duration of the vowel in stressed syllables; (6) tempo; and (7) tempo variability. These acoustic parameters appear rather exhaustive for this sort of acoustic comparison. Nevertheless, results of the comparison revealed that infant-directed singing and non-infant-directed singing could be distinguished from one another using a few of these parameters. For both play-songs and lullabies the tempo was slower, there was relatively more energy at lower frequencies, inter-phrase pauses were lengthened, and pitch was higher in infant-directed singing than in non-infant-directed singing. Pitch variability was higher and rhythm was exaggerated (as measured by the relative duration of stressed to unstressed syllables) in the infant-directed versions than in the non-infant-directed versions. Overall, the acoustic features of infant-directed singing provide an interesting parallel to those of infant-directed speech.

Infant-directed singing can serve an affective function. This claim is not all that surprising, given that music can communicate information about emotion and evoke direct emotional responses. In their experiment, Trehub et al. (1997) asked 100 adults (fifty males and fifty females) to evaluate a singer's emotional engagement in infant-directed singing versus a simulated version. Participants rated emotional engagement on a nine-point scale ranging from 1 (very low) to 9 (total). Listeners reported more emotional engagement in the infant-directed song than in the simulated version of the same song by the same singer. Simple regression analyses were used to determine whether untrained listeners' accuracy of identifying infant-directed singing in the previous identification experiment was related to differences in emotional engagement ratings between simulated and infant-directed versions; the regression analyses revealed that rating differences were highly predictive of percentage correct identification. The greater the difference in emotional engagement ratings between infant-directed and simulated versions, the higher the accuracy was in identifying infant-directed excerpts.

Further, the higher the pitch of the infant-directed songs relative to simulated versions, the greater the difference in emotional engagement. Tempo differences between infant-directed and simulated excerpts also predicted differences in emotional engagement between the two versions. Specifically, the more parents slowed the tempo of their singing from infant-directed to simulated versions, the greater the differences in perceived emotional engagement. Absolute tempo values, however, were unrelated to emotional engagement. Similarly, only relative differences in tonic pitch between infant-directed and simulated versions were predictive of differences in emotional engagement. Finally, a multiple regression analysis revealed that, together, changes in pitch and tempo were more predictive of reported differences in emotional engagement between infant-directed and simulated versions than either factor alone. Obviously, the behavioral tactics used to achieve effective vocal performances differ between speech and song. Typically, pitch and pitch contour are considerably less constrained in speech than in song. The temporal pattern of adult speech to non-comprehending listeners is, in principle, free of the metrical and rhythmic constraints of particular songs. Despite the pitch and temporal patterning constraints imposed by musical as opposed to spoken communication, infants perceive infant-directed singing affectively and along the same acoustic dimension as they perceive infant-directed speech.

Possible predispositions for perceptual sensitivity in infant-directed speech and singing

Data available to date indicate that the prosodic properties characterizing infant-directed speech and singing are prevalent components of language input to preverbal infants and that they serve important social and attentional functions in early development. Hence, with respect to infant-directed speech, several researchers have explored the possibility that the effectiveness of its exaggerated properties in modulating infant attentional and affective responsiveness results from innate predispositions to respond selectively to these properties. Cooper and Aslin (1990) examined behavioral preferences for infant-directed over adult-directed speech in two groups of infants. One group consisted of twelve one-month-old infants and the other consisted of sixteen two-day-old infants. Both groups of infants were tested according to the same visual-fixation-based auditory-preference procedure. The results showed that both one-month-olds and newborns preferred infant-directed speech to adult-directed speech. Although the absolute magnitude of the infant-directed speech preference was significantly greater, with the older infants showing longer durations of looking than the younger infants, subsequent analyses showed no significant difference in the relative magnitude of this effect, indicating that infants' preference for the exaggerated prosodic features of infant-directed speech is present from birth and may not depend on any specific postnatal experience. From these results, it appears that postnatal experience with language does not have to be extensive for the infant to learn about the prosodic features of their native language. It has also been shown that newborns prefer the intonational contour and temporal patterning of a melody that they experienced prenatally (Panneton, 1985). The possibility remains that both prenatal and postnatal auditory experience could affect the relative salience of prosodic cues for young infants.

In a subsequent study, four- and nine-month-old English-learning infants were reported to show robust attentional and affective preferences for infant-directed over adult-directed speech in Cantonese, even though the language was completely foreign to them (Werker, Pegg and McLeod, 1994). Similarly, four- to seven-month-old English-learning infants were reported to show as strong attentional and affective responsiveness to infant-directed singing in foreign languages as in English (Trainor, 1996). However, the infants included in these experiments had heard speech and song before. In fact, as early as the prenatal period, all hearing infants of hearing parents are exposed to some form of speech and song (DeCasper et al., 1994). Masataka (1999) investigated attentional responsiveness to infant-directed speech and song in two-day-old healthy hearing infants who were born to congenitally deaf parents. A total of fifteen infants participated in the experiment. All infants lived in nuclear families. The parents had acquired Japanese Sign Language as a first language and they used it exclusively when they communicated with one another. They lived in deaf communities. Since prenatal auditory experience with speech and song comes mostly from parents, these studies on the hearing infants of deaf parents were undertaken to explore more rigorously whether or not infants have a predisposed preference for infant-directed speech and song.

The experimental stimuli included infant-directed and adult-directed speech as well as infant-directed and adult-directed songs. Both speech samples and song samples included a Japanese version and an English version. Speech samples and song samples were recorded from ten adult females. Five native speakers of Japanese and five of English were instructed to direct identical short scripts and play-songs either towards an infant or towards an adult. Acoustical comparisons of the speech and song samples revealed that when directed to the infant, both speech and song showed modifications like those reported to be typical to infant-directed speech or song: the pitch was elevated, the pitch contour was exaggerated, and the tempo became slower. When infant-directed and adult-directed speech or song stimuli were presented, the infants were found to look longer at the infant-directed version than the adult-directed version regardless of whether or not the stimuli were speech or singing samples. Since intrauterine recordings taken near term have revealed that maternal voice and heartbeats are audible *in utero* but that non-maternal voices are rarely audible due to attenuation by maternal tissue and/or masking by intrauterine sounds (Querleu and Renard, 1981; Querleu, Renard and Crepin, 1981), these results strongly suggest a predispositional perceptual preference by human infants for exaggerated prosodic properties, whether they are in speech or song.

Are prosodic features of infant-directed speech or song universal across cultures?

As compared with the cross-cultural universality of preferences for perceptual features of infant-directed speech, evidence for cross-cultural universality of the production of motherese is less convincing and actually very controversial. Since the pioneering study by Ferguson (1964), a number of studies have reported exaggerated prosodic properties as the most prominent feature of infant-directed speech (e.g. Ferrier, 1985; Halliday, 1975). However, the results presented in these investigations were all based on unmeasured and subjective estimations of acoustic qualities. Once instrument-based measurements of speech samples became available, Fernald et al. (1989) conducted cross-language comparisons of prosodic modifications in infant-directed speech. A cross-language analysis of French, Italian, Japanese, German, British English and American English revealed that fathers as well as mothers modified their prosody when addressing preverbal infants, contrasting with their typical adult-directed speech. Based on these findings, Fernald and her colleagues argued for the universality of prosodic modifications in speech addressed to infants. However, Fernald (1992) herself later admitted that in the Fernald et al. (1989) study, Japanese mothers seemed to show less expansion of the fundamental frequency range than did the American and European mothers and she pointed out the possibility of cultural variation in the "display rule" for the prosodic modification. This could also be the case for the Mandarin Chinese sample collected by H. Papoušek and M. Papoušek (1991).

Ingram (1995) more strongly argued against the universality of prosodic modification. Referring to work by Bernstein-Ratner and Pye (1984), which measured the fundamental frequency in Guatemalan maternal speech to children, Ingram states that their small sample of three Quiche-Mayan speakers did not raise their pitch when addressing children. He proposed that prosodic modifications in child-directed speech are the result of a set of conventions that may vary from culture to culture. Ingram also reinterpreted the data published by Fernald (1987) on adult identification of infant affective states, which was originally used to support the universality of child-directed speech. He also sees this as being interpretable in terms of a set of culturally transmitted rules.

Indeed, one must take effect size and individual differences into account when interpreting the results of cross-cultural studies. Although the research by Fernald et al. (1989) filled a gap in the literature in view of the difficulties of making detailed comparisons across different studies that were earlier discussed, their sample sizes of parents chosen from each cultural-linguistic groups were still small. Shute and Wheldall (1989, 1995) examined the child-directed speech of British women using a larger sample than Fernald et al. in order to clarify issues related to the size of the typical prosodic modification effect. They recorded a total of twenty-four British women while they interacted with their children ranging in age from one to three years and with another adult; they then individually examined the degree of prosodic modifications in their child-directed speech. The interactions recorded included both a reading aloud and a free speech condition. Results revealed overall increases in pitch and pitch range when talking to or reading a book with young children. However, the group averages that showed this result were also found to mask a wide range of individual differences. For several participants, their average pitch and pitch range when they interacted with a child did not differ substantially from and was often even lower than, when they interacted with an adult. Most previous studies had not considered individual differences between subjects, which might have created an unspoken assumption that raised pitch and exaggerated pitch excursions are typical of all subjects within a cultural-linguistic group. In other words, even within a single cultural-linguistic group, more variability likely exists than has been conventionally assumed. This could, in turn, affect variability across cultural-linguistic groups.

Women's experience with siblings as a variable relating to individual differences in child-directed speech

Shute and Wheldall (1989, 1995) pointed out that characteristics of the adult woman, particularly her familiarity and experience with children in general, might account for some individual differences in her prosodic modification in child-directed speech. They anecdotally described dramatic modifications of prosody in infant-directed speech by some women who were highly experienced with childcare. Subsequently, Ikeda and Masataka (1999) attempted to substantiate this finding quantitatively, with a larger sample of Japanese women, for the purpose of establishing the range of individual differences between women in infant-directed speech and specifying possible characteristics correlating with the differences. In order to examine whether a woman's experience with childcare affects her prosodic modifications, participants were asked to respond to several questions concerning this issue. Each woman was also recorded while interacting with a very young child and with another adult. We included the number of siblings that the women had as a possible variable. We hypothesized that the absence or presence of siblings might influence individual differences because siblings would commonly have lived in family environments since early infancy, where there would commonly have been peers with whom they would have shared an abundance of varied experiences. We assumed that for adults who grew up with siblings, such family environments would tend to be associated with the development of a characteristic attitude towards children, which would be reflected in the pattern of their child-directed speech.

The study participants included sixty-one women between the ages of eighteen and twenty-six years. All of the participants were single university students, had no children, and spoke Japanese as their first language. At least until eighteen years of age, they had lived with their biological parents. In the experiment, each participant was recorded as she read one of seven picture books aloud (each was approximately twenty pages long) to a child (adult-to-child sample) and as she conversed with another Japanese-speaking adult woman (adult-to-adult sample). All of the participants interacted with the same child and adult, with whom they were unfamiliar. When the experiment began, the adult and the child were thirty years old and nineteen months old, respectively. It usually took participants four–five minutes to read the book to a child. After that, the participant was required to answer a standard set of open-ended questions about her views on the role of reading books to young children with respect to their cognitive development. The questions that were asked during the interview were: (1) How old are you? (2) Do you like playing with young children? (3) How often have you had experience with baby-sitting? (4) Do you like reading picture books? (5) How much experience have you had with having picture books read to you? (6) How much experience have you had reading picture books by yourself? and (7) How many siblings did you grow up with? For questions 2 to 6, participants answered using five-point scales. For questions 2 and 4, the scales ranged from 1 (very much) to 5 (not at all); for questions 3, 5 and 6, the scales ranged from 1 (very often) to 5 (very rare).

For analysis, a continuous vocalization by a participant that was bounded by pauses of longer than 0.3 sec was defined as an utterance; ten such utterances were randomly chosen from each of the adult-to-child and the adult-to-adult samples. For each utterance, the average pitch and the pitch range were measured in terms of its fundamental-frequency element. When differences between samples in the values of the two parameters were examined statistically for each participant, individual differences were found in both parameters. For one cohort, seventeen of the sixty-one participants, both parameters were significantly increased in the adult-to-child sample. For a second cohort, another eight participants, either one or the other of the two parameters showed an increase. For the remaining cohort of thirty-six participants, neither parameter differed between the two samples. Subsequently, participants' answers to the interview questions were compared retrospectively across the three cohorts to examine correlations between the characteristics of the participants and the individual differences found above.

No significant differences were found with respect to the responses to questions 1 through 6. However, response scores did differ significantly across cohorts for question 7. In the first cohort, where modifications were recorded in terms of both the average pitch and the pitch range, the mean number of siblings was the greatest, while in the third cohort, where neither of the two parameters showed a significant difference between the two experimental conditions, the mean number of siblings was the smallest. Of the sixty-one participants, nineteen had grown up as only children. Of the remaining forty-two participants, thirty-four had grown up with one sibling and eight with two siblings. In sixteen of the nineteen only-children (84.2 percent), none of the acoustic parameters differed significantly between the adult-to-child and adult-to-adult samples. The rate was 52.9 percent for those participants who had grown up with one sibling (eighteen out of the thirty-four) and 25 percent for those that had grown up with two siblings. When the rates were compared between women who had grown up as only-children and those who had grown up with siblings, there was a significant difference.

Next, we examined whether findings from our analysis of the interaction between being a single woman and being unfamiliar with children could be extended to the interaction between mothers and their own infants. This time, speech samples of mothers were recorded as each mother addressed her four-month-old infant and as she addressed her adult female friends. For the study, we employed two groups of participants, each consisting of 100 women; one group was comprised of women who had grown up as only-children and the other of women who had grown up with one sibling. For each participant, we acoustically measured the speech samples in terms of the average pitch and pitch range using the same procedure as in our previous study. In ninety-five of the 100 women who grew up with siblings, we found a significant increase in pitch when they interacted with their infants as compared with when they interacted with their adult friends. However, in the 100 women who grew up as only-children, the rate was 47 percent. In ninety-three of the 100 women who had grown up with siblings, the average pitch range increased significantly when they interacted with their infants; for the women who grew up as only-children, the rate was only 54 percent.

Clearly, these results demonstrate fairly wide individual variation in prosodic modification among Japanese single women reading a picture book aloud to a child as well as among Japanese mothers talking to their own preverbal infants. In the experiment involving the single women, retrospective attempts to relate the findings to the participants' preference for picture books, previous experience with reading books, having been read books, or with childcare experience did not successfully account for the individual differences. The one variable that might have accounted for the variability was whether the participants had grown up with siblings or as only-children. These results were further confirmed in a subsequent experiment on Japanese mothers. Therefore, the family environment in which a woman grew up appears to exert a profound influence on the acoustic characteristics of her maternal speech. The finding was also confirmed with another participant group of Japanese-speaking women (Masataka, in press).

During the 1920s, several objective investigations of birth order and family size were conducted (e.g., Fenton, 1928). As of the mid-1980s, as many as 500 studies had been published in psychological, medical, sociological and educational journals in Europe and North America, comparing the personality and social outcomes of only-children to those of their peers with siblings (Falbo and Polit, 1986). Since the mid-1980s, however, very few articles on this topic have appeared, particularly with respect to comparing the behavioral qualities of only-children and children with siblings; in fact, virtually only one study has been reported (Jiao, Ji and Jing, 1986). Hence, current knowledge related to this issue is extremely limited. In any case, based on peer-ratings of behavioral qualities, it is apparent that only-children are perceived as more egocentric than children with siblings. On the other hand, children with siblings are more likely than only-children to be perceived as possessing the positive qualities of persistence and cooperation. Items assessing persistence asked whether or not the individual carries through on a task from beginning to end and whether or not the individual uses every effort necessary to overcome difficulties. Items assessing cooperation asked whether or not the individual likes to play games or perform tasks with others and whether or not the individual is happy to do things for others when asked.

Arguably, persistence and cooperation are the behavioral qualities that adults must possess in order to interact effectively with young children. For example, these qualities would be useful in encouraging young children to attend to a picture book for a four–five-minute period. Study participants who possessed these qualities more strongly would presumably be more successful in maintaining children's attention. Their efforts would include raising the pitch of their voice as well as injecting more dramatic emphasis in their speech. The behavioral characteristics of individuals who had grown up with siblings are thought to underpin a high degree of prosodic modification in their child-directed speech as compared to those who had grown up as only-children.

The lack of evidence for motherese as an emotional indicator

Caregivers of infants and young children do not necessarily have a predisposition for prosodic modification in their infant-directed speech; rather, this process is learned through certain postnatal experiences. Although some researchers have attempted to associate prosodic modification in infant-directed speech with caregivers' emotions, virtually no evidence has been presented thus far in support of the argument that the voice qualities that characterize infant-directed speech reflect specific underlying types of affect in caregivers, such as pleasure or joy. The general consensus about predispositional patterns in the vocal signaling of affect in humans is that emotional change appears in these acoustic parameters of voice: the relative differences in intensity between stressed and unstressed syllables, the relative proportion of energy in the higher frequency range, and the amount of jitter (variation in the fundamental frequency at the smallest time period) and shimmer (variation in intensity at the smallest time period). However, previous efforts to relate the characteristics of motherese with any of these parameters (e.g., Trainor et al., 1997) were unsuccessful. Furthermore, Banse and Sherer (1996), having conducted meticulous acoustic analyses on a number of vocal samples corresponding to fourteen different emotions, reported that speech rate tended to decrease as the emotion of pleasure increased in speakers, a finding quite contradictory to what has commonly been seen in motherese. Such findings suggest why there is difficulty viewing infant-directed speech as a behavior that caregivers are compelled to do.

The interaction between caregiver and infant can be regarded as a system of communication in which each influences the other. Some components in the system (e.g., infants' attentional and affective responsiveness to specific acoustic qualities of speech sounds) are certainly predispositional. They basically function to enhance the development of certain aspects of the system over others. Therefore, motherese is very likely to emerge as a form of parenting behavior that meshes with the caregiver-directed actions of the infant. However, motherese still remains just one of the options for infant-directed responses. When adjusting the acoustic quality of their speech to the predispositional, attentional and affective sensitivities of their infants, caregivers must have learned such modifications in order to manipulate their speech quality relative to these sensitivities. Even though motherese has occasionally been regarded as some sort of "intuitive" parenting, just because parental behavior appears intuitive does not necessarily imply that it is genetically preprogrammed. The error of regarding the two as equivalent stems from confounding one dichotomy – automatic, nonconscious versus conscious processes governing behavior – with a second dichotomy – learned versus genetically determined processes governing behavior.

As already noted, caregiver calls in some nonhuman primate species can be regarded as phylogenetically antecedent forms of caregiver motherese in humans. It is difficult to see even these nonhuman primate vocalizations as an expression directly reflecting the underlying emotional or arousal level of a calling animal. Masataka and Symmes (1986) recorded vocalizations by separating squirrel monkey infants from their mothers as well as other natal group members and then permitting vocal contact between the "lost" baby and the group at systematically varied distances. In response to lost calls given by the infants, mothers and other relatives gave caregiver calls in which the acoustic structure varied according to the distance between callers and infants. As the distance increased, the overall pitch of the vocalizations elevated, which was considered to enhance the localizability of the sounds. No evidence was found that callers at a greater distance were more aroused or frustrated than those closer to the infants (but prevented from joining them by cages). The rate of calling, the nonvocal behavior of separated individuals, and the use of vocal signals other than caregiver calls did not differ with the amount of distance separating the callers from the infants. None of these observations offers a clue as to the effect of distance on the acoustic modification of calls. The notion that modification reflects emotional changes in callers was concluded to be untenable. The functional explanation is that animals vary the localization cues in their vocalizations according to their expectations about the distance of potential listeners.

Changes in call structure that accompany differing demands vis-à-vis localizability have been reported in other New World primates. Pola and Snowdon (1975) found that captive pygmy marmosets (*Cebuella pygmaea*) used three trill variants of isolation calls that were physically different from one another and yet appeared to convey identical messages. These trill variants could be ordered according to their cues for sound localization. In a subsequent field study in Peru, Snowdon and Hodun (1985) reported that the most localizable trill variant was heard most frequently when calling and responding animals were far apart, whereas the least localizable variant was used by animals in close proximity, and that such exchanges occurred most often between mothers and their infants. Further, in both squirrel monkeys and pygmy marmosets, flexible usage of acoustic vocalization variants is thought to be acquired by animals of each species through postnatal experience with conspecifics. They need to learn the manner in which they can choose the localization variants of calls that are most suitable for maintaining others' attention at appropriate levels. Even in nonhuman primates, the pattern of vocal interaction between caregivers and infants varies to some extent and the ability to be flexible in vocal usage develops through learning. Humans have apparently inherited this feature, which is reflected in the context-sensitive nature of vocal interaction between human caregivers and prelinguistic infants.

Context-sensitive properties of infant-directed speech

Masataka (1992a) compared the fundamental frequency speech patterns of six Japanese-speaking mothers when they addressed their four-month-old infants and when they addressed their adult friends. The unit of analysis for mother–infant interaction was an interaction episode, operationally defined as a series of exchanges with a focus on a specific topic and set off by periods of verbal inactivity; an utterance was used as the unit of acoustic measurement and was defined as a continuous vocalization of a mother or an infant bounded by pauses of longer than 0.3 sec. Each episode began with the mother attempting to attract her infant's attention through her speech; hence each episode was ultimately constrained by the infant's attention level. Once the infant responded, the mother would usually continue the vocal interaction as long as the infant remained attentive and responsive. When the infant directed its attention elsewhere, the episode would end. The first mother's utterance that elicited an infant's response was considered the beginning of an episode; if the infant vocalized within 3.0 sec of the mother's utterance, it was counted as an infant response. In each episode, the mother's utterance was defined as an "initial maternal utterance." When the mother was unsuccessful, she would make a few utterances that were punctuated by silence on the infant's part. Even when she was successful, she would frequently have to make more than one utterance before the infant responded. In the study, only the initial maternal utterance and the initial vocal response of the infant to that utterance in each episode were used for analysis. The number of utterances that the mother needed to make in order to initiate the episode was also counted.

Fig. 5.1 presents the average pitch and pitch range for the six mothers' utterances in their adult-directed speech and all initial maternal utterances in their infant-directed speech. For the infant-directed speech, the data are presented in terms of the number of utterances the mother made before successfully eliciting an infant response in each episode (represented on the abscissa of fig. 5.1). Comparisons of the average pitch for the adult- and the infant-directed speech showed that, overall, the mothers' average pitch in their infant-directed speech significantly exceeded that in their adult-directed speech. However, post-hoc examination revealed that each mother demonstrated a significant increase in her pitch values only when she made more than two utterances before eliciting the infant's response. When the infant responded to the first one or two utterances by the mother, the mother's pitch did not differ significantly from the pitch she used in her adult-directed speech.

Similar results were obtained from the analysis of the pitch range for the adult- and the infant-directed speech. Overall, the mothers' average pitch range in their infant-directed speech significantly exceeded that observed in their adult-directed speech. Again, follow-up tests revealed that each mother demonstrated a significant increase in her pitch range values only when she made more than two utterances before her infant responded. When the mother made only one or two utterances before her infant responded, her pitch range did not differ significantly from the pitch range she used in her adult-directed speech. The pattern of vocal interaction between a caregiver and preverbal infant is therefore context-sensitive and flexible. When an infant is very eager to respond to a

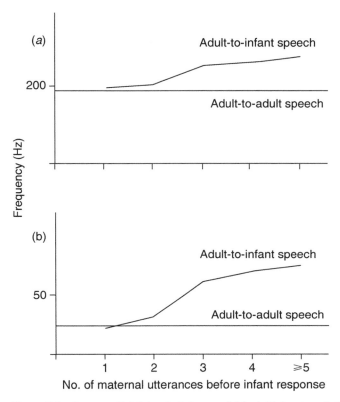

Figure 5.1   Average pitch (a) and pitch range (b) for initial maternal utterances in A-I speech. (Average values of the mothers' utterances in A-A speech are given by the horizontal straight lines.) (cited from Masataka, 1992c).

caregiver's behavior with a high level of underlying communicative intent, the typical motherese acoustic feature does not characterize maternal speech. The mother resorts to maternal speech with this feature in cases where her infant is initially unresponsive. As a consequence, the infant's arousal level is maintained optimally. This pattern would be hard to interpret from the perspective that motherese is a behavior that directly expresses the underlying emotions of the signaler.

Implications of infant-directed speech for the acquisition of voluntary use of pitch contours in preverbal vocalizations

The context-sensitive nature of motherese allows us to investigate the differential effects of the acoustic properties of maternal speech on immediately subsequent infant vocal utterances; that is, it becomes possible to examine whether

Table 5.1(a) *Distribution of maternal speech/infant's response sequences when the mother made only one or two utterances before infant's response*

Contour type of initial maternal utterance	Contour type of subsequent infant's response			
	Rising	Falling	Bell-shaped	Flat or complex
Rising	72	88	41	50
(N = 251)	(68.0)	(91.5)	(42.5)	(49.0)
Falling	77	102	51	51
(N = 281)	(76.2)	(102.4)	(47.6)	(54.9)
Bell-shaped	37	63	22	25
(N = 147)	(39.8)	(53.6)	(24.9)	(28.7)
Flat or complex	43	55	29	39
(N = 166)	(45.0)	(60.5)	(28.0)	(32.4)
Total N	229	308	143	165

$G(9) = 5.64$, $P > 0.10$. Expected values calculated from marginal totals are given in parentheses.

or not the elevation of maternal pitch affects the pitch of subsequent infant vocalizations. I hypothesized in a study that the pitch contour of exaggerated maternal speech would significantly affect the pitch contour of immediately subsequent infant vocalizations and that the pitch contour of less exaggerated speech would not have this effect. Analyses were conducted independently on two different subsets of data and were classified according to the following criteria: (1) when the mother made only one or two utterances before her infant responded and (2) when the mother made more than two utterances before her infant responded. We classified all contours in the maternal and infant utterances according to five contour categories: rising, falling, flat, bell-shaped and complex. Rising and falling contours were typically marked by relatively small upward and downward frequency shifts, respectively. A pitch rise or fall was recognized only when the frequency modulation range of a continuous slope exceeded 15 Hz in maternal speech and exceeded 10 Hz in infant vocalizations.

In all, rising contours accounted for 32 percent of maternal speech and 36 percent of infant speech. Bell-shaped contours containing both a rise and a fall accounted for 17 percent of the data in maternal speech and 18 percent of the data in infant speech. The remaining two contour types, complex and flat, occurred less than 10 percent of the time in both maternal and infant speech. Therefore, the latter two have been combined in tables 5.1(a) and 5.1(b). The tables present the distributions of maternal speech/infant response sequences when the mother

Table 5.1(b) *Distribution of maternal speech/infant's response sequences when the mother made more than two utterances before infant's response*

Contour type of initial maternal utterance	Contour type of subsequent infant's response			
	Rising	Falling	Bell-shaped	Flat or complex
Rising	114	73	23	9
($N = 219$)	(69.1)	(78.6)	(44.4)	(26.9)
Falling	44	109	28	8
($N = 189$)	(59.7)	(67.5)	(38.3)	(23.2)
Bell-shaped	16	29	55	7
($N = 107$)	(33.8)	(38.4)	(21.7)	(31.1)
Flat or complex	24	14	21	53
($N = 112$)	(35.4)	(40.2)	(22.7)	(13.8)
Total N	198	225	127	77

$G(9) = 239.5$, P < 0.001. Expected values calculated from marginal totals are given in parentheses.

made only one or two utterances before the infant's response versus when she made more than two utterances before the infant's response, respectively. When the number of maternal utterances was one or two, these distributions did not deviate significantly from those predicted by chance alone. However, when the number of maternal utterances was greater than two, the distributions of maternal speech/infant response sequences deviated highly significantly from those predicted by chance. More often than expected, infants responded to rising pitch contours in maternal speech with vocalizations likewise marked by rising pitch contours. Other types of pitch contours seldom occurred but similarly, more frequently than expected, each of the other three types of pitch contours was followed by an infant vocalization of the same contour type. When infants responded to maternal speech that had exaggerated pitch patterns, they tended to mimic those patterns; however, they tended not to do so in response to maternal speech with nonexaggerated pitch patterns. As discussed in chapter 4, infants develop the ability to imitate the pitch contour of the speech they hear during the first six months of their lives. Subsequently, maternal speech helps infants to modify their own vocal responses by presenting exaggerated contours as well as elevated overall pitch levels.

The voluntary use of pitch contour is apparently one of the earliest linguistic features a child must acquire. Stern et al. (1982) argued that pitch contour is the earliest and most basic unit of interpersonal signaling in the auditory domain. The pitch contour variations in preverbal infant vocalizations are systematically related to context (Delack, 1976; D'Odorico, 1984; Furrow, 1984). In a study on his own son, Halliday (1975) made the first systematic attempt to examine the use of pitch contour as a means of signaling different communication functions. Halliday related the contrastive pitch contours that his son as a preverbal infant produced to various functions. Rising terminal contours were associated with "pragmatic" functions (i.e., those that sought to change the environment or that required a response, such as requests for objects) while falling terminal contours were associated with "mathetic" functions (such as labeling or commenting on objects or events). However, Halliday did not report on the use of these contours for the same functions in earlier prelinguistic vocalizations so that it is not clear if there was any continuity in the association of intonational contours with communicative functions from the preverbal period through the single-word-utterance period.

Influenced by Halliday (1975), Flax et al. (1991) observed three children interacting with their English-speaking mothers at three different times: before the onset of single words (exact age varied individually from eleven to four-teen months), when vocabulary consisted of ten words (fifteen–sixteen months of age), and when vocabulary consisted of fifty words (eighteen–twenty-two months of age). In each of the three study periods, each of the three mother–infant dyads was observed in a laboratory for approximately a one-hour period. When the mother was playing with her infant, a standard set of toys was pro-vided and the mother was asked to interact with her infant as they normally might in private. From these sessions, which were recorded, all noncry vocal-izations recorded from the children were transcribed in terms of their pitch contours and each of them was assigned to one of ten communicative func-tions: (a) response (RESP); (b) comment-label (COM-L); (c) request-attention (RQ-A); (d) request-object or action (RQ-OA); (e) request-attention (RQ-A); (f) protest (PRO); (g) request-command (RQ-C); (h) give (G); (i) comment-non-interactive (COM-NI); and (j) comment-interactive (COM-I).

These data revealed considerable individual variability between the three children when the number of utterances characterized by each pitch contour class was compared. Nevertheless, the use of each pitch contour was fairly consistent among the three children and was constant over time. Overall, rises (rising contours) were produced relatively more frequently than nonrises in functions requiring a response from the listener; nonrises were produced more frequently than rises in functions involving commenting on or labeling exter-nal objects or persons. Masataka (1993b) confirmed these findings in a study on the nine-month-old preverbal infants of Japanese-speaking mothers. In this study, more than 3,000 utterances were recorded from six infants while they in-teracted with their mothers during a consecutive four-day period. The data collection and data transcription procedures were adapted from Flax et al. (1991).

The association between terminal contours of vocalizations and communicative functions was analyzed quantitatively, using a three-way (infants × pitch contours × contexts) G test for goodness of fit (Sokal and Rohlf, 1981). The analysis did not show a significant interaction among the three factors. Infants × pitch contours and infants × contexts interactions were also not significant. There was, however, a highly significant pitch contours × contexts interaction. Tests for the complete independence of infants versus pitch contours and versus contexts were not significant, indicating that the "infants" variable was completely independent of the "pitch contours" and "contexts" variables. These results were taken to justify pooling the data regardless of infant differences; results for the pooled data are presented in table 5.2. The distribution of all recorded vocalizations in terms of their pitch contours and contexts shows that rising terminal contours were more frequently used in response to utterances that demanded a response, such as requests and protests, whereas nonrising terminal contours were more frequently used in response to utterances that did not demand a response. Given that Japanese is a very different language from English, this phenomenon appears to be fairly robust and not specific to certain linguistic environments. Rather, since it occurs in infants whose mothers speak a nonWestern, tonal language, the association between terminal vocalization contours and communicative function should be regarded as cross-linguistically universal as well as developmentally stable after the age of, at least, nine months. Its onset is assumed to depend upon the development of the infants' ability for vocal imitation of pitch contour.

Phonetic features of infant-directed speech

In addition to the finding that linguistic input directed to infants is modified prosodically, evidence has been presented indicating the possibility of phonetic modification in motherese in such a way as to enhance language learning. Kuhl et al. (1997) audiotaped ten native-speaking women from each of the United States, Russia and Sweden while they spoke to their two–five-month-old infants and while they spoke to their adult friends. Native-language words containing the vowels /i/, /a/, and /u/ were preselected for analysis in the three languages and, with regard to each of the three vowels in each of the languages, the vowel triangle was compared between the speech sample recorded in the infant-directed condition and that recorded in the adult-directed condition.

Results showed that phonetic modifications in maternal speech were more likely to occur in interactions with infants than in communication with adults. In all three languages, mothers were found to produce acoustically more extreme vowels when addressing their infants, resulting in an expansion of the vowel triangle in the speech sample collected in the infant-directed condition. Mothers did not simply raise all formant frequencies when speaking to their infants as

Table 5.2 *Distribution of three terminal contour variants by ten communicative function categories*

					Communicative function					
Pitch contour variant	RESP	COM-L	RQ-A	RQ-OA	RQ-R	PRO	RQ-C	G	COM-NI	COM-I
Rising	21	14	268	241	153	262	31	11	8	10
	(113.5)	(106.1)	(120.9)	(119.3)	(114.5)	(120.3)	(69.4)	(57.1)	(109.0)	(88.5)
Falling	302	257	88	91	96	78	23	116	114	75
	(149.3)	(139.5)	(159.5)	(156.9)	(150.5)	(158.2)	(91.3)	(75.1)	(143.3)	(16.4)
Flat	27	56	18	36	104	31	60	49	214	188
	(87.2)	(81.5)	(93.2)	(91.7)	(88.0)	(92.5)	(53.3)	(43.9)	(83.7)	(68.0)
Total	350	327	374	368	353	371	114	176	336	273

Expected values calculated from marginal totals are given in parentheses.

they might have done if they were mimicking child speech. Rather, formant frequencies were selectively modified to achieve an expansion of the acoustic space encompassing the vowel triangle. When vowel triangle areas were compared between the infant-directed sample and the adult-directed sample for each mother, the results were highly consistent across individuals. For each of the thirty mothers, the area of the vowel triangle was greater in the infant-directed condition than in the adult-directed condition. On average, they expanded the vowel triangle by 92 percent when addressing their infants (English, 91 percent; Russian, 94 percent; Swedish, 90 percent). The ratio of the scores did not differ across languages, suggesting that the phonetic modification took place in a similar manner regardless of differences in language.

An expanded vowel triangle is thought to increase the acoustic distance between vowels, which eventually enables the infants to distinguish them more easily. Moreover, it is possible that by stretching the triangle, mothers come to produce vowels beyond those they produce in a typical adult conversation. From both an acoustic and articulatory perspective, these vowels are "hyper-articulated"; hyper-articulated vowels are perceived by adults as "better instances" of vowel categories. Indeed, a laboratory test showed that when infants listened to good instances of phonetic categories, they demonstrated greater phonetic categorization ability (Iverson and Kuhl, 1995). When the prosodic properties of maternal speech are exaggerated, listening infants are able to imitate the prosodic pattern more easily. Given that, as described in chapter 3, infants' ability for vocal imitation proceeds simultaneously for prosody and for phonetics during their first six months of life, it is not difficult to predict that the same exaggeration in maternal speech would occur for phonetic properties as for prosodic ones: when the vowel triangle is expanded in maternal speech, it facilitates the infant's effective imitation of the vowel heard.

The facilitating effects of infant-directed speech on infants' learning about causal relationships

The infant's imitation of the prosodic pattern of maternal speech is possible because of the infant's predisposed attentional and affective preference for speech with exaggerated prosodic properties. However, since no such predisposed perceptual preferences have been detected for the phonetic features of motherese, phonetic exaggeration in maternal speech would be faced with the difficulty of facilitating imitation of whatever pattern the infant detects in listening to the speech. Rather, in order to facilitate imitation of the phonetic pattern of maternal speech, the infant should learn to associate exaggerated speech with patterns with other positive stimuli. One possibility is that both the phonetic and prosodic properties of maternal speech are modified simultaneously so that the phonetic characteristics are highlighted on the basis of the infant's positive attentional and affective responsiveness to its prosodic characteristics. However, Kuhl et al. (1997) also reported that mothers occasionally decrease the overall pitch of their speech directed to their infants in order to make the sounds more distinguishable. In this case, the phonetic modification was performed at the expense of the prosodic modification in the speech. The pattern of phonetic modification is certainly context-sensitive, as is the pattern of prosodic modification, and apparently, both properties can be modified in such a manner as to contradict one another.

In this regard, the results of an experiment by Kaplan et al. (1996) are noteworthy. Prior to this experiment, Kaplan, Fox and Huckeby (1992) showed that a tone that preceded the presentation of a smiling face acquired the ability to increase the subsequent duration of looking at a novel checkerboard pattern. In the pairing phase of the experiment, four-month-old infants received six pairings of a pure tone and a smiling face. For one group of infants, the tone preceded the face, and for the second group, it followed the face. For the third group, the two stimuli were randomly intermixed, and in the fourth group infants saw a face but heard no tone. In the summation test phase, all infants received four ten-second presentations of a novel 4 × 4 checkerboard pattern. The tone was combined with the checkerboard pattern on its first and fourth presentation only. Results of the summation test showed that infants looked significantly longer in response to presentations of the tone plus the checkerboard than to the checkerboard alone, but only when the tone had preceded the face in the pairing phase. In a subsequent experiment (Kaplan et al., 1996), infant-directed speech and non-infant-directed speech segments were substituted for the pure tone and the differential effects on conditioned attention were assessed. Results of the experiment showed that responses elicited by conditioned stimuli in the form of an infant-directed speech segment were greater than those elicited by those in the form of a non-infant-directed speech segment, indicating that infant-directed maternal speech facilitates learning more than non-infant-directed speech. This finding has significant implications for the effects of infant-directed speech characterized by phonetic modification on infants' responses, as different from the effects of infant-directed speech characterized by prosodic modification. The study suggests that if speech produced with an expanded vowel triangle is initially paired with something that functions as a positive unconditioned stimulus for the infant (such as a smiling face), then subsequent presentation of the speech itself could elicit infant imitative responses as conditioned responses.

Overall, the acoustic modifications that are characteristic of maternal speech enhance the infant's language learning in different ways when they occur phonetically than when they occur prosodically; further, the occurrence of one of the two can occasionally hinder the occurrence of the other. Additionally, the processes by which each facet of motherese affects the infant's response might differ from one another. In order to explore this possibility, Ikeda and Masataka (in press) examined the degree of phonetic modification in the infant-directed speech of 100 mothers who grew up as only-children and 100 mothers who grew up with siblings; the same sample was employed in the Ikeda and Masataka (1999) study. Analysis of the speech samples showed that when we compared the vowel triangle recorded in the infant-directed condition with the vowel triangle recorded in the adult-directed condition, we found a significant expansion in the infant-directed speech of ninety-six mothers who grew up with siblings and thirty-eight mothers who grew up as only-children. Again, we confirmed that the family environment in which a woman grew up (i.e., with or without siblings) affects the acoustic characteristics of her infant-directed speech. Of these 134 mothers, seven did not modify the prosodic property of their speech significantly in the infant-directed condition. However, 142 of the total of 200 mothers investigated were found to modify both the overall pitch and the pitch range of their speech significantly in the infant-directed condition. Among them, nine did not modify the phonetic property significantly in this condition. Subsequently, in a further analysis, we more closely examined the data concerning these sixteen atypical mothers for the purpose of disentangling the differential effects of prosodic and phonetic modifications in infant-directed speech on the behavior of infants listening to it.

In the analysis, we transcribed the data in terms of aspects other than the vocal quality of the maternal utterances. In particular, we employed a functional approach because it is the most prevalent way in which to compare styles of caregiver–infant communication in different settings. Although a variety of functional category systems have been used in the analysis of mother–infant interaction (see Rondal, 1985), Penman et al. (1983) categorized maternal speech into two modes: information-salient (fully propositional sentences that are not stereotyped expressions and that are acceptable in normal adult conversation) and affect-salient (expressive and affective; generally non-propositional, idiomatic or meaningless content). Since this system has been used most commonly, we broadly followed this classification system. The sentence categories classified as information-salient were Direct, Interpret, Question, Report, Answer, Didactic and Label. The utterance categories defined as affect-salient were Encourage, Convention, Discourage, Nonsense, Greeting, Call by name, Game, Song and Onomatopoeic.

When the overall frequencies for each of the two functional categories were compared between mothers who modified prosodic features of their infant-directed speech and mothers who modified phonetic features of their infant-directed speech, a different communicative style was found. Mothers who modified prosodic features of their speech tended to be more affect-oriented than mothers who modified phonetic features of their speech. Mothers who modified only prosodic features of their infant-directed speech used "Nonsense,"

"Onomatopoeic" and "Call by name" significantly more than mothers who modified phonetic features. On the other hand, mothers who modified only phonetic features of their speech were more information-oriented than mothers who modified prosodic features; "Direct" and "Question" were used significantly more by the former than by the latter. When mothers exaggerated prosodic properties of infant-directed speech, they were likely to use short and simple utterances such as Nonsense or Onomatopoeic sounds, or Call by name, for example, "ba ba ba ba" or "pon pon pon," but rarely to use grammatically complete utterances. When mothers exaggerated their infant-directed speech in terms of its phonetic properties, they used grammatically complete utterances, such as "talk to me" (Direct) or "are you hungry?" (Question).

Finally, the likelihood that nonvocal maternal stimulation (e.g., visual stimulation such as smiling and tactile stimulation such as tickling) accompanied speech was compared between mothers who talked to their infants with prosodically modified speech and mothers who talked to their infants with phonetically modified speech. Obviously, preverbal infants are able to access their mothers' affective feelings via this sort of stimulation. We computed the mean probability for each situation (nonvocal stimulation accompanied prosodically or phonetically modified speech) and found it was 22 percent for prosodically modified infant-directed speech whereas it was 53 percent for phonetically modified infant-directed speech. When modifying the phonetic features of their speech, mothers were more likely to stimulate their infants nonvocally while simultaneously directing their speech to their infants.

Possible variables producing different styles of maternal speech

The process by which each speech style was employed by each of the mothers cannot be determined from the present analysis. However, it would not be difficult to predict that the difference is closely related to individual-specific beliefs and values related to childrearing. A previous cross-cultural observation of mother–infant communication in the US and in Japan reported that US mothers are more likely than Japanese mothers to be information-oriented and that Japanese mothers are more likely than US mothers to be affect-oriented (Toda, Fogel and Kawai, 1990). More information-oriented US mothers show extremely distinct prosodic modification in their maternal speech. Shute and Wheldall (1989) reported a lack of prosodic modification in maternal speech in two of eight British mothers they observed. One of the two mothers included in the study who exhibited only very small pitch alternations, when asked to discuss parental influences on child language development in an interview, attributed this to her focus on the parental teaching of linguistic structure. In her interview, the second of the two mothers claimed that she deliberately talked to children in a manner that made "everything more wow."

When they are information-oriented mothers tend to question their infants more often than when they are affect-oriented. It is unlikely that they believe that their preverbal infants will answer their questions, or even need to, because many of their questions are asked about ongoing activities or about things in plain view. Rather, asking questions of infants might be a way for mothers to emphasize the informational components of speech. For instance, asking, "What does this car do?" goes beyond merely posing a question; it also conveys information through labeling. Simultaneously, the use of questions allows the mother to get the infant's attention efficiently through prosodic modification. In contrast to the use of descriptions, questions emphasize the infant's participation in his or her own language development; this is a "distancing strategy" thought to promote cognitive development (Sigel, 1982).

When they are affect-oriented mothers frequently use grammatically incomplete utterances and play with sounds in speaking to their infants (e.g., by using nonsense, onomatopoeia, song, etc.). This has been reported as the typical and traditional style of childrearing in Japanese mothers (e.g., Fogel, Toda and Kawai, 1988). The goal of the affect-oriented mother in childrearing is to empathize with her infant's needs and, rather than show authority as a mother, to meet her infant at the infant's level. This mother tries to distinguish children from adults in order to teach age and status differences from an early age. She often uses so-called "baby-talk," which, through identification with the baby might also reflect an expression of affection. The speaker's consideration of the listener's situation appears to be important to affect-oriented mothers (Toda et al., 1990). Nevertheless, prosodic modification in their speech was much less distinctive than in the speech of information-oriented mothers. Again, such observations make it difficult for one to assume that the prosodic features characteristic of motherese are a direct reflection of the underlying affective states of the speaker. Although there are cultural variations in the degree to which individual mothers tend to be information- or affect-oriented, most mothers, regardless of cultural differences, become somehow more affect-oriented under some circumstances and more information-oriented under others. When they are affect-oriented, mothers attempt to elicit and maintain attention from their infants through the acoustic content of their utterances themselves; when they are information-oriented, they attempt to capture the infant's attention through nonverbal behavior accompanying their speech. The two styles also serve to offer linguistic input to infants in different as well as compensatory manners.

As already described in chapter 4, maternal echoic responding to infant cooing plays an important role in the onset of true imitation in the infant; this echoic responding occurs either prosodically or phonetically. The type of responding performed by each mother is related to earlier responsiveness on the part of the infant to prosodically and phonetically echoed maternal utterances.

The above findings suggest that an infant's responsiveness might also be partly determined by whether the mother herself is more affect-oriented or more information-oriented. The more information-oriented mother and the more affect-oriented mother might attend more strongly to the phonetic and the prosodic properties of the infant vocalizations, respectively. Moreover, early infant vocal responsiveness to the mother may be influenced by the quality of the maternal speech that the infant has experienced since its birth; i.e., if the mother is more information-oriented, the infant could be exposed to phonetically characterized speech more often, which will, in turn, facilitate the sensitivity of the infant to sounds in terms of this dimension, and vice versa. Regardless of which speech style characterizes a given mother, her infant will eventually acquire the ability to imitate both the phonetic and prosodic qualities of speech sounds.

Even with respect to the earliest stage in the development of prosodic and phonetic aspects of preverbal vocalizations, parental teaching of language to infants is flexible. System theorists in general, and von Bertalanffy (1968) in particular, have placed considerable emphasis on the self-correcting features of development and have called the convergence of different routes to the same steady state "equifinality." While this is a well-known concept, empirical quantitative data to support the applicability of this notion to behavioral development have been meager. Therefore, instead of empirical data demonstrating the plausibility of the theory, anecdotal accounts have been presented. For example, children show astonishing differences in the age at which language development begins. Some may begin developing before the end of their first year whereas others may not utter a recognizable word until they are three years of age or more. However, despite these enormous differences, it is remarkably difficult to pick out the early developers when children are older (Nelson, 1973). Put very cautiously, behavior at one stage of development is an exceedingly poor predictor of behavior at another. The development of prosodic or phonetic aspects of linguistic behavior in preverbal infants is not a very good predictor of their degree of later development in these aspects of behavior. Regardless of whether one aspect of behavior develops earlier than another, the development of the behavior as a whole ultimately reaches the equivalent, predetermined goal. In other words, to enable infant development that is equifinal, parental speech itself provides variable characteristics.

6   From laughter to babbling

A major milestone in the vocal development of preverbal hearing infants is the emergence of reduplicated consonant-vowel sequences such as *da da da*. In these series, the consonant initially remains the same. This is known as reduplicated babbling but it is more frequently referred to simply as babbling. Although infants might babble in the communicative context of infant–caregiver interaction, no meaning or reference can be assigned to the babble itself. Babbling must also be word-like. It is thought that babbling is characterized by the use of a subset of all possible sounds and syllable organizations found in spoken languages. As a consequence, the regular emergence of babbling has been interpreted as evidence of a biological preparedness for speech. According to Lenneberg (1967), babbling is a phenomenon of speech development that does not depend on the availability of input and all children begin babbling between the ages of six and eight months, whether or not they are hearing or deaf. While such traditional perspectives regarded babbling as a true precursor to speech, other infant vocalizations were regarded as random collections of miscellaneous sounds unrelated to the later emergence of true speech. More recent research, however, does not support this view. For example, with respect to rhythmic vocal production, there is continuity between babbling and earlier vocalizations. Prior to the onset of true babbling, infants come to utter sequences of vowel-like sounds without distinctive consonant-like elements. Since this seemed to serve as a transition between earlier vocalizations and true babbling, it has been referred to as marginal babbling (Stark, 1980). Several subsequent studies have attempted to link babbling as rhythmic sound production with earlier nonrhythmic vocal behavior. In this chapter, we will first look at these continuity issues, then relate them to issues concerning how babbling is acquired by the infant. It will be argued that babbling is by no means a maturational process for language acquisition.

The development of crying as the earliest rhythmic vocal behavior

Arguably, one might see the earliest developmental precursors of babbling in the first vocal productions that satisfy the criterion of rhythmicity: crying in

157

newborns. Crying is the most common sound pattern, other than vegetative sounds, that a newborn produces. Infant crying is widely viewed as an emotional expression with an attachment function that promotes proximity to or contact with the caregiver, usually the mother. This form of attachment behavior originally evolved to perform a protective function by bringing the infant into close proximity with the mother.

Lester and Boukydism (1992) were the first to provide an integrated view of the complex interaction between the biological and social aspects of infant crying and they sought to examine the transition from infant crying to babbling. Initially, the infant has restricted signaling options available through crying, probably pain and nonpain. The pain cry seems to be unique in both newborn and older infants. Through interactions with infants, adult listeners easily learn to distinguish the pain cry from the nonpain cry on the basis of acoustic cues. If a nonpain cry is heard, adults learn to use contextual cues in order to provide appropriate caregiving responses to the sound. Usually, hunger is the adult's first interpretation of infant crying since satisfying this physical need is crucial for the infant's survival. As the infant develops and becomes more interested in social interaction with caregivers, nonpain cries become more differentiated, each expressing a different need, and individual caregiver–infant dyads develop more complex cry communication through a negotiated history of interactions. Lester and Boukydism argued that contrary to the traditional view of crying as merely stereotypic and reflexive, as the infant develops, crying behavior becomes differentiated and modulated according to infant needs and caregiver interpretations. Therefore, crying might serve as the cornerstone for developing the ability to produce more complicated rhythmic sounds.

Once the infant reaches four–five months of age, the frequency of the pain cry drops significantly and the infant begins to use identifiably different types of cries. Wolff (1969) reported that as early as the infant's second month, a qualitatively different type of cry is heard, the so-called irregular or fussy cry. Subsequently, as the infant develops, crying behavior becomes more elaborated with the addition of novel acoustical features such as variation of vocal intensity and bilabial friction noises. These changes in the ability to produce acoustical variability in crying is linked with each individual infant's goal-directed action through the idiosyncratic forms of interaction that develop within each caregiver–infant dyad. As the infant grows, it acquires the ability somehow to control the variable acoustic features of its cries according to different social demands. Fogel and Thelen (1987) argued that once cry variations come to be perceived differentially by the caregiver as demands for particular objects or actions, the acoustic variations become coordinated with the goal-directed actions of the infant. They refer to developmental changes in the respiratory apparatus as a possible initial control parameter providing newborn cries with acoustic variability. During the first month after birth, the basic structure of a cry is assumed to merely reflect the infant's respiratory cycles. Physiologically, crying is basically generated by the larynx when air is expired from the lungs (Zemlin, 1968). Subglottal respiratory pressure causes the laryngeal vocal folds to vibrate, producing a fundamental frequency, which determines the pitch of the cry heard. Increases in fundamental frequency are predominantly modulated by tension in the vocal folds, resulting from contraction of the intrinsic laryngeal muscles, which are innervated by both sympathetic and parasympathetic (vagal) input from the autonomic nervous system (Berne and Levy, 1983).

The model of newborn cry production proposed by Golub (1980) and Lester (1984) states that variations in vagal influence on the muscles of the larynx are responsible for variations in fundamental frequency. This model has received empirical support from a study relating vagal tone to fundamental frequency (Porter, Porges and Marchall 1988). Vagal tone plays two primary roles. First, during sleep or quiet states, the vagus fosters physiological homeostasis to promote growth and restoration. Second, during states influenced by environmental challenges, the vagus acts as a brake by rapidly regulating cardiac metabolic output. By increasing vagal output to the heart and actively inhibiting sympathetic influences, this vagal brake functions to keep the heart rate slow. Releasing the vagal brake reduces vagal inhibition on the cardiac pacemaker and heart rate increases due to the intrinsic rate of the pacemaker, mechanical reflexes, and sympathetic influences. Using routine unanesthetized circumcision as a model of stress, Porter et al. (1988) examined the relationship between cry acoustics and vagal tone in normal healthy newborns undergoing this acutely stressful event. They found that vagal tone, as measured by the amplitude or respiratory sinus arrhythmia extracted from heart period data, was significantly reduced during circumcision and that these reductions were paralleled by significant increases in the pitch of the infants' cries. However, this relationship has been experimentally demonstrated exclusively with the cries of newborns but not with cries of older infants (Masataka, 1991).

In cry perception studies, the most frequent focus has been on fundamental frequency. Comparisons of the mean ratings of groups of newborn cries that differ in fundamental frequency show a high correlation between aversiveness ratings and cry pitch (e.g., Zeskind and Marshall, 1988). However, Gustafson and Green (1989) stated that with respect to cries produced by older infants, no studies have yet found significant correlations between any measure of fundamental frequency and perceived aversiveness. In newborn infants, painful stimuli, such as heel-stick or immunization, are known to result in a variety of distress reactions. The typical response to acute pain lasts approximately one minute (Holmes, 1990) and is characterized by an initial drop in heart rate associated with breath-holding, a high-pitched cry and the facial expression of pain (Kaitz et al., 1992). When this pain-induced distress was compared in two-week-old infants who underwent heel-sticks and two-month-old infants who received injections, facial expression was found to be a reliable indicator of heart rate change in each infant at each age. In two-week-old infants, pitch of crying also showed a significant correlation with heart rate; the more distinctive the initial heart rate drop, the higher the pitch of the cry. However, such a tendency has not been found in two-month-old infants (Gustafson and Green, 1991). Around two months of age, the explosive respiratory phenomenon develops, the forced expulsion of air, which enables the infant to perform some sort of cough–cry combination. Thus, changes in the respiratory apparatus might underlie the developmental shift in crying seen at two months of age; i.e., the shift from the newborn cry to the irregular, fussy cry. The unsuccessful attempt to relate acoustic qualities of cries to physiological measures in infants around this age suggests that the cries were no longer a direct manifestation of infants' internal states, such as arousal.

At three months of age, a more distinctive change occurs in the respiratory apparatus. As discussed in chapter 3, respiratory control develops dramatically with the aid of skeletal repositioning of the rib cage and increased neuromotor control. Increased lung strength and efficiency, in particular, provide the infant with the morphological capability to produce cries of varying pitch and duration (Prescott, 1975). Through learning to vary the acoustic parameters of its cries in order to express particular demands, via the reinforcing responses of caregivers, the infant acquires voluntary control over its neuromotor system with respect to vocal production. Crying comes to serve as a social signal rather than as a biological indicator. Individuality becomes more distinctive than it previously was (Gustafson et al., 1994). The pattern of associating each variant of an infant's cry with its corresponding context is also individual-specific. This is because the association is determined by how the variant is interpreted and reinforced by the caregivers of the crying infant. The cry becomes more complex, particularly in terms of the manner in which it is temporally organized; for instance, an intermittent brief distress cry, a longer arrhythmic cry, and then a cry with a regularly rhythmic pattern with higher intensity progressively emerge. This modification relates profoundly to the development of the respiratory apparatus, which induces the voluntary control of respiration, i.e., the capability to produce uninterrupted inspirations, to slow the breathing rate, to increase lung air pressure, and to keep a volume of unexpired air in the lungs (Oller, 1980). It is thought that it is through the development of these capabilities that preverbal infants come to produce speech-like vocalizations. Actually the capability also concerns the ontogeny of crying, which in turn contributes to the development of segmental features in speech-like vocalizations, as will be seen later. Interestingly, as the cry behavior pattern becomes increasingly differentiated, the frequency of the behavior itself declines. Longitudinal quantitative observations of crying consistently show that while overall frequencies of crying had waned sharply in three-month-old infants, its variability proved remarkably robust (Gustafson, Green and Cleland, 1994; Murray, 1979). With the decline in crying, another rhythmic vocal behavior appears: laughter.

The emergence of laughter

For adults, smiling and laughing are often regarded as expressions of pleasure without any particular distinction between the two; indeed, in many human languages, including Japanese, there is no distinction between laughing and smiling in the lexicon. Several authors have often implicitly regarded smiling and laughing as behavior patterns that differ only in degree with smiling being a less intense or diminutive form of laughter. Typically, it is thought that smiling involves situations which exclusively affect facial musculature whereas laughing involves situations which affect other muscles and induce greater excitation. Darwin (1872) argued that laughing preceded smiling in human evolution, with smiling being a subdued version or a diminutive form of laughing. However, ontogenetically, infants smile just after birth while laughter first appears at about four months of age (Sroufe and Waters, 1976). Newborn smiling is not thought to result from external stimulation. Emde, McCartney and Harmon (1971) argued that smiling in newborns occurs "spontaneously" as a manifestation of endogenously determined physiological rhythms during the rapid eye movement (REM) state of sleep. Like newborn cries, newborn smiles should be regarded as biological indicators rather than as social signals. Numerous studies have been conducted on the ontogeny of smiling. The general consensus about its overall developmental time course is the very famous notion of a transition from endogenous or spontaneous smiling to responsive or social smiling. At its onset, it is assumed that smiling by newborns functions to draw the attention of caregivers intermittently. Caregivers are supposed to be able to defend newborns against predators and other dangers. Although close proximity between infants and caregivers is not necessary to ensure protection in our present society, infants are nevertheless genetically programmed to smile – they even smile in their sleep. Their smiling therefore appears to reflect a rudimentary adaptation to prototypical ancestral caregiving environments. It is difficult to determine the adaptive significance of many human characteristics, however, because we have modified our environments so drastically from those in which we originated. Adopting an anthropological perspective on contemporary societies, comparative studies might provide us with the kinds of evidence necessary to support this view of the adaptive basis for early infant smiling.

In contrast to smiling, laughter is a social signal even at its onset. Hence, very little attention has been paid to ontogenetic aspects of this behavior. Laughter has been mostly investigated by social psychologists when adults perform it during social encounters because solitary laughter seldom occurs except in response to media. Among all our expressive behaviors, the so-called audience effect is most robust in laughter. The frequency of occurrence of other expressive behaviors is smaller when subjects stay together versus alone, whereas the frequency of laughter is greater in groups than in individual situations (Fridlund and Loftis, 1990). Chovil (1991) examined the frequency of laughter in response to hearing about a close-call experience, across four communicative situations. In one condition, participants were required to listen to a tape-recording of an individual telling about a close-call event. In two interactive but nonvisual conditions, participants listened to another person over the telephone or in the same room but separated by a partition. In the final condition, participants were told to listen to another person in a face-to-face interaction. The results of the experiment showed that the frequency of laughing varied monotonically with the level of sociality represented by the four conditions.

Clearly, laughter is a human behavior that has evolved as a powerful and pervasive communicative tool for adults and infants alike. Caregivers primarily use three important vocal modes to initiate and maintain contact with their prelinguistic infants: sounds, talk and laughter (Ziajka, 1981). Each of the three vocal modes might play an equally important role as a reinforcer in caregiver–infant interactions. However, in contrast to the two other vocal modes, laughter has been relatively neglected in the research literature. Laughter has likely been neglected because it has not been regarded as an integral part of any linguistic system. Further, there are practical concerns in studying laughter; in contrast to language, the various meanings communicated by variants of laughter are not precise or rigorously analyzable.

In spite of the meager empirical evidence, philosophers and scientists from antiquity to the present day have been fascinated with determining what evokes laughter, perhaps more so than any other human expressive behavior. Their views commonly emphasize some contrast, unexpected change or contradiction in the situation as the key that elicits laughter. Early authors (e.g., Spencer, 1892) regarded laughter as merely a means of discharging surplus tension, which tended to accumulate if its proper release was prevented. From this perspective, laughter functions solely to restore normal physiological equilibrium. Later, some scientists questioned whether or not all such cases necessarily elicited laughter as well as whether or not the causes of all laughter could be interpreted in this fashion. They emphasized that a certain emotional appreciation must be involved in the cognitive processes of those from whom laughter is elicited.

As a biologist, independently of other scientists investigating laughter, Charles Darwin (1872) believed that many common expressions were habits that were associated with and derived from serviceable acts, including: startle, head-scratching during problem solving, wincing upon attack, tearing in sadness, and laughter. He also thought it was quite possible that these expressive habits were heritable. Subsequently, he attempted to connect tickling to humor both by virtue of the responses they both produced and by virtue of their qualities as elicitors (Darwin, 1872). Darwin (1872, pp. 201–2) wrote:

The touch must be light, and an idea or event, to be ludicrous, must not be of grave import. It seems that the precise point to be touched must not be known; so with the mind, something unexpected – a novel or incongruous idea which breaks through an habitual train of thought – appears to be a strong element in the ludicrous.

Interestingly, experimental evidence supporting Darwin's hypothesis was only recently presented. In a questionnaire study of 100 college students, Fridlund and Loftis (1990) found that there were strong correlations between participants' reported ticklishness and their propensities to laugh. In interpreting the findings, the study also suggested a second ontogenetic mechanism: the chronic abdominal reflex and its autonomic and facial accompaniments that are seen in laughter and crying are variable and heritable. Caregivers commonly attempt to initiate laughter in their infants by tickling them. Infants respond to these overtures by leading caregivers to try visual puns. Thereafter, as children acquire language, caregivers come to use wordplay involving humor. Consequently, the adults' sense of humor would be dependent, at least partly, upon the degree of reflexive responding to their initial tickling.

Nwokah and Fogel (1993) examined the role of maternal laughter in a longitudinal study of mothers' free-play with infants from four to fifty-two weeks old. They found that the main elicitor of maternal laughter was the onset of specific types of infant behavior and that the actual types of infant behavior preceding laughter dramatically changed as the infant developed. Further, newly appearing behaviors in the infant's repertoire were the most frequent causes of maternal laughter. The researchers' detailed analyses of when and at what point maternal laughter appears during social games with their infants revealed that the occurrence of this behavior was mediated by an alert responsive state in the infant and that it functioned as a positive maternal reaction to the infant's state. The novelty of the infant's behavior is a crucial component in eliciting maternal laughter. However, it was not only new infant behaviors that elicited maternal laughter, but also old behaviors displayed in new contexts. Based on these findings, a theory was proposed that laughter might develop as an important learned social signal that is affected by imitation and parental influence (Argyle, 1987; Malatesta and Haviland, 1982).

It is well known that by the time infants reach three months of age, caregivers and infants come to engage in the simultaneous exchange of similar behavior. From as early as three–six weeks of age, caregivers show a strong tendency to respond contingently to infant facial expressions with their own positive expressions, which are again responded to positively by infants. Cohn and Tronick (1987) found that positive maternal expressions always preceded positive infant expressions when infants were aged three–six months; however, by nine months of age, they found a significant increase in the probability that positive infant expressions preceded positive maternal expressions. In both these types of interaction, both the caregiver and the infant were likely to laugh. That the tendency to laugh spreads contagiously from one to another and that vocalizing in unison is a noticeable feature of laughter may be considered very important patterns that are part of the development of early attachment behavior and contribute to the ties between caregiver and infant. Indeed, in a longitudinal study of six children aged six–twelve months, Ziajka (1981) found that the more mothers laughed, the more infants laughed, and vice versa. In adult-to-adult interactions, co-occurrence, matching and possible contagion in laughing interchanges are also observed frequently, where the stronger the feeling of rapport or intimacy, the more likely adults are to make similar postures and movements and to match their vocal pitch and intensity in their interactions (Argyle, 1987).

Phylogenetic antecedents of human laughter

While the social stimulus dimension of human laughter is relatively well understood, surprisingly little research attention has been focused on laughter as a motor action. A series of studies on "pathological laughter" is perhaps the only relevant research that exists pertaining to this issue, although pathological laughter is frequently a rather vaguely described medical symptom in the literature. Damage to a wide variety of brain regions is known to produce abnormal laughter, a result consistent with the diverse emotional, respiratory, motor, cognitive and communicative aspects of the behavior. Pathological laughter is most commonly found in pseudobulbar palsy, gelastic epilepsy and psychiatric illness (Bickley and Hunnicutt, 1992). However, despite tremendous improvement in our descriptive tools over the past decade, little is known about the motoric aspects of abnormal or pathological laughter.

Ethologists, who are interested in whether or not it is possible to determine the phyletic origins of laughter in nonhuman animals, have studied the motoric aspects of laughter in greater depth than psychologists and psychiatrists. Van Hooff (1972) hypothesized that laughter fits neatly into the phylogenetic developmental range of the "relaxed open-mouth" display, which is a meta-communicative signal that designates any associated behavior as mock-aggression or play. Specific rhythmic vocalizations usually accompany occurrences of these relaxed open-mouth displays. Darwin (1872) noted that chimpanzees (*Pan troglodytes*) and other great apes perform laugh-like vocalizations when tickled or during play.

In chimpanzees, so-called "pant-hooting" has been the most intensively studied of several types of laugh-like vocal behaviors. The pant-hoot call is a contact call between spread-out individuals and groups. Like other long-distance nonhuman primate calls, individuals utter pant-hoot calls during foraging or

Mahale

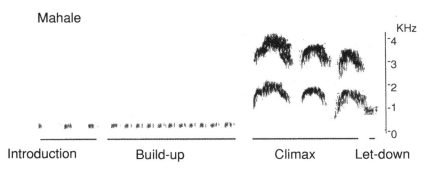

| Introduction | Build-up | Climax | Let-down |

JMC

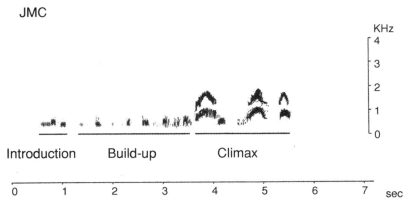

| Introduction | Build-up | Climax |

Figure 6.1   Representative sonagrams of pant-hoot vocalizations of chimpanzees in two populations, Mahale and JMC (cited from Kajikawa and Hasegawa, 2000).

progression. When a pant-hoot call is heard, other individuals often respond with pant-hoots of their own. This behavior has been reported to occur with extremely high frequency on occasions of eating prey after capture and reuniting groups after separation (Teleki, 1973). Based on observations of wild chimpanzees at Gombe National Park, Tanzania, van Lawick-Goodall (1968) found that marked individuality might exist in these vocalizations. Subsequently, Marler and Hobbett (1975) acoustically investigated this issue in more detail. A typical pant-hoot sequence lasts between seven and eleven seconds. As the term suggests, it is acoustically characterized by rhythmic repetition of voicing on inhalation and exhalation. As shown in fig. 6.1, in a given sequence, four different types of phases can be distinguished: introduction, build-up, climax and let-down. A sequence typically begins with a brief "introduction" phase, in which one or more calls are made that are longer and lower in pitch than those in other phases and that are not usually accompanied by frequency modulation. Phonation on inhalation is weak or totally missing. Next, a build-up phase follows. The build-up phase is comprised of several notes, each of which involves an inhalation and an exhalation. The notes are repeated rhythmically but there are often progressive changes in stress, duration, pitch and intensity as the build-up proceeds. Following the build-up phase is the climax phase, the loudest part of the sequence that forms a distinct crescendo. The climax phase can be differentiated from the build-up phase by differences in the patterns of frequency, duration and harmonic structure. Finally, a let-down phase follows the climax phase. Acoustically, the let-down phase resembles the introduction phase.

Within this basic pattern considerable variation is found (e.g., occasionally the introduction phase is omitted). Variation exists even among vocalizations produced by the same individual. For example, within individuals there is variation in the timing and morphology of the build-up and let-down phases. There are also marked sex differences. Female pant-hooting lacks a climax. On the other hand, the harmonic structure of the build-up phase is the most stereotyped and individually distinctive aspect of the pant-hoot sequence. Mitani et al. (1992) compared the vocalizations collected by Marler and Hobbett (1975) with the same type of vocalizations recorded from chimpanzees living in Mahale Mountain National Park, Tanzania. The Mahale study site is along the eastern shore of Lake Tanganyika and approximately 150km south of the Gombe study population. To exclude the possibility that variation in acoustic features as a function of the age or sex of individuals could bias results, only calls from adult males were studied. Analysis revealed some acoustic differences between the two populations. The most noticeable difference related to the manner in which each note that consisted of an inhalation and exhalation was temporally organized in the build-up section. Individuals from Mahale uttered notes at a faster rate in this phase than individuals from Gombe who uttered notes relatively slowly in this phase. Although the authors attempted to relate this finding to genetic factors, anatomical differences, variations in the use of calls at the two sites and changes in calling over time, none of the four explanations was found to account for the variability convincingly. Perhaps the differences were due to learning. Kajikawa and Hasegawa (2000) reported similar findings.

The chimpanzee's social system might have facilitated the evolution of vocal learning in this species. Because chimpanzees of neighboring communities are quite hostile to one another, variation in vocalizations that serve as long-distance calls would be favored as an effective means of discriminating individuals of their own community from others, if variation were locale-specific. This hypothesis is very intriguing. It is also noteworthy that populational differences in particular show the temporal sequencing pattern of rhythmic notes. Flexibility in the production of laugh-like vocalizations in nonhuman primates presumably leads us to developmental questions about human laughter. However, we know little about this developmental process. Only meager evidence has been presented from observations of a few congenitally deaf-blind children, showing that at least some features of laughter develop without benefit of auditory and visual stimulation; this suggests the presence of a strong maturational and genetic basis for the behavior (Eibl-Eibesfeldt, 1989). However, these results were based on poor-resolution analysis.

Provine (1996) examined this issue in greater detail. Based on his own observations of captive chimpanzees, he argued that their laugh-like behavior differs from human laughter primarily in terms of two acoustic characteristics. First, chimpanzee panting sounds are generated by repetitive movements of expiration and inspiration while the vowel-like notes of human laughter are produced solely by the abrupt chopping of a single expiration. Second, while vowel-like elements can be recognized in each note of human laughter, they are ambiguous in chimpanzee sounds. Chimpanzees produce sounds that can be thought of as possessing the "cadence of a handsaw cutting wood." Such differences reflect morphological constraints in chimpanzees that preclude their production of speech-like vocalizations. Provine hypothesized that human laughter evolved from a breathy panting vocalization, a primal form of modern laughter, which became manifest in its modern form when human beings adapted to bipedal walking after diverging from their common ancestor with chimpanzees. Laughter can be regarded as almost speech-like vocal behavior in that the production of laughter is exclusively possible via those sound-producing systems that enable humans to produce speech sounds.

It should be noted that the onset of laughter as a rhythmic vocalization occurs at three–four months of age. Further, the onset of laughter apparently precedes the onset of any other type of speech-like vocalization with segmental features. Given that contagious laughter involves the perceiver's (i.e., the infant's) replication of the vocal motor pattern that the sender (i.e., the caregiver) originally generated, and that this vocal motor pattern functions as a powerful reinforcer for the perceiver, it does not appear unreasonable to assume a close and specific functional connection between the ontogeny of laughter and the ontogeny of speech-like vocalizations.

Continuities between the ontogeny of laughter and the onset of babbling

In a longitudinal observational study, I investigated possible continuities between the ontogeny of laughter and the emergence of babbling by recording the vocalizations of infants between the ages of three and eight months. I performed sound spectrographic analyses of the infants' laughter and speech-like vocalizations. In addition, I recorded the frequencies and types of motor actions that the infants performed simultaneously; I did this because several studies have recently reported that the most reliable event predicting the onset of canonical babbling is the emergence of rhythmic hand movement, typically, banging action (Eilers and Oller, 1994; Eilers et al., 1993; Locke, 1993).

Regardless of the language to which the infant is exposed, the onset of canonical babbling is known to be quite abrupt, typically occurring some time after the age of six months. Based on this observation, it has been thought that the onset of canonical babbling is a deeply biological phenomenon, driven predominantly by maturation, and virtually invulnerable to the effects of auditory experience or other environmental factors (Lenneberg, 1967). In a longitudinal investigation, Eilers et al. (1993) examined recordings of babbling and other motor milestones in term and preterm infants of middle and low socioeconomic status and found that neither preterm infants, whose ages were corrected for gestational age, nor infants of low socioeconomic status were delayed in the onset of canonical babbling and that the infants' hand banging was an important indicator of a certain kind of readiness to produce babbling; the onset period of the babbling coincided with that of the banging. Other motor milestones showed neither delayed nor accelerated onset in the same infants. Babbling and hand banging share the property of rhythmicity. Therefore, Eilers et al. argued that the auditory feedback generated by hand banging might influence the development of the babbling ability in hearing infants.

In fact, since it gives us the impression of reduplicated consonant-vowel syllables (e.g., *dadada*), babbling is thought to be the preverbal infant's first rhythmic speech-like vocal activity. In babbling, mandibular depressions alternate with elevations that briefly narrow the vocal tract, the specific points of obstruction being determined by the positioning of the tongue and lips. The most widely accepted definition of canonical babbling is that of Oller (1986), which includes the following seven criteria:
1. Power envelope with peaks (nuclei) and valleys (margins) differing by at least 10 dB.
2. Peak-to-peak duration 100–500 ms.
3. Nuclei produced by periodic source and relatively open vocal tract to yield full resonance.
4. At least one margin of low resonance and relatively closed vocal tract.
5. Smooth formant transition between margin(s) and nucleus; transition duration 25–120 ms.
6. Intensity range = or <30 dB.
7. Fo range equal or less than two-fold.

These criteria have been provided in technical, acoustic and articulatory terms, but essentially what distinguishes canonical babbling from previous speech-like vocalizations lies in the rapid transition (in general, <120 ms) that separates at least one consonant and a vowel (Eilers et al., 1993). For instance, a pronunciation transcribable as "ta" would be deemed canonical if articulated with a rapid transition duration, but would be deemed noncanonical if articulated with a slow transition duration. Syllables of the latter form have conventionally been termed marginal babbling (Oller, 1986), the connotation obviously being that they are intermediate between canonical babbling and earlier speech-like vocalizations. Because human listeners are extremely sensitive to differences between canonical babbling and earlier speech-like vocalizations, meticulous acoustical analyses suggest that the onset of babbling is not as abrupt as has been generally assumed.

Babbling is certainly the first rhythmic activity during vocal ontogeny, if vocal activity is restricted to the domain of so-called speech-like vocalizations. However, if we expand the category of vocal activity to include non-speech-like vocalizations, it appears that rhythmic vocal activity emerges during a much earlier period in the form of laughter. The influence of preceding vocal activity on the subsequent onset of truly speech-like rhythmic sounds remains largely unexplored. If exposure to external stimulation is necessary for the process of babbling development, such exposure might include auditory experience as well as previous experience in performing motor action, particularly rhythmic motor action. This possibility was explored in the following study.

Eight firstborn infants (three males and five females) who had uncomplicated prenatal and perinatal histories were observed between the ages of three and eight months while they interacted with their mothers. The mothers were monolingual in Japanese. All of the mothers were middle-class full-time homemakers between twenty-four and thirty years of age. Every month, each mother–infant dyad was observed for a total of six days, three days in the first week of the month and three days in the third week of the month. On a given observation day, the mother–infant dyads were simultaneously audio and videotaped in their homes for approximately two one-hour sessions, using a portable video camera and recorder and a wireless FM microphone and audiocassette recorder. During each session, a standard set of toys was presented to the infant. The observer instructed the mother to play with her infant as she normally might when they were alone together.

Four raters, none of whom was told the purpose of the research, coded the infants' behaviors. Nonvocal and vocal behaviors were coded independently by different pairs of coders using two different methods: videotapes for non-vocal behaviors and audiotapes for vocal behaviors. With respect to nonvocal behaviors, the coding categories included: gaze at mother (action of looking at mother's face), smile, mouthing (movements of the mouth such as chewing, sucking, puckering), sitting, reaching, crawling, stereotyped kicking, and rhythmic hand banging. In coding vocalizations, the occurrence and quality of the sound were analyzed first. A vocalization was operationalized as a discrete, continuously voiced sound occurring within a single respiration, excluding non-verbal sounds (sneezes, coughs, hiccoughs) and other vegetative sounds. With respect to vocalizations, the coding categories included: crying, laughing, coo-ing, marginal babbling and canonical babbling. Inter-rater reliabilities, defined as the percentage of instances for which there was agreement on the classifica-tion of visual movements (nonvocal behaviors) and sounds, were 88 percent and 85 percent, respectively. After all the ratings were completed, the tape record-ings of laughter, marginal babbling, and canonical babbling were submitted to an acoustical analysis. There is no doubt that babbling should show rhythmic pattern frequently. Using a sonagraph with a 59-band filter and frequency scale up to 4000 Hz, we counted the number of repetitions in a given bout of utter-ances (conventionally described as syllable). The length in ms of each syllable was measured to an accuracy of 0.5 ms. The acoustic characteristics of laughing also include a deep inspiration followed by a short interrupted expiration. A vowel sound is produced with a glottal stop consonant that often interrupts the vocalization several times so that there is an abrupt and sharp cut in the flow of air to the mouth; this is usually accomplished by a sudden and complete closure and quick separation of the vocal cords. Borrowing a term from speech analysis for convenience, each such recognizable unit in a laugh was called a "syllable." The number of "syllables" in each laugh was counted and the length of each of the syllables was measured according to the same procedure used to assess babbling.

When we compared the number of occurrences of each type of vocalization with the infants' age in months, laughing, marginal babbling and canonical babbling showed remarkable changes over the infants' ontogeny. The onset of laughter occurred between three and four months of age and its frequency increased as the infants developed. Marginal babbling appeared abruptly at the age of six months and was observed most often in the next month; thereafter, its frequency waned dramatically. Canonical babbling, which appeared at the age of seven months, came to be performed more frequently with increasing age. These developmental patterns are quite consistent with previous findings (e.g., Sroufe and Waters, 1976; Oller, 1986).

In order to examine temporal associations between occurrences of vocal and nonvocal behaviors, the written records of vocalizations obtained from coding the audiotapes were compared with the records of nonvocal behaviors obtained from an independent coding of the videotapes. If any nonvocal be-havior was found to temporally overlap a vocalization for a minimum of 0.5 s, the nonvocal behavior was considered to co-occur with the vocal behavior. When we computed the rate of co-occurrence for each vocal type according to this criterion, the scores were found to be relatively high for laughter (overall rate: 47.3 percent) and marginal babbling (39.5 percent) but low for canonical

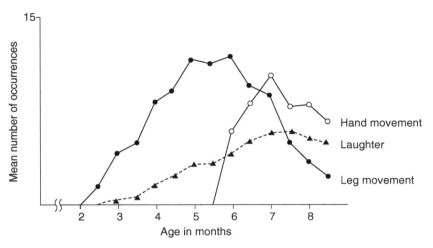

Figure 6.2   Overall developmental patterns in the occurrence of rhythmic leg
and hand movements and laughter.

babbling (9.6 percent). The former two were significantly more likely to co-
occur than the latter one. With respect to the types of nonvocal behavior recorded
in co-occurrences, laughter often tended to be associated with stereotyped kicking and hand banging, i.e., 34 percent of all recorded co-occurrences involved
kicking and 41 percent involved hand banging. In contrast, marginal babbling
co-occurred extremely frequently with hand banging alone (76 percent of the
total co-occurrences).

Fig. 6.2 shows the patterns of developmental change in overall occurrences
of laughter, kicking and banging. Compared with banging, kicking emerged
earlier and was observed most often between the ages of five and six months.
However, after its onset, banging occurrences tended to decline sharply. Fig. 6.3
shows the patterns of co-occurrence of laughter with stereotyped kicking and
with hand banging. Laughter co-occurred solely with kicking until the age
of five months, when its frequency sharply declined. Then, co-occurrence
with banging started. Thelen (1981), studying the rhythmic motor behaviors
in normally developing infants, reported that the onset of stereotyped kicking
occurred between two and three months of age, a finding confirmed by the
present investigation. With respect to the development of locomotor behavior,
two developmental transitions are known to occur during the first year of life,
namely disappearance of newborn stepping and the subsequent onset of independent locomotion. The onset of independent locomotion coincides with the
onset of stereotyped kicking (Thelen, Skala and Kelso, 1987), although this
takes place long before the onset of bipedal walking. Once kicking emerges,

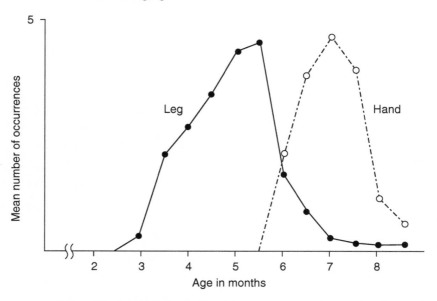

Figure 6.3   Developmental changes in co-occurrences between laughter, and rhythmic leg and hand movement.

infants are able to perform well-coordinated stepping movements when supported over a motorized treadmill. Although involuntary, this movement is not considered to be merely reflexive because infants are able to adjust these steps exquisitely to the demands of a task and, specifically, to maintain bilateral coordination when each leg is on a treadmill belt driven at a different speed. Also, a very sharp increase in the number of occurrences has been reported for rhythmic hand movements around six months of age (Thelen, 1991), which was again confirmed in the present observation. According to this change, the frequency of co-occurrences between laughter and kicking dramatically decreased as co-occurrences between laughter and hand banging appeared rather abruptly.

Further, detailed acoustical analyses revealed that through its co-occurrence with kicking and hand banging, the motor pattern of laughter tended to change in its rhythmic patterning. Stereotyped kicking is essentially alternate-leg kicking, which is "the simultaneous bending of the hip and knee of one leg and extending of the hip and knee of the other leg" (Thelen, 1979, p. 703). Whenever laughter co-occurred with kicking, the number of alternate-leg kicking bouts within the kicking session was counted. For analysis, the number of such bouts minus the number of syllables in the co-occurring laughter was computed, and the

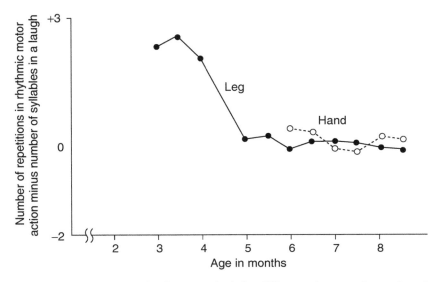

Figure 6.4   The development of relative differences between the number of syllables in a laugh and the number of repetitions in co-occurring kicking and banging.

computed scores were averaged for the infants at each age level. The results of this analysis are presented in fig. 6.4. When the infants were three–four months old, their scores were relatively high. That means that the number of kick bouts exceeded the number of syllables in the co-occurring laughter. Basically, the scores ranged between two and three, i.e., if there were six bouts of kicking, there would often be three or four syllables of laughter. After the age of four months, the scores started to decrease, they almost reached the zero level once the infants were five months old, and they no longer exhibited significant changes thereafter, i.e., the number of syllables produced in a laugh tended to coincide exactly with the number of kick bouts in a simultaneously occurring action.

When the average number of kick bouts in a given action was examined as a function of infants' age, there were no significant differences with age. However, when the average number of syllables in laughter was examined as a function of infants' age, there were highly significant differences with age. The number of syllables tended to increase with age. During earlier periods, the laughter that infants produced consisted of a relatively small number of syllables. To continue laughing, infants must keep subglottal air pressure or vocal fold tension rather constant while performing the repetitive movement of opening and closing the glottis. Presumably, this would not be an easy task for younger infants. Subsequently, some voluntary control over this phonatory movement is enabled or facilitated by timing the phonatory movement to co-occur with other rhythmic motor actions such as stereotyped kicking. In other words, with the aid of another rhythmic motor action that appears earlier in ontogeny, infants achieve rhythmic vocal production.

The period when rhythmic vocal production is achieved coincides with the period when the frequency of kicking declines and hand banging appears. Hand banging is basically "a rhythmical, vertical movement of the arm from the shoulder, and occasionally with additional bending at the elbow" (Thelen, 1979, p. 705). Whenever banging and laughter co-occurred, the number of vertical movement bouts in a banging session as well as the number of syllables in a laughing session was counted and a score was again computed as the difference between the two counts. This average score is also presented as a function of infants' age in fig. 6.4. This time, unlike the relationship found between kicking and laughter, both counts were extremely close to one another at the very onset of hand banging, at the age of six months. At the onset of banging, the infants were already able to match the rhythmic feature of their vocal production with the rhythmic feature of their ongoing motor activity. This also confirms that the ability to produce rhythmic sounds is acquired in part by making vocal activity co-occur with stereotyped kicking.

After the onset of co-occurrences between laughter and hand banging, a further change in the motor pattern of laughter was also identified. The change concerned the average duration of the syllables comprising each laughter session. Fig. 6.5 presents the average duration of syllables within laughter sessions as a function of infant age. Until the age of six months, there was no significant change in this measure. Overall, the average duration was 0.92 sec. During this period, measurements of the duration of a single bout of kicking within a stereotyped kicking session likewise did not reveal any significant change. Overall, the average kicking bout duration was 0.86 sec, which did not differ significantly from laughter syllable duration. However, once laughter began to co-occur with hand banging, syllable length tended to become shorter. Furthermore, when measuring the average duration of single bouts of vertical movements within a banging session, these average scores showed a similar tendency. Thus, as the tempo of hand banging accelerated, so did the tempo of laughter syllable production. The mean duration of syllable production in eight-month-old infants was 0.34 sec and the tempo became more than twice as rapid as it had been during the preceding two-month-period. Although data concerning older infants' tempo in laughter were not obtained in the present study, Nwokah et al. (1994) reported that the average score was 0.27 sec in one-year-olds. Such sharp acceleration may not occur thereafter.

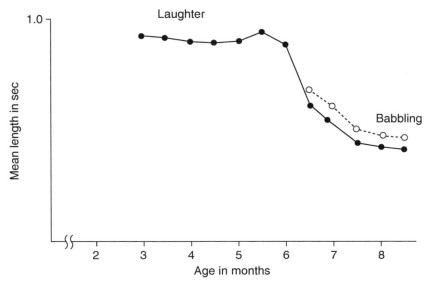

Figure 6.5   Developmental changes in syllable length, laughter and babbling.

"Truly" speech-like rhythmic vocalizations appear between six and seven months of age, i.e., babbling. Interestingly, when the average tempo of syllable production in babbling was plotted against the same infants' age in months, a similar pattern of acceleration was found to the average tempo of syllable production in laughter (as shown in fig. 6.5). The average duration was 0.66 sec at the onset of babbling while it was 0.37 sec when the infants were eight months old, again roughly twice as rapid as two months before. When the temporal change of syllable production was compared with the infants' development in terms of babbling and laughter, the effects of the infants' age were highly significant while the effects of the type of vocal behavior (i.e., laughter versus babbling) were not significant.

In order to compare the tempo of syllable production by infants with that by adults, twenty utterances were randomly chosen from each of the nine mothers who had been audiotaped in the present investigation. Durations of all syllables included in their utterances were measured and a mean score was computed for each mother. The average duration score for the mothers was 0.23 sec. In a previous study (Provine and Young, 1991), it was reported that the speed at which English-speaking adults produce a single syllable during conversation is 0.17 sec. This difference should not be surprising since it is well known that Japanese speakers participate in conversation at a slower tempo than do English speakers and speakers of other European languages (Beckman, 1982). Rather, what is noteworthy is that the tempo of the infants' syllable production in babbling at six months of age was more than twice as slow as the tempo of their mothers' syllable production in speech; the tempos became similar over the next two months, at which time canonical babbling emerged.

During the two-month-period of accelerated syllable production in babbling and laughter, canonical babbling had not appeared yet and all instances of recorded babbling were classified as marginal babbling.

Marginal babbling was recorded most frequently around the age of seven months, one month after its onset. Thereafter, the frequency of marginal babbling declined, essentially to be replaced by canonical babbling. However, even after the onset of canonical babbling, marginal babbling was still observed with relatively high frequency, at least, during the following six-week period. Until the onset of canonical babbling, marginal babbling also showed a strong tendency to co-occur with hand banging. The probability that marginal babbling would co-occur with hand banging (a motor action) was 63.8 percent during the first six-week period. However, as shown in fig. 6.6, this value suddenly dropped to less than 10 percent in the next one-month period. Interestingly, the co-occurrence of laughter and hand banging, which had been observed often, came to be observed at much lower frequencies (see fig. 6.3). The probability of co-occurrence exceeded 50 percent before the age of eight months while it was less than 10 percent thereafter.

After the onset of canonical babbling, rhythmic vocal production was no longer accompanied by rhythmic motor action, but each of the two occurred independently of one another. Finally, we analyzed recordings in fine detail to determine whether or not the onset of the motor action (stereotyped kicking or hand banging) temporally preceded the onset of the vocal behavior (laughter or marginal babbling), or followed it. Of course, under such circumstances, the occurrences of the two types of behaviors exhibited temporal overlapping to some extent with one another, but one of the two had to have preceded the other temporally even if only marginally. If their temporal relationship were random, the probability that one would occur earlier than the other would be close to 50 percent. However, when the probability with which laughter preceded stereotyped kicking and hand banging was computed in all cases where laughter co-occurred with kicking and banging, scores were 26 percent and 23 percent, respectively, which is significantly lower than expected by chance alone. When recordings of co-occurrences of marginal babbling and hand banging were examined, the probability that babbling preceded banging was 21 percent, again significantly lower than expected by chance alone. In all of the three co-occurrence patterns, the rhythmic motor actions were found to occur temporally earlier than the vocal behaviors.

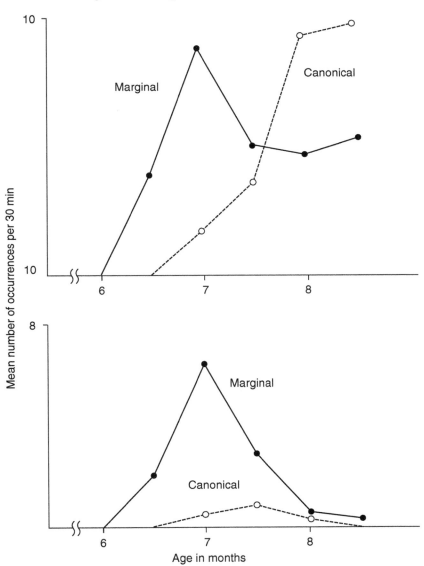

Figure 6.6 Overall developmental patterns of marginal babbling and canonical babbling (upper) and of co-occurrences between babbling and banging (lower).

The functional significance of co-occurrences between marginal babbling and hand banging

The finding that a specific temporal association exists between occurrences of marginal babbling and hand banging but not between occurrences of canonical babbling and hand banging was also independently confirmed by Ejiri (1998). Ejiri longitudinally observed four healthy infants (two males and two females) between the ages of four–five months and eleven months. Each infant was video-taped for a total of twelve–twenty hours per month while his/her vocalizations were simultaneously audiotaped. From these data, a forty–minute recorded segment was randomly chosen; all motor actions and vocalizations were transcribed for this segment. The motor actions were classified into five categories: manipulative act, mouthing, hand banging (defined as a single downward vertical movement of an arm, a definition slightly different from mine), any rhythmic action ("banging" used in my study was included here if it was performed repetitively), and others. The vocal behaviors were first divided into non-speech-like and speech-like and then further subdivided into cooing, marginal babbling and canonical babbling. The co-occurrence of a motor action and a vocal behavior was defined when the two temporally overlapped for at least a one-second period.

When the rate of co-occurrence was computed for each category of motor actions, the values were higher for rhythmic action and banging than for the others. The rates of co-occurrence for rhythmic action and banging did not differ significantly. When scores were compared across the three categories of speech-like vocal behaviors, marginal babbling was found to co-occur significantly more frequently than cooing and canonical babbling; in particular, there were frequent co-occurrences between marginal babbling and rhythmic action. Longitudinal analyses of the likelihood of such co-occurrences showed that they were recorded almost exclusively during a one-month period after the onset of marginal babbling. For each infant, this was also the period that preceded the onset of canonical babbling by one month, i.e., the onset of canonical babbling was delayed from the onset of marginal babbling by one month. The actual age in months that the onset of canonical babbling was recorded varied for the four infants: seven months for two infants, six months for one infant and five months for the final infant. Regardless of when canonical babbling appeared, co-occurrences between marginal babbling and rhythmic motor action or banging were recorded most often one month earlier than the onset of canonical babbling. For instance, if the onset of canonical babbling was recorded at six months of age, the co-occurrence of marginal babbling and banging was recorded most often at five months of age. The probability that marginal babbling co-occurred with the motor action was 65 percent during this period, but fell to 5 percent in the following month.

Ejiri also examined whether the onset of the manual motor action temporally preceded the onset of marginal babbling, or vice versa, whenever co-occurrences were recorded. The probability that occurrences of manual action preceded occurrences of vocalizations was 78 percent, which is significantly greater than expected by chance. These results, taken together with my findings, suggest that preverbal infants exploit rhythmic motor actions as a vehicle for developing the ability to produce sounds such as those in the consonant–vowel series.

Results of my acoustical analysis on laughter revealed that the temporal pattern of laughter was affected by the temporal characteristics of co-occurring motor actions. It is therefore reasonable that a similar acoustical modification might have occurred in marginal babbling before the onset of canonical babbling. The perceptual system of human adults is extremely keen to differences between the two types of babbling. However, perception of these differences would have made us insensitive to within-category differences in each type of babbling. To explore this possibility, Ejiri and Masataka (2001) performed a sound spectrographic analysis on samples of marginal babbling that had been collected in Ejiri's previous study. From the corpus, seventy–ninety utterances were randomly chosen for each of the four infants. The sounds were divided into three categories of marginal babbling: (1) recorded before the onset of canonical babbling and co-occurring with rhythmic manual action; (2) recorded before the onset of canonical babbling and not co-occurring with rhythmic action; and (3) recorded after the onset of canonical babbling and not co-occurring with manual action. For each utterance, a sonagraph was used to measure the duration of its first syllable and the frequency transition duration of its first formant (F1). The average values of these parameters were compared across the three categories of marginal babbling for each infant. These parameters were chosen for analysis because important features that distinguish marginal from canonical babbling pertain to the intervals in an utterance that separate a syllable from the syllable that immediately follows and the intervals that separate a consonant element from a vowel within a syllable.

Results of this analysis revealed that before the onset of canonical babbling, the average utterance duration of marginal babbling that did not co-occur with motor action was significantly longer than that which did co-occur with motor action. The duration of utterances of marginal babbling recorded after the onset of canonical babbling, that did not co-occur with motor action, did not differ significantly from the duration of marginal babbling recorded before the onset of canonical babbling, that did co-occur with motor action; the former duration was significantly shorter than the duration of non-co-occurring marginal babbling before the onset of canonical babbling. Similarly, before the onset of canonical babbling, the average duration of the formant frequency transition in non-co-occurring marginal babbling was significantly longer than that in co-occurring babbling. However, the duration of the formant frequency

transition in marginal babbling recorded after the onset of canonical babbling did not differ significantly from the comparable duration in co-occurring
marginal babbling before the onset of the canonical babbling, but it was significantly shorter than the comparable duration in non-co-occurring marginal
babbling before the onset of the canonical babbling.

A dynamic view of rhythmic vocal production

So far, evidence has been presented to indicate that a particular type of motor
action and babbling appear around the same developmental period. A study
by Ramsay (1985) further supports this possibility. In observations of eight infants from five months of age through eight weeks after the onset of babbling,
Ramsay found that the infants frequently performed rhythmic action during earlier periods but that nonrhythmic or unimanual manipulative actions appeared
during the week of babbling onset. Ramsay interpreted the results in terms of
developmental change in hemispheric specialization at the subcortical level and
assumed there was some sort of reorganization at this level.

The Supplementary Motor Area, located on the medial surface of the superior frontal gyrus, has been shown to control various rhythmic action patterns.
Electrical stimulation of this area evokes involuntary body movements as well
as involuntary iterative vocalizations. Penfield and Welch's (1951) classic experiment revealed that stimulation of this area evoked stepping movements,
waving of the hand, and complex movements of the hand involving successive
flexion and extension of the fingers and wrist. The motor patterns were repeated
during continued stimulation. Brickner (1940) reported that stimulation of the
Supplementary Motor Area caused a patient to suddenly utter "err" sounds that
were rhythmically repeated.

Based on these findings, a theory on the production of babbling was proposed. MacNeilage and colleagues (MacNeilage and Davis, 1990; Davis and
MacNailage, 1995) argued that production of the consonant–vowel sequences
of babbling is mechanically controlled by repetitive opening and closing of the
jaw. They called this movement a syllable frame, which should be generated in
the Supplementary Motor Area. According to their hypothesis, these syllable
frames are determined only by the immature motor capabilities of the infants.
Consequently, the acoustic quality or content of the syllable during this period should be under involuntary control. For infants to acquire motor control
over their vocal production requires further development. Individual segments
must come under the infant's voluntary control and be inserted into syllable
frames. The hypothesis would attribute the strong synchronizing tendency between laughter or earlier babbling and rhythmic motor action to the notion that
all their temporal organization patterns are governed by the same rhythmic os-
cillator that is localized in a specific area of the brain. One possibility may be to

attribute this synchronizing tendency to the undifferentiated manner in which each of these behaviors is generated; as infants develop further, specialization occurs and their occurrences became differentiated. However, if we follow this line of reasoning, it becomes difficult to account for the finding that whenever co-occurrences between motor action and vocal production have been identified, the former has been found to be significantly more likely to precede than follow the latter temporally.

Locke (1993) also noted the chronological concordance between the onset of rhythmic motor action involving banging and the onset of canonical babbling. He interpreted this on the basis of so-called "sound motivation" hypothesis. The hypothesis assumes that infants have an auditory preference for rhythmic sounds at this point, so they babble because they like these sounds. To reinforce babbling behavior endogenously, such a preference is supposed to develop in infants. To support his idea, Locke referred to the culturally universal tendency for infants to be attracted to noisemakers and noisy toys. The preference is most robust when infants are eight–ten months old; six-month-olds might show less attraction to these items.

Further evidence on the developmental underpinnings of canonical babbling comes from studies of vocal development in congenitally deaf infants. Until recently, no systematic comparisons had been made between deaf infants and hearing infants in terms of their vocal development, in part because babbling had been assumed to appear under maturational control. Since the mid-1990s, several systematic studies have been published that report quite consistent findings (Locke, 1993; Clement and Koopmans van Beinum, 1995). Using Oller's (1980) terms for preverbal infant vocal development, no significant differences in vocal behavior have been found between deaf and hearing infants during the phonation stage (0–1 month), the GOO stage (2–3 months), or the expansion stage (4–6 months). As infants pass through these stages, overall frequencies of vocalizations increase. Thereafter, hearing infants proceed to the next stage, the reduplicated babbling stage (7–10 months), whereas deaf infants rarely do, i.e., deaf infants produce marginal babbling as well as hearing infants but deaf infants rarely come to produce canonical babbling. For instance, Clement and Koopmans van Beinum (1995) longitudinally investigated six congenitally deaf infants between two or three months of age and twelve months of age and reported that of the six infants, canonical babbling was found in only one infant. Ejiri (1999) longitudinally examined the vocal recordings of a single deaf infant whose parents were also deaf from the age of five months to eighteen months. Though the study sample size was extremely small (i.e., one individual), Ejiri recorded not only the infant's vocal behavior but also all occurrences of simultaneous motor action; the temporal relationship between the two was then examined. Results of her analysis were consistent with previous findings: the infant passed through phonation, GOO and expansion stages by the age of six months. The frequency of the deaf infant's marginal babbling was approximately half the average frequency expected in hearing infants. This marginal babbling was very likely to co-occur with a motor action, specifically, a rhythmic motor action. Nonetheless, reduplicated babbling was not recorded, at least not during the following twelve-month period.

According to Locke's sound motivation hypothesis, both the motor action and babbling emerge together because the two are commonly motivated or sustained by their audibility. Accordingly, their chronologically concurrent emergence during development could certainly be accounted for in terms of age, and shown by independently plotting the frequencies of each as a function of infant age. However, even if this explanation were generally plausible, it cannot explain the fine synchronization between the two during this period. If infants babble or perform rhythmic motor action due to underlying sound motivation, either the babbling or the performance of the motor action would be sufficient to satisfy the motivation. Logically, one would expect that when the babbling is produced, the motor action would not occur and vice versa. The motor action and the babbling should take place alternately, without temporal overlap. Their temporal relationship should be somewhat mutually exclusive.

In order to investigate the sound motivation hypothesis, Locke et al. (1995) observed sixty-one infants around the onset of canonical babbling. In the experiment, an audible or inaudible rattle was offered to each of the infants. When the frequencies of infants' shaking actions using each of the two rattles were compared, no significant difference was found. Ejiri (1999) also presented both audible and inaudible toys to seven infants during the marginal babbling period and compared the frequencies of their banging actions between the two conditions. Again, no significant difference was found. One of the infants was even experimentally heavily bandaged so that any rhythmic action produced almost no audible sound. Despite this manipulation, the bandaged infant performed banging as often as other same-aged infants without a bandage. These results contradicted the hypothesis that preference for audibility is the underlying motivation for the performance of rhythmic motor action.

On the other hand, the notion that auditory experience is crucial for preverbal infants to acquire the ability to produce a consonant-vowel series is supported by other researchers. Kuhl and Meltzoff (1996) examined developmental change in infant vocal responses to adults' vowels at twelve, sixteen and twenty weeks of age and tested them for vocal imitation. In this experiment, three different vowels (/a/, /i/, and /u/) were presented to infants via videotapes of an adult uttering the sounds. In previous studies, sound stimuli were presented to infants via audiotape recorders. The vocalizations the infants produced in response to the presentation were sound spectrographically analyzed. Kuhl and Meltzoff reported that when the videos were presented to the infants, vocal imitation occurred: infants listening to a particular vowel produced vocalizations resembling that vowel. The results of this study imply that the earliest form of vocal imitation is guided primarily by the visual rather than by the auditory modality. In this vein, it should be noted that even neonates are capable of imitating some facial expressions of adults around them (Meltzoff and Moore, 1983). Indeed, even vocalizations produced by deaf infants are hardly distinguishable from those produced by hearing infants during this period, at least to our ears.

Conversely, the acquisition of abilities enabling the production of canonical babbling, specifically, the ability for complicated articulation, could not be guided by the visual modality alone. Auditory feedback becomes crucial in this regard. This does not mean, however, that performance of rhythmic action is a by-product of the infant's auditory preference for rhythmic sounds. Infants could certainly master the production of well-articulated sounds by listening to their self-produced sounds and by using their ability to match their own sounds with the sounds they select as models. The consonant–vowel series produced by caregivers and others in the ambient environment often serve as models for infants. The occurrence of rhythmic motor actions is not triggered by their audibility, but rather by their rhythmic nature, which is the basis for controlling the regulatory oscillation of vocal production. In this regard, the implications of the dynamic principles of development derived from studies of the ontogeny of infant locomotion are of relevance.

Ontogenetic changes in infant locomotor movements

From birth, infants are able to produce patterned movements of the legs such as cyclic kicking and stepping. This pattern is even generated *in utero* (Prechtl, 1984). The first dramatic change in this behavior occurs around the age of three months. In the motor pattern of leg movements that had previously been totally under autonomic control, some intentionality emerges around the three-month mark. Piaget (1952) first documented the conversion of early spontaneous autonomic kicking into intentional kicking when he described Lucienne's repeated shaking of her bassinet by kicking. Rovee-Collier and colleagues successfully demonstrated that infants could be conditioned to perform harness kicking in order to repeat a pleasurable event. Interestingly, the age in months at which infants can first be conditioned this way clearly corresponds to the age at which co-occurrences appear between sound production and rhythmic kicking. The modifiability of their kicking pertains to its frequency and intensity dimensions. Thelen and Smith (1994) pointed out that although three-month-old infants achieve some voluntary control over the frequency and intensity of their kicking, other motor aspects of kicking remain autonomous. The basic topography of the kicking movement remains unchanged: alternating or single legs moving and synchronous flexions and extensions of the joints. In order to perform limb movement for support and locomotion, infants obviously must free themselves from the compulsory nature of this movement topography; they spend several months achieving this goal.

Thelen and Smith regards our locomotor activity as the dynamic assembly of several skills and as the mutual interaction of heterogeneous components. For each component to interact with the others dynamically, it must first come under independent control. This process is thought to occur during early infancy and is called "uncoupling." Presumably, we could extend the notion of uncoupling in the leg movements of three-month-old infants to their development of rhythmic vocal production; for example, the co-occurrence of stereotyped kicking with laughter and of banging with marginal babbling. That is, both rhythmic activities are initially governed conjointly in infants and subsequently become uncoupled during development. This represents another version of the undifferentiated explanation for co-occurrences, but this is the explanation that did not appear plausible above.

In the view of Thelen and Smith, the development of a behavior starts from its "unique set of intrinsic dynamics." This notion seems similar to the concept of species-specificity in ethology. However, while species-specificity is an attribute that should predispose all members of a species uniformly, classified into the same species, intrinsic dynamics is defined as "a collective of temperament, attention span, abilities, muscle physiology, energy level, and so on" (Thelen and Smith, 1994, p. 152). Consequently, intrinsic dynamics vary between individuals even within a species and "this is what they had to work with, the space in which their system lived, and from which they must autonomously and individually discover a solution" (p. 152). During their first five–six months, infants have been thought to perform rhythmic leg movements under minimal or non-specific task demands. Presumably then, the topography of their rhythmic leg movements should reflect the initial state of the underlying intrinsic dynamics. Viewing the co-occurrence of rhythmic vocal production and rhythmic motor action as being in an uncoupled state apparently emerges from this notion. However, according to the dynamic principles of behavioral development theory, it is also possible that the development of rhythmic motor action itself could provide vocal production with a specific demand and that with this demand, the initial state of intrinsic dynamics surrounding vocal production would become unstable and seek a solution.

In Thelen's previous argument, morphological variables such as body weight and the balance between muscle and fat were regarded as factors that could render the intrinsic dynamics for locomotor behavior in a given age period unstable. For instance, the development of intentionality in kicking around the age of three months is considered to be profoundly related to rapid weight gain in infants during the first two–three postnatal months. The weight gain is mostly due to subcutaneous fat that is absolutely necessary for temperature regulation in infants. Increases in nonmuscle tissue would serve as a contextual change for leg movement. Applying this logic to other nonmorphological factors, another independently developing behavior pattern could interact with early locomotor activity in a similar manner as these morphological variables.

Individuality in laughter as a manifestation of intrinsic dynamics

As proposed by Thelen and Smith (1994), if the intrinsic dynamics underlying a behavior vary individually at a given developmental stage, the pathway by which the dynamics become transient will also vary individually. In order to test this hypothesis, one must deconstruct the pathway by collecting longitudinal data on individuals and by comparing dynamic changes in pathways across individuals. However, the data analyzed in my aforementioned experiment were exclusively cross-sectional, except for nine infants who were observed longitudinally. As long as the overall ontogenetic relationship between vocal activity and rhythmic motor action is examined without taking individual differences into account, dynamical change in vocal activity relative to the development of rhythmic motor activity in each individual seems hard to study. Therefore, as a next step of investigation, these data were reanalyzed by splitting the entire participant infant group into three subgroups; the degree of co-occurrence of vocal behavior with motor actions was then compared for these subgroups.

In the previous analysis, the number of "syllables" in a laugh was found to match the number of repetitions in co-occurring kicking as the infants developed. This matching was achieved by gradual developmental increases in the number of syllables in laughter. However, when individual data were examined in detail, there was considerable individual variability in behavior patterns at the very onset of laughter. Thus, the nine infants were divided into three groups based on the average number of syllables in the laughter that they produced during a one-month period after the onset of laughter. The three infants who produced laughter with the smallest number of syllables relative to the other six infants were assigned to Group 1. Similarly, the three infants who produced laughter with the greatest number of syllables relative to the other six infants were assigned to Group 3. The remaining three infants fell in the middle and were assigned to Group 2.

Results of the reanalysis are presented in table 6.1. When the probability of co-occurrence between laughter and kicking was compared for the three groups, a statistically significant tendency was found. Group 1 obtained the highest score and Group 3 obtained the lowest score, i.e., on average, the smaller the number of syllables in these infants' laughter at the onset of laughter, the more frequently their laughter co-occurred with kicking. The degree to which laughter co-occurred with kicking could be predicted at the onset of laughter by measuring the number of syllables in their laughter. The data on co-occurrences between laughter and hand banging were also reanalyzed. The

Table 6.1 *Variability of the degree of co-occurrence of laughter with rhythmic leg movement according to variability of syllables included in a laugh*

	Group*		
	1	2	3
Number of syllables	3.14	3.92	5.37
Probability of co-occurrence (%)	42.8	30.6	22.6

*For grouping of the infants, see text.

Table 6.2 *Variability of the degree of co-occurrence of laughter with rhythmic hand movement according to variability of syllable length of a laugh*

	Group*		
	A	B	C
Syllable length (ms)	628	750	971
Probability of co-occurrence (%)	21.8	34.2	46.6

*For grouping of the infants, see text.

nine infants were divided into three groups based on the average duration of syllables they produced in their laughter at the onset of its co-occurrence with hand banging. Three infants who produced laughter with syllables of shorter duration than the other six infants were assigned to Group A. Similarly, three infants who produced laughter of longer duration than other six were assigned to Group C. The remaining three infants fell in the middle and were assigned to Group B.

When the probability that laughter co-occurred with banging was compared for the three groups, Group C obtained the highest values and Group A obtained the lowest values. The degree to which laughter co-occurred with banging could be predicted at the very onset of the co-occurrence by measuring the duration of the syllables in the infants' laughter. Overall, individuality in the degree of co-occurrence of laughter with stereotyped kicking and hand banging was found to correlate with individuality in the acoustic quality of laughter. In this regard, it should be noted that the number of syllables comprising a given session of laughter and the average duration of the syllables did not significantly correlate with one another across the nine infants. Each of the acoustic parameters, individually heterogeneous and independent of one another, has influenced the pattern of co-occurrence with leg movement and hand movement, respectively.

For infants, acquiring the ability for articulatory movement should be regarded as acquiring the ability for some sort of gesturing movement and the production of rhythmic sounds must be comparable, as a movement, to performing gestures of other kinds, such as banging. For instance, when the consonant "b" is pronounced, the movements of vocal fold vibration, glottis opening, lip closure and so forth must be performed in a certain sequence. Various neuromuscular activities must be spatiotemporally organized into a functional unit, which is an equivalent class of coordinated movements that achieve some goal. Although gesture is often used to mean a symbolic but nonlinguistic structure, a gesture can also be defined as any equivalent class of coordinated movements that accomplishes some end. Thus, rhythmic leg and hand movements as well as vocal articulatory movements are all gestural. The difference is that a vocal gesture results in a primarily acoustic signal while the others result primarily in a visual signal. Moreover, the systems controlling each activity are separate from and independent of one another, but share rhythmicity as a common physical property. As described above, motor organization regulating rhythmicity develops earlier in the system controlling leg and hand movements than in the system controlling vocal movements, and with the help of information generated in the leg and hand system, articulatory gesturing is accomplished in the vocal apparatus of hearing children. During this process, the problems that each infant faces in acquiring adult movement patterns are idiosyncratic, and the manner in which each infant discovers solutions to the problem of how to adapt his/her spontaneous movement dynamics to their ultimate goals may be individually specific. This idea will be explored in more detail in the next chapter by comparing the early development of vocal and signing behavior in hearing and deaf infants.

7 Earliest language development in sign language

This chapter is devoted to identifying the signed equivalents of hearing pre-verbal infant–caregiver interactions in deaf infant–caregiver interactions and to overviewing this latter developmental process, which appears to play an important role in language acquisition of deaf infants. Thus far, studies have examined early parent–infant interaction from a variety of perspectives. However, virtually all of them have focused on hearing infants while very little attention has been focused on deaf infants. What can the study of early sign language acquisition tell us about the human capacity for language? Linguists have not hesitated to propose theories of human language based on data drawn only from spoken language. Several theories of very early language development are based on the hypothesis that infants' emerging linguistic abilities are determined by the mechanisms underlying the production and perception of speech and/or the mechanisms of general perception. Given that most studies focus only on spoken language, it is in principle impossible to find data that would do anything but support this hypothesis. Only by examining language in another modality would it be possible to determine fully the relative contributions of motor production and perception constraints to the time course and nature of early human language acquisition. By considering all natural human language, both signed and spoken, we can gain a better understanding of the essential prerequisites for language acquisition, how language evolved, and how its use is conditioned by natural limitations on the organs of articulation and the sensory mechanisms for perception.

Comparisons between the development of vocal and gestural language might provide clues to questions concerning how language interacts with more general cognitive and motor abilities in the developmental process. The logic behind such comparisons is that since language has traditionally been treated as synonymous with speech, as might have also been implied in previous chapters of this book, it is possible that inaccurate perceptions exist concerning the relationship between general motor and cognitive milestones and language-specific milestones. Typically, causative explanations are offered for data showing that a specific cognitive or motor skill immediately preceded a specific milestone in spoken language. Such conclusions, however, would need to be reevaluated if the same language milestones were achieved significantly earlier in the gestural modality. Given the long history of regarding language as exclusively vocal in nature, extensive reevaluation might be required. The empirical question of whether or not language development proceeds differently in the vocal and gestural modalities is of pressing theoretical import. This chapter is devoted to conducting preliminary investigations to address this sort of question; in addressing this issue, I will examine the motherese phenomenon and the development of babbling.

The significance of research on sign language acquisition

Linguistic and psycholinguistic research on American Sign Language (ASL) over the past three decades has established without question that ASL is a form of natural human language. Studies of several other indigenous sign languages have led to the same conclusion: primary sign languages, used mainly by deaf people, are fully developed human languages that are more or less independent of the spoken languages used for linguistic communication in the same region. That signed languages employ the hands, face and body, rather than the vocal tract as articulators, suggested that vocal and signed language vastly differ from one another. Such differences were thought to relate to the structure of signed languages. Actually, signed languages were found to lack certain grammatical properties that were shared across spoken languages. However, the task of identifying these differences and representing them in explicit ways turned out to be more difficult than anticipated. Presently, the general consensus is that the unique characteristics of signed languages are restricted mainly to the area of phonology and to the role of space in the grammar (in addition to hands and body as articulators, the space in front of the signer's body plays a role in the forms of signs and sign sentences). In other aspects, however, signed languages have been demonstrated to be highly constrained, following general restrictions on structure and organization comparable to those posited for spoken languages (Armstrong, Stokoe and Wilcox, 1995; Padden, 1988).

With respect to sign language acquisition, psychologists' and psycholinguists' interests stem from the fact that language-learning children in all cultures are exposed to models of a particular language and, not surprisingly, acquire that language. Linguistic input clearly has an effect on children's acquisition of language. However, it is possible that linguistic input does not affect all aspects of language development uniformly and that variations in linguistic input will alter the course of development of some properties of language but not of others. In their pioneering studies, Feldman, Goldin-Meadow and Gleitman (1978) and Goldin-Meadow and Mylander (1984) attempted to isolate the properties of language whose development could withstand wide variations in learning conditions – the "resilient" properties of language. They observed children who had not been exposed to conventional linguistic input in order to determine the properties of language that children could develop under a set of degraded input conditions. The researchers studied children who had hearing losses so severe that they could not acquire spoken language naturally. The children were born to hearing parents who had not exposed them to a manual language. Despite their impoverished language-learning conditions, these deaf children were found to develop a gestural communication system that was structured in many ways like the communicative systems developed by young children who acquired language in traditional linguistic environments.

The above findings suggest that in addition to the hearing parents' inclination to use gestures when interacting with their deaf children, the children themselves are to some extent responsible for introducing language-like structure into their gestures. Subsequently, Goldin-Meadow and Mylander (1998) explored the robustness of this phenomenon by observing the deaf children of hearing parents in two cultures, American and Chinese; the two cultures differed in their child-rearing practices and in the way gestures were used in relation to speech. Despite these differences, the spontaneous sign systems that developed in the two cultures shared a number of structural similarities, including: patterned production and deletion of semantic elements in the surface structure of a sentence; patterned ordering of those elements within the sentence; and concatenation of propositions within a sentence. These structural properties are universally robust in almost all naturally developing signed languages, indicating that their development is buffered against large variations in environmental conditions and, in this sense, can be considered "innate."

This argument could be consistent with recent understandings about signed languages that are shared by most linguists. Indigenous signed languages existing over generations of deaf signers are quite widespread and have been reported in various parts of the world (Ahlgren and Bergman, 1980; Kyle and Woll, 1983; Stokoe and Volterra, 1985). One of the most extensively investigated signed languages is ASL, which is used as a primary mode of communication by deaf individuals in the United States and parts of Canada. Limited contact between separate areas of the United States has resulted in distinct varieties of ASL, including one used by many southern black deaf signers. In North America, geographic and other forms of isolation have led to many distinct signed languages, including French Canadian Sign Language, Alaskan Native Sign Language and Nova Scotian Sign Language. ASL and French Sign Language are historically related, having shared key educators who introduced French Sign Language to schools for young deaf children in America (Lane, 1984). In contrast, British Sign Language is not related to ASL because of little historical contact between signers of the two countries. Nevertheless, ASL and British Sign Language share a number of linguistic properties. Moreover, their linguistic properties are shared by the gestural systems used by the deaf children of hearing parents who were studied by Goldin-Meadow and Mylander (1998) in China and America.

Such similarities suggest the presence of a unitary language capacity that underlies human signed and spoken language acquisition. That language capacity might be internally constrained with regard to the structures that it can realize but, in the face of environmental variation, it appears to be flexible with regard to the expressive modality it can employ to realize this capacity. The degree to which the capacity is modality-free and modality-specific can be determined only by comparing the acquisition processes of signed and spoken languages. However, despite the increasing research on communication between hearing mothers and their hearing infants, there has been little comparable research on communication between deaf parents and their deaf infants. In particular, little information is available on the first six months after birth; data are relatively abundant on mother-infant interaction at six months of age and later. Hence, this chapter aims to review previous research with deaf infants around these ages, specifically focusing on motherese and babbling in the manual mode, which clearly corresponds to the spoken motherese and vocal babbling that have been discussed so far.

Preliminary studies of signed motherese

Maestas y Moores (1980) first examined interactions between deaf infants and their deaf parents, quantitatively and systematically comparing their interactions with those between hearing infants and their hearing parents. She described the communication of these deaf parents as relying heavily on physical and visual contact with the infants and as incorporating a variety of strategies to gain and maintain the infants' attention. She concluded that tactile stimulation might be the fundamental modality by which the parents communicated with their infants; for example, she noted that parents signed while holding their infants, physically oriented the infant so that the infant might attend to visual-gestural communication, and tapped and patted the infant's body. She noted that deaf parents employed a variety of communicative strategies with their deaf infants. In particular, they frequently positioned themselves behind or beside the infant with their signing hands moving in front of the infant's body. Moreover, their signing was often modified through repetition, holding a sign in location, and producing a sign very slowly.

Launer (1982) hypothesized that this phenomenon was analogous to motherese in spoken languages. As already described, when hearing adults address hearing infants and young children, they tend to modify their speech in an unusual and characteristic fashion. Launer investigated the nature of ASL motherese in her study of four deaf mother–child pairs, the youngest participant being nine months old when the experiment began. Launer found that the communicative strategies used by deaf mothers consistently included "positioning the body to maximize attention, interspersing nonvocal affective acts with language acts, and using alternate or simultaneous sensory modalities to communicate to a young child" (Launer, 1982, p. 1). She described this early input as highly redundant and simple in structure, usually comprising only one or two signs per string. Launer concluded that these features of signing "represent efforts to increase the clarity of sign production for young children" (1982, p. 140), with mothers focusing on a root form consisting of the hand-shape, location and basic movement of the sign. However, it should be noted that her entire data sample was only one hour long and that the conditions under which she collected the data were not strictly controlled (e.g., during interactions with toys in some cases and during interactions with snacks or meals in others). Therefore, the results should be viewed with an appropriate degree of caution.

Launer's findings were confirmed by Kantor (1982), who collected data on two profoundly deaf infants interacting with their deaf mothers at three-week intervals over a ten-month period of time. The youngest child was twelve months of age at the beginning of the study. Each of the two mother–infant dyads was videotaped at home in both a free-play situation and a play situation with a predetermined set of toys. Kantor reported that these mothers modified their signing behavior during interactions with their infants so that it was simpler and more linear. Kantor stated that the mothers "do not use the rich fundamental modulation system of adult ASL with their young deaf children, but instead offer a model of ASL that separates out these highly analytic units into their simple components" (1982, p. 234). However, neither Launer nor Kantor compared the signing behavior mothers directed to their children with the signing behavior they directed to other adults, nor did they analyze the signing quantitatively. More importantly, it should be taken into account that even the youngest infant Launer and Kantor investigated was ten months old and it is well known that several different functions that have been assumed to exist in the motherese used in spoken language are not necessarily active at the same time. It is possible that the particular functions that the manual motherese served changed with the developmental status of the infant, and that according to changes in the infant, the parental style of manual motherese varied. Still unknown is the extent to which the robust features of infant-directed signs that Launer found generalized to younger infants. Further, it is essential to investigate whether deaf infants really are able to perceive these characteristics of the manual motherese.

Characteristics of deaf mothers' signs when interacting with their deaf infants

Erting, Prezioso and O'Grady-Hynes (1990) reported the first systematic attempt to analyze the signing of deaf parents to their deaf infants. Since 1985, they have collected videotapes of deaf mothers interacting with their deaf infants. Their preliminary observations supported previous researchers' findings that deaf mothers vary in their signing in terms of type of movement, location on the infant's body, intensity and speech of movement, and rhythmic patterning, so that they effectively attract and maintain the infant's attention. Their results appeared consistent with the claim that motherese in spoken language is mainly concerned with prosodic modification. Based on their findings, they focused on the American sign for "mother" produced by two deaf mothers, who had acquired ASL as their first language, during interactions with their deaf infants when the infants were between five and twenty-three weeks of age as well as during interactions with their adult friends. When a total of twenty-seven "mother" signs directed to the infants were compared with the same number of the signs directed to the adults, the mothers were found to: (1) place signs closer to the infants, perhaps the optimal signing distance for visual processing; (2) orient their hands so that the full hand-shape was visible to the infants; (3) position their faces so that they were fully visible to the infants; (4) direct their eye gaze at the infants; and (5) lengthen signs by repeating the same movement. The results appeared to support the idea that parents, including those from a visual culture whose primary means of communication is visual-gestural rather than auditory-vocal, use special articulatory features when communicating with their infants.

Following this study, I began a series of experiments on sign motherese between deaf infants and their deaf parents who had acquired Japanese Sign Language (JSL) as their first language. In this series of experiments on sign motherese, I attempted to replicate this finding, using a larger sample, participants who lived in different cultural background from those studied by Erting et al., and a more exhaustive methodology. In most signed languages investigated thus far, facial expression has been found to play a multifunctional role in transmitting the meaning embedded in each signing movement. As in spoken language, facial expression is used to express affect. However, unlike spoken language, signed languages employ specific facial behaviors as part of the required grammatical morphology for numerous linguistic structures (e.g., in the case of ASL, relative clauses, questions, conditional sentences). This poses tremendous difficulty for the quantitative analysis of signing behavior. In this regard, JSL has a practical advantage over ASL in that it relies on cues produced by hand movements exclusively. Consequently, it appears relatively easy to separate the linguistic from the paralinguistic dimensions in sign production.

In all, fourteen mothers participated in the study. Eight of the mothers were recorded while freely interacting with their deaf infants and also while interacting with their deaf adult friends (Masataka, 1992a). The remaining five mothers were instructed to recite seven prepared sentences either to their infants or to their adult friends (Masataka, 1996). Each mother and her infant or her friend were seated in chairs in a face-to-face position. The height of each chair was

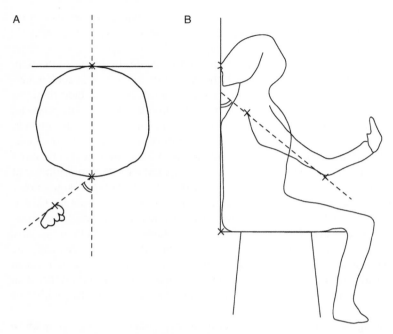

Figure 7.1   Schematic representation of the plane view (A) and the side view (B) of the mothers as recorded on film. The points marked by a light pen on the digitizer are indicated by an X (cited from Masataka, 1992a).

adjusted so that the eyes of the mothers, their infants and their friends were about ninety-five centimeters above the floor. The infants were fastened to the seat with a seat belt. Two video cameras were used to monitor the mothers' behavior. One camera provided the plane view, and the other provided the right side view. At the beginning of each recording session, each mother was instructed to interact with her infant or friend as she normally might when they were in private and not to move her head during the session.

For each recognized sign recorded, the following four measurements were performed: (a) duration (number of frames); (b) average angle subtended by the right hand with respect to the sagittal plane of the mother; (c) average angle subtended by the right elbow with respect to the body axis of the mother; and (d) whether the mother repeated the same sign consecutively or not. For each sign, the duration was measured by counting the frames on which the sign was filmed. Moreover, for each of the frames recorded by the camera located above the mother, the position of the right hand in relation to the head (angle subtended by the right hand with respect to the sagittal plane) was noted (fig. 7.1). For a given sign, the mean value of this angle was estimated. For each of the frames recorded by the camera on the right of the mother, the position of the right elbow (angle subtended by the right elbow with respect to the vertical axis) was noted. Values were averaged for each sign. Subsequently, measured values were averaged for each sign by the mother. These measurements were performed in order to analyze the degree of exaggeration in signing by the mother. Since signed languages are processed by deaf infants in the visual mode whereas spoken languages are processed by hearing infants mainly by the auditory mode, it was hypothesized that exaggeration of signing behavior should appear in the pattern of movements of hands and arms that made the signing gestures.

As shown in table 7.1, statistically significant differences were found between conditions on all four parameters. To analyze the duration of signs, values were averaged across participants then compared for each condition. Durations were longer for signs directed to infants than for signs directed to adult friends.

When the angle of the hand and elbow subtended to the sagittal plane or body axis was calculated across mothers for each condition, the same tendency was apparent. Mean scores for the maximum angles for each sign directed to infants significantly exceeded those for signs directed to adults, with respect to both the hand and the elbow. Similarly, mean scores of averaged values of angles for signs directed to infants significantly exceeded those for signs directed to adults. With regard to these three parameters, post-hoc comparisons revealed that each mother demonstrated a significant increase in these scores when she interacted with her infant versus her friend. Rates of repetition for signs directed to her infant versus her adult friend also differed; rates of repetition for the thirteen mothers when interacting with their infant exceeded their rates of repetition when interacting with their adult friend; and each mother significantly increased her repetitions when interacting with her infant.

Overall, the results revealed that the sign language Japanese deaf mothers used in interactions with their infants was strikingly different from the sign language they used in interactions with their adult friends. In comparison to when interacting with their friends, when interacting with their infants, mothers signed at a relatively slower tempo and were more likely to repeat signs and movements for exaggeration. Hence, this experiment revealed a phenomenon analogous to motherese in maternal speech. Currently, it is well known that signed languages are organized in an identical fashion to spoken language with respect to most linguistic aspects (Klima and Bellugi, 1979). When adults produce manual activities that are part of the phonetic inventory of signed languages in communicating with young deaf children, who have only rudimentary knowledge of language, one would predict that the social interactions should have qualities as distinctive as those seen when adults speak to young hearing children. That is, if interactions are to be established and maintained, adults must be led to apply special constraints to their activities and to produce signals,

Table 7.1 *Average duration, size (by angle degree) and repetition rates for infant-directed and adult-directed signs*

Condition	Duration (no. of frames)		Angle (in degrees)						Repetition rate (%)	
			Hand-sagittal plane		Elbow-body axis					
	Infant	Adult	Infant	Adult	Infant	Adult			Infant	Adult
Interacting freely (n = 8)	39.1	32.8	23.6	17.9	16.4	11.5			6.6	2.9
Reciting prepared script (n = 5)	41.2	31.0	26.5	20.4	18.9	15.5			5.9	2.5

in either the signed or spoken modalities, in a manner commensurate with the infants' level of attention and comprehension. The results of my experiments described above provide strong support for this conclusion.

It is particularly important to note that mothers manipulated the duration, scope (angle) and repetition rate of their signs when signing to their infants as opposed to their adult friends. This "sign motherese" is considered to be parallel to "speech motherese" in its manipulating or varying the prosodic patterns of the signal because duration, scope and repetition rate are all dimensions of prosody in sign, roughly analogous to duration, pitch and repetition in speech. The fact that mothers in our study clearly manipulated or changed these dimensions of their sign production indicated that they were doing something in addition to and, presumably, apart from, their manipulation of the affective dimensions of sign production. Speech motherese is often accompanied by pronounced modifications in facial expression (i.e., more frequent and more exaggerated smiling, arched eye-brows, rhythmical head movement; Gusella, Roman and Muir, 1986; Sullivan and Horowitz, 1983). Nevertheless, all these components can be regarded as paralinguistic in speech as well as in JSL; their occurrences, if they do occur, do not influence mother–infant communication from a grammatical perspective. Thus, we concluded that motherese is a property of an amodal language capacity, at least with regard to its prosodic dimensions.

Perception of sign motherese

I consider that a phenomenon quite analogous to speech motherese has therefore been identified. In terms of the spoken modality, the available data indicate that motherese is a prevalent form of language input to infants; however, it is still unclear whether the same is true for sign motherese. Certainly, in the studies introduced above, experimenters were able to distinguish infant-directed signing from adult-directed signing on behavioral and physical grounds. However, the question of whether deaf infants can perceive the difference remains unanswered. By continually monitoring their infants' degree of attention and understanding, mothers might modify various features of their signing so as to maintain their infants' responsiveness at an optimal level. This leads to the hypothesis that these signing modifications enhance their infants' acquisition of the basic units of signed language. In order to test this hypothesis, I undertook the following perception study of sign motherese.

The experiment examined the congenitally deaf infants of deaf mothers as well as the hearing infants of hearing mothers. In the first experiment, a stimulus videotape was presented to seven deaf six-month-old infants; the videotape comprised excerpts of the infant- and adult-directed signs produced by the five deaf mothers described above. All the deaf mothers, whose husbands were also deaf, were signers of JSL as their first language. In the stimulus tape, the following seven sentences were recited to the mothers' infants or adult friends: Good morning; How are you today? Get up; Come on now; If you get up right away, we have a whole hour to go for a walk; What do you want to do? Let's go for a walk.

The question being asked in this study is whether or not deaf infants will attend to and prefer infant-directed signing to adult-directed signing. Therefore, infants' reactions to the stimulus presentations were videotaped and later scored in terms of attentional and affective responsiveness to the different video presentations. The stimulus presentation and recording took place in a black booth. Throughout the experiment, each of the twelve infants was presented the stimulus tape only once. During each session, the mother stood with her back to the video monitor and held her infant over her shoulder to allow the infant to face the video display from a distance of approximately sixty centimeters. Each session was conducted only when the infant was quiet and alert. During the session, the mother was instructed to wear a music-delivering headphone and to direct her gaze to a picture on the wall, ninety degrees to her right. Although deaf, the mothers were asked to wear the headphone so that they could be compared to hearing mother–infant dyads with no exposure to sign language, as described below.

The infants' reactions were evaluated by four raters, two of whom rated attentional responsiveness and two of whom rated affective responsiveness. As an indicator of attentional responsiveness, the percentage of the total video display time spent looking at the video screen, averaged between the two raters, was measured. To measure attentional responsiveness, two raters independently watched the infant on video and pushed a button whenever the infant fixated on the video display. These button presses were counted and timed by a computer. To measure affective responsiveness, the other two observers independently attended to the infant's facial features and vocalizations and rated the infant using a set of nine-point scales on the three dimensions that were used in the perception study of spoken motherese described in chapter 4 (Werker and McLeod, 1989). The three dimensions were treated as indexes of a single underlying factor: affective responsiveness. One cumulative affective responsiveness score was created for each infant by summing each rater's ratings on the three dimensions then averaging across the two raters. Thus the maximum and minimum cumulative scores would be twenty-seven and three, respectively, for each infant for each stimulus condition. The higher the scores received by the infants on these three dimensions, the more positive emotions they were judged to be experiencing.

The results of the experiment are summarized in fig. 7.2. When the amounts of time each infant fixated on the videotape during depictions of infant-directed versus adult-directed signing were analyzed statistically, a significant difference

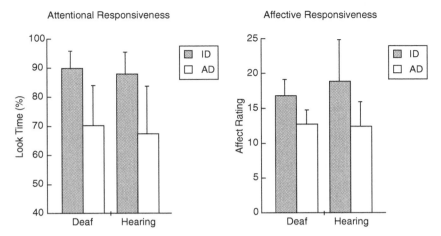

Figure 7.2 Comparison of responsiveness for infant-directed (ID) signing versus adult-directed (AD) signing between hearing infants and deaf infants. Error bars represent standard deviations (cited from Masataka, 1998).

was found. The overall mean proportion of time that each infant fixated on the videotape was 90.4 percent (SD = 6.3) for infant-directed signing and 69.8 percent (SD = 14.7) for adult-directed signing. When the videotape segment of infant-directed signing was presented, infants apparently looked at it longer than when the segment of adult-directed signing was presented. With respect to affective responsiveness, scores for the segment of infant-directed signing exceeded those for the segment of adult-directed signing in every infant. The overall mean affect rating scores were 16.9 (SD = 2.5) for infant-directed signing and 12.8 (SD = 2.1) for adult-directed signing. The infants were affectively more responsive to infant-directed signing than to adult-directed signing.

Results of this experiment showed that signed motherese evoked more robust responsiveness from deaf infants than adult-directed signing did. This offers the long-term prospect of identifying the features of motherese that are not specific to a particular language modality. Of course, one cannot discount the possibility that the attractiveness of sign motherese was due to the way deaf mothers manipulated their affective behavior rather than to characteristics of the signs themselves. In this regard, it should be noted that the mothers' head movements were limited in the initial videotaping. As already noted, this restriction did not influence mother–infant communication from a grammatical perspective. From the paralinguistic perspective, however, communicative samples obtained from the mothers under these circumstances might have been affected by this restriction. However, infants showed greater responsiveness to infant-directed than to adult-directed signing; human infants might also possess equal capacities to attend to motherese characteristics in speech or sign. Infants might be predisposed to attend to appropriately modified input, regardless of the modality of the input.

Clearly, to determine whether or not modality-specific capacities must be triggered by some amount of experience, we must examine responses to these patterns by infants who lack substantive experience (linguistic exposure) in that modality. Indeed, several researchers have addressed this issue with respect to spoken motherese. Among others, Cooper and Aslin (1990) showed that infants' preference for exaggerated prosodic features is present at the age of two days. Based on their results, postnatal experience with language did not have to be extensive for infants to learn about the prosodic features of their native language. It has also been shown that newborns continue to show preferences for the intonational contour and/or temporal patterning of melodies they experienced prenatally (Panneton, 1985). Both prenatal and postnatal auditory experiences affect the relative salience of prosodic cues for young infants. In a subsequent study, four- and nine-month-old English-learning infants were reported to show robust attentional and affective preferences for infant-directed over adult-directed speech in Cantonese, even though Cantonese was completely "foreign" to them (Werker, Pegg and McLeod, 1994); but these infants had heard speech before. No convincing evidence has ever been presented to assess the hypothesis about modality-specific experience. As long as hearing infants remain the primary focus of investigations, it will be extremely difficult, if not impossible, to address the question of whether or not exposure to any language is necessary for infants to be able to react to the motherese form of the language.

Therefore, I conducted the following experiment to determine whether or not hearing infants with no exposure to signed language also prefer signed motherese. If such a preference exists, this might indicate that human infants lock onto particular kinds of patterned input in a language modality, completely independent of prior experience. Participants were forty-five sets of hearing mothers and their first-born, full-term hearing infants who had no prior exposure to a signed language (twenty-one boys, twenty-four girls). All of the infants were six months of age. The infants' mothers were all middle-class monolingual women, between twenty-two and twenty-nine years of age, who spoke Japanese exclusively. The stimulus tape shown to each of the forty-five infants was the same videotape used in the experiment on deaf infants. Stimulus presentation and scoring protocols were also the same as those used in the previous experiment (Masataka, 1998).

Analysis of the data from these forty-five infants revealed that there was a significant main effect for stimulus type on their attentional responsiveness. Infants looked at the videotape of infant-directed signing longer that at the tape of adult-directed signing. The overall mean proportion of time that each infant fixated on the stimulus tape was 87.5 percent (SD = 8.2) for infant-directed signing and 66.0 percent (SD = 17.3) for adult-directed signing. Moreover, when comparing hearing infants' responsiveness for infant-directed versus adult-directed signing with that of the deaf infants in the above experiment, no significant difference was found (see fig. 7.2). A similar tendency was also found for affective responsiveness. For the forty-five hearing infants, overall mean affect rating scores were 18.9 (SD = 6.1) for infant-directed signing and 12.6 (SD = 3.4) for adult-directed signing. This represents a statistically significant difference between the two stimulus conditions. Comparing the scores of the hearing and the deaf infants, again no significant difference was found.

Hearing infants who have had no exposure to any form of signed language are attracted to motherese in JSL in a manner strikingly similar to deaf infants who have been exposed to signed language from birth. Infants are attracted to signed motherese, regardless of whether or not they have ever seen signed language. Space and movement are known to be the means for transmitting morphological and syntactic information in signed languages. The continuous, analogue properties of space and movement are used in systematic, rule-governed ways in virtually all signed languages that have been investigated thus far (Armstrong, Stokoe and Wilcox, 1995; Newport, 1981), JSL is no exception. Abstract spatial and movement units are analogous in function to the discrete morphemes found in spoken languages. Among the properties of spoken languages, it is grand sweeps in fundamental frequency (dynamic peak-to-peak changes) that are thought to attract hearing infants to spoken motherese (Fernald and Simon, 1984). As a visual analogue to such features, it is likely to be the sweeps in peak visual movement of signed motherese that attract deaf infants. These special properties, evident in infant-directed communication, might have universal attentional and affective significance; human infants might be predisposed to attend to these properties even if they have had no prior exposure to them in a given modality.

The emergence of manual babbling

The above findings might lead us to question how the presence or absence of such linguistic input affects the linguistic behavior infants acquire. Concerning how the ontogenetic process for vocal behavior differs between deaf and hearing infants over the first year of life, little is known to date, partly because the emergence of babbling had been considered under maturational control on the basis of incidental data. As noted in chapter 5, however, recent observations have revealed that vocal ontogeny proceeds in an essentially similar manner in deaf and hearing infants until the end of the marginal babbling stage. Thereafter, hearing infants come to produce canonical babbling whereas deaf infants do not.

This was thought to be due to the necessity for auditory feedback in acquiring articulatory ability, through which the pronunciation of reduplicated consonant–vowel syllables is made possible.

Interestingly, Petitto and Marentette (1991) proposed that the onset of canonical babbling in hearing infants coincides exactly with the onset of manual babbling in deaf and in hearing infants. In the course of conducting research on signing deaf infants' transition from prelinguistic gestures to their first signs, Pettito and Marentette closely analyzed the "articulatory" variables (analogous to "phonetic" variables) of all manual activity produced by deaf infants from six months of age and their deaf parents who were users of ASL. A number of researchers had noted the presence of manual babbling prior to Petitto and Marentette. Based on their observations of a hearing infant between the ages of seven and twenty-one months who was born to a deaf mother, Prinz and Prinz (1979) reported a group of manual behaviors that appeared to be the result of the infant's imitating its mother's signing. In another dyad comprised of a hearing infant and its deaf mother, Griffith (1985) observed the infant clapping and rubbing its hands in a circular motion. Griffith interpreted this behavior as a prelexical form of an ASL sign. However, neither Prinz and Prinz nor Griffith conducted analyses as systematic and quantitative as those that Petitto and Marentette conducted. Petitto and Marentette observed a class of manual activity unlike anything else that had been reported previously in the literature. This class of manual behaviors included linguistically relevant units produced in entirely meaningless ways. Further, their pattern was wholly distinct from all other manual activity, i.e., general motor activity, communicative gestures and signs. Deaf infants performed these manual behaviors between nine and twelve months of age, the period corresponding to hearing infants' canonical babbling stage. Indeed, subsequent analyses revealed that in hearing infants, this class of manual activity was characterized by identical patterns in timing, patterning, structure and use of the vocal behavior to those universally identified as babbling. As a result, this class of manual behavior was termed "manual babbling." Further, a comparison of the ontogeny of manual action between hearing infants who were acquiring spoken language with no exposure to a signed language and deaf infants who were acquiring ASL as their first language revealed that both groups produced a roughly equal proportion of communicative gestures (e.g., arms raised to request being picked up) at approximately eight–fourteen months of age. Nevertheless, the deaf infants produced more forms of manual babbling (e.g., hand shape movement combinations exhibiting the phonological structure of formal signed language) than did the hearing infants, and manual babbling accounted for approximately 40 percent of the manual activity in deaf infants but less than 10 percent of in hearing infants.

Takei (2001) sought to replicate the above findings in deaf infants who had grown up with exposure to JSL. He observed one male and one female infant

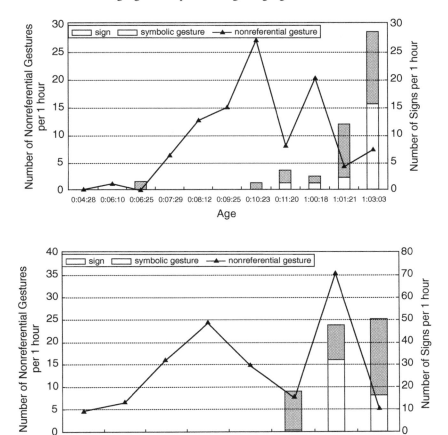

Figure 7.3   Number of occurrences of signs and nonreferential gestures in two deaf infants, S1 (top) and S2 (bottom), as a function of age in months (cited from Takei, 2000).

whose parents had both acquired JSL as their first language. Using a video-recorder, Takei observed each infant for at least one hour at home while the infant and its mother freely interacted with prearranged toys. Subsequently, the video-recordings were transcribed in the laboratory. All recorded manual activities were transcribed according to the same classification categories employed by Pettito and Marentette. As shown in fig. 7.3, the results revealed that in the male infant, manual babbling first appeared at the age of six months and occurred most often when he was ten months old. Immediately following this period, the first recognizable signs that were meaningful as JSL signs were recorded. After the onset of the first signs, the frequency of manual babbling tended to decline. The same tendency was found in the female infant. Essentially, in the two infants, the peak of manual babbling was found to be a reliable predictor for the onset of meaningful signs.

Taken together, deaf infants with exposure to signed language demonstrated a higher frequency of manual babbling than their hearing counterparts. Further, the deaf infants' manual babbling was most robust just prior to the onset of meaningful vocabulary in their signed language. In spite of this quantitative difference, however, even hearing infants with no exposure to a signed language were found to produce manual babbling (Petitto and Marentette, 1991). Given that manual babbling precedes the onset of the first recognizable signs just as vocal babbling precedes the onset of the first meaningful words, Takei concluded that the language capacity could manifest itself equally as sign or speech in human infants, i.e., in hearing infants, the ability of vocal and gestural language can develop simultaneously and in a similar manner, at least during the preverbal period. The balance between the two modalities can apparently vary, however, because some infants come to produce almost equal amounts of first words both in speech and in sign around the identical period (Goodwyn and Acredolo, 1993). For deaf infants, progression in acquiring spoken language is hindered earlier. To some extent this is because auditory feedback, which deaf infants lack, is crucial for the acquisition of the articulatory ability for speech. Therefore, deaf infants rely on the manual mode to realize their linguistic capacity. This could partly account for the richer repertoire of manual babbling in the sign-exposed infants described by Petitto and Marentette (1991). However, it is not the only variable determining the difference.

I recently tracked the ontogeny of manual activity in three preverbal deaf infants of hearing parents who had no exposure to signed language. I found that these infants performed manual babbling, and the frequency of their manual babbling was greater than that of hearing infants but much lower than that of deaf infants exposed to JSL (Masataka, in press). In my study, I examined the developmental pattern of manual activity for infants between the ages of eight and twelve months. There were three groups in the study: (1) three deaf infants of deaf parents with exposure to JSL; (2) three deaf infants of hearing parents with no exposure to any signed language; (3) two hearing infants of hearing parents with no exposure to any signed language. All of the infants' manual activities were transcribed in an identical manner and were classified into two types: syllabic manual babbling and gestures. Infants in the three groups produced similar types and quantities of gestures during the study period. However, the groups differed in their production of manual babbling. Manual babbling accounted for 25–56 percent of manual activity in deaf infants with exposure to JSL and a mere 2–6 percent of the manual activity in hearing infants.

Manual babbling as a percentage of manual activity (manual babbling/(manual babbling + gesture)) showed a significant increase in the deaf infants as they developed, but not in the hearing infants. The percentage of manual babbling for deaf infants with no exposure to any signed language was intermediate between these two groups, ranging between 10 and 15 percent. Moreover, the value was greatest at the age of eight months in all three of these infants and showed a significant decrease as they developed.

Thus, the existence of manual babbling does not necessarily imply that babbling is purely an expression of a "brain-based language capacity" that is amodal. Neither does it imply that babbling is not a phenomenon of motor development but is strongly associated with the abstract linguistic structure of language. As described in chapter 5, even vocal babbling arises with the aid of properties of motor organization that are shared by the motor system that controls manual articulators. The parallel progression of manual and spoken babbling over the course of their development should not then be that surprising.

The development of deaf infants' intentional use of sign space

In the above research on manual babbling, the presence or absence of a linguistically relevant unit in an observed manual activity was determined using the transcription system of adult patterns of signed language, i.e., ASL when investigated in North America and JSL when studied in Japan. For the development of these transcription systems, each sign was described in terms of three dimensions: (1) location (where on the body or in space the sign is being made – on the cheek, the chest, in front of the body, etc.); (2) hand shape (how the fingers are extended and bent in this particular sign – the hand makes a fist, has some fingers extended, etc.); (3) movement (how the hand (or hands) move(s) – in a circle, up-and-down, forward, etc.). For ASL, the basic system comprises twelve different symbols for location, nineteen different symbols for hand shape and twenty-four different symbols for type of movement (Battison, 1974). For JSL, the basic system comprises twenty-one symbols for location, forty-five for hand shape and twenty-one for movement (Yonekawa, 1984). The manual systems are regarded as equivalent to a group of phonemes constituting a spoken language. When the manual activity of each deaf infant exposed to JSL was transcribed in this manner, on average 29 percent of the location symbols were identified, 53 percent of the hand shape symbols, and 57 percent of the movement symbols (Takei, 2001).

This identification of signing dimension symbols is an approach analogous to that of analyzing preverbal vocalizations by focusing on those elements of the sounds that conform to the patterns of adult speech. However, in addition to this "phonetic transcriptional analysis," there is another procedural approach: instrumental/acoustic analysis. Instrumental/acoustic analysis has been the approach consistently employed to investigate infant vocalizations in this book. This approach allows researchers to divorce themselves from the stricture of phonetics and to describe infant vocalizations in terms of parameters that are comparable regardless of speakers' age differences. Exclusively based on this type of analysis, developmental continuity has been revealed between those preverbal vocalizations that could be adequately described with a phonetic alphabet and those vocalizations that could not. The question is whether an approach analogous to instrumental/acoustic analysis is possible for assessing developmental change in signing behavior.

In order to explore this possibility, Masataka (2000) examined the degree to which manual babbling occurred within so-called sign space in two congenitally deaf infants and in two hearing infants. This was conducted because adult signers are known to perform their signing movements within a constrained sign space extending from the waist to the top of the head regardless of which signed language they acquired. The outward boundary of this sign space is "the reach of the arms from side to side (with elbows bent)" (Klima and Bellugi, 1979, p. 51). Thus, if manual activity is regarded as sign-like, it should take place within the space as well as be somehow articulated. Occurring within a limited space imposes constraints on any hand shape, location of hand, and hand movement that must be recognized for that manual activity to be considered a linguistically relevant phonetic element. Each infant's interactions with its mother were recorded twice, once when the infant was six months of age and again when the infant was nine months of age. The infants were chosen from the three deaf infants and the two hearing infants included in the previous study (Masataka, 2000). Each mother and her infant were seated in a face-to-face position. The video-recording protocol was essentially the same as the one previously employed to investigate sign motherese. However, this time the entire figure of the infant instead of the mother was monitored by two video cameras; one of the cameras monitored the plane view of the infant and the other monitored the side view. By combining the images recorded by the two cameras, I could reconstruct the spatial movement of the infant's manual action. The sign space can be visualized as a hollow disk in front of the infant, the bottom half flattened when the infant is seated. Occurrences of manual activity can be represented as densities within this sign space, following procedures developed by McNeill (1992). For transcription purposes, the sign space was divided into sectors using McNeill's system of concentric squares. The sector directly in front of the infant's chest was Center–Center; surrounding this was the Center; then the Periphery; and finally, at the outer limit, the Extreme Periphery. With respect to each activity filmed in continuous frames of the videotape, the right hand's position was identified in the sign space in each frame when the angle it subtended was at its maximum with respect to the sagittal plane.

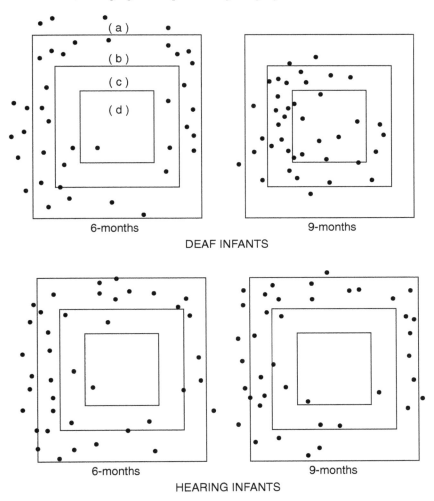

Figure 7.4   Density of space usage in manual babbling of deaf infants and hearing infants at the ages of 6 months and 9 months. The spaces are divided into four sectors: (a) Extreme Periphery, (b) Periphery, (c) Center, and (d) Center–Center.

Surprisingly, no known systematic study has been conducted focusing on how adult users of any sign language use this sign space. However, it appears that adults usually perform signing around the Center–Center space and the Center space. As shown in fig. 7.4, results of the analysis revealed that, as in adults, the manual babbling of the deaf infants tended to occur around the Center–Center or Center space when they were observed at the age of nine months; however, their activity was more likely to extend into the Periphery when they were observed earlier, at six months of age. The manual babbling of hearing infants often tended to occur around the Periphery at both six and nine months of age. The spatial pattern of manual babbling occurrences changed over the three-month period only for the deaf infants. For manual babbling, this strongly suggests development in the use of limited space towards the pattern seen in signed language.

Since intentional use of the sign space in signing could be considered the visual analogue of voluntary use of phonatory characteristics in speech production, these results indicated that the analogues of phonation and articulation progress almost simultaneously in the acquisition of signed language by deaf infants. This is not the case for the acquisition of spoken language by hearing infants, in which the development of phonatory abilities precedes the development of articulatory abilities. This is because when newborn babies expire air through their vocal chamber, a natural resonance is produced so that vocal output is provided with a characteristic frequency and temporal envelope. "Fully resonant" vowel-like vocalizations that appear by six months of age represent progress that is due to enormous anatomical remodelling of the vocal apparatus and increased respiratory control. Sequenced articulation does not begin by that time. For sign-like activity to be provided with phonatory-like characteristics, development of skilled manual action is the prerequisite. Bruner (1990) argued that acquiring manual skills consists of gaining voluntary control over a preestablished eye–hand coordination. Contemporary research tends to favor the view that basic eye–hand coordination is innate. However, static balance is also a prerequisite for the emergence of visually guided manual action. Consequently, infants must reach five–six months of age in order to gain control over a relatively variable pattern of manual activity. For language development in the manual mode, poor static balance works as a constraint against the earlier onset of phonatory-like ability that is seen in language development in the vocal mode. It should be noted that this delay does not work as a constraint to delay articulation because the expression of phonetic elements does not necessarily presuppose the onset of phonation in signing behavior.

Individual-specific transitions to babbling

Next, manual actions of the two deaf infants at the age of nine months were analyzed in more detail to determine how their intentional use of sign space arose from their previous manual activity. Indeed, the use of sign space appears to require a set of very complicated motor skills. Thus, the development of this ability is an important motor milestone like other milestones such as reaching,

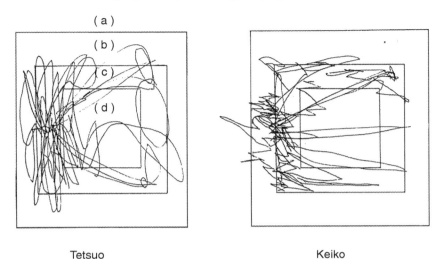

Tetsuo   Keiko

Figure 7.5   Comparison of trajectories of the right hand in the frontal plane in manual babbling between two deaf infants at the age of 9 months. Imagine the infants facing the page.

walking, crawling, etc. In order to investigate how these infants acquired their manual babbling ability, I mapped the trajectories of all manual activities for each infant; these results are shown in fig. 7.5. Comparisons of these mappings for the two infants tell us that how each infant modulated its previous manual activity for babbling was idiosyncratic. The problems each infant had to solve for this accomplishment differed. As noted earlier, the motor activity most commonly seen in six- to nine-month-old infants is banging and similar types of rhythmic movement. However, the spatial pattern characterizing this movement varies individually; according to these individual differences, the developmental process of acquiring the ability to control manual action to a predefined space appears to differ. One of the deaf infants in my study, Tetsuo, was very active. His banging was characterized by raising both hands overhead at arms' length and moving them up and down repeatedly. Initially, he always moved both hands simultaneously. The movement was so vigorous that both hands had high velocity as they passed down through the sign space. The trajectories of his activities (see fig. 7.5) displayed several notable features. First, the pattern by which his arms were driven showed rather regular cycling in an equivalent but larger space. Second, both hands moved in smooth ellipses, like a damped spring with a periodic forcing function. When this infant was excited, the timing and pattern of his arm movements were topographically similar to those of a physical spring. This was obviously inappropriate for intentional use of the limited space required for signing.

The task for Tetsuo was to disrupt this spring-like motor pattern, hopefully in the vicinity of the Center–Center space. In other words, to perform manual babbling, he had to hold his arms at a single point in the space. Thus, he had to convert this ongoing motor activity into a new form more suitable for goal-directed behavior. What he needed to learn was how to slow down and dampen his banging movements around the Center–Center space. To do so, he flexed and extended his elbows and wrists before the arms approached the Center–Center space. Through the movement, massive co-contraction of both shoulder and upper arm movements seemed to occur during the downward swinging of his arms. Such cocontraction had the effect of stiffening the arms, reducing their compliance, and thereby damping his vigorous movement. Consequently, the initial pattern of his movement, characterized by high velocities, high motion-dependent torques, and using extensive cocontraction, was successfully tamed: a damped spring will finally come to rest at a single point, in an infant's case, in front of the chest.

The situation for another infant, Keiko, was quite different from that for Tetsuo. Keiko did not exhibit vigorous repeated up and down movements. With respect to the horizontal coordinate, Keiko's hand speed and muscle torque were much lower than Tetsuo's. She did not need to tame uncontrolled forces. Rather, her initial movements were characterized by the repeated swinging of her arms frontward and backward. Her movement somewhat resembled the sweeping gesture of adults, but it was more nearly spherical and centered on her own position, and her movement occurred even behind her body. The task she faced in maintaining her hands within the sign space for some time differed from the task Tetsuo faced. The task for Keiko was to generate sufficient force in her shoulder to deliberately lift her arms against gravity and, using her elbow, to counteract the natural flexor positions of her arms. While phasic cocontraction at the first bang and tonic cocontraction at the bang were noticeable in Tetsuo as he worked towards sign-like behavior, slow adjustments confined to the elbow and wrist were characteristic for Keiko. A typical sign-like movement for Keiko, depicted in the figure, was initiated from a quiet position with a small lateral and backward loop, followed by the hand movement moving directly in the vicinity of her chest. Keiko's movement was relatively slow in duration and speed, with few changes in direction, and it looked more like the adult pattern of signing than Tetsuo's initial attempts did.

Whereas Tetsuo mostly kept his elbow stiff, Keiko showed more compliant joints that occasionally moved in a coordinated fashion. Keiko's shoulder movement was not as great as Tetsuo's and her muscle torque was supposed to work primarily against gravity. Nevertheless, her muscle-firing pattern appeared quite similar to Tetsuo's in primarily involving coactivation. While the problem

Keiko faced was visibly different from the problem Tetsuo faced, it was also the same in some senses. Both infants had to adjust the energy or the forces moving their arms so that they could produce sign-like activity within a sign space. Therefore, what Tetsuo and Keiko achieved in common was the ability to modulate the forces provided in their individually specific motor activity, so that they could alter their ongoing nonfunctional movements into communicatively functional movements. The communicatively functional movements they achieved are elements of the phonetic inventories that comprise a linguistic system of signs, and parts of linguistically relevant units. The solution each infant discovered was adaptive in relation to the circumstances it faced. The significance of the solution was evident only when we traced each infant's development longitudinally.

Individual specificity of intrinsic dynamics

The findings described above appeared analogous to those of Thelen et al. (1993) concerning individually specific development of reaching actions. Their study examined how intentional reaching arises from infants' ongoing, intrinsic movement dynamics and how infants' first reaches were successively adapted to the task. Four infants were observed longitudinally performing a standard reaching task. The week when the first arm-extended reach occurred as well as the two weeks before and after that onset were identified for each infant. The assumption underlying this research was that "reaching could be acquired through the soft assembly of mutually interacting, equivalent, multiple-component structures and processes within a context" (Thelen et al. 1993, p. 1090). For each reaching attempt, three-dimensional position-time data were collected from the joints of both arms, along with electromyographic (EMG) recordings from one arm and the lower back. These recordings provided a large amount of kinematic (time-space), kinetic (force) and muscle data. Detailed analyses of these data showed that the four infants used different reaching strategies to reach for a toy presented in front of them.

When adults were given the same reaching task as the infants, the kinematic, kinetic and muscle activation pattern accompanying their actions showed little individual variation. Typically, the extending hand's trajectories traced a reproducible path, the hand's pattern of velocity change was smooth, joint coordination occurred with some regularity, and so on. Comparisons revealed that these characteristics were totally absent in the four infants' reaching acts at the onset of reaching. The way in which the EMG feature of infants' reaching deviated from the typical adult pattern differed from one infant to another. For instance, one of the four infants, Gabriel, was very active motorically. Initially, his reaching attempt resulted in vigorous flapping movements. When the target toy captured his attention, his arms behaved like springs so he could not get the toy successfully. However, as Gabriel repeated his reaching attempts, he mastered massive cocontraction movements of both his shoulder and his upper arm during the reaching trial. Such cocontraction served to stiffen his arm. Consequently, he succeeded in adjusting his muscle patterns to exploit the spring-like system. In contrast to Gabriel, Hannan, another of the four infants, showed much lower than average hand speed and muscle torque in her spontaneous movements than the other three infants. Hannan did not need to slow down her flapping movements, but rather needed to generate sufficient force in her shoulder to lift her arm and her elbow against gravity to counteract the natural flexor position of her arms; this is what she actually did.

Thelen and colleagues proposed that the differences found in the initial motor patterns used by the four infants to reach reflected individual differences in the intrinsic dynamics underlying the behavior. The problem that each infant faced in acquiring the adult pattern of reaching was idiosyncratic. The manner in which each infant discovered solutions to the problem of how to adapt his/her spontaneous movement dynamics to their ultimate goals was unique. The same could apply to the ontogeny of the ability to use the sign space in manual babbling in the deaf infants investigated above. The initial state of the intrinsic dynamics of their manual activity was as variable as it was in those infants studied by Thelen and her colleagues, and the initial state characteristics for Tetsuo and Keiko were similar to those for Gabriel and Hannan, respectively. This is not very surprising because expressions of signed words can be understood as intentional muscular gestures. Since the expression of words is a form of intentional movement, it requires motor control as complicated as the performance of reaching.

According to Thelen and Smith (1994), when infants convert their spontaneous manual action into intentional reaching, a time-locked association of neural activations coheres because of the repeated, varied and re-entrant nature of the neural activations within a functional task context. In a series of studies by Thelen and colleagues on infants' motor development, movement was treated as a perceptual category. Within certain task contexts, infants act and, through acting, learn what levels of arm stiffness, trunk stabilization, bilateral damping and so on best meet the task demands of the motor activity required to perform in a given context; Gabriel, for instance, learned to convert the natural spring-like qualities of his arms to produce efficient reaching.

Thelen regarded this learning as knowledge, like knowledge about the physical properties of objects in the world such as their edges, contours, collisions, etc. Of course, the world in which infants live exists not only on a physical level, but on a social level as well. The findings on the development of sign space usage implicated social forces in early motor development, and the social construction of knowledge. Fogel (1993) argued that meaning is imparted through relationships within the family, school, community and culture in ways identical to those by which bodily actions become "embodied" in thought. Because social information and opportunities for social problem solving are so prevalent, commonalities across such encounters create a large attractor basin that pervades all aspects of thought and language. According to Vygotsky (1978), children's cognitive processes can only be understood in terms of social activity. Indeed, for the deaf infants we studied, learning specific patterns of manual activity was enabled by the activity of interacting partners. As successful reaching for and obtaining a target object function contingently at each attempt, so socially contingent responding by a partner also serves to reinforce repeated attempts. Clearly, the communication partner is as intimately a part of the infant's world as the objects and surfaces with which it lives. Essentially, the process by which activity is modified does not differ between reaching and using sign space. However, in using sign space, unlike the physical counterpart, humans create an intrinsic dynamic with both partners mutually changing as their relationship proceeds. Consequently, as they modified their manual activity, the infants appeared to discover that communicative meaning was conveyed by the activity. Through social interaction within a culture (e.g., through JSL), infants actively participate in and absorb the sociocultural context, which they apparently incorporate into their thought and language. At the very onset, socially embodied knowledge has common roots with individually embodied knowledge.

Continuities between manual babbling and the first signs

Because the solution that each deaf infant discovered for converting intrinsic movement dynamics into communicatively functional behavior was idiosyncratic, the developmental process from babbling to the first signs is also likely to be specific to each individual infant. Takei (2001) longitudinally observed the manual activities of two congenitally deaf infants between six and twenty months of age who had been exposed to JSL. In the first infant (S1), "Up and Down Movement" (as defined by Wilbur, 1987) was identified as the first recognizable nonreferential gesture, at eight months of age. "Right and Left Movement" was identified in the following month, "Wrist Flexing" and "Clapping" at ten months of age, and "Elbow Rotation" and "Up and Down Movement with Hands Linking" two months later. In the second infant (S2), "Right and Left Movement" followed "Banging" in the next month. "Up and Down Movement" occurred at ten months of age, which was followed by "Face Touching" at thirteen months, then by "Forward and Backward Movement" at fourteen months. Takei reported observing the first meaningful signs at twelve months of age for S1 and fourteen months of age for S2. Fig. 7.6 presents the infants' signs and their developmental precursors. The movement of "Elbow

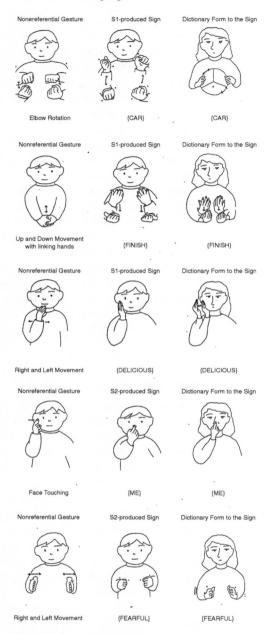

Figure 7.6 Comparison of five types of manual babbling and the first recognized signs that appear to have developed from each, as produced by deaf infants (cited from Takei, 2001).

Rotation" was observed in S1, in accompaniment with the hand shape G, and initially categorized in ASL. Subsequently, a slight modification of the movement took place; while "Elbow Rotation" occurred simultaneously in both hands and was repeated several times at its onset, eventually it occurred alternately, i.e., in one hand and then in the other hand, then it was repeated. When the modification was noted, the caregiver interpreted it as a meaningful sign, "car" in JSL. S1's "Up and Down Movement" was observed with linking hands but apparently without any recognizable hand shape in either hand. Subsequently, the behavior occurred without the linking. When the hands were swung down simultaneously, fists were formed with the thumbs lightly closed against the knuckles. As the hands swung up, the thumbs opened. This was interpreted as the sign representing "finish." S1's "Right and Left Movement" was first performed in front of the chest and involved both hands simultaneously. Soon, it was performed unimanually, involving only the right hand, and around the mid Center–Center area. However, during the movement, S1 suddenly shifted the hand up around the cheek and paused. Thereafter, S1 lowered the hand. After the hand was lifted up to the cheek, it never swayed again. This behavior was recorded exclusively during feeding time, which apparently signaled that the infant was enjoying the feeding. From commonalities in the location element, the behavior was interpreted as a sign meaning "delicious."

"Face Touching" by S2 was accompanied by the hand shape for G on the right hand. Initially, the behavior was performed at the height of S2's eyes so that it looked something like eye-poking. Two months later, S1 modified the movement by allowing the extended fingertip to touch the infant's nose. The movement resembled the JSL sign representing "me." However, in the sign "me," the fingertip approaches from the front towards the nose; S2 never performed such a movement. S2 was also observed to perform "Right and Left Movement," initially in the form of simultaneously swaying both hands. S2 modified the behavior into a form wherein the degree of swaying was less exaggerated. However, fists were made by both hands. This was interpreted by the caregiver as the sign for "fearful."

Although each babbling element reported by Takei was subsequently incorporated into a meaningful sign system in each infant, not every "first sign" was always performed as perfectly as a correct (adult-like) sign. In the case of the sign "car" by S1, for example, rotating the elbows of both hands is far from the adult gesture of wheeling, shivering of both elbows is absent in S2's "Right and Left Movement," etc. Importantly, adult signers nonetheless interpreted these as equivalent to adult signs, which resulted in further linguistic modulation of the infant's sign-like behavior.

In all, although there is continuity in development from the production of babbling to the production of first signs in sign language acquisition, the development of early vocabulary in the manual mode is closely linked to each infant's individually specific intrinsic movement dynamics and to each infant's experience with adult signers' use of signs in familiar contexts. There is no single route to the mastery of the language and deaf infants show a large range of individual variation in their pattern of acquisition. The progress of deaf infants can be conceptualized as another example of development through the epigenetic landscape as depicted by Waddington (1957).

8   From babbling to speaking

Chapters 2 to 6 of this book have been devoted to understanding how hearing infants increasingly develop vocal control over the first six years of their lives. The process appears to take a crucial step when babbling begins. Reduplicated babbling refers to the alternating depression and elevation of the mandible, with points of oral contacts, while phonating. To the ear, this activity produces syllabic elements that sound like speaking. In fact, though early researchers claimed that babbling and speaking were clearly separated in time, no support for this claim has emerged; indeed, there is now considerable evidence that babbling typically merges with and continues well beyond the beginning of speaking. For example, Locke (1986) listed five characteristics that are similar for babbling and speaking in the domain of consonant development: (1) singletons outnumber clusters; (2) prevocalic exceed postvocalic consonants; (3) stops, nasals and glides exceed fricatives, affricatives and liquids; (4) prevocalic stops are apical and unaspirated, rather than dorsal or aspirated; and (5) final obstruents are voiceless and either velar or glottal. These similarities fed the assumption that babbling is a real precursor of speech. However, subsequent research has revealed divergent individual heterogeneity in other acoustic parameters of speaking at the beginning of meaningful speech, such as the diversity of segments used in words. A similar phenomenon has also been revealed in early language development in the manual mode. This chapter examines how hearing infants' phonological capabilities, which show considerable individual variability in organization at their onset, nevertheless develop into a common system of speech as the infant develops in a language-culture.

Implications of pattern perception of the speech stream

With respect to production, Locke (1997) designated infant language development during first six months of life as the vocal learning phase, during which infants become acquainted with the vocal cues that characterize the expression of their native language. The vocal learning phase is followed by the storage phase, which is mostly dedicated to the storage of utterances. In the storage phase, infants typically develop their long-term retention of the sound patterns of a fair number of words. Only after a long period of such lexical storage are infants able to speak. A somewhat analogous period has been observed in the vocal development of songbirds (Locke and Snow, 1997).

The first recognizable speech that an infant produces is comprised of a single word or what may appear to be a phrase (Peters, 1983). Some infants have been found to emphasize single words, simple productive rules for combining words, nouns and noun phrases, and referential functions, while others use whole phrases and formulas, pronouns, compressed sentences and expressive or social functions. Phrases are usually a rote or nearly rote copy of sentences that infants have heard often in their caregivers' speech. Such "holistic phrases not subjected to or requiring grammatical analysis in either comprehension or production" (Van Lancker, 1987, p. 85) are regarded as formulaic. Almost all children produce this type of phrase during the period when they are acquiring their first words though there are individual variations in frequency. The fifty-word vocabulary of children includes on average nine such formulaic phrases and their 100-word vocabulary contains approximately twenty (Lieven, Pine and Barnes, 1992). They are not aware that the words they produce have constituent elements such as phonemes (Echols, 1993) and they do not understand the notion of word or lexical meaning.

The question that then arises relates to the segmentation problem: how do children discover the structural components of the fluent speech stream without knowing the identity of the target elements (Peters, 1983)? Although adult speech contains a wealth of phonetic and prosodic cues that facilitate lexical segmentation, these cues are often ambiguous and distorted as a result of performance factors. Other linguistic cues transmitted in the speech signal often interfere with these cues as well. Children have to overcome these difficulties by bootstrapping their way into the linguistic system, utilizing any information they can extract from the surrounding environment and their capabilities for processing linguistic information. In order to investigate how children solve the problem, we need to know what constitutes an appropriate unit of speech for them at that moment and what properties make up this unit.

One approach to understanding the process is through artificially segmenting speech for the infants by inserting pauses at different locations. If the speech stream is perceived as completely unstructured, it should not matter where these pauses are inserted. However, if there is some psychologically salient organization of continuous speech into perceptual segments that correspond to syntactically relevant units, an artificial segmentation of speech that coincides with the boundaries between such units might be preferable to one that disrupts the units. The rationale for this approach is supported by experiments on adults who judged samples containing pauses that coincided with boundaries of large units to be more natural than ones that disrupted these units (Wakefield, Doughtie and Yom, 1974; Pilon, 1981). Clause boundaries were clearly marked by prosodic changes such as a rise and fall in fundamental frequency and a lengthening of the syllable preceding the clause boundary. Hirsh-Pasek et al. (1987) provided evidence for a comparable effect in infants varying in age between seven and twelve months. Using a head-turning procedure, the infants' preferences were assessed while they listened to a mother speaking to her nineteen-month-old daughter. They listened to speech that was segmented either at major clause boundaries or within clauses by the inclusion of short pauses. The reasoning was that pauses inserted within a clause, a perceptual unit, or an auditory group would be better detected than pauses of identical duration placed between clauses, perceptual units, or auditory groups. A clear preference for speech with pauses inserted at clause boundaries over speech with pauses inserted within clauses was found.

Subsequently, Jusczyk et al. (1992) examined infant sensitivity to the acoustic correlates of phrasal units in their native English language; in particular, they assessed the role of intonation contour. Infants six–ten months of age were tested using a preference procedure. In the first experiment, nine-month-old infants were found to prefer listening to speech samples segmented at major phrase boundaries. Next, the stimuli used in the first experiment were low-pass filtered in order to eliminate cues to linguistic content while leaving the prosodic information intact. When such stimuli were presented, the infants still showed a strong preference for speech samples segmented at major phrase boundaries. However, there were no significant differences in the responses of six-month-olds regardless of where the stimuli were segmented. This indicates the possibility that by nine months infants have a greater familiarity with the prosodic structure of language and that the detection of speech segments related to phrase units might depend on experience with a specific language. In these experiments, the stimuli were taken from a conversation between a mother and her two-year-old child; these conversations are likely to differ from those with younger infants, being much more like adult-directed speech. Given that nine-month-old infants have more experience with speech of this sort than six-month-old infants, it is possible that age-group differences in the responses to the stimuli might be due to differences in the sensitivity of each infant cohort to adult- and infant-directed speech. However, Kemler Nelson et al. (1989) demonstrated greater sensitivity to prosodic cues in infant-directed speech that would help segment the speech stream into perceptual units that correspond to clauses than to the same acoustic cues in adult-directed speech, even in seven–ten-month-old infants.

Overall, infants around nine months of age already parsed the speech stream into units like clauses and phrases, which are important syntactic units. The results also showed that infants perform this segmentation based on prosodic information. Prosody, in turn, is the most prominent aspect of child-directed speech that provides infants of this age with efficient cues to units of speech, and contributes to the segmentation of words within a stream of fluent speech. As argued by Fassbender (1996), this segmentation becomes possible based on the Gestalt principle. According to theory, incoming perceptual information is analyzed and grouped into configurations early in the perceptual process on the basis of simple principles (Wertheimer, 1923). This view is supported by research on auditory grouping, which has shown that infants structure tonal sequences on the basis of frequency similarity as well as on similarity of amplitude and spectral content (Demany, 1982; Thorpe and Trehub, 1989).

A logical prediction of this view might be that infants are not only sensitive to speech units but that they are also sensitive to relevant units of any hierarchically organized sound sequences, such as music. Just as speech can be divided into clauses, clauses into phrases, and phrases into words, music can be divided into sections, sections into smaller musical phrases, and smaller phrases into melodic and rhythmic figures. The notion that prosody is crucial for speech segmentation is in line with this prediction. Indeed, Palmer and Krumhansl (1987a, 1987b), and Clark and Krumhansl (1990) have shown that changes in melodic line, lengthening of tone durations, contrasts in pitch range and dynamics, and tonal and harmonic stress contribute to the perceptual segmentation of music by adults. Further, infants older than seven months are known to discriminate tone sequences readily as well as tunes differing in pitch contour (up/down/same pattern of pitch changes; Chang and Trehub, 1977). They can categorize such sequences on the basis of contour (Thorpe, 1986).

Characteristics of infants' music perception

Other evidence exists suggesting parallels between the development of music processing and speech processing that appear crucial for speech segmentation. One line of experimental evidence pertains to the infant's preference for consonance over dissonance. As a dimension of perceptual pitch space, consonance/dissonance obviously plays a very important role in virtually all musical systems. Consonance/dissonance is a dimension that refers to the degree of pleasingness of two or more frequencies occurring together. The most basic example is an interval, which is the difference in pitch between two tones. Some intervals are considered dissonant, others consonant. Several studies have shown that nine–eleven-month-old infants and adults alike find it much easier to discriminate a small change to one note of a melodic pattern with a prominent perfect fifth pitch interval (i.e., a 2:3 ratio) than to discriminate a melodic pattern without this feature, whether or not the patterns conform to Western musical structure (Cohen, Thorpe and Trehub, 1987; Trainor and Trehub, 1993a, 1993b). In such experiments, participants were typically asked to listen to repeated transpositions of either a prototypical melody that was based on the major triad or a nonprototypical melody that was based on the augmented triad. In both cases, the transpositions were either to related keys (standing in a 2:3 frequency ratio) or to unrelated keys (more complex frequency ratios). For the prototypical melody, infant and adult participants readily discriminated a change to the melody in the context of related keys. For the nonprototypical melody, infants were found to perform better in the context of related keys, but adults performed worse. Thus, the global context of auditory patterns influences the processing of pattern details both for infants and adults. That such effects occurred before infants had knowledge of Western musical structure suggested that the auditory system is designed to be able to process these intervals particularly well very early in development.

Trainor (1997) tested the effects of frequency ratio simplicity on infants' and adults' processing of simultaneous pitch intervals with component sine wave tones. Both six–eight-month-old infants and adults showed superior performance at detecting a change from a perfect fifth (2:3) to either a tri-tone (one semitone smaller in pitch distance, with a ratio of 32:45) or a minor sixth (5:8) interval than at detecting the reverse discrimination (minor sixth or tri-tone to perfect fifth). Similarly, both infants and adults exhibited superior performance at detecting a change from an octave (1:2) to either a major seventh (8:15) or a minor ninth (15:32) interval than at detecting the reverse discriminations. Considered together with the previous finding of infants' superior performance on tone sequences with prominent perfect fifth intervals, the results strongly indicate that both simultaneous and sequential intervals with simple ratios are easy to process early in development.

Trainor and her colleague further examined preferences for consonant versus dissonant intervals that were matched for average interval size and transposed to a number of different pitch levels (Trainor and Heinmiller, 1998). In their study, relative looking time to consonant versus dissonant intervals was employed as the measure of infants' preference because there is much evidence that looking time is a good measure of affective response as well as attentional preference. In the first experiment, twelve six-month-old infants were found to look longer in order to listen to a set of consonant intervals than to a set of dissonant intervals. In the second experiment, sixteen six-month-olds preferred to listen to the original version of a Mozart minuet than to a version altered to contain many dissonant intervals. By the age of six months, the infants did not appear to acquire the musical-system-specific knowledge of scale structure that is involved in adult's emotional reactions to music. Nevertheless, they were similar to adults in their evaluative reactions to consonance and dissonance. In fact, considerable controversy surrounds the origins of the perception of consonance and dissonance in music. While von Helmholtz (1954) believed that judgments of consonance rested on genetically predisposed preparedness, Schönberg (1984) argued that judgments of consonance are acquired through exposure to the music of a particular culture. Actually, it is practically impossible to disentangle the degree to which the perception is based on genetic predisposition versus learning. However, apart from issues surrounding the degree to which the perception develops based on a predisposition, it should be pointed out that infants generally acquire knowledge of the system of harmonic rules by the age of six–seven months. Such knowledge is crucial in order to segment melodies into musical phrase units.

The phrase is a basic structural unit in music insofar as it presents a syntactically complete musical idea that acts in a balanced relationship with other components in a composition. Characteristically, phrases end with a pattern of notes called a cadence, which suggests movement towards a point of harmonic closure. All tones have a tendency to support or progress in temporal order towards tones of greater stability. The cadence constitutes an important stylistic means by which temporal movement towards more stable points is achieved. There are several types of cadence; they differ with respect to their point of harmonic arrival. For example, a full cadence arrives at the tonic chord (the I chord of the key and the central point in the schema of tonal relationships) and implies strong closure. A semi-cadence involves movement toward the dominant chord (the V chord of the key) and implies partial but not complete closure, since the dominant is secondary to the tonic in the tonal order. The type of cadence concluding a phrase largely determines the degree of finality associated with the phrase. Structural units normally incorporate dynamic movement through characteristic patterns of harmonic change.

The quality of a phrase as determined by the cadence has an important bearing on the overall effect of the larger structure. For this reason, normative structures are commonly found that achieve resolution through harmonic means, wherein the cadence is critical. Therefore, for instance, the musical period, a two-phrase unit, often consists of a first phrase ending in a semi-cadence and a second phrase ending in a full cadence. In the experiment of Tan, Aiello and Bever (1981), sixty adults (thirty musicians and thirty nonmusicians) heard a series of items, each item consisting of a two-phrase melody followed by a two-note probe. After each item, participants indicated whether the probe occurred in the melody. The probes were taken from three locations in the melody, with the two notes: (1) preceding the phrase boundary (the last two notes of the first phrase); (2) straddling the phrase boundary (the last note of the first phrase and the first note of the last phrase); and (3) following the phrase boundary (the first two notes of the last phrase). Participants were tested in groups. Their task was to indicate if the two-note sequence (probe) presented directly after each melody had occurred in the melody by placing a check in the appropriate space on an answer sheet. Initially, they were presented with two example items after which the experimenter stopped the tape to answer questions about the task. When scores for each participant were obtained by computing the percentage of correctly recognized items for each probe type, the probe that straddled the phrase boundary was found to be more difficult to recognize than either of the within-phrase probes. Moreover, this tendency was more robust for musicians than for nonmusicians.

The methodology employed in the above study was originally developed for research that revealed the importance of segmentation in sentence perception: as listeners process incoming sequences of words, the words become grouped together and reorganized into phrases and elementary propositional units of meaning (see Fodor, Bever and Garrett, 1974, for review). Typically, this has been experimentally demonstrated by the presentation of a brief click, which is generally reported as having occurred between clauses even when it occurred during a clause. There is a formal similarity between the distinctions of full versus semi-cadence in melodies and main versus subordinate clauses in sentences. In each case, one structure is complete and independent of the other (full cadence/main closure), whereas the other structure (semi-cadence/subordinate clause) is relatively incomplete and dependent on the former structure (full/main) for resolution. In adults, the way that knowledge of harmonic structure influences perceptual organization of melodies is analogous to the way that clause relations influence the perceptual organization of sentences. Training plays an important role in refining listeners' sensitivity to harmonic variables. By developing strong positive responsiveness to harmonic sounds, preverbal infants are facilitated in abstracting pattern regularities from temporally structured sound sequences, whether they are presented in the form of music or speech. Thus, it is thought that through the development of the perceptual ability to discriminate consonance/dissonance in music, infants become predisposed to segment fluent speech into small, discrete packets with little understanding of the reference it makes to extrinsic, real-world objects and events. The notion is also confirmed by the findings presented by Hayashi, Tamekawa and Kiritani (2001), who tested Japanese infants using the head-turn preference procedure in order to investigate whether or not infants are sensitive to prosodic cues in clausal units. In the experiment, two types of Japanese speech samples were prepared. The first sample was called the "Natural" sample, which was created by inserting one-second pauses at all clause boundary locations in natural speech. The second sample was called the "Unnatural" sample, which was created by inserting the same number of pauses as were inserted in the Natural sample but placing them between words within clauses. When the results of six- and ten-month-old infants were compared, only the ten-month-olds were found to demonstrate a significant preference for the Natural over the Unnatural sample, indicating that sensitivity to the clausal units in fluent speech sequences develops during a four-month-period after the age of six months.

Development of the recognition of words in native language

Along with the development of the ability to segment listening speech into word-sized units, infants almost simultaneously become able to recognize the particular phonetic and prosodic characteristics of their native language. To date, this has been experimentally demonstrated in three languages: English, French and Japanese. Jusczyk and colleagues reported results of a series of experiments on infants as young as seven months, which showed that the infants were able to code and recognize a few words on which they had been trained even when these words were embedded in short sentences (Hohne, Jusczyk and Redanz, 1994; Jusczyk and Aslin, 1995). In order to determine infants' capacity to code, recall and recognize words, two sets of words were presented to the infants. Both were equal in the number of syllables, but one of the two was presented to the infants during a limited period of "Training" while infants were not exposed to the other during a training period. Thereafter, infants' responses to both groups of words were tested using the head-turn preference procedure. For half of the infants, all stimulus words used were those used relatively frequently in adult conversation, whereas for the other half of the infants, the stimulus words were those used less frequently. Testing was conducted using both monosyllabic words and disyllabic words. However, no matter what type of word was used as a stimulus, very similar results were obtained: infants were likely to listen to the familiar words longer than to the unfamiliar words. It could hardly be the case that infants had already associated such disyllabic words with their meanings. Nevertheless, they were able to code and retain in memory the sound patterns of the words they had heard during the training phase.

Similar results were also obtained in a study of ten-month-old French infants that was conducted under more "naturalistic" circumstances than previous studies (Hallé and Boysson-Bardies, 1994). The hypothesis tested was that, around ten months of age, infants would have noticed in their linguistic environments words that occurred frequently in ecologically relevant situations; they would have extracted words heard in their environment in various referential situations where they could be associated to some sort of meaning. Such words would not simply be those words frequently experienced by children but, more relevantly, words that would be especially appealing to them, i.e., those meeting certain communication demands. These words would presumably be among the words they would soon attempt to produce. The study, therefore, used early words drawn from infants' production data as "familiar words" to test infants' word recognition. A second underlying hypothesis was that despite some individual variability, a "core set" of words would be shared by most infants. Thus, the authors chose those early words that had been attempted by a majority of French children. Indeed, their results revealed that this core set of frequently attempted familiar words was recognized by infants as young as ten months old.

In the Japanese language study (Tamekawa et al., 1997), no specific training was conducted on participant infants. A total of twenty-four ten-month-old infants were presented with a total of twenty-four Japanese words. They called half of the words "Familiar words" and the other half, "Rare words." Such categorization was based on officially established frequencies of public usage compiled in a nationwide survey (National Language Research Institute, Japan, 1984). The number of moras in each word was matched between the groups. Word accent was also counterbalanced. When mean listening time was compared between the two word groups, scores were found to be significantly greater when familiar words were presented than when rare words were.

More recently, Jusczyk and Hohne (1997) tested infants' long-term retention of the sound patterns of words by exposing them to recordings of three children's stories for ten days during a two-week period, when the infants were eight months old. The authors visited fifteen infants in their homes and, on each occasion, presented thirty minutes of prerecorded speech consisting of three short stories for young children to each infant, who was seated in a chair. In addition to the three stories, a list of seventy-two content words was tape-recorded by the same talker, half of which consisted of the most frequently repeated content words in the three stories. The other half of the list was made up of foil words that never occurred in the stories. Two weeks after the last of the ten home visits, each infant was brought to the laboratory in order to test his or her retention of the sound patterns of words in the stories. When tested for his or her listening preferences for lists of words that either occurred frequently or did not occur in the stories, the infants were found to listen significantly longer to the lists of story words. A possible explanation for these results is that the infants' prior experiences with the story and foil word lists might be different; that is, perhaps the story words were simply more intrinsically interesting than the foil words. Therefore, to check this possibility, an additional group of fifteen nine-month-old infants was tested according to the same procedure with the same materials but with no previous exposure to the stories. Results of the testing revealed no display of specific preference for the lists of story words over those of the foil words, though they may have been overridden by the memory of the talker's voice because only two talkers were used.

Interestingly, findings from the above-mentioned series of experiments suggest that infants are able to code word forms in a more abstract format than a purely acoustic format; for instance, despite various acoustic variations in the same phone generated by the speaker's voice or speech context, infants can recognize the phone heard during training in a later test. On the other hand, infants could no longer recognize trained words when just one segment was phonetically changed just as Jusczyk and Aslin (1995) reported that infants trained on "cup" and "dog" showed no recognition for "tup" and "bawg" presented in the test phase. The coding format that the infants used probably depended upon a detailed phonetic description of the word forms on which they had been trained, not upon an acoustic description. With respect to how infants segment speech into words, this evidence supports the proposal that they first learn to recognize some words by hearing them spoken in isolation and then match their representations of these words to subsequent speech input (Pinker, 1984). In contrast to the common notion of prosodic bootstrapping that language learners use supra-segmental cues to locate boundaries in the speech stream, this is basically a top-down or analytic approach to segmentation. How can we reconcile the two notions with one another?

Development of phonemic discrimination

As already argued, infants as young as eight months can voluntarily produce preverbal vocalizations that vary in prosody according to different communicative functions. With regard to segmental features of their vocalizations, they become able to produce canonical babbling only later. The period of the onset of canonical babbling coincides with the period when infants become able to segment words from fluent speech. Producing a limited, sequentially organized phonemic segment entails extracting words from some portion of the speech stream, which in turn is segmented according to prosodic and more global supra-segmental characteristics. Extracting words enables infants to code them, which in turn enables them to recognize them as familiar words. This notion appears to be confirmed by the results of a series of experiments reported by Myers et al. (1996), who examined infants' sensitivity to word units in fluent speech by inserting one-second pauses either at boundaries between successive words (coincident versions) or between syllables within words (noncoincident versions). Eleven-month-old infants were found to listen preferentially to the coincident versions whereas younger infants were not. Even eleven-month-olds showed no preference for coincident versions when they were low-pass filtered, which suggests that they rely on more than prosodic cues. On the other hand, new stimulus materials introduced in a subsequent experiment indicated that responses by eleven-month-olds did not depend solely on prior familiarity with the stimuli. This finding is intriguing because eleven-month-old infants are sensitive to word boundaries in the speech stream, but their sensitivity depends on more than just prosodic information or prior knowledge of the words. The final test included in the study revealed that two groups of eleven-month-olds were as sensitive to boundaries for Strong/Weak words as for Weak/Strong words, suggesting the possibility that the infants came to rely on multiple sources of information in the signal in order to help locate word boundaries.

This possibility was explored in more detail by Hallé and Boysson-Bardies (1996) on eleven-month-old infants learning French. In their first experiment, bisyllabic French words were used as stimuli. Two groups of words were prepared, one made up of familiar words and the other of rare words. However, each of the familiar words was altered by a small change in the word-initial consonant. Voiced consonants were changed into their unvoiced counterparts, and vice versa. For example, /gato/ became /kato/, /pupe/ became /bupe/, and so on. The words were unknown to the eleven-month-old infants. When looking time was compared between the two groups using the head-turn preference procedure, the average score was significantly greater when altered familiar words were presented than when rare words were presented. Infants of this age should have no difficulty in perceiving a voicing contrast as long as it is phonemic in the language they learn. Otherwise, they are insensitive to the difference between altered and unaltered familiar words and deaf to certain phonemic changes. Therefore, in the next experiment, the infants were tested on their preference for unaltered over altered familiar words. Results revealed that the average looking time did not differ significantly between the two stimulus conditions and, therefore, the familiarity explanation is more plausible than the phonemic contrast explanation. In fact, looking time did not differ significantly either when the familiar words were presented with their first consonant suppressed or when the rare words were presented after the suppression.

However, when looking time for familiar words with their first consonant suppressed was compared to looking time for unaltered familiar words, scores did not differ significantly. Apparently, infants tolerated such a gross deformation as the suppression of an initial consonant, although they did not recognize familiar words without an initial consonant when compared to rare words. Presumably, the process of recognizing words let infants overlook, or perhaps made them insensitive to, otherwise salient phonotactic changes. Finally, Hallé and Boysson-Bardies altered familiar words rather severely and again tested infants' preferences for altered familiar words over rare words. The experimental alteration concerned the manner of articulation of the word-initial or word-medial consonant. Plosives were exchanged with fricatives and liquids and glides were exchanged with their nasal counterparts. When mean looking time was compared between the two stimulus conditions, the infants were found to look at the familiar words altered in their word-initial consonant longer than at the rare words. On the other hand, they did not look at the familiar words altered in their word-medial consonant longer than at the rare words. Thus, in recognizing a word, the infants loosely specified the word-initial consonant but not the word-medial consonant, to the extent that they tolerated variations in voicedness and in the manner of articulation.

This was confirmed by my study on the memory of eleven-month-old Japanese infants for tape-recorded words (Masataka, 2002a). Essentially, in my study I employed the same methodology that was developed by Jusczyk and Hohne (1997). However, in my study, thirty infants were divided into two groups at the beginning of the experiment. Each of the fifteen infants in the first group was exposed to recordings of three children's stories presented in adult-directed speech for ten days during a two-week period; each of the 15 infants in the second group was exposed to the same stories presented in child-directed speech over the same period. The words tested were all trisyllabic. When I tested the retention of words that had occurred in the stories, using the head-turn procedure, both groups of infants had significantly longer mean listening times for the lists of story words than for the lists with the foils. However, mean listening times to the list of story words were significantly longer for the group of infants exposed to the stories presented in infant-directed speech than for the group of infants exposed to the stories presented in adult-directed speech. Subsequently, on another two groups of eleven-month-old infants, I examined the effects of supra-segmental parameters on the discrimination of a pair of rare Japanese trisyllabic words that differed from one another only in terms of a single consonant (target consonant) (for example /gaburu/ versus /kaburu/). The target consonant was located either in the first or the second syllable. Infants in one of the groups were required to discriminate the two syllable sequences when supra-segmental characteristics typical of infant-directed speech emphasized the syllable in which the target consonant occurred, whereas those in the other groups were required to discriminate the same stimuli presented in adult-directed speech. The results showed that infants failed to demonstrate discrimination when adult-directed supra-segmentals were used. However, when the stimuli were presented in infant-directed speech, the infants could easily discriminate roughly 40 percent of the pairs of words when the target consonant was word-initial; in most of these pairs, targets were voiced versus unvoiced consonants. The pattern of results suggests that the exaggerated supra-segmentals of infant-directed speech enhance long-term retention of the words occurring in the speech and that they facilitate discrimination by focusing the infant's attention on a specific consonant contrast on a distinctive syllable within polysyllabic sequences.

Two different paths to the first words

It has been reported that infants between one and four months of age have not demonstrated discrimination of three-syllable sequences that differ by one speech sound. Using the high-amplitude sucking technique, Trehub (1974) presented naturally spoken versions of [atapa] and [adapa]. She did not find significant recovery of the sucking response with these stimuli. In contrast to these results, Goodsitt et al. (1984) found that seven-month-old infants could discriminate a variety of three-syllable sequences. Discrimination performance was significantly better with more redundant segmental contexts such as [kobako] versus [koduko] than with less redundant contexts such as [kobati] versus [koduti]. Fernald and Kuhl (1982) first demonstrated the role played by supra-segmental features in phonemic discrimination. They found that seven-month-old infants could discriminate five-syllable sequences (galasalaga versus galatalaga) in both of the intonation conditions tested, i.e., infant-directed and adult-directed speech; however, preliminary observation suggested that performance was slightly better in the infant-directed condition.

Fernald and Kuhl's preliminary work influenced me in designing my experiment described above (Masataka, 2002a). My hypothesis was that supra-segmental parameters enhance discrimination performance but the degree to which they affect performance may depend on characteristics of the selected stimuli. Two characteristics were addressed. For example, it has been pointed out that the context of the phonemic contrast might influence the effectiveness of supra-segmental highlighting (Karzon, 1985). Several context variables may be considered, including magnitude of phonemic contrast, number of syllables surrounding the syllable of contrast, phonemes within those syllables, and location of the syllable of contrast within a sequence. Among them, position within a sequence was chosen for the analysis because this variable has been considered important in three-syllable sequences, such as those tested in a series of phonemic discrimination studies. Presumably, a contrast placed in the initial position of the sequence was assumed to benefit from "primacy" effects as compared with the same contrast placed in other positions. Phoneme class is another stimulus variable assumed to be very important in determining the effectiveness of supra-segmental highlighting. Therefore, experimental stimuli were prepared so as to be able to examine the possibility that contrasts between members of other phoneme classes would be differentially affected by the supra-segmental cues used. Indeed, results revealed that a distinction between voiced versus unvoiced consonants was most amenable to enhancements by the exaggeration of supra-segmental features in eleven-month-old infants and that the distinction was possible when the "target" syllable was located in the initial position of the sequence. It has often been said that infant-directed speech acts as a vehicle for the infant's language learning by enhancing segmentation of the speech stream, holistically enhancing the infant's attention to the prosodic property of the utterance. In addition to this prosodic function, the supra-segmental aspect of infant-directed speech, by interacting with the segmental aspect under specific circumstances, also enhances segmentation of the speech stream. The supra-segmental aspect affects segmentation analytically, facilitating phonemic discrimination by focusing the infant's attention on the distinctive syllable of polysyllabic sequences.

The effectiveness of infant-directed speech analytically, for segmentation, largely depends on the context in which the speech occurs. It should show much more individual variability than the effectiveness of the infant-directed speech in a holistic approach (Masataka, 2002b). Further, such individual variability seems to be strongly associated with individual variability in the acquisition of phonology and words in infants who are beginning to produce meaningful speech. Vihman (1993) typographically classified the supra-segmental variability in infant-directed speech into two types: (1) a loose gestalt pattern characterized by boldness, richness of phonological elements, variability of pronunciation, and lack of harmony, and (2) a more analytical pattern, cautious, more limited in phonological elements, and characterized by consistency in pronunciation and widespread harmony.

In terms of different patterns in early word use by children, Nelson (1973) identified two distinctive styles in early language development. These were the referential style and the expressive style. According to her classification, children who adopted the referential style had a larger proportion of object names in their first fifty words than did children who adopted an expressive style. Children who adopted an expressive style had a larger proportion of action words and people's names than did children who adopted a referential style. The style differences mentioned by Vihman and Miller (1988) are, of course, reminiscent of this distinction by Nelson.

Generally, children's production of their earliest words is considered to be closely related to the speech that they hear every day. Harris et al. (1988) found a very close relationship between children's initial use of words and the way that their mothers most frequently used them. For example, one of the children they studied first used "mummy" only when he was holding out a toy for his mother to take. Analysis of his mother's speech revealed that her most frequent use of "mummy" when speaking to the child was when she held out her hand to take a toy from him and asked "Is that for mummy?" Referential children acquire a large number of object names due to their abundant experience of looking at objects that are singled out and of hearing an accompanying verbal label by caregivers. To be able to associate the objects seen with the label heard, they argued that establishing joint attention between the caregiver and the child and developing the child's understanding of reference are crucial.

Joint visual attention is common in the first year of life and caregivers and infants tend to look at the same objects. Butterworth and Grover (1989) and Butterworth and Jarrett (1991) have shown that infants as young as six months are able to follow their mother's line of regard successfully providing that the object of attention is in front of the infant and that the object is the first one the infant encounters when turning to look. Some time later, infants become capable of locating a target even when it is not the first object encountered in turning to look, although they are still unable to locate a target that is behind them. The developmental milestone of establishing joint reference occurs coincidentally with the infant's developing an understanding of pointing; that is, the infant comes to look in the appropriate direction when someone else points (Leung and Rheingold, 1981; Schaffer, 1984). Indeed, pointing has been regarded as crucial for the development of referential communication because this gesture provides an important nonverbal procedure for picking out an object in the environment for the benefit of both another person and oneself.

Bates et al. (1979) argued that infant proffering of objects and communicative pointing (pointing followed by checking) are associated with the quality of subsequent language development. How this infant proffering and communicative pointing is actually achieved was illustrated by Masur (1982) and Baldwin and Markman (1989). They argued that this development is initially elicited by very specific adult responses to infant pointing. When they closely analyzed mothers' responses to their infants' first pointing gestures, they found that the mothers' responses involved labeling objects at which the infants pointed. Furthermore, infants as young as ten months of age spent significantly longer looking at novel objects when they were pointed at than when they were merely presented without pointing. The amount of time an infant spent looking was greatest when an object was pointed to and verbally labeled. Under such circumstances, labeling was most frequently done in the form of infant-directed speech in which the supra-segmental aspect was exaggerated. Such speech is supposed to facilitate infants in learning particular words (i.e., referential words) in the speech stream, as a form of top-down approach to segmenting the speech stream.

Overall, the caregivers' speech style is predictive of the nature of the words an infant acquires soon afterwards. The infant's experience with caregiver labeling of and pointing to objects is predictive of the infant's subsequent development of an understanding of reference. However, caregiver pointing is predictive of infant pointing in itself, which, in turn, is predictive of the development of referential communication between the infant and the caregiver. Obviously these arguments are circular. Relationships among the variables remain correlational, however, so in order to disentangle cause and effect, Masataka (2003) longitudinally investigated the development of the pointing gesture and compared it to the subsequent development of vocabulary.

While the average onset of the pointing gesture is at twelve months of age (327 days for girls, 350 days for boys), individual differences are known to be considerable. Although pointing develops as a referential gesture in more than 80 percent of the world, it is not performed at all in some cultures (Butterworth and Castillo, 1976). Pointing is regarded as uniquely human because it has been claimed that no other animal species, including chimpanzees, is capable of performing this indicative gesture. Thus, it is assumed that humans are somehow predisposed to develop the pointing gesture; however, the predisposition needs some experience to manifest itself as an indicative behavior. In other words, the development of pointing in each infant should be profoundly related to how the infant is provided with the necessary experience. This issue had not been investigated in detail and appeared to be closely related to issues surrounding the pattern in which infants begin to produce meaningful speech.

Development of pointing as a referential gesture

With respect to the developmental origin of the pointing gesture, Leung and Rheingold (1981) proposed that it differentiates from the movement of reaching and grasping. They argued that pointing is the movement that replaces reaching and grasping in order to economize the movement as a reference gesture. Bruner (1983), however, proposed that the gesture does not appear as an extension or modification of reaching, but rather appears, at least partly, as a primitive marking system for singling out the noteworthy. Vygotsky (1961) saw pointing as originating in the failed reaching activities of the infant. Through the intervention of adults around the infant, this failure occasionally results in successful access to the object that the infant originally attempted to reach. Consequently, it is assumed that the infant is thereby notified of the different communicative function of the failed reaching. Although these researchers presented conflicting arguments, all presupposed that cognitive developments around the one-year period induced the child to acquire the pointing. This was a purely cognitive interpretation based on traditional reports of infants around the onset of the gesture. However, little is known about the early developmental processes that underlie the subsequent emergence of the gesture.

In this regard, Masataka (1995) pointed out the strong temporal connection between the occurrence of index-finger extension and the production of speech-like vocalizations in three-month-old infants. As already discussed in chapter 2, due to the tendency of the caregiver to contingently respond to these infant vocalizations, the manual activity itself is inadvertently conditioned. Moreover, insofar as adults use index-finger pointing as a referential gesture, index-finger extension performed by the infant provides adults with a strong affordance for their own impression of the infant as socially favorable and communicatively intentional; this, in turn, selectively reinforces this infant activity.

Consequently, when the manual activities of eight first-born Japanese infants were longitudinally observed between the ages of three and sixteen months, the mean number of index-finger extension occurrences was found to differ significantly as a function of the infants' ages (Masataka, 2002a). As shown in fig. 8.1, the infants were more likely to show the behavior with increasing age and the behavior was observed with the highest frequency when they were eleven–twelve months old. Interestingly, this period coincided precisely with the onset of pointing (index-finger pointing) in these same infants. Once index-finger pointing emerged, the frequencies of index-finger pointing increased dramatically whereas index-finger extension decreased dramatically. On the other hand, the number of reaching occurrences did not differ significantly as a function of the infants' ages. This might be evidence against the notion that pointing is an abbreviated form of reaching: if the explanation is plausible, the patterns of occurrences of the two activities should developmentally change in

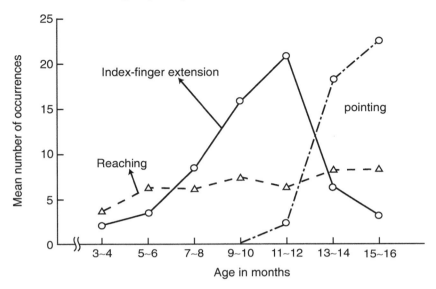

Figure 8.1   Mean number (per 30 min) of infants' manual activities as a function of their ages (cited from Masataka (2003)).

relation to one another. Rather, the results indicate that we should regard the onset of index-finger pointing as an extension of learning to produce index-finger extension.

The view that index-finger pointing develops from failed reaching is based on the assumption that such motor activity develops as an indicative gesture first, then is replaced by pointing (Lock, 1980). It is thought that young infants are unable to perceive whether or not an object is positioned at a distance that makes contact possible. As a result, failed reaching occurs relatively frequently. Nevertheless, adults around them understand the infant's intent rather appropriately and, finally, the infants become aware of the "true" communicative significance of their failure. However, this view has been based on pure speculation thus far; systematic and quantitative investigations are necessary to determine whether or not the indicative gesture ontogenetically supersedes failed reaching and whether or not it is functionally equivalent to later pointing.

In this vein, Masataka (2002a) conducted an experiment in which a variety of objects were presented to eight-month-old infants, and their responses were observed. Ten first-born male infants and their mothers participated in the experiment. Each infant was tested while seated in an infant chair. An experimenter, who was blind to the purpose of the experiment, presented one of the following three types of toys: a familiar toy bear, an unfamiliar toy automobile with one randomly blinking colored light, or an unfamiliar toy automobile with three blinking colored lights. The latter two toys were different from one another only in the number of lights blinking. The toy automobile with three lights is expected to elicit more intense interest in the infant than that with a single light.

Manual action related to exploration and self-regulation of attention is expected to be produced by the infant most frequently in response to the unfamiliar toys, especially to the automobile with three lights, and least often in response to the familiar toy. Furthermore, attempts to bring the object closer to the infant are expected to occur most often in response to the familiar toy and least often in response to the automobile with three lights, which is unfamiliar and in some sense more intimidating.

Each of the three toys was presented to each infant in two different conditions. In one condition, it was presented within reach (approximately 15cm away from the infant), and in the other condition it was presented beyond reach (approximately 60cm away from the infant). On the basis of video-recording, the infants' behaviors were categorized into the following three types: (1) reaching, (2) failed reaching/ indicative gesture and (3) index-finger extension.

A movement was classified as a "reaching" when the infant reaches out to the stimulus, and the infant's hand touches it. A movement was classified as a "failed reaching/indicative gesture" when the arm was extended towards the stimulus with an open hand, without reaching it. This movement was often accompanied by an alternating look between the stimulus and the mother. An index-finger extension is characterized by extension of the index finger and nonextension of the arm. A movement is assigned to this category, regardless of whether the finger is directed toward the stimulus or not.

The results are shown in fig. 8.2. Let us consider the within-reach condition first. Not surprisingly, reaching was observed frequently, and failed reaching/indicative gesture was not observed. The number of occurrences of reaching was greatest when the presented toy was familiar, and was smallest when it was the unfamiliar toy with three blinking lights. The number of occurrences of index-finger extension, in contrast, showed the opposite tendency. It was smallest when the presented toy was familiar, and was greatest when it was the unfamiliar one with three blinking lights.

Let us now turn to the beyond-reach condition. In this case, failed reaching/indicative gesture was observed fairly abundantly. Like reaching in the within-reach condition, it occurred most often when the presented toy was familiar and least frequently when the toy was the unfamiliar one with three blinking lights. Index-finger extension was also observed relatively often, but for different types of stimuli than failed reaching/indicative gesture. Index-finger extension again occurred most frequently when the presented object was the toy with three blinking lights and least often when it was a familiar one.

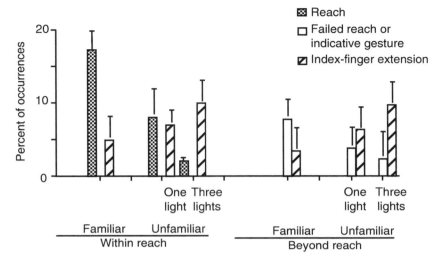

Figure 8.2   Percentage of occurrences of infants' manual activities when familiar and unfamiliar toys were presented, within reach and beyond reach (cited from Masataka (2003)).

Index-finger extension occurred more often when the presented object calls for exploration more intensely. The pattern of frequency was reversed for the manual acts that are aimed at bringing the object to the infant, namely reaching and failed reach/indicative gesture. They occurred more often for the objects that are more familiar and less intimidating. This indicates that index-finger extension is related to exploration and self-regulation of attention, and not to the infant's desire to bring the object to him-/herself. In other words, index-finger pointing emerges from a manual act related to exploration and self-regulation of attention. When infants develop the desire to share the exploration and attention intersubjectively, index-finger extension develops into index-finger pointing. However, this view might lead one to question why, if index-finger extension was originally exploratory behavior, the infants showed the activity in response to the out of reach object despite their being able to precisely perceive the distance separating themselves from the object.

Clues to answering this question lie in further responses by the mother to her infant's manual activity, which also relate to questions about why the pointing gesture occurs with index-finger extension in most cultures. Coding of the mother's behavior following the infant's manual action revealed that when the infant performed an indicative gesture, the act of holding the toy accounted for 74 percent of all of the mothers' responses. Mothers were observed to hand the toy to their infants in 32 percent of their responses. Pointing accounted for only 8 percent of all mothers' responses. On the other hand, when index-finger extension was performed, the act of holding the toy accounted only for 23 percent of all their responses. On the other hand, pointing accounted for 55 percent of all their responses. Moreover, in 74 percent of all instances in which mothers pointed, they simultaneously responded verbally to their infant's manual action by labeling the object. Such behavior was never observed when the infants performed indicative gestures. Concerning the indicative gesture, interpretations of the functions of this manual action were consistent between the researcher and the mothers, i.e., request-attention or request-object. With respect to index-finger extension, however, mothers and the researcher interpreted its communicative function differently, with mothers regarding it as referential. This probably happened because the mothers themselves extended their index-fingers as a referential gesture. Possibly, infants' index-finger extensions would be shaped into the referential gesture. The way that adults interact with infants depends on how members of the culture in which the adults live view child development; the development of pointing from index-finger extension is no exception. This was confirmed through observation of the subsequent development of the pointing gesture in the ten infants.

The relationship between the development of pointing and the development of the early lexicon in infants

When the above experiment was completed, the mothers of each of the ten infants were asked to participate with their infants in a study of "gestural development" and "language development." All the mothers were full-time housewives between the ages of twenty-three and thirty. They were asked to record the context in which their infants produced the adult-like pointing gesture, whenever they recognized it. They were also asked to identify all words or phrases their infants used as well as all adult-like pointing gestures their infants produced. Mothers were presented with diary forms and asked to write down every novel word or phrase that their infants said together with as much detail as possible about the context in which the utterance occurred. This information was used in order to conduct further analyses on the relationship between the development of pointing and the development of the early lexicon. The researcher visited each mother at her home every two weeks to "go over" the diaries. Data continued to be collected until each child reached one year of age.

All words and phrases noted were classified according to the coding schema constructed by Lieven et al. (1992). The category system consisted of: (1) single-word utterances (one word as defined by the adult language) and (2) multiword utterances (more than one word). The single-word utterances were further divided into five subcategories: common nouns, onomatopoeic, proper nouns, interactive words (words with no referential value whose meaning is derived from the interactive situation in which they occur, such as greeting), and other words. The multiword utterances were divided into three subcategories: frozen phrases (utterances that contained two or more words which had not occurred alone previously in the child's vocabulary); constructed phrases (utterances that contained two or more words, each of which had occurred alone previously in the child's vocabulary); and intermediate phrases (utterances that had characteristics between frozen and constructed phrases).

The data revealed relatively large individuality in the development of pointing. While the average age of onset of pointing was 334 days, individual differences spanned a seventy-eight-day period. Thus, we first analyzed how these individual differences related to early interactions between each infant and its mother. It is possible that the more often an infant produced index-finger extension at the age of eight months, the earlier the pointing gesture developed in that infant. For the ten infants in the study, we found no significant relationship when we compared the frequency of the infants' index-finger extension recorded in response to their mothers' presentations of three types of toys with the infants' age in days at the onset of pointing. However, the likelihood of a mother responding to her infant's index-finger extension with a pointing gesture correlated highly with individual differences in the onset of pointing in the infants: the more often the mother responded with pointing, the earlier pointing developed in her infant. The likelihood of a mother's responding to her infant's index-finger extension with behaviors other than pointing did not significantly correlate with the onset of pointing in her infant.

Next, we analyzed the relationship between the rate of the development of pointing and the rate of the development of language. With respect to the tempo of the development of early vocabulary, individual differences were also distinctive. While the mean age at which the infants reached fifty words was 569 days on average, individual differences spanned a 112-day period. This finding is comparable to previous reports (Lieven et al., 1992; Nelson, 1981). However, in contrast to English-learning children, Japanese-learning children had, overall, significantly smaller noun vocabularies (21 percent on average). Instead, in Japanese children, the proportion of unanalyzed phrases was larger (14 percent on average). When this form of individual difference was compared with individual differences in the onset of pointing, no significant correlation was found, and the overall rate of the acquisition of the first fifty words or phrases was independent of whether the development of pointing was early or late. Nevertheless, the quality of the early lexicon as categorized by the coding system was significantly related to the onset of pointing. When the proportion of each of the seven categories in the lexical system was compared with the age in days when pointing first occurred in each infant, two of the categories correlated with the onset of pointing, common nouns and frozen phrases. As shown in fig. 8.3, the proportion of common nouns was positively correlated with the

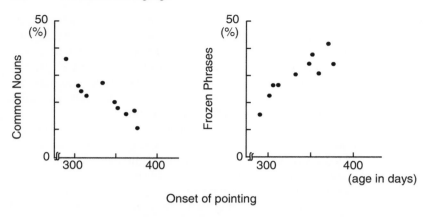

Figure 8.3   Relation between the onset of pointing and the proportion of common nouns and frozen phrases in the first 50 words in 10 children.

onset of pointing whereas the proportion of frozen phrases was negatively correlated with its onset. The earlier that pointing developed in an infant, the more likely the infant was to produce common nouns and the less likely it was to produce frozen phrases.

We analyzed the maternal speech to ten eight-month-old infants that had been recorded in the experiment in which three types of toys were presented; as a basis for evaluating its acoustic qualities comparatively, each of the ten mothers was asked to talk with one of her adult friends over a telephone. Results of the analysis confirmed that compared to the utterances they directed to their adult friends, mothers used exaggerated prosodic features, higher pitch, wider pitch excursion, and lengthened vowels in the utterances they directed to their infants. No doubt, verbally labeling objects by such utterances would enhance or highlight particular phonemes included in the objects' names. Infant-directed speech provides the infant with this linguistic benefit, which facilitates the acquisition of the lexicon in a referential style.

Although Nelson's original dichotomy of referential versus expressive style in early vocabulary acquisition has generated a great deal of interesting research, several major problems have been raised. In particular, confusion has been pointed out in the literature as to whether the categories are functionally or formally defined. The confusion exists in part because the people recording infants' lexical development are inevitably the infants' own caregivers, who have difficulty documenting in detail the context in which a new word is produced. Moreover, the same vocabulary item can often be used in more than a single context. Therefore, in order to avoid confusion, classification of infants' early lexicon was undertaken in the present analysis based on nonfunctional, formal categories; stylistic variation between infants in the early stages of language acquisition was still evident.

As a variable predictive of the quality of the lexicon that a child subsequently acquires, the degree to which the caregiver responds to the child's index-finger extension at the age of eight months was found to be useful. Culture shapes input and affects the style of infants' early lexical development. As potential determinants of the content of children's early vocabularies, the nonlinguistic cognitive understandings that children bring to bear on word learning tasks have been mentioned. In explaining the overall universal noun bias in children's vocabularies, for instance, one traditional theory has argued that children acquire nouns before other parts of speech because the meanings of nouns are easier for them to encode than the meanings of other words. Nouns refer to entities or things and young children can have an understanding of things based on their perception of the physical world. Pointing no doubt plays an important role in enhancing this sort of cognitive understanding. However, it is difficult to account fully for the variation in the style of early language development described above using this variable alone. Nonlinguistic cognition is a factor in lexical development but it is only one of several factors. Since cross-cultural and cross-linguistic evidence against the universality of the noun bias has been presented, the nature of the target language has been mentioned as one additional factor underlying variability in early language development. For example, in Asian languages (see Hayashi et al., 2001), where there does not seem to be a noun bias in children's early vocabularies, a verb is often the final word in a sentence; it is possible that this position is particularly salient to children.

Fernald and Morikawa (1993) explored this possibility by investigating speech directed to the six-, twelve-, and nineteen-month-old children by their American and Japanese mothers. This maternal speech shared common characteristics in both cultures, such as linguistic simplification and frequent repetition, and the mothers made similar adjustments in their speech to infants of different ages. However, American mothers labeled objects more often and consistently than did Japanese mothers, whereas Japanese mothers used objects to engage infants in social routines more often than did American mothers. The researchers concluded that the greater emphasis on object nouns in American mothers' speech is only partially attributable to structural differences between Japanese and English. In addition, cultural differences in interaction style and beliefs about child rearing strongly influence the structure and content of speech to infants.

As an intervening variable between the actual interaction the caregiver directs to the infant and the prevailing culture as a factor affecting the linguistic input the caregiver prepares for the infant, the caregiver's impression of the infant may be important. As noted in chapter 3, cultural differences influence perceptions of the infant as a communicative partner. Further, the degree to which infant behavior affects adult perceptions is modulated by the adult's own characteristics as well as the adult's willingness to overgeneralize various characteristics of his/her own behavior to the infant's behavior. In those cultures where index-finger pointing is prevalent as a referential gesture, preverbal infants' production of index-finger extension could generate strong affordances for adults' impressions of the infants, which could lead infants in turn to show the early stages of language acquisition that have been characterized as "referential" by Nelson (1981) or "analytic" by Peters (1983). Conversely, it is not very difficult to predict that if the same infant index-finger extension were observed by people living in cultures where index-finger pointing is regarded as taboo, the index-finger extension would generate extremely weak affordances for adults' impressions. In a culture, the style of children's language acquisition could be "expressive" or "holistic." The infant-directed speech of caregivers living in a given culture should play an affective role in an efficient manner. Of course its linguistic benefit is also exerted but probably only holistically, in suggesting how to segment the speech and by using prosodic properties only to locate the boundaries of the speech stream. Moreover, such variability does not necessarily occur only between cultures; it can also occur within cultures in terms of variability in parental beliefs and values about child rearing as well as individual characteristics of linguistic performance.

Clearly, the distinctions of holistic versus analytic, or expressive versus referential, are always relative to one another. Each child acquires language somehow referentially or analytically and, simultaneously, somehow expressively or holistically. This process can again be depicted as a rolling ball that progresses downhill. The landscape for the ball is provided by some characteristics of early infant behaviors and adults' response to them. From individual to individual, the ball might occasionally pass through different junctions. However, as infants develop to adjust their linguistic capabilities closer to adult speech, the qualities of infants' capabilities move closer to one another. The path to language acquisition is variable and yet no matter which route is taken, it is equifinal.

9   Summary and conclusion

The relationship between cognitive and motor aspects of language development

In this book, I have examined how preverbal infants acquire languages during their first year of life, focusing primarily on communication between them and their caregivers. In the domain of communication, the advent of an interest in objects places the infant, cognitively, at the entry to referential communication. After the age of five months, infants and caregivers as their communication partners negotiate the process of importing objects and events into the interpersonal sphere. This is regarded as an important step in infants' language acquisition because by the end of their first year, they are able to share in object-focused communications and elaborate upon common interests in their surroundings. Infants and their caregivers can request objects from one another and they can direct one another's attention to interesting events. Further, infants at this age begin to comment on these events, conveying messages about details and their affective significance. Thus, as long as the subject of the communication remains physically present, infants near the end of the first year and their social partners are able to enter into episodes of joint object involvement that serve a range of fundamental communicative functions.

The developmental pathway to such communication is full of many challenges. Some challenges arise because infants must master new communicative acts that pertain primarily to objects rather than to communication itself. For example, as described in chapter 8, infants must come to look where an extended index-finger points rather than at the digit itself. An additional challenge is posed by the inherent attentional complexity of joint object involvement. In order to comprehend the meaning of caregivers' acts of pointing appropriately, infants must coordinate their attention to both caregivers and objects and learn the communicative functions of referring or requesting. Otherwise, a singular focus would result in either interpersonal engagement (as infants attend to caregivers) or in severing the communicative channel (as infants attend to objects restrictively).

Only with the development of this ability do infants become able to understand the meaning of referential messages such as "Look at this" and requests such as "Give me that." The observational and experimental findings presented in this book illustrate that by the end of their first year, infants develop the ability to understand and produce acts that allow them to communicate with caregivers about objects. As objects are drawn into communicative episodes, infants and their caregivers use earlier-developing communicative acts including speech-like vocalizations such as cooing and babbling. In addition, they begin to use gestures composed of manual movements and gaze patterns as well as speech-like vocalizations, to communicative intentions such as requests for and reference to objects.

Moreover, as infants master this rudimentary from of object-focused communication, they also acquire the motor skills necessary to produce language. Since the utterance of even a simple one-syllable word requires the coordination in time and space of numerous muscles and body parts, the acquisition of language can be regarded as a preeminent achievement of coordination and control of articulators as well as an achievement of human cognition. Nonetheless, until the present, little attention has been focused on the motor aspects of early language development. In this book, I reviewed the transitional process from the preverbal to the acquisition stages of language development with respect to its motoric aspects, on the assumption that linguistic motor skills develop according to the same general priciples as other motor skills. In order to address how human linguistic ability develops as a complex process over time, a dynamic systems perspective was used to explain various observations and experimental results.

A possible explanation for the conventional "missing link" in the early cognitive development underlying language acquisition

Successful introduction to object-focused communication, in turn, results in filling the "missing link" that has been identified in previous explanations of how cognitive development leads towards the acquisition of language. A puzzling pattern that has been identified across various studies on the emergence of object-focused communication is a breach in the developmental time line. According to models of the early development of communication, by five months of age infants share intricately textured episodes of interpersonal engagement with their caregivers. During this period, both partners actively contribute to these episodes and appear to find them amusing. Nevertheless, these episodes suddenly wane. Infants who just weeks before had enjoyed face-to-face conversation, begin to turn their attention away from their caregivers and towards objects. Several researchers have reported such observations. Among them was Piaget (1952), who was struck by the suddenness with which infants turned towards objects.

However, it has also been shown that infants exhibit interest in objects well before they can intentionally draw them into communicative episodes. This delay may be explained by the actions of caregivers, who embed object-absorbed infant episodes within periods of supposed joint engagement. However, several months are needed for infants to master the new triadic arrangement of infant–partner–object communication. This long delay has puzzled researchers and several theories have been proposed to explain the delay.

Piaget inspired theoretical development in this area. Traditional Piagetians have tended to seek an overarching new structure of action (e.g., the coordination of secondary circular reactions) that might enhance new accomplishments in all cognitive domains (Demetriu, 1988). Others have searched for local homologies (Bates et al., 1979), constellations of specific abilities that undergo change simultaneously, probably because they are dependent upon the development of a common structure. Scientists who adopted this second approach have noted some particular relationships between intentional communication and certain aspects of cognition, specifically, the temporal parallel between the emergence of intentional object-focused communication and changes in an infant's appreciation of causality. Harding and Golinkoff (1979) found that infants who attempted to communicate intentionally with their mothers using vocalizations during a frustrating encounter with an inoperative toy were more likely to pass two Piagetian tasks designed to probe their understanding of the idea that effects (e.g., the sudden movement of their chair) have causes (e.g., an examiner who shifted the chair) than infants who did not call upon their mothers for help. Bates et al. (1979) also found correlated changes in gestural communication between nine and thirteen months of age and in intentional tool use (as well as changes in imitation), but not in other cognitive domains such as object permanence and spatial relations. Thus, on the basis of this pattern of findings, Bates et al. proposed that as infants achieve an appreciation of means–ends relations, they might come to realize that they can act both to influence people and to manipulate objects in pursuit of specific outcomes.

As satisfying as these demonstrations of local homologies are, they account for the delay described above on only one level. Their argument concerns what "software" the child has in the form of cognitive structures. But, as Bates and colleagues explained, they make "no claims whatsoever about the role of environment versus genetic factors in bringing about the set of relationships observed" (1979, p. 131). In response, Trevarthen (1988) proposed a theory of innate cognition in which he argued that a genetic factor underlies the emergence of intentional object-focused communication. Trevarthen did not disagree with the neo-Piagetian perspective on regularities in development between, for example, causal understanding and intentional communication. However, he was concerned not to blur the distinction between causal knowledge about inanimate objects and communicative knowledge about the human world. In his view, this crucial distinction is built into the structure of the human brain, which may contain a "real system" specific to communication (Trevarthen and Hubley, 1978, p. 213).

Moreover, Trevarthen suggested that maturation in this system directly results in the emergence of new levels of communicative competence, at predictable times. The first transformation-producing maturational event takes place at about six–eight weeks of age and a second takes place at about nine–ten months of age. The second shift is thought to expand the infant's intersubjectivity, pushing him or her to become interested in sharing objects as well as in interpersonal engagement. Obviously, this theory was profoundly influenced by ethology. Like other ethologists studying humans, Trevarthen regarded crosscultural research as crucial to evaluating the claim that maturation is primarily responsible for the onset of each new stage of communicative action during early infancy. Unfortunately, few cross-cultural studies were available at the time Trevarthen published his theory of innate cognition. In his own cross-cultural study, Trevarthen (1988) found that Yoruba infants of Lagos proceeded eagerly along the same developmental path as infants he had observed previously in Edinburgh, even though their mothers were strikingly different communicative partners when they played with their infants and objects. Later, Bakeman et al. (1990), based on their systematic observations of Kung San caregiver–infant interactions, reached the similar conclusion that the developmental time course of this communicative pattern is not necessarily different for infants raised in Western versus nonWestern cultures.

However, this book demonstrated that the developmental communication process cannot be determined in isolation. Children, particularly during early infancy, show great variability in terms of both the rate and the pattern of their development. This variability apparently relates to the diverse array of environments in which infants develop. A seemingly single route in their developmental process, if it is seen as such, is actually due to equifinality, an essential feature of this development process. Misconceptions about equifinality have resulted in attempts to identify maturation as the single factor responsible for the onset of intentional object-focused communication.

The theory of innate cognition is probably correct insofar as it claims that human infants are, in extremely diverse ways, genetically predisposed to communicate with adults who surround them. This book has also repeatedly demonstrated this phenomenon. In this regard, the ethological approach, which was originally formulated in the field of nonhuman animal behaviors, is also very useful for understanding human behavior. Nevertheless, that young infants almost "innately" possess an impetus to communicate with adults does not necessarily imply an overall universal pattern of communicative development; rather, the way in which each innate component is organized with others is determined flexibly as infants develop. The transition from one level of development to the next requires overarching cognitive reorganization that is flexible; the process by which this reorganization occurs in each infant is far from maturational. The strategy employed by each infant in accomplishing this task is dependent upon its environmental conditions. Many traditional Piagetians adhere to this notion (Adamson, Bakeman and Smith, 1990; Nelson, 1991), but they have had difficulty determining the specifics of this process. At issue has been how broad a reorganization to seek. The theory of innate cognition might be understood historically as appearing in response to the issue raised by Piagetians. Unfortunately, such attempts were unsuccessful owing to their inclination to locate the change primarily within the infant itself.

In fact, long before the theory of innate cognition was formulated, Bernstein (1967) pointed out that a central executive, such as a motor program, could not master the many redundant degrees of freedom nor the indeterminacy involved in the control of movement. There are simply too many components for all possible contingencies to be stored in the central nervous system. According to Bernstein, the central nervous system controls the motor system by forming movement synergies that are also known as coordinative structures. He defined coordinative structures as the temporary marshaling of many degrees of freedom into a task-specific functional unit. Although redundant degrees of freedom were considered as a problem at that time, they are actually prerequisites for biological systems to adjust flexibly to changing environmental conditions. This is a particularly important point for motor equivalence, which depends on the motor system having many degrees of freedom, so that a variety of movements and their different muscle contractions and joint rotations can produce the same outcome (Hebb, 1949).

I expected approaches of this sort to compensate for what the theory of innate cognition had dismissed by focusing on the orchestration of multiple factors that are present both within (innately) and outside (environmentally) the infant, rather than by focusing on the characteristics of any single factor. As such, in this book I introduced a dynamic systems perspective. A dynamic systems approach addressed the issue of how to situate the cause of a new form of activity in the changing relations between numerous elements during periods of reorganization. These elements include factors that have been considered by earlier investigators, namely, the maturation of genetically predisposed traits that humans possess and new cognitive insights. Further, factors related to contributions from communicative partner and the inanimate environment were also taken into consideration. In this sense, my explanation does not dispute previous perspectives but rather expands upon them by placing the developing infant within a wider system of influences.

From a dynamic systems perspective, although one element might be the controlling factor that ushers in a new accomplishment, the same function might be served by other elements under other conditions. The development of pointing behavior described in this book provides a good example. The onset of communicative pointing often depends on the infant's degree of motivation to explore a distant object with its index-finger. However, another element, such as the caregiver's interpretation of what the index-finger extension means, might help the infant realize that its index-finger extension can refer to the object across space. Of course, genetic elements must also be taken into account in the development of the behavior. From its onset, index-finger extension is very likely to co-occur temporally with speech-like vocalization. This can serve to canalize this referential gesture along one certain route rather than along others, the phenomenon that has been primary focus of investigators adhering to the theory of innate cognition. However, it should also be noted that any of a whole host of elements could limit an infant's performance in a particular situation. Typically, the rate-limiting element for the production of pointing might be the infant's ability to perform specific motor acts such as extending its index-finger.

Not only the onset of intentionally communicative gestures but also the basic developmental process of acquiring speech motor control were formulated within the dynamic systems framework. Originally, the approach was developed from studies of nonsocial, perceptual motor activities such as the spontaneous movements of newborns and the onset of bipedal walking and manual reaching of infants. In this book, I sought to clarify early vocal development and the onset of referential communication as extensions of the development of such motor actions.

Combining a dynamic systems approach with the notion of direct perception

From a dynamic systems perspective, the behavior of a system can be explained only in terms of complex interactions between different factors that contribute to the system's functioning. Thelen and Ulrich (1991) pointed out that those studying motor activity erroneously seek to explain it purely in terms of some neural substrate; the complexity of motor activity is as much a function of the biodynamic properties of the limbs and muscles as it is a function of the functional characteristics of the motor cortex. For instance, much of the complexity involved in walking derives from bipedal dynamics and it is not necessary to look for a neural control system for the key to the whole process. This is important when we compare the dynamic systems approach with more conventional Piagetian cognitive approaches to the development of referential communication, since the implication is that any behavior in the system cannot be explained by referring to a single element alone (e.g., the cognitive onset of causal understanding). Instead, behavior, even if it is social, is an emergent property of a whole system composed of not only psychological components, but also of biological and physiological components.

Proponents of the dynamic systems approach claim that it can be applied at any level, from physical systems alone to systems composed of physical, biological and psychological factors. Thus, from this perspective, it is important when performing a psychological analysis to include physical and biological factors or constraints as part of the system. However, the actual application of the dynamic systems approach in infant development has thus far been largely limited to the area of motor development. In this research, it is argued that the development of complex motor achievements such as crawling, walking and grasping can be understood in terms of a complex interaction between emergent properties of a system composed of physical and biological factors or constraints. In this book, I have applied the dynamic systems perspective to social behavior, based on the assumption that there is scope for applying the same analysis more broadly so that it incorporates communicative activities. Using this approach, I empirically demonstrated that when one considers intention in communication, it is necessary to treat the infant's intent as just one component of a system that also includes the physical dynamics of the vocal apparatus and the way the muscles are controlled by the motor regions of the brain. From this type of analysis, it is clear that complex behaviors do not call for a conventional psychological or cognitive interpretation in terms of some mental representation for the behavior. Although there is certainly some form of representation of the act, the representation is distributed throughout the system and cannot be identified as residing in a particular place.

However, there are limitations to the dynamic systems approach that should be mentioned. It could be argued that the detail involved in a dynamic system analysis might lead one to be overly occupied with minute aspects of behavior; the danger is being unable to see the psychological forest for the physical and biological trees. In order to avoid this danger, I introduced the Gibsonian concept of affordance in the present analysis. The affordance concept implies that in addition to perceiving the world objectively, individuals also perceive connections between features of the world and their own action. Both the dynamic systems approach and Gibsonian theory are essentially ecological systems theories. It is already widely recognized that both approaches have much in common and might profitably be combined (Reed, 1982; Turvey, 1990). In fact, recent ecological accounts of the development of affordances use terminology that has much in common with dynamic systems accounts. However, the link appears to stop at the level of common terminology, partly due to the tendency of the Gibsonian school to stick with rather vague generalities rather than specifying developmental processes with the quantifiable precision characteristic of dynamic systems approaches.

Indeed, the strength of the dynamic systems approach is that it seeks to specify precisely what sorts of processes are involved in the detection of affordances. While most previous investigations on the perception of affordances have been concerned with affordances in terms of the inanimate physical world (e.g., nonsocial actions), I applied the concept to social perception in the communicative behavior of infants and caregivers, and investigated how each of them as a communicative partner perceived affordances in the behavior of the other and its functional implications for the development of the linguistic ability of the infant. I found that the progressive detection of "partnership" with one another, by both the infant and the caregiver, was crucial for the development of communication between them.

The basic notion underlying the dynamic systems analysis was that it must encompass factors composing the action system, the perceptual system, and those environmental features providing perceptual structure. Whenever new action systems emerge, whether they are social or nonsocial, they either mesh or do not mesh with certain features of the perceptual world. Meshing is achieved through action. The action should not be construed as a mental construction but rather as an emergent property of the perceptuomotor system. It is perhaps inappropriate to call this direct perception of affordances, because this places too much stress on perceptual activities. Nonetheless, the link between the structure of the world and the structure of action is certainly detected through action that includes perceptual activity.

In fact, a growing literature proposes that movement is the "engine" driving developmental change. Since Spelke (1990), many authors have agreed that movements are essential for the development of fundamental cognitive abilities, and also for the development of linguistic production ability. Rhythmic motor activities (e.g., burst/pause repetition in sucking, stereotyped kicking and hand banging) provide typical examples of movement driving events. Through learning to perform each of the movements in a skillful manner, infants use the information as a basis for elaborating their speech motor control. Once acquired, the temporal co-occurrence of the newly acquired pattern of vocal production with the rhythmic motor activity creates new perceptual experiences, which in their turn afford further developmental changes. These perceptual experiences also include caregiver responses to the infant behavior, which are evoked by the detection of affordances in the infant as a communicative partner. For instance, the incidental matching of the vocal quality in infant cooing with temporally preceding maternal utterances in some acoustic dimension is interpreted by the mother as the infant's intentional imitation of her vocal activity, which actually enhances the emergence of the infant's awareness of imitation.

Without question, humans as a biological species are genetically preprogrammed, variably, with capabilities to acquire linguistic abilities. This also applies to the perceptual experiences confronting them during development.

In the words of Adolph, Eppler and Gibson (1993), "an affordance is the fit between an animal's capabilities and the environmental supports that enable a given action to be performed" (p. 1159). Any given environmental feature is species-specific and holds one type of affordance for one species and a different type for another. Importantly, this notion has a developmental parallel in the sense that the affordances detected will depend on the infant's ability to act. For instance, as new achievements come on the scene, new affordances emerge for both the infant and the caregiver, where the possibility that the emerging flexibility of the infant's achievements is developmentally generated. The affordances are essentially relationships between the structure of the environment and the structure of action; here, the implication of the dynamic systems perspective is present. This book illustrated how the dynamic systems perspective helps us to understand the developmental process of early language acquisition during the first year of an infant's life. New affordances are picked up progressively not only by the infant but also by its caregiver through the meshing of organismic and environmental facets of the overall system.

References

Adamson, L. B., Bakeman, R. and Smith, C. B. (1990). Gestures, words, and early object sharing. In V. Volterra and C. Erting (eds.), *From Gesture to Language in Hearing and Deaf Children* (pp. 31–41). New York: Springer-Verlag.

Adolph, K. E., Eppler, M. A. and Gibson, E. J. (1993). Crawing versus walking. *Child Development*, 64, 1158–74.

Ahlgren, I. and Bergman, B. (eds.) (1980). *Papers from the First International Symposium on Sign Language Research.* Stockholm: The Swedish National Association of the Deaf.

Alley, T. R. (1981). *Caregiving and the Perception of Maturational Status.* Storrs, CT: University of Connecticut.

Anisfeld, M. (1984). *Language Development from Birth to Three.* Hillsdale, NJ: Erlbaum.

Argyle, M. (1987). Social cognition and social interaction. Jaspers Memorial Lecture, Oxford, September 1987. *The Bulletin of the British Psychological Society*, 1, 117–83.

Armstrong, D. F., Stokoe, W. C. and Wilcox, S. E. (1995). *Gesture and the Nature of Language.* Cambridge: Cambridge University Press.

Armstrong, E. A. (1963). *A Study of Bird Song.* Oxford: Oxford Univrsity Press.

Bahrick, L. E. (1983). Infants' perception of substance and temporal synchrony in multimodal events. *Infant Behavior and Development*, 6, 429–51.

Bakeman, R., Adamson, L. B., Konner, M. and Barr, R. G. (1990). Kung infancy: the social context of object exploration. *Child Development*, 61, 794–809.

Baldwin, D. A. and Markman, E. M. (1989). Establishing word-object relations: a first step. *Child Development*, 60, 381–98.

Banse, R. and Scherer, K. R. (1996). Acoustic profiles in vocal emotion expression. *Journal of Personality and Social Psychology*, 70, 614–36.

Bargh, J. A. and Pietromonaco, P. (1982). Automatic information processing and social perception: the inflence information presented outside of conscious awareness on impression information. *Journal of Personality and Social Psychology*, 43, 437–49.

Barton, R. A. (1996). Neocortex size and behavioural ecology in primates. *Proceedings of the Royal Irish Academy Section B: Biological, Geological and Chemical Science*, 263, 173–7.

Barton, R. A. and Dunbar, R. I. M. (1997). Evolution of the social brain. In A. Whiten and R. Byrne (eds.), *Machiavellian Intelligence II* (pp. 240–63). Cambridge: Cambridge University Press.

Bates, E., Benigni, B., Bretherton, I., Camaioni, L. and Voktera, V. (1979). Cognition and communication from nine to thirteen months: correlational things. In E. Bates (ed.), *The Emergence of Symbols: Cognition and Communication in Infancy* (pp. 69–140). New York: Academic Press.

Bates, E., Camaioni, L. and Voltera, V. (1975). The acquisition of performatives prior to speech. *Merrill-Palmer Quarterly*, 21, 105–226.

Bates, E., Elman, J., Johnson, M., Karmiloff-Smith, A., Parisi, D. and Plunkett, K. (1996). *On Innateness*. Cambridge, MA: MIT Press.

Battison, R. (1974). Phonological delection in ASL. *Sign Language Studies*, 5, 1–19.

Bauer, H. R. and Philip, M. M. (1983). Facial and vocal individual recognition in the common chimpanzee. *Psychological Record*, 33, 161–70.

Beckman, M. E. (1982). Segment duration and the mora in Japanese. *Phonetica*, 39, 113–35.

Berger, J. and Cunningham, C. C. (1983). Development of early vocal behaviours and interactions in Down's Syndrome and nonhandicapped infant-mother pairs. *Developmental Psychology*, 19, 322–31.

Berne, R. M. and Levy, M. N. (1983). *Physiology*. St. Louis: Mosby.

Bernstein, N. A. (1967). *The Coordination and Regulation of Movements*. Oxford: Pergamon Press.

Bernstein-Ratner, N. and Pye, C. (1984). Higher pitch in BT is not universal: acoustic evidence from Quiche Mayan. *Journal of Child Language*, 11, 515–22.

Berry, D. S. and Zebrowitz-McArthur, L. (1988). What's in a face? Facial maturity and the attribution of legal responsibility. *Personality and Social Psychology Bulletin*, 14, 23–33.

Biben, M., Symmes, D. and Bernhards, D. (1989). Contour variables in vocal communication between squirrel monkey mothers and infants. *Developmental Psychology*, 22, 617–31.

Biben, M., Symmes, D. and Masataka, N. (1986). Temporal and structural analysis of affiliative vocal exchanges in squirrel monkeys (*Saimiri sciureus*). *Behaviour*, 98, 259–73.

Bickley, C. and Hunnicutt, S. (1992). Acoustic analysis of laughter. *Proceeedings of the International Conference on Spoken Language Processes*, 2, 927–30.

Blaustein, A. R. and O'Hara, R. K. (1981). Genetic control for sibling recognition? *Nature*, 290, 246–8.

(1982). Kin recognition in *Rana cascadae* tadpoles: maternal and paternal effects. *Animal Behaviour*, 30, 1151–57.

(1983). Kin recognition in *Rana cascadae* tadpoles: effects of rearing with non-siblings and varying the strength of the stimulus cues. *Behavioral and Neural Biology*, 39, 259–67.

Bloom, K. (1977). Patterning of infant vocal behaviour. *Journal of Experimental Child Psychology*, 23, 367–77.

(1988). Quality of adult vocalizations affects the quality of infant vocalizations. *Journal of Child Language*, 15, 469–80.

Bloom, K. and Esposito, A. (1975). Social conditioning and its proper control procedures. *Journal of Experimental Child Psychology*, 19, 209–22.

Bloom, K. and Lo, E. (1990). Adult perceptions of vocalizing infants. *Infant Behavior and Development*, 13, 209–19.

Bloom, K., Russell, A. and Wassenberg, K. (1987). Turn-taking affects the quality of infant vocalizations. *Journal of Child Language*, 14, 211–27.

Blurton-Jones, N. (1972). Characteristics of ethological studies of human behavior. In N. Blurton-Jones (ed.), *Ethological Studies of Child Behavior*. London: Cambridge University Press.

Boinski, S. and Mitchell, C. L. (1995). Wild squirrel monkey (*Saimiri sciureus*) "caregiver"calls: contexts and acoustic structure. *American Journal of Primatology*, 35, 129–37.

Bornstein, R. F., Leone, D. R. and Galley, D. J. (1987). The generalizability of subliminal mere exposure effects: inflence of stimuli perceived without awareness on social behavior. *Journal of Personality and Social Psychology*, 53, 1070–9.

Bowen-Jones, A., Thompson, C. and Drewett, R. F. (1982). Milk flw and sucking rates during breast-feeding. *Developmental Medicine and Child Neurology*, 24, 626–33.

Brickner, R. (1940). A human cortical area producing repetitive phenomena when stimulated. *Journal of Neurophysiology*, 3, 128–30.

Brown, C. H., Beecher, M. D., Moody, D. B. and Stebbins, W. C. (1979). Locatability of vocal signals in Old World monkeys: design features for the communication of position. *Journal of Comparative and Physiological Psychology*, 93, 806–19.

Bruner, J. (1990). *Acts of Meaning*. Cambridge, MA: Harvard University Press.

Bruner, J. S. (1983). *Child's Talk: Learning to Use Language*. Cambridge: Cambridge University Press.

Bullowa, M. (1979). *Before Speech: The Beginning of Interpersonal Communication*. Cambridge: Cambridge University Press.

Bushnell, E. M. and Boudreau, J. P. (1993). Motor development in the mind: the potential role of motor abilities as a determinant of aspects of perceptual development. *Child Development*, 64, 1005–21.

Butterworth, G. E. and Castillo, M. (1976). Coordination of auditory and visual space in newborn human infants. *Perception*, 7, 513–25.

Butterworth, G. E. and Grover, L. (1989). Joint visual attention, manual pointing, and preverbal communication in human infancy. In M. Jeannerod (ed.), *Attention and Performance XIII*. London: Erlbaum.

Butterworth, G. E. and Harris, M. (1994). *Principles of Developmental Psychology*. Hillsdale, NJ: Erlbaum.

Butterworth, G. E. and Jarrett, N. (1991). What minds have in common is space: spatial mechanisms serving joint attention in infancy. *Developmental Psychology*, 9, 55–72.

Byrne, R. W. (1995). *The Thinking Ape: Evolutionary Origins of Intelligence*. Oxford: Oxford University Press.

Cameron, E. Z. (1998). Is suckling behavior a useful predictor of milk intake? A review. *Animal Behaviour*, 56, 521–32.

Carpenter, C. R. (1934). A field study of the behavior and social relations of howling monkeys (*Alouatta palliata*). *Comparative Psychological Monograph*, 10, 1–168.

Caudill, W. and Weinstein, H. (1969). Maternal care and infant behavior in Japan and America. *Psychiatry*, 32, 19–43.

Chang, H. W. and Trehub, S. E. (1977). Auditory processing of relational information by young infants. *Journal of Experimental Child Psychology*, 24, 324–31.

Charlesworth, W. R. (1980). Teaching ethology of human behavior. *Human Ethology Newsletter*, 28, 7–9.

Cheney, D. L. and Seyfarth, R. M. (1980). Vocal recognition in free-ranging vervet monkeys. *Animal Behaviour*, 28, 362–7.

Chovil, N. (1991). Social determinants of facial displays. *Journal of Nonverbal Behavior*, 15, 141–54.

Clark, E. F. and Krumhansl, C. L. (1990). Perceiving musical time. *Music Perception*, 7, 213–52.

Clement, C. J. and Koopmans-van Beinum, F. J. (1995). Inflence of lack of auditory feedback: vocalizations of deaf and hearing infants compared. *Proceedings of the Institute of Phonetic Sciences, University of Amsterdam*, 19, 25–37.

Cleveland, J. and Snowdon, C. T. (1982). The complex vocal repertoire of the adult cotton-top tamarin, *Saguinus oedipis oedips*. *Zeitschrift für Tierpsychologie*, 58, 231–70.

Cohen, A. J., Thorpe, L. A. and Trehub, S. E. (1987). Infants' perception of musical relations in short transposed tone sequences. *Canadian Journal of Psychology*, 41, 33–47.

Cohn, J. F. and Tronick, E. Z. (1987). Mother-infant face-to-face interaction: the sequence of dyadic states at 3, 6, and 9 months. *Developmental Psychology*, 23, 38–77.

Cooper, R. P. and Aslin, R. N. (1990). Preference for infant-directed speech in the first month after birth. *Child Development*, 61, 1584–95.

D'Odorico, L. (1984). Non-segmental features in prelinguistic communications: an analysis of some types of infant cry and noncry vocalizations. *Journal of Child Language*, 11, 17–27.

Dang, J. and Honda, K. (1997). Acoustic characteristics of the priform fossa in models and humans. *Journal of the Acoustical Society of America*, 101, 456–65.

Dang, J., Shadle, C., Kawanishi, Y., Honda, K. and Suzuki, H. (1998). An experimental study of the open end correction coefficient for side branched with an acoustic tube. *Journal of the Acoustical Society of America*, 104, 1075–84.

Darwin, C. (1872). *The Expression of Emotions in Man and Animals*. London: Murray. (1877). A biographical sketch of an infant. *Mind*, 2, 286–94.

Davis, B. L. and MacNeilage, P. F. (1995). The articulatory basis of babbling. *Journal of Speech and Hearing Research*, 38, 1199–211.

DeCasper, A. J., Lecanuet, J. P., Busnel, M. C., Garnier-Deferre, C. and Maugeais, R. (1994). Fetal reactions to recurrent maternal speech. *Infant Behavior and Development*, 17, 159–64.

Delack, J. B. (1976). Aspects of infant speech development in the first year of life. *Canadian Journal of Linguistics*, 21, 17–37.

Demany, L. (1982). Auditory stream segregation in infancy. *Infant Behavior and Development*, 5, 261–76.

Demetriou, A. (ed.) (1988). *The Neo-Piagetian Theories of Cognitive Development: Toward an Integration*. Amsterdam: Elsevier Science.

Dore, J. (1974). A pragmatic description of early language development. *Journal of Psycholinguistics Research*, 4, 343–50.

Dumond, F. (1968). The squirrel monkey in a seminatural environment. In L. A. Rosenblum and R. W. Cooper (eds.), *The Squirrel Monkey* (pp. 88–145). New York: Academic Press.

Dunbar, R. I. M. (1993). Coevolution of neocortex size, group size and language in humans. *Behavioral and Brain Sciences*, 16, 681–735.

(1996). Towards a general model for primate social groups. In G. Runciman, J. M. Smith and R. I. M. Dunbar (eds.), *Evolution of Social Behavior Patterns in Primates and Man* (pp. 33–58). Oxford: Oxford University Press.

Dunbar, R. I. M. and Bever, J. (1998). Neocortex size predicts group size in carnivores and some insectivores. *Ethology*, 104, 695–708.

Echols, C. H. (1993). A perceptually-based model of children's earliest productions. *Cognition*, 46, 245–96.

Edelman, G. M. (1987). *Neural Darwinism*. New York: Basic Books.

Eibl-Eibesfelt, I. (1970). *Ethology: The Biology of Behavior*. New York: Holt, Rinehart and Winston.

(1989). *Human Ethology*. New York: Aldine de Gruyter.

Eilers, R. E. and Oller, D. K. (1994). Infant vocalizations and the early diagnosis of severe hearing impairment. *Journal of Pediatrics*, 124, 199–203.

Eilers, R. E., Oller, D. K., Levine, S., Basinger, D., Lynch, M. P. and Urbano, R. (1993). The role of prematurity and socioeconomic status in the onset of canonical babbling in infants. *Infant Behavior and Development*, 16, 297–315.

Eimas, P. D., Siqueland, E., Jusczyk, P. and Vogorito, J. (1971). Speech perception in infants. *Science*, 171, 303–6.

Ejiri, K. (1998). Relationship between rhythmic behavior and canonical babbling. *Phonetica*, 55, 226–37.

(1999). Inflence of lack of auditory feedback on the synchronization between preverbal vocal behaviors and motor actions: deaf and hearing infants compared. *Japanese Journal of Educational Psychology*, 47, 1–10 (in Japanese with English summary).

Ejiri, K. and Masataka, N. (2001). Co-occurrence of preverbal vocal behavior and motor action in early infancy. *Developmental Science*, 4, 40–8.

Elias, G. and Broerse, J. (1989). Timing in mother-infant communications: a comment on Murray and Trevarthen. *Journal of Child Language*, 16, 703–6.

Elowson, A. M. and Snowdon, C. T. (1994). Pygmy marmosets, *Cebuella pygmaea*, modify vocal structure in response to changed social environment. *Animal Behaviour*, 47, 1267–77.

Emde, R. N., McCartney, R. D. and Harmon, R. J. (1971). Neonatal smiling in REM states, IV: premature study. *Child Development*, 42, 1657–61.

Erting, C. J., Prezioso, C. and O'Grady Hynes, M. (1990). The interactional context of deaf mother–infant communication. In V. Voltera and C. J. Erting (eds.), *From Gesture to Language in Hearing and Deaf Children* (pp. 97–106). Berlin: Springer.

Falbo, T. and Polit, D. (1986). A quantitative review of the only-child literature: reseach evidence and theory development. *Psychological Bulletin*, 100, 176–89.

Fantz, R. L. (1963). Pattern vision in newborn infants. *Science*, 140, 296–7.

Fassbender, C. (1996). Infants' auditory sensitivity towards acoustic parameters of speech and music. In I. Deliege and J. Sloboda (eds.), *Musical Beginnings: Origins and Development of Musical Competence* (pp. 56–87). Oxford: Oxford University Press.

Feldman, H., Goldin-Meadow, S. and Gleitman, L. R. (1978). Beyond Herodotus: the creation of language by linguistically deprived deaf children. In A. Lock (ed.), *Action, Gesture, and Symbol* (pp. 351–414). London: Academic Press.

Fenton, N. (1928). The only child. *Journal of Genetic Psychology*, 35, 546–58.

Ferguson, C. A. (1964). Baby talk in six languages. *American Anthropologist*, 66, 103–14.

Fernald, A. (1984). The perceptual and affective salience of mother's speech to infants. In L. Feagans, C. Garvey and R. Golinkoff (eds.), *The Origins and Growth of Communication* (pp. 249–306). Norwood: Ablex.

  (1985). Four-month-old infants prefer to listen to motherese. *Infant Behavior and Development*, 8, 181–95.

  (1987). Intonation and communicative intent in mothers' speech to infants: is the melody the message? *Child Development*, 60, 1497–510.

  (1992). Meaningful melodies in mothers' speech to infants. In H. Papoušek, U. Jürgens and M. Papoušek (eds.), *Nonverbal Vocal Communication: Comparative and Developmental Approaches* (pp. 262–82). Cambridge: Cambridge University Press.

Fernald, A. and Kuhl, P. (1982). Discrimination of five-syllable sequences (gala*sa*laga versus gala*ta*laga) by infants. Unpublished data.

  (1987). Acoustic determinants of infant preference for motherese speech. *Infant Behavior and Development*, 10, 279–93.

Fernald, A. and Morikawa, H. (1993). Common themes and cultural variations in Japanese and American mothers' speech to infants. *Child Development*, 64, 637–56.

Fernald, A. and Simon, T. (1984). Expanded intonation contours in mothers' speech to newborns. *Developmental Psychology*, 20, 104–13.

Fernald, A., Taeschner, T., Dunn, J., Papoušek, M., de Boysson-Bardies, B. and Fukui, I. (1989). A cross-linguistic study of prosodic modifications in mothers' and fathers' speech to preverbal infants. *Journal of Child Language*, 16, 477–507.

Ferrier, L. J. (1985). Intonation in discourse: talk between 12-month-olds and thier mothers. In K. Nelson (ed.), *Child Language* (pp. 35–60). Hillsdale, NJ: Erlbaum.

Finan, D. S. (1999). Intrinsic dynamics and phase-dependent mechanosensory modulation of non-nutritive sucking in human infants. *Dissertation Abstracts International; B: The Sciences and Engineering*, 60, 0609.

Flax, J., Lahey, M., Harris, K. and Boothroyd, A. (1991). Relations between prosodic variables and communicative functions. *Journal of Child Language*, 18, 3–19.

Fletcher, J. M., Rice, W. J. and Ray, R. M. (1978). Linear discriminant function analysis in neuropsychological research: some uses and abuses. *Cortex*, 14, 564–77.

Fodor, J. A., Bever, T. G. and Garrett, M. F. (1974). *The Psychology of Language*. New York: McGraw-Hill.

Fogel, A. (1993). *Developing Through Relationships: Communication, Self, and Culture in Early Infancy*. Cambridge: Harvester Press.

Fogel, A. and Hannan, T. E. (1985). Manual actions of nine- to fifteen-week-old human infants during face-to-face interaction with their mothers. *Child Development*, 56, 1271–9.

Fogel, A. and Thelen, E. (1987). The development of expressive and communicative action in the first year: reinterpreting the evidence from a dynamic systems perspective. *Developmental Psychology*, 23, 747–61.

Fogel, A., Toda, S. and Kawai, M. (1988). Mother-infant face-to-face interaction in Japan and the United States: a laboratory comparison using 3-month-old infants. *Developmental Psychology*, 24, 398–406.

Fooden, J. (1975). Taxonomy and evolution of liontail and pigtail macaques (Primates: Cercopithecidae). *Fieldiana Zoology*, 67. Chicago: Field Museum of Natural History.

Fox, N. A. and Calkins, S. D. (1993). Multiple-measure approaches to the study of infant emotion. In M. Lewis and J. Haviland (eds.), *Handbook of Emotions* (pp. 167–84). New York: Guilford Press.

Fraiberg, S. (1977). *Insights from the Blind: Comparative Studies of Blind and Sighted Infants*. New York: Basic Books.

Frant, G. (1960). *Acoustic Theory of Speech Production*. The Hague: Mouton.

Fridlund, A. J. and Loftis, J. M. (1990). Relations between tickling and humorous laughter: preliminary support for the Darwin–Hecker hypothesis. *Biological Psychology*, 30, 141–50.

Furrow, D. (1984). Young children's use of prosody. *Journal of Child Language*, 11, 201–13.

Furuichi, T. (1983). Interindividual distance and inflence of dominance on feeding in a natural Japanese macaque troop. *Primates*, 24, 445–55.

Garnica, O. (1977). Some prosodic and paralinguistic features of speech to young children. In C. E. Snow and C. A. Ferguson (eds.), *Talking to Children: Language Input and Acquisition* (pp. 189–224). Cambridge: Cambridge University Press.

Gibson, E. J. and Walk, R. D. (1960). The Visual cliff." *Scientific American*, 202, 64–71.

Gibson, E. J. and Walker, A. (1984). Development of knowledge of visual and tactile affordances of substance. *Child Development*, 55, 453–60.

Gibson, J. J. (1966). *The Senses Considered as Perceptual Systems*. Boston: Houghton Miffh.

(1979). *The Ecological Approach to Visual Perception*. Boston: Houghton Miffh.

Ginsburg, G. P. and Kilbourne, B. K. (1988). Emergence of vocal alternation in mother-infant interchanges. *Journal of Child Language*, 15, 221–35.

Goldin-Meadow, S. and Mylander, C. (1984). Gestural communication in deaf children: the effects and noneffects of parental input on early language development. *Monographs of the Society for Research in Child Development*, 49, Washington, DC.

(1998). Spontaneous sign systems created by deaf children in two cultures. *Nature*, 391, 279–81.

Golub, H. L. (1980). A physioacoustic model of the infant cry and its use for medical diagnosis and prognosis. Ph.D Dissertation. Boston, MA: Massachusetts Institute of Technology.

Goodsitt, J. V., Morse, P. A., Ver Hoeve, J. N. and Cowan, N. (1984). Infant speech recognition in multisyllabic contexts. *Child Development*, 55, 903–10.

Goodwyn, S. W. and Acredolo, L. P. (1993). Symbolic gesture versus word: is there a modality advantage for onset of symbol use? *Child Development*, 64, 688–701.

Gouzoules, S., Gouzoules, H. and Marler, P. (1984). Rhesus monkey (*Macaca mulatta*) screams: representational signalling in the recruitment of agonistic aid. *Animal Behaviour*, 32, 182–93.

Green, S. (1975). Variation of vocal pattern with reference to social situation in the Japanese monkey (*Macaca fuscata*): a field study. In L. A. Rosenblum (ed.), *Primate Behavior: Developments in Field and Laboratory Research*. New York: Academic Press.

Griffith, P. L. (1985). Mode-switching and mode-finding in a hearing child of deaf parents. *Sign Language Studies*, 48, 195–222.

Gusella, J., Roman, M. and Muir, D. (1986). Experimental manipulation of mother–infant actions. Paper presented at the International Conference of Infant Studies, Los Angels, September.

Gustafson, G. E. and Green, J. A. (1989). On the importance of fundamental frequency and other acoustic features in cry perception and infant development. *Child Development*, 60, 772–80.

(1991). Developmental coordination of cry sounds with visual regard and gestures. *Infant Behavior and Development*, 14, 51–7.

Gustafson, G. E., Green, J. A. and Cleland, J. W. (1994). Robustness of individual identity in the cries of human infants. *Developmental Psychobiology*, 27, 1–9.

Haccou, P. and Meelis, E. (1992). *Statistical Analysis of Behavioural Data: An Approach Based on Time-structured Models*. New York: Oxford University Press.

Hallé, P. A. and Boysson-Bardies, B. de (1994). Emergence of an early receptive lexicon: infants' recognition of words. *Infant Behavior and Development*, 17, 19–129.

(1996). The format of representation of recognized words in infants' early receptive lexicon. *Infant Behavior and Development*, 19, 463–81.

Halliday, M. A. K. (1975). *Learning How to Mean: Explorations in the Development of Language*. London: Edward Arnold.

Hansen, E. W. (1976). Selective responding by recently separated juvenile monkeys to the calls of their mothers. *Developmental Psychology*, 9, 83–8.

Harding, C. and Golinkoff, R. M. (1979). The origins of intentional vocalizations in prelinguistic infants. *Child Development*, 50, 33–40.

Harris, M., Barrett, M., Jones, D. and Brookes, S. (1988). Linguistic input and early word meaning. *Journal of Child Language*, 15, 77–94.

Hauser, M. D. (1992). Articulatory and social factors inflence the acoustic structure of rhesus monkey vocalizations: a learned mode of production? *Journal of the Acoustical Society of America*, 91, 2175–79.

(1996). *The Evolution of Communication*. Cambridge, MA: MIT Press.

Hayashi, Y., Hoashi, E. and Nara, T. (1997). Ultrasonographic analysis of sucking behavior of newborn infants: the driving force of sucking pressure. *Early Human Development*, 49, 33–8.

Hayashi, A., Tamekawa, Y. and Kiritani, S. (2001). Developmental change in auditory preferences for speech stimuli in Japanese infants. *Journal of Speech, Language, and Hearing Research*, 44, 1189–200.

Hebb, D. O. (1949). *The Organization of Behavior: A Neurophysiological Theory*. New York: Wiley.

Hirsh, I. J. and Watson, C. S. (1996). Auditory psychophysics and perception. *Annual Review of Psychology*, 47, 461–84.

Hirshberg, L. M. and Svejda, M. (1990). When infants look to their parents: 1. Infants' social referencing of mothers compared to fathers. *Child Development*, 61, 1175–86.

Hirsh-Pasek, K., Kemler Nelson, D. G., Jusczyk, P. W., Wright Cassidy, K., Druss, B. and Kennedy, L. (1987). Clauses are perceptual units for young infants. *Cognition*, 26, 269–86.

Hockett, C. F. (1960). The origin of speech. *Scientific American*, 203, 88–96.

Hohmann, G. and Herzog, M. O. (1985). Vocal communication in lion-tailed macaques (*Macaca silenus*). *Folia Primatologica*, 45, 148–78.

Hohne, E. A., Jusczyk, A. M. and Redanz, N. J. (1994). Do infants remember words from stories? Paper presented at the meeting of the Acoustical Society of America, Boston, MA, June.

Holmes, W. G. (1990). Parent-offspring recognition in mammals: a proximate and ultimate perspective. In N. A. Krasnegor, and R. S. Bridges (eds.), *Mammalian Parenting: Biochemical, Neurobiological, and Behavioral Determinants* (pp. 441–60). New York: Oxford University Press.

Huffman, M. K. (1990). Implementation of nasal timing and articulatory landmarks. *UCLA Working Papers in Phonetics*, 75, 1–149.

Ikeda, Y. and Masataka, N. (1999). A variable that may affect individual differences in the child-directed speech of Japanese women. *Japanese Psychological Research*, 41, 203–8.

Ingram, D. (1995). The cultural basis of prosodic modifications to infants and children: a response to Fernald's universalist theory. *Journal of Child Language*, 22, 223–33.

Iverson, P. and Kuhl, P. K. (1995). Mapping the perceptual magnet effect for speech using signal detection theory and multidimensional scaling. *Journal of the Acoustical Society of America*, 97, 553–62.

Jakobson, R. (1941). *Kindersprache, Aphasie, und allgemeine Lautgesetze (Child Language, Aphasia, and Phonological Universals)*. Uppsala, Sweden: Almqvist and Wiksell.

Jerison, H. J. (1973). *Evolution of the Brain and Intelligence*. New York: Academic Press.

Jiao, S., Ji, G. and Jing, Q. (1986). Comparative study of behavioral qualities of only children and sibling children. *Child Development*, 57, 357–61.

Johnson, P. and Salisbury, D. M. (1975). Breathing and sucking during feeding in the newborn. In *Parent-infant interaction, Chiba Foundation Symposium 33* (pp. 119–35). Amsterdam: Elsevier.

Jusczyk, P. W. (1997). *The Discovery of Spoken Language*. Cambridge, MA: MIT Press.

Jusczyk, P. W. and Aslin, R. N. (1995). Infants' detection of the sound patterns of words in flent speech. *Cognitive Psychology*, 29, 1–23.

Jusczyk, P. W., Hirsh-Pasek, K., Kemler Nelson, D. G., Kennedy, L., Woodward, A. and Piwoz, J. (1992). Perception of acoustic correlates of major phrasal units by young infants. *Cognitive Psychology*, 24, 252–93.

Jusczyk, P. W. and Hohne, E. A. (1997). Infants' memory for spoken words. *Science*, 277, 1984–6.

Kaitz, M., Lapidot, P., Bronner, R. and Eidelman, A. I. (1992). Parturient women can recognize their infants by touch. *Developmental Psychology*, 28, 35–9.

Kajikawa, S. and Hasegawa, T. (2000). Acoustic variation of pant hoot calls by male chimpanzees: a playback experiment. *Journal of Ethology*, 18, 133–9.

Kantor, R. (1982). Communicative interaction: mother modification and child acquisition of American Sign Language. *Sign Language Studies*, 38, 233–82.

Kaplan, J. M., Winchip-Ball, A. and Sim, L. (1978). Maternal discrimination of infant vocalizations in squirrel monkeys. *Primates*, 19, 187–93.

Kaplan, P. S., Fox, K. B. and Huckeby, E. R. (1992). Faces as reinforcers: effects of pairing condition and facial expression. *Developmental Psychology*, 25, 299–312.

Kaplan, P. S., Goldstein, M. H., Huckeby, E. R., Owren, M. J. and Cooper, P. P. (1995). Dishabituaion of visual attention by infant- versus adult-directed speech: effects of frequency modulation and spectral composition. *Infant Behavior and Development*, 18, 209–23.

Kaplan, P. S., Jung, P. C., Ryther, J. S. and Zarlengo-Strouse, P. (1996). Infant-directed versus adult-directed speech as signals for faces. *Developmental Psychology*, 32, 880–91.

Karzon, R. G. (1985). Discrimination of polysyllabic sequences by one- to four-month-old infants. *Journal of Experimental Child Psychology*, 39, 326–42.

Kaye, K. (1977). Toward the origin of dialogue. In H. R. Schaffer (ed.), *Studies in Mother-Infant Interaction* (pp. 68–94). London: Academic Press.

(1982). *The Mental and Social Life of Babies: How Parents Create Persons*. Chicago: Chicago University Press.

Kaye, K. and Wells, A. J. (1980). Mothers' jiggling and the burst-pause pattern in neonatal feeding. *Infant Behavior and Development*, 3, 29–46.

Kemler Nelson, D. G., Hirsh-Pasek, K., Jusczyk, P. W. and Wright Cassidy, K. (1989). How prosodic cues in motherese might assist language learning. *Journal of Child Language*, 16, 55–68.

Kent, R. D. (1981). Articulatory-acoustic perspectives on speech development. In R. E. Stark (ed.), *Language Behavior in Infancy and Early Childhood* (pp. 105–26). Amsterdam: Elsevier North Holland.

(1992). The biology of phonological development. In C. A. Ferguson, L. Menn and C. Stoel-Gammon (eds.), *Phonological Development: Models, Research, Implications* (pp. 65–90). Timonium, MD: York Press.

Kent, R. D. and Murray, A. D. (1982). Acoustic features of infant vocalic utterances at 3, 6, and 9 months. *Journal of the Acoustical Society of America*, 72, 353–65.

Klima, E. S. and Bellugi, U. (1979). *The Signs of Language*. Cambridge, MA: Harvard University Press.

Kudo, H. and Dunbar, R. I. M. (2001). Neocortex size and social network size in primates. *Animal Behaviour*, 62, 711–22.

Kuhl, P. K., Andruski, J. E., Chistovich, I. A., Chistovich, L. A., Kozhevnikova, E. V., Ryskina, V. L., Stolyarova, E. I., Sundberg, U. and Lacerda, F. (1997). Cross-language analysis of phonetic units in language addressed to infants. *Science*, 277, 684–6.

Kuhl, P. K. and Meltzoff, A. N. (1996). Infant vocalizations in response to speech: vocal imitation and developmental change. *Journal of the Acoustical Society of America*, 100, 2425–38.

Kyle, J. and Woll, B. (eds.) (1983). *Language in Sign: An International Perspective on Sign Language*. Beckenham: Croom Helm.

Lane, H. (1984). *When the Mind Hears*. New York: Random House.

Launer, P. (1982). 'A plane' is not 'to fly': acquiring the distinction between related nouns and verbs in ASL. Ph.D dissertation, City University of New York.

Lavelli, M. and Poli, M. (1998). Early mother–infant interaction during breast- and bottle-feeding. *Infant Behavior and Development*, 21, 667–83.

Lebra, T. S. (1976). *Japanese Patterns of Behavior*. Honolulu: University Press of Hawaii.

Legerstee, M. (1991). The role of person and object in eliciting early imitation. *Journal of Experimental Child Psychology*, 51, 423–33.

Lenneberg, E. H. (1967). *Biological Foundations of Language*. New York: Wiley.

Lester, B. M. (1984). A biosocial model of infant crying. In L. P. Lipsitt and C. Rovee-Collier (eds.), *Advances in Infant Research* (pp. 167–212). Norwood: Ablex.

Lester, B. M. and Boukydism, C. F. Z. (eds.) (1985). *Infant Crying: Theoretical and Research Perspectives*. New York: Plenum.

Lester, B. M. and Boukydism, C. F. Z. (1992). No language but a cry. In H. Papoušek, U. Jürgens and M. Papoušek (eds.), *Nonverbal Vocal Communication: Comparative and Developmental Approaches* (pp. 145–73). Cambridge: Cambridge University Press.

Leung, E. H. L. and Rheingold, H. (1981). Development of pointing as a social gesture. *Developmental Psychology*, 17, 215–20.

Lewis, M. M. (1936). *Infant Speech: A Study of the Beginnings of Language*. New York: Harcourt Brace.

Lieberman, P. (1984). *The Biology and Evolution of Language*. London: Harvard University Press.

Lieven, E. V. M., Pine, J. M. and Barnes, H. D. (1992). Individual differences in early vocabulary development: redefining the referential–expressive distinction. *Journal of Child Language*, 19, 287–310.

Lock, A. (1980). *The Guided Reinvention of Language*. London: Academic Press.

Locke, J. L. (1986). The linguistic significance of babbling. In B. Lindblom and R. Zetterstorm (eds.), *Precursors of Early Speech* (pp. 48–96). New York: Stockton Press.

  (1993). *The Child's Path to Spoken Language*. Cambridge, MA: Harvard University Press.

  (1994). Phases in the child's development of language. *American Scientist*, 82, 436–45.

  (1997). A theory of neurolinguistic development. *Brain and Language*, 58, 265–326.

Locke, J. L., Bekken, K. E., McMinn-Larson, L. and Wein, D. (1995). Emergent control of manual and vocal-motor activity in relation to the development of speech. *Brain and Language*, 51, 498–508.

Locke, J. L. and Snow, C. (1997). Vocal learning in human and nonhuman primates. In C. T. Snowdon and M. Hausberger (eds.), *Social Influences on Vocal Development* (pp. 274–92). Cambridge: Cambridge University Press.

Lorenz, K. (1943). Die angeborenen Formen möglicher Erfahrung. *Zeitschrift für Tierpsychologie*, 5, 235–409.

Loske, J. L. (1993). Learning to speak. *Journal of Phonetics*, 21, 141–6.

Lucas, A., Lucas, P. J. and Baum, J. D. (1979). Pattern of milk flw in breast-fed infants. *Lancet*, 2, 57–8.

Macedonia, J. M. (1990). Vocal communication and antipredator behavior in ring-tailed lemurs (*Lemur catta*). Ph.D dissertation. Durham, NC: Duke University.

MacNeilage, P. F. and Davis, B. L. (1990). Acquisition of speech production: the architect of segmental independence. In W. J. Hardcastle and A. Marchal (eds.), *Speech Production and Speech Modeling* (pp. 55–68). Dordrecht, Netherlands: Kluwer.

  (2000). Evolution of speech: the relation between phylogeny and ontogeny. In J. R. Hurford, C. Knight and M. G. Studdert-Kennedy (eds.), *The Evolutionary Emergence of Language* (pp. 146–60). Cambridge: Cambridge University Press.

MacWhinney, B. (1999). *The Emergence of Language*. Mahwah, NJ: Erlbaum.

Maeda, T. and Masataka, N. (1987). Locale-specific vocal behaviour of the tamarin (*Saguinus I. labiatus*). *Ethology*, 75, 25–30.

Maestas y Moores, J. (1980). Early linguistic environment: interactions of deaf parents with their infants. *Sign Language Studies*, 26, 1–13.

Malatesta, C. and Haviland, J. M. (1982). Learning display rules: the socialization of emotion expression in infancy. *Child Development*, 53, 991–1033.

(1985). Signals, symbols, and socialization: the modification of emotional expression in human development. In M. Lewis and C. Sarrni (eds.), *The Socialization of Emotions* (pp. 89–116). New York: Plenum Press.

Malatesta-Magai, C. (1991). Development of emotion expression during infancy: general course and patterns of individual difference. In J. Garber and K. A. Dodge (eds.), *The Development of Emotion Regulation and Dysregulation* (pp. 49–68). New York: Cambridge University Press.

Marcel, A. J. (1983). Conscious and unconscious perception: experiments on visual masking and word recognition. *Cognitive Psychology*, 15, 197–237.

Marler, P. and Hobbett, L. (1975). Individuality in the long range vocalizations of wild chimpanzees. *Zeitschrift für Tierpsychologie*, 38, 97–109.

Maruhashi, T. (1980). Feeding behavior and diet of Japanese monkey (*Macaca fuscata yakui*) on Yakushima Island, Japan. *Primates*, 21, 141–60.

Masataka, N. (1983a). Categorical responses to natural and synthesized alarm calls in Goeldi's monkeys (*Callimico goeldii*). *Primates*, 24, 40–51.

(1983b). Psycholinguistic analysis of alarm calls of Japanese monkeys (*Macaca fuscata fuscata*). *American Journal of Primatology*, 5, 111– 25.

(1985). Development of vocal recognition of mothers in infant Japanese macaques. *Developmental Psychobiology*, 18, 107–14.

(1988). The response of red-chested moustached tamarins to long calls from their natal and alien populations. *Animal Behaviour*, 36, 55–61.

(1991). Cortisol level and acoustic features of cries in Japanese newborns. *Journal of the Anthropological Society of Nippon*, 99, 363–9.

(1992a). Early ontogeny of vocal behavior of Japanese infants in response to maternal speech. *Child Development*, 63, 1177–85.

(1992b). Motherese in a signed language. *Infant Behavior and Development*, 15, 453–60.

(1992c). Pitch characteristics of Japanese maternal speech to infants. *Journal of Child Language*, 19, 213–23.

(1993a). Effects of contingent and noncontingent maternal stimulation on the vocal behaviour of three- and four-month-old Janapese infants. *Journal of Child Language*, 20, 303–12.

(1993b). Relation between pitch contour of prelinguistic vocalizations and communicative functions in Japanese infants. *Infant Behavior and Development*, 16, 397–401.

(1993c). Sucking behavior of newborns as a first step of language learning. *Japanese Journal of Pediatrics*, 64, 48–51 (in Japanese).

(1995). The relation between index-finger extension and the acoustic quality of cooing in three-month-old infants. *Journal of Child Language*, 22, 247–57.

(1996). Perception of motherese in a signed language by 6-month-old deaf infants. *Developmental Psychology*, 32, 874–9.

(1998). Perception of motherese in Japanese Sign Language by 6-month-old hearing infants. *Developmental Psychology*, 34, 241–6.

(1999). Preference for infant-directed singing in 2-day-old hearing infants of deaf parents. *Developmental Psychology*, 35, 1001–5.

(2000). The role of modality and input in the earliest stage of language acquisition: studies of Japanese sign language. In C. Chamberlain, J. P. Morford and R. I. Mayberry (eds.), *Language Acquisition by Eye* (pp. 3–24). Hillsdale, NJ: Lawrence Erlbaum.

(2002a). Long-term retention of spoken words in preverbal infants. Paper presented at the fifth congress of the International Society of Spoken Languages Processing, Chiba, Japan.

(2002b). Pitch modification when interacting with elders: Japanese women with and without experiences with children. *Journal of Child Language* (in press).

(2003). From index-finger extension to index-finger pointing: ontogenesis of pointing in preverbal infants. In S. Kita (ed.), *Pointing: Where Language, Culture, and Cognition Meet* (pp. 69–84). Mahwah, NJ: Lawrence Erlbaum.

Masataka, N. and Biben, M. (1987). Temporal rules regulating affiliative vocal exchanges of squirrel monkeys. *Behaviour*, 101, 311–19.

Masataka, N. and Bloom, K. (1994). Acoustic properties that determine adults' preferences for 3-month-old infant vocalizations. *Infant Behavior and Development*, 17, 461–4.

Masataka, N. and Fujita, K. (1989). Vocal learning of Japanese and rhesus monkeys. *Behaviour*, 109, 191–9.

Masataka, N. and Symmes, D. (1986). Effect of separation distance on isolation call structure in squirrel monkeys (*Saimiri sciureus*). *American Journal of Primatology*, 10, 271–8.

Masataka, N. and Thierry, B. (1993). Vocal communication of tonkean macaques in confined environments. *Primates*, 34, 169–80.

Masur, E. F. (1982). Mothers' responses to infants' object-related gestures: inflences on lexical development. *Journal of Child Language*, 9, 23–30.

McArthur, L. Z. and Baron, R. M. (1983). Toward an ecological theory of social perception. *Psychological Review*, 90, 215–38.

McGurk, H. and MacDonald, J. (1976). Hearing lips and seeing voices. *Nature*, 264, 746–8.

McNeill, D. C. (1992). *Hand and Mind*. Chicago: Chicago University Press.

Meltzoff, A. N. and Borton, R. W. (1979). Intermodal matching by human neonates. *Nature*, 282, 403–4.

Meltzoff, A. N. and Moore, M. K. (1983). Newborn infants imitate adult facial gestures. *Child Development*, 54, 702–9.

Merikle, P. M. and Rheingold, E. M. (1988). Using direct and indirect measures to study perception without awareness. *Perception and Psychophysics*, 44, 563–75.

Meyer, D. E., Schvaneveldt, R. W. and Ruddy, M. G. (1972). Activation of lexical memory. Paper presented at the meeting of the Psychonomic Society, St Louis, MI, November 1972.

(1975). Loci of contextual effects on visual word-recognition. In P. M. A. Rabbit and S. Dornic (eds.), *Attention and Performance* (pp. 98–118). New York: Academic Press.

Mitani, M. (1986). Voiceprint identification and its application to sociological studies of wild Japanese monkeys (*Macaca fuscata yakui*). *Primates*, 27, 397–412.

Mitani, J. C., Hasegawa, T., Gros-Louis, J., Marler, P. and Byrne, R. (1992). Dialects in wild chimpanzees? *American Journal of Primatology*, 27, 233–43.

Moon, C., Cooper, R. P. and Fifer, W. P. (1991). Two-day-olds prefer the maternal language. Presentation at the 1991 Biennial Meeting of the Society for Research in Child Development, Seattle, WA.

Moynihan, M. (1970). The control, suppression, decay, disappearance, and replacement of displays. *Journal of Theoretical Biology*, 29, 85–112.

Murphy, C. M. (1978). Pointing in the context of a shared activity. *Child Development*, 49, 371–80.

Murray, A. (1979). Infant crying as an elicitor of parental behavior: an examination of two models. *Psychological Bulletin*, 86, 191–215.

Myers, J., Jusczyk, P. W., Nelson, D. G. K., Charles-Luce, J., Woodward, A. L. and Hirsh-Pasek, K. (1996). Infants' sensitivity to word boundaries in flent speech. *Journal of Child Language*, 23, 1–30.

National Language Research Institute (1984). A study of fundamental vocabulary for Japanese language teaching. *The National Language Research Institute Report*, 78. Shuei-Shoseki.

Neely, J. H. (1977). Semantic priming and retrieval from lexical memory. *Journal of Experimental Psychology: General*, 106, 226–54.

Nelson, K. (1973). Structure and strategy in learning to talk. *Monographs of the Society for Research in Child Development*, 38. Chicago: Chicago University Press for the Society for Research in Child Development.

  (1981). Individual differences in language development: Implications for development and language. *Developmental Psychology*, 17, 170–87.

  (1991). Concepts and meaning in language development. In N. A. Krasnegor, D. M. Rumbaugh, R. L. Schiefelbusch and M. Studdert-Kennedy (eds.), *Biological and Behavioral Determinants of Language Development* (pp. 89–115). Hillsdale, NJ: Erlbaum.

Netsell, R. (1981). The acquisition of speech motor control: a perspective with directions for research. In R. E. Stark (ed.), *Language Behaviour in Infancy and Early Childhood* (pp. 134–61). Amsterdam: Elsevier.

Newport, E. (1981). Constraints on structure: evidence from ASL and language learning. In W. Collins (ed.), *Minnesota Symposia on Child Psychology* (pp. 65–128). Hillsdale, NJ: Erlbaum.

Nie, N. H., Hull, C. H., Jenkins, J. G., Steinbrenner, K. and Bent, D. H. (1975). *SPSS*. New York: McGraw-Hill.

Nisbett, R. E. and Wilson, T. D. (1977). Telling more than we can know: verbal reports on mental processes. *Psychological Review*, 84, 231–59.

Nozawa, K., Shotake, T., Minezawa, M., Kawamoto, Y., Hayasaka, K., Kawamoto, S. and Ito, S. (1991). Population genetics of Japaneze monkeys: III. Ancestry and differentiation of local populations. *Primates*, 32, 411–36.

Nwokah, E. and Fogel, A. (1993). Laughter in mother-infant emotional communication. *Humor*, 6, 137–61.

Nwokah, E. E., Hsu, H.- C., Dobrowolska, O. and Fogel, A. (1994). The development of laughter in mother–infant communication: timing parameters and temporal sequences. *Infant Behavior and Development*, 17, 23–35.

Oda, R. and Masataka, N. (1996). Interspecific responses of ringtailed lemurs to playback of antipredator alarm calls given by Verreaux's sifakas. *Ethology*, 102, 411–53.

Okayasu, N. (1987). Coo sound communication. *Kikan Jinruigaku*, 19, 12–30 (in Japanese).

Oller, D. K. (1980). The emergence of the sounds of speech in infancy. In G. Yeni-Komshian, J. Kavanagh and C. Ferguson (eds.), *Child Phonology* (pp. 93–112). New York: Academic Press.

(1986). Metaphonology and infant vocalizations. In B. Lindblom and R. Zetterstorm (eds.), *Precursors of Early Speech* (pp. 21–36). New York: Stockton Press.

(2000). *The Emergence of the Speech Capacity*. Mahwah, NJ: Erlbaum.

Padden, C. A. (1988). Grammatical theory and signed languages. In F. Newmayer (ed.), *Linguistics: The Cambridge Survey* (pp. 250–66). Cambridge: Cambridge University Press.

Palmer, C. and Krumhansl, C. L. (1987a). Independent temporal and pitch structures on determination of musical phrases. *Journal of Experimental Psychology: Human Perception and Performance*, 13, 116–26.

(1987b). Pitch and temporal contributions to musical phrase perception: effects of harmony, performance timing, and familiarity. *Perception and Psychophysics*, 1341, 505–18.

Panneton, R. K. (1985). Prenatal experience with melodies: effect on postnatal auditory preference in human newborns. Ph.D dissertation. Greeensboro: University of North Carolina.

Papoušek, H., Jürgens, U. and Papoušek, M. (eds.) (1992). *Nonverbal Vocal Communication*. Cambridge: Cambridge University Press.

Papoušek, H. and Papoušek, M. (1991). Innate and cultural guidance of infants' integrative compentencies: China, the United States, and Germany. In M. H. Bornstein (ed.), *Cultural Approaches to Parenting* (pp. 23–44). Hillsdale, NJ: Erlbaum.

Papoušek, M. (1994). *Von ersten Schrei zum ersten Wort; Anfänge der Sprachentwicklung in der vorsprachlichen Kommunikation (From the First Cry to the First Word: The Beginning of Language Development in Prespeech Communication)*. Bern, Switzerland: Verlag Hans Huber.

Papoušek, M. and Papoušek, H. (1989). Forms and functions of vocal matching in interactions between mothers and their precanonical infants. *First Language*, 9, 137–58.

(1991). Preverbal vocal communication from zero to one: preparing the ground for language acquisition. In M. E. Lamb and H. Keller (eds.), *Perspectives on Infant Development: Contributions from German-speaking Countries* (pp. 299–328). Hillsdale, NJ: Erlbaum.

Papoušek, M., Papoušek, H. and Bornstein, M. H. (1985). The naturalistic vocal environment of young infants: on the significance of homogeneity and variability in parental speech. In T. Field and N. Fox (eds.), *Social Perception in Infants* (pp. 269–97). Norwood, NJ: Ablex.

Patterson, M., Muir, D. W. and Hains, S. (1997). Infant sensitivity to perturbations in adult infant-directed speech during social interactions with mother and stranger. Paper presented at the Society for Research in Child Development, New Orleans.

Paul, K., Dittrichová, J. and Papoušek, H. (1996). Infant feeding behavior: development in patterns and motivation. *Developmental Psychology*, 29, 563–76.

Penfield, W. and Welch, K. (1951). The supplementary motor area of the cerebral cortex. *Archives of Neurology and Psychiatry*, 66, 289–317.

Penman, R., Cross, T., Milgrom-Friedman, J. and Meares, R. (1983). Mothers' speech to prelingual infants: a pragmatic analysis. *Journal of Child Language*, 10, 17–34.

Perreira, M. (1986). Maternal recognition of juvenile offspring coo vocalizations in Japanese macaques. *Animal Behaviour*, 34, 935–7.

Peters, A. M. (1983). *The Units of Language Acquisition*. Cambridge: Cambridge University Press.

Peterson, G. E. and Barney, H. L. (1952). Control methods used in the study of vowels. *Journal of the Acoustical Society of America*, 24, 175–84.

Pettito, L. A. and Marentette, P. F. (1991). Babbling in the manual mode: evidence for the ontogeny of language. *Science*, 251, 1493–6.

Piaget, J. (1951). *Play, Dreams and Imitation in Childhood*. New York: Norton.
  (1952). *The Origins of Intelligence in Children*. New York: Routledge and Kegan Paul.

Pilon, R. (1981). Segmentation of speech in a foreign language. *Journal of Psycholinguistic Research*, 10, 113–21.

Pinker, S. (1984). *Language Learnability and Language Development*. Cambridge, MA: Harvard University Press.

Pisoni, D. (1977). Identification and discrimination of the relative onset time of two component tones: implications for voicing perception in stops. *Journal of the Acoustical Society of America*, 61, 1352–61.

Pisoni, D. R. and Lazarus, J. H. (1974). Categorical and un-categorical models of speech perception along the voicing continuum. *Journal of the Acoustical Society of America*, 55, 328–33.

Pola, Y. V. and Snowdon, C. T. (1975). The vocalization of pygmy marmosets (*Cebulla pygmaea*). *Animal Behaviour*, 26, 192–206.

Porter, F. L., Porges, S. W. and Marchall, R. E. (1988). Newborn pain cries and vagal tone: parallel changes in response to circumcision. *Child Development*, 59, 480–505.

Posner, M. I. (1969). Abstraction and the process of recognition. In G. H. Bower and J. T. Spence (eds.), *The Psychology of Learning and Motivation: Advances in Reseach and Theory* (pp. 175–244). New York: Academic Press.

Pouthas, V., Provasi, J. and Droit, S. (1996). Biobehavioral rhythms: development and role in early human ontogenesis. In J. T. Fraser and M. P. Soulsby (eds.), *Dimensions of Time and Life* (pp. 19–30). Madison, CT: International Universities Press, Inc.

Power, T. G., Hildebrandt, K. A. and Fitzgerald, H. E. (1982). Adults' responses to infants varying in facial expression and perceived attractiveness. *Infant Behavior and Development*, 5, 33–4.

Prechtl, H. F. R. (1984). Contituity and change in early neural development. In H. F. R. Prechtl (ed.), *Continuity of Neural Functions from Prenatal to Postnatal Life* (pp. 1–15). London: Spastics International.
  (1990). Qualitative changes of spontaneous movements in fetus and preterm infant are a marker of neurological dysfunction. *Early Human Development*, 23, 151–8.

Prescott, R. (1975). Infant cry sound: developmental features. *Journal of the Acoustical Society of America*, 57, 1186–91.

Prinz, P. M. and Prinz, E. A. (1979). Simultaneous acquisition of ASL and spoken English: phase I: early lexical development. *Sign Language Studies*, 25, 283–96.

Provine, R. R. (1996). Laughter: the study of language provides a novel approach to the mechanisms and evolution of vocal production, perception and social behavior. *American Scientist*, 84, 38–45.

Provine, R. R. and Yong, Y. L. (1991). Laughter: a stereotyped human vocalization. *Ethology*, 89, 115–24.

Querleu, D. and Renard, K. (1981). Les perceptions auditives du foetus humain (Auditory perception of the human fetus). *Journal de Gynécologie Obstétrique et Biologie de la Reproduction*, 10, 307–14.

Querleu, D., Renard, K. and Crepin, G. (1981). Perception auditive et réactive foetale aux stimulations sonores. *Journal de Gynécologie Obstétrique et Biologie de la Reproduction*, 10, 307–14.

Ramsay, D. S. (1985). Fluctuations in unimanual hand preference in infants following the onset of duplicated syllable babbling. *Developmental Psychology*, 21, 318–24.

Rao, C. R. (1948). *Advanced Statistical Methods in Biometric Research*. New York: Wiley.

Reed, E. S. (1982). An outline of a theory of action systems. *Journal of Motor Behavior*, 14, 98–134.

Reicher, G. M. (1969). Perceptual recognition as a function of stimulus material. *Journal of Experimental Psychology*, 21, 275–80.

Robson, K. S. (1967). The role of eye-to-eye contact in maternal–infant attachment. *Journal of Child Psychology and Psychiatry*, 8, 13–25.

Rondal, J. (1985). *Adult–Child Interaction and the Process of Language Acquisition*. New York: Praeger.

Rovee-Collier, C. (1990). The memory system of prelinguistic infants. In A. Diamond (ed.), *The Development and Neural Bases of Higher Cognitive Functions* (pp. 517–42). New York: Academy of Sciences.

Rovee-Collier, C. K. and Gekoski, M. J. (1979). The economics of infancy: a review of conjugate reinforcement. In H. W. Reese and L. P. Lipsitt (eds.), *Advances in Child Development and Research* (pp. 195–255). New York: Academic Press.

Rovee-Collier, C. K. and Hayne, H. (1987). Reactivation of infant memory: implications for cognitive development. In H. W. Reese (ed.), *Advances in Child Development and Behavior* (pp. 185–238). New York: Academic Press.

Rowell, T. A. and Hinde, R. (1962). Vocal communication in the rhesus monkey (*Macaca mulatta*). *Proceedings of the Zoological Society of London*, 138, 279–94.

Saslow, C. A. (1972). Behavioral definition of minimal reaction time in monkeys. *Journal of Experimental Analysis of Behavior*, 18, 87–106.

Sawaguchi, T. and Kudo, H. (1990). Neocortical development and social structure in primates. *Primates*, 31, 283–90.

Schaffer, H. R. (1977). *Studies in Mother–Infant Interaction*. New York: Academic Press.

Schaffer, R. (1984). *The Child's Entry into the Social World*. London: Academic Press.

Schieffelin, B. B. and Ochs, E. (1983). A cultural perspective on the transition from prelinguistic communication. In R. M. Golinkoff (ed.), *The Transition from Prelinguistic to Linguistic Communication* (pp. 48–76). Hillsdale, NJ: Erlbaum.

Schönberg, A. (1984). *Style and Idea*. Berkeley: California University Press.

Sekiyama, K. and Tohkura, Y. (1991). McGurk effect in non-English listeners: few visual effects for Japanese subjects hearing Japanese syllables of high auditory intelligibility. *Journal of the Acoustical Society of America*, 90, 1797–805.

Seyfarth, R. M. and Cheney, D. L. (1986). Vocal development in vervet monkeys. *Animal Behaviour*, 34, 1640–58.

Seyfarth, R. M., Cheney, D. L. and Marler, P. (1980). Vervet monkey alarm calls: semantic communication in a free-ranging primate. *Animal Behaviour*, 28, 1070–94.

Shute, B. and Wheldall, K. (1989). Pitch alternations in British motherese: some preliminary acoustic data. *Journal of Child Language*, 16, 503–12.

(1995). The incidence of raised average pitch and increased pitch variability of British motherese speech and the inflence of maternal characteristics and discourse form. *First Language*, 15, 35–55.

Sibly, R. M., Nott, H. M. and Fletcher, D. J. (1990). Splitting behaviour into bouts. *Animal Behaviour*, 39, 63–9.

Siegal, M. and Cowen, J. (1984). Appraisals of intervention: the mother's versus the child's behavior as determinants of children's evaluations of discipline techniques. *Child Development*, 55, 1760–6.

Sigel, I. E. (1982). The relationship between distancing strategies and the child's cognitive behaviour. In L. Laosa and I. E. Sigel (eds.), *Families as Learning Environment for Children* (pp. 47–87). New York: Plenum.

Skinner, B. F. (1957). *Verbal Behavior*. New York: Appleton-Century-Crofts.

Smith, H. J., Newman, J. D., Hoffman, H. J. and Fatterly, K. (1982). Statistical discrimination among vocalizations of individual squirrel monkeys (*Saimiri sciureus*). *Folia Primatologica*, 37, 267–79.

Smith, H. J., Newman, J. D. and Symmes, D. (1982). Vocal concomitants of affiliative behavior in squirrel monkeys. In C. T. Snowdon, C. H. Brown and M. R. Petersen (eds.), *Primate Communication* (pp. 30–49). Cambridge: Cambridge University Press.

Smith, W. J. (1977). *The Behavior of Communicating*. Cambridge, MA: Harvard University Press.

Snowdon, C. T. (1982). Linguistic and psycholinguistic approaches to primate communication. In C. T. Snowdon, C. H. Brown and M. R. Petersen (eds.), *Primate Communication* (pp. 212–38). Cambridge: Cambridge University Press.

Snowdon, C. T. and Cleveland, J. (1980). Individual recognition of contact calls by pygmy marmosets. *Animal Behaviour*, 28, 717–27.

Snowdon, C. T. and Hodun, A. (1981). Acoustic adaptations in pygmy marmoset contact calls: locational cues vary with distances between conspecifics. *Behavioral Ecology and Sociobiology*, 9, 295–300.

(1985). Troop-specific responses to long calls of isolated tamarins (*Saguinus mystax*). *American Journal of Primatology*, 8, 205–13.

Snowdon, C. T. and Pola, Y. V. (1978). Interspecific and intraspecific responses to synthesized pygmy marmoset vocalizations. *Animal Behaviour*, 26, 192–206.

Sokal, R. R. and Rohlf, F. J. (1981). *Biometry* (2nd ed.). New York: Freeman.

Speidel, G. E. and Nelson, K. E. (1989). *The Many Faces of Imitation in Language Learning*. New York: Springer.

Spelke, E. S. (1979). Perceiving bimodally specified events in infancy. *Developmental Psychology*, 15, 626–36.

(1990). Principles of object perception. *Cognitive Science*, 14, 29–56.

Spencer, H. (1892). *The Physiology of Laughter*, vol. II. New York: Appleton.

Sroufe, L. A. and Waters, E. (1976). The ontogenesis of smiling and laughter: a perspective on the organization of development in infancy. *Psychological Review*, 83, 173–89.

Stampe, D. L. (1973). A dissociation of natural phonology. Ph.D dissertation. Chicago: University of Chicago.

Stark, R. E. (1980). Stages of speech development in the first year of life. In G. Yeni-Komshian, J. Kavanagh and C. Ferguson (eds.), *Child Phonology* (pp. 73–90). New York: Academic Press.

Stephan, C. W. and Langlois, J. H. (1984). Baby beautiful: adult attributions of infant competence as a function of infant attractiveness. *Child Development*, 55, 576–85.

Stern, D. N., Spieker, S., Barnett, R. K. and MacKain, K. (1983). The prosody of maternal speech: infant age and context related changes. *Journal of Child Language*, 10, 1–15.

Stern, D. N., Spieker, S. and MacKain, K. (1982). Intonation contours as signals in maternal speech to prelinguistic infants. *Developmental Psychology*, 18, 727–35.

Sternglanz, S. H., Gray, J. L. and Murakami, M. (1977). Adult preferences for infantile facial features: an ethological approach. *Animal Behaviour*, 25, 108–15.

Stokoe, W. and Volterra, V. (eds.) (1985). *Proceedings of the Third International Symposium on Sign Language Research*. Silver Spring: Linstok Press.

Struhasaker, T. T. (1967). Auditory communication among vervet monkeys (*Cercopithecus aethiops*). In S. A. Altmann (ed.), *Social Communication among Primates* (pp. 218–34). Chicago: Chicago University Press.

Sugiura, H. (1993). Temporal and acoustic correlates in vocal exchange of coo calls in Japanese macaques. *Behaviour*, 124, 207–25.

  (1998). Matching of acoustic features during the vocal exchange of coo calls by Japanese macaques. *Animal Behaviour*, 55, 673–87.

Sugiura, H. and Masataka, N. (1995). Temporal and acoustic flexibility in vocal exchanges of coo calls in Japanese monkeys (*Macaca fuscata*). In E. Zimmermann, J. D. Newman and U. Jürgens (eds.), *Current Topics in Primate Vocal Communication* (pp. 121–40). London: Plenum Press.

Sullivan, J. W. and Horowitz, F. D. (1983). Infant intermodal perception and maternal multimodal stimulation: implication for language development. In L. P. Liositt and C. K. Rovee-Collier (eds.), *Advances in Infancy Research* (pp. 184–239). Norwood, NJ: Ablex.

Takei, W. (2001). How do deaf infants attain first signs? *Developmental Science*, 4.

Tamekawa, Y., Deguchi, T., Hallé, P. A., Hayashi, A. and Kiritani, S. (1997). Acquisition of word-sounds pattern of native language by Japanese infants. *Bulletin of Tokyo Gakugei University Section I Science of Education*, 48, 249–54.

Tan, N., Aiello, R. and Bever, T. G. (1981). Harmonic structure as a determinant of melodic organization. *Memory and Cognition*, 9, 533–9.

Tanaka, Y. and Shimojo, S. (1996). Location versus feature: reaction time reveals dissociation between two visual functions. *Vision Research*, 36, 2125–40.

Tankova-Yampol'skaya, R. V. (1973). Development of speech intonation in infants during the first two years of life. In C. A. Ferguson and D. I. Slobin (eds.), *Studies of Child Language Development* (pp. 214–50). New York: Holt, Rinehart and Winston.

Teleki, G. (1973). *The Predatory Behavior of Wild Chimpanzees*. Lewisburg: Bucknell University Press.

Tenaza, R. R. and Tilson, R. L. (1977). Evolution of long-distance alarm calls in Kloss's gibbon. *Nature*, 268, 233–5.

Thelen, E. (1979). Rhythmical stereotypes in normal human infants. *Animal Behaviour*, 27, 299–715.

(1981). Rhythmical behavior in infancy: an ethological perspective. *Developmental Psychology*, 17, 237–57.

(1991). Motor aspects of emergent speech: a dynamic approach. In N. A. Krasnegor, D. M. Rumbaugh, R. L. Schiefelbusch and M. Studdert-Kennedy (eds.), *Biological and Behavioral Determinants of Language Development* (pp. 339–62). Hillsdale, NJ: Erlbaum.

Thelen, E., Corbetta, D., Kamm, K., Spencer, J., Schneider, K. and Nernicke, R. F. (1993). The transition to reaching: mapping intention and intrinsic dynamics. *Child Development*, 64, 1058–98.

Thelen, E., Skala, K. and Kelso, J. A. (1987). The dynamic nature of early coordination: evidence from bilateral leg movements in young children. *Developmental Psychology*, 23, 179–86.

Thelen, E. and Smith, L. B. (1994). *A Dynamic Systems Approach to the Development of Cognition and Action*. London: MIT Press.

Thelen, E. and Ulrich, B. D. (1991). Hidden skills: a dynamic systems analysis of treadmill stepping during the first year. *Monographs of the Society for Research in Child Development, Serial No. 223*, 56.

Thorpe, L. A. (1986). Infants categorize rising and falling pitch. Paper presented at the meeting of the International Conference on Infant Studies, Los Angeles, April.

Thorpe, L. A. and Trehub, S. E. (1989). Duration illusion and auditory grouping in infancy. *Developmental Psychology*, 25, 122–7.

Thurlow, W. R. (1971). Audition. In J. W. King and L. A. Riggs (eds.), *Experimental Psychology* (pp. 223–59). New York: Holt, Rinehart and Winston.

Tinbergen, N. (1951). *The Study of Instinct*. London: Oxford University Press.

Toda, S., Fogel, A. and Kawai, M. (1990). Maternal speech to three-month-old infants in the United States and Japan. *Journal of Child Language*, 17, 279–94.

Tomkins, S. (1962). *Affect, Imagery, Consciousness*. Vol. I. *The Positive Affect*. New York: Springer.

Trainor, L. J. (1996). Infant preferences for infant-directed versus non-infant-directed playsongs and lullabies. *Infant Behavior and Development*, 19, 83–92.

(1997). Effect of frequency ratio on infants' and adults' discrimination of simultaneous intervals. *Journal of Experimental Psychology: Human Perception and Performance*, 23, 1427–38.

Trainor, L. J., Clark, E. D., Huntley, A. and Adams, B. (1997). The acoustic basis of preference for infant-directed singing. *Infant Behavior and Development*, 20, 383–96.

Trainor, L. J. and Heinmiller, B. M. (1998). The development of evaluative responses to music: infants prefer to listen to consonance over dissonance. *Infant Behavior and Development*, 21, 77–88.

Trainor, L. J. and Trehub, S. E. (1993a). Musical context effects in infants and adults: key distance. *Journal of Experimental Psychology: Human Perception and Performance*, 19, 615–26.

(1993b). What mediates infants' and adults' superior processing of the major over the augmented triad? *Music Perception*, 11, 185–96.

Trehub, S. E. (1974). Auditory-linguistic sensitivity in infants. Ph.D dissertation, McGill University, 1973. *Dissertation Abstracts International*, 34 (pp. 6254B).

Trehub, S. E., Trainor, L. J. and Unyk, A. M. (1993). Music and speech processing in the first year of life. In H. W. Reese (ed.), *Advances in Child Development and Behavior* (pp. 1–35). Orlando, FL: Academic Press.

Trehub, S. E., Unyk, A. M., Kamenetsky, S. B., Hill, D. S., Trainor, L. J., Henderson, J. L. and Saraza, M. (1997). Mothers' and fathers' singing to infants. *Developmental Psychology*, 33, 500–7.

Trevarthen, C. (1988). Universal cooperative motives: how infants begin to know the language and culture of their parents. In G. Jahoda and I. M. Lewis (eds.), *Acquiring Culture: Cross Cultural Studies in Child Development* (pp. 37–90). London: Croom Helm.

Trevarthen, C. and Hubley, P. (1978). Secondary intersubjectivity: confidence, confiding and acts of meaning in the first year. In A. Lock (ed.), *Action, Gestures and Symbol* (pp. 183–229). London: Academic Press.

Turvey, M. T. (1990). Coordination. *American Psychologist*, 45, 938–53.

Valentine, C. W. (1930). The innate basis of fear. *Journal of Genetic Psychology*, 37, 394–419.

van der Stelt, J. M. and Koopmans van Beinum, F. J. (1986). The onset of babbling related to gross motor development. In B. Lindblom and R. Zetterstorm (eds.), *Precursors of Early Speech* (pp. 138–62). New York: Stockton Press.

van Hoof, J. (1972). A comparative approach to the phylogeny of laughter and smiling. In R. Hinde (ed.), *Non-verbal Communication* (pp. 209–41). Cambridge: Cambridge University Press.

Van Lancker, D. (1987). Nonpropositional speech: neurolinguistic studies. In A. Ellis (ed.), *Progress in the Psychology of Language*. Hillsdale, NJ: Erlbaum.

van Lawick-Goodall, J. (1968). The behavior of free-living chimpanzees in the Gombe stream reserve. *Animal Behaviour Monographs*, 1, 161–311.

van Schaik, C. P. and van Noordwijk, M. A. (1985). Evolutionary effects of the absence of felids on the social organization of the macaques of the island of Simeulue (*Macaca fascicularis fusca*, Miller 1903). *Folia Primatologica*, 44, 138–47.

Vauclair, J. (1997). Mental states in animals: cognitive ethology. *Trends in Cognitive Sciences*, 1, 35–9.

Vihman, M. M. (1993). Variable paths to early word production. *Journal of Phonetics*, 21, 61–82.

Vihman, M. M. and Boysson-Bardies, B. de (1994). The nature and origin of ambient language inflence on infant vocal production and early words. *Phonetica*, 51, 159–69.

Vihman, M. M. and Miller, R. (1988). Words and babble at the threshold of language acquisition. In M. D. Smith and J. L. Locke (eds.), *The Emergent Lexicon: The Child's Development of a Linguistic Vocabulary* (pp. 151–83). San Diego: Academic Press.

von Bertalanffy, L. (1968). *General Systems Theory*. New York: Braziller.

von Helmholtz, H. L. F. (1954). *On the Sensations of Tone as a Physiological Basis for the Theory of Melody* (2nd ed.). New York: Dover.

Vygotsky, L. S. (1961). *Thought and Language*. Boston, MA: MIT Press.

(1978). *Mind in Society: The Development of Higher Psychological Processes*. Cambridge, MA: Harvard University Press.

Waddington, C. H. (1957). *The Strategy of the Genes*. London: Allen and Unwin.

Wakefield, J. R., Doughtie, E. B. and Yom, L. (1974). Identification of Structural Components of an Unknown Language. *Journal of Psycholinguistic Research*, 3, 262–9.

Waser, P. M. and Waser, M. S. (1977). Experimental studies of primate vocalizaion: specializations for long-distance propagation. *Zeitschrift für Tierpsychologie*, 43, 239–63.

Watson, J. (1985). Contingency perception in early social development. In T. M. Field and N. A. Fox (eds.), *Social Perception in Infants* (pp. 157–76). Norwood, NJ: Ablex.

Watson, J. S. (1972). Smiling, cooing and the game." *Merrill-Palmer Quarterly*, 18, 323–39.

Werker, J. F. and McLeod, P. J. (1989). Infant preference for both male and female infant-directed talk: a developmental study of attentional and affective responsiveness. *Canadian Journal of Psychology*, 43, 320–46.

Werker, J. F., Pegg, J. E. and McLeod, P. J. (1994). A cross-language investigation of infant preference for infant-directed communication. *Infant Behavior and Development*, 17, 323–33.

Wertheimer, M. (1923). Untersuchung zur Lehre von der Gestalt II. *Psychologische Forschung*, 4, 301–50.

Wheeler, D. D. (1970). Processes in word recognition. *Cognitive Psychology*, 1, 59–85.

White, M. (1993). *The Material Child: Coming of Age in Japan and America*. New York: Free Press.

Wilbur, R. (1987). *American Sign Language: Linguistic and Applied Dimensions*. Boston, MA: Little, Brown.

Wiley, R. H. and Richards, D. G. (1978). Physical constraints on acoustic communication in the atomosphere: implications for the evolution of animal vocalizatoins. *Behavioral Ecology and Sociobiology*, 3, 69–94.

Winter, P., Ploog, D. and Latta, J. (1966). Vocal repertoire of the squirrel monkey (*Saimiri sciureus*). *Experimental Brain Research*, 1, 359–84.

Wolff, P. (1969). The natural history of crying and other vocalizations in early infancy. In B. Fox (ed.), *Determinants of Infant Behavior* (pp. 81–109). London: Methuen.

Wolff, P. H. (1968). Sucking patterns of infant mammals. *Brain, Behavior and Evolution*, 1, 354–67.

Yonekawa, A. (1984). *Shuwa gengo no kijutsuteki kenkyu (A Descriptional Study of Japanese Sign Language)*. Tokyo: Meiji-shoin.

Zahn-Waxler, C., Friedman, R. J., Cole, P. M., Mizuta, I. and Hiruma, N. (1996). Japanese and United States preschool children's responses to conftt and stress. *Child Development*, 67, 2462–77.

Zebrowitz, L. A. (1990). *Social Perception*. Pacific Cove, CA: Brooks.

Zebrowitz, L. A. and McDonald, S. (1991). The impact of litigants' baby-facedness and attractiveness on adjudications in small claims courts. *Law and Human Behavior*, 15, 603–23.

Zebrowitz, L. A. and Montepare, J. M. (1992). Impressions of babyfaced individuals across the life span. *Developmental Psychology*, 28, 1143–52.

Zebrowitz, L. A., Tenenbaum, D. R. and Goldstein, L. H. (1991). The impact of job applicants' facial maturity, sex, and academic achievement on hiring recommendations. *Journal of Applied Social Psychology*, 21, 525–48.

Zemlin, W. R. (1968). *Speech and Hearing Science: Anatomy and Physiology.* Englewood Cliffs: Prentice-Hall.

Zeskind, P. S. and Barr, R. G. (1997). Acoustic characteristics of naturally occurring cries of infants with colic." *Child Development*, 68, 394–403.

Zeskind, P. S., Klein, L. and Marshall, T. R. (1992). Adults' perceptions of experimental modifications of durations of pauses and expiratory sounds in infant crying. *Developmental Psychology*, 28, 1153–62.

Zeskind, P. S. and Marshall, T. R. (1988). The relation between variations in pitch and maternal perception of infant crying. *Child Development*, 59, 193–6.

Ziajka, A. (1981). *Prelinguistic Communication in Infancy.* New York: Praeger.

Index

For EU product safety concerns, contact us at Calle de José Abascal, 56–1°,
28003 Madrid, Spain or eugpsr@cambridge.org.

www.ingramcontent.com/pod-product-compliance
Ingram Content Group UK Ltd.
Pitfield, Milton Keynes, MK11 3LW, UK
UKHW010034140625
459647UK00012BA/1365